Alternate Ways of Organizing the Contents of this Book

Process and Thought in Composition

SECOND EDITION

Frank J. D'Angelo

Arizona State University

Winthrop Publishers, Inc.

Cambridge, Massachusetts

Acknowledgments begin on page xiii.

Library of Congress Cataloging in Publication Data

D'Angelo, Frank J
    Process and thought in composition.

    Includes index.
    1. English language—Rhetoric. I. Title.
PE1408.D15 1980   808'.042   80–10240
ISBN 0–87626–662–6

Cover and interior design by Susan Marsh

© 1980, 1977 by Winthrop Publishers, Inc.
17 Dunster Street, Cambridge, Massachusetts 02138

10 9 8 7 6 5 4 3 2 1

Contents

Preface

The second edition of *Process and Thought in Composition* retains the original emphasis on writing as a thinking process, but it also includes the following features:

1. New material on aims, modes, and kinds of discourse, introduced in the opening chapter and reinforced throughout the book.
2. A completely rewritten chapter on invention (Chapter Two).
3. Two new chapters on persuasion as an aim (Chapters Eight and Nine), emphasizing logical thinking as it relates to writing essays, not merely to analyzing arguments.
4. Interesting new paradigms, based on the enthymeme, for writing arguments, with a step-by-step illustration of the process.
5. New material on paragraphing as a process, in relation to the writer's intention, audience, and kinds of discourse (Chapter Ten).
6. Expanded material on analysis, description (Chapter Four), and narration (Chapter Seven).
7. New professional and student models, exercises, and suggestions for student writing throughout the book.

The plan of the book is similar in many respects to that of the first edition. I have divided the main part of the text into three parts: invention, arrangement, and style. In each of these parts, I have tried to show how invention, arrangement, and style are organically related by providing connecting links wherever possible, especially in those chapters titled "Patterns of Thought."

The two chapters on "Persuasion as an Aim" may seem to depart from the original plan, but they do not. Rather they reinforce the new emphasis on aims introduced in the opening chapter and reinforced throughout. Because persuasion is such an important aim, I devote two chapters to it and to the writing of arguments. I continue the emphasis on aims in the new material on paragraphing which follows.

The chapter on the paragraph is almost twice the size as that of the original. It includes a discussion of paragraphing as a process, not just a discussion of the paragraph as a separate unit. There is also new material on beginning and ending paragraphs and on transitions.

In making these changes to the first edition, I have tried to write with my audience in mind. I am grateful for the constructive criticism I have gotten from my readers over the past few years. Whatever success I have had with the first edition, I owe to you, my readers.

*   *   *

I have been truly fortunate, in preparing both editions of this text, to have received the kind of helpful advice so necessary to making a book a critical success.

Richard Larson, Robert Gorrell, Gary Tate, and William Lutz were among those who helped with the first edition. Their influence is still a strong one in the second edition.

Many of those who helped with the second edition have used the first edition, and their criticisms have helped to make the second edition a better book. Among those who gave of their time and help are Erika Lindemann of the University of South Carolina, Constance F. Gefvert of Virginia Polytechnic Institute and State University, Tommy J. Boley of the University of Texas at El Paso, David E. Fear of Valencia Junior College, Kris Gutierrez of the University of Colorado, Melinda G. Kramer of Purdue University, Carolyn B. Matalene of the University of South Carolina, Roberta Pritchard of Texas Christian University, Richard Raspa of the University of Utah, and Woodruff Thompson of Brigham Young University.

In the preparation of both the first and second editions of this manuscript, I have received invaluable assistance from Terri Garchow, Robin Ruiz, and Robin Kendrick. They did an excellent job in typing and helping to edit the manuscript. I thank them for their patience and their unfailing good humor. Deborah Lay did a very fine job of helping me with various aspects of the text, as did Bob Johannsen and Rob Archer.

Herbert Nolan of Winthrop Publishers is one of the best editors I have worked with, and I thank him for his patience, humor, and good sense.

Special thanks again go to Paul O'Connell of Winthrop Publishers, who first encouraged me to write this book several years ago and who is largely responsible for an improved second edition. His warmth, friendship, and sincerity go far beyond the bounds of a single textbook.

I would also like to thank the many students whose essays I have used. When the essays of professional writers seemed difficult for some students to emulate, their writing always seemed inviting, accessible, and interesting.

Finally, I would like to thank my daughters, Susan and Lori, and my sons, Frank, Marc, and Stephen for their patience and understanding, and my wife, Sylvia, for her love and support, and her unfailing sense of humor and great wit. "Holy, fair, and wise is she;/The heaven such grace did lend her."

F.J.D.
Tempe, Arizona

Acknowledgments

Aetna advertisement, from *Time* magazine, November 21, 1977. Reprinted by permission of Aetna Life & Casualty.

The Animal Kingdom, "Mollusks," August 1972; published by Bantam Books, by arrangement with Grosset & Dunlap, Inc., July 1971. Reprinted with permission of Grosset & Dunlap, Inc.

AP Newsfeatures, "7,000 Stolen Books Found in New York." Reprinted by permission of The Associated Press.

Arizona Republic. "Shoplifting Is A Crime," public service message from The Arizona Republic. Reprinted by permission.

Arrow Liquors advertisement, "Caramella by Arrow." Reprinted by permission of Arrow Liquors Company.

Isaac Asimov, "UFOs, Are They Visitors from Space—or Unreliable False Observations?" From TV GUIDE magazine, December 14, 1974. Reprinted with permission from TV GUIDE® Magazine. Copyright © 1974 by Triangle Publications, Inc., Radnor, Pennsylvania.

James Baldwin, "Go Tell It On the Mountain." From *Go Tell It On the Mountain* by James Baldwin. Copyright © The Dial Press, 1963. Reprinted by permission.

Ray Allen Billington, "The Frontier Disappears." In *The American Story* edited by Earl S. Miers. Copyright © 1956 by Broadcast Music, Inc. Reprinted by permission.

Ray Allen Billington and James B. Hedges, *Westward Expansion: A History of the American Frontier, 3rd edition.* Copyright © Macmillan Publishing, Inc., 1960. Reprinted by permission.

Ray Bradbury, "A Sound of Thunder." In *Golden Apples of the Sun* by Ray Bradbury. Copyright 1952 by Ray Bradbury. Reprinted by permission of Harold Matson Co., Inc.

Charles S. Brooks, "On the Difference Between Wit and Humor." From *On the Difference Between Wit and Humor* in Chimney Pot Papers (1919). Reprinted by permission of Yale University Press.

Bulova Watch advertisement, "Do You Have An Unfaithful Watch?" Reprinted by permission of the Bulova Watch Company, Inc.

Dinah Calhoon, "Rubbing Concepts." Reprinted by permission.

Willa Cather, "My Antonia." From *My Antonia* by Willa Cather. Copyright renewed 1954 by Edith Lewis. Reprinted by permission of Houghton Mifflin Co.

Stuart Chase, "Mexico: A Study of Two Americas." From *Mexico: A Study of Two Americas* by Stuart Chase in collaboration with Marian Tyler Chase. Copyright 1931, renewed 1959 by Stuart Chase. Reprinted by permission of Macmillan Publishing Co., Inc.

Chesebrough-Pond's advertisement, for "Ultra Vera" lotion. Reprinted by permission of Chesebrough-Pond's Inc.

Christian Children's Fund advertisement, from *Time* magazine, January 10, 1972. Reprinted by permission of the Christian Children's Fund.

Marchette Chute, "Shakespeare of London." From *Shakespeare of London* by Marchette Chute, copyright 1949 by E. P. Dutton & Co., Inc., and reprinted with their permission.

Coach Leatherware advertisement, from the *New Yorker*, November 8, 1976. Reprinted by permission of Coach Leatherware.

The New Columbia Encyclopedia, 1975. Entries for "pidgin" and "lingua franca." Reprinted by permission of Columbia University Press.

Joseph Conrad, "The Lagoon." From *Tales of Unrest* by Joseph Conrad. "The Secret Sharer." Excerpt from *The Secret Sharer* by Joseph Conrad. Copyright 1910 by Harper Bros. In the book *Twixt Land and Sea* by Joseph Conrad. Both reprinted by permission of Doubleday & Company, Inc.

Norman Cousins, "The Conquest of Pain." From the *Saturday Review*, March 17, 1979. Reprinted by permission of Norman Cousins.

Stephen Crane, *The Red Badge of Courage.* From the University of Virginia Edition of *The Works of Stephen Crane.* Reprinted by permission. "The Open Boat" in *The Open Boat and Other Tales,* Alfred A. Knopf, Inc., publisher. Also in *The Complete Short Stories & Sketches of Stephen Crane* edited by Thomas A. Gullason, Doubleday & Co., Inc., publisher.

Charles Dickens, *The Works of Charles Dickens.* From *Bleak House* in *The Works of Charles Dickens,* P. F. Collier & Son, publishers.

Gerald Durrell, *The Overloaded Ark.* Copyright 1953 by Gerald Durrell. Reprinted with permission from The Viking Press, Inc.

Empire Machinery advertisement, from *Time* magazine, July 3, 1978. Reprinted by permission of the Empire Machinery Company.

Leonard Engel, "The Sea." From Life Nature Library—*The Sea* by Leonard Engel and The Editors of Time-Life Books © 1961 Time Inc. Reprinted by permission.

Kenan T. Erim, "Aphrodisias: Awakened City of Ancient Art." From National Geographic Society magazine, June 1972. Reprinted by permission of the National Geographic Society.

Martin Esslin, *The Theater of the Absurd,* revised updated edition. Copyright © 1961, 1968, 1969 by Martin Esslin. Reprinted by permission of Doubleday & Co., Inc.

The Fantastiks, "Try to Remember." Copyright © 1960 by Tom Jones & Harvey Schmidt. Chappell & Co., Inc., owner of publication and allied rights throughout the world. International Copyright Secured. ALL RIGHTS RESERVED. Used by permission.

Ralph H. Faulkingham, "Where the Lifeboat Ethic Breaks Down." From "Where the Lifeboat Ethic Breaks Down" by Ralph H. Faulkingham, from *Human Nature,* October 1978. Copyright © 1978 by Human Nature, Inc. Used by permission of the publisher.

Ford Motor Company advertisement, from *Psychology Today,* October 1977. Reprinted by permission of Ford Motor Company.

E. M. Forester, "Aspects of the Novel." THE PLOT from *Aspects of the Novel* by E. M. Forster, copyright 1927 by Harcourt Brace Jovanovich, Inc., renewed 1955 by E. M. Forster. Reprinted by permission of the publishers.

W. Nelson Francis, "Revolution in Grammar," in The Quarterly Journal of Speech, Vol. XL no. 3 (October 1954). Reprinted by permission of the University of Wisconsin, Madison. *The English Language,* An Introduction by W. Nelson Francis. By permission of W. W. Norton & Company, Inc. Copyright © 1963, 1965 by W. W. Norton & Company, Inc. From "Usage and Variety in English."

Frontier Airlines advertisement, from Frontier Airlines inflight magazine, 1978. Reprinted by permission.

General Foods International Coffees advertisement. Reprinted by permission of General Foods Corporation. © General Foods Corporation 1976.

Edward T. Hall, "Let's Heat People Instead of Houses," from *Human Nature,* January 1979. Reprinted with permission of the author.

Robert Harr, essay on the composing process (untitled). Reprinted by permission.

Head & Shoulders shampoo advertisement. Reprinted by permission of Procter & Gamble Company.

Nancy Hechinger, "Discovering Human Nature." From "Discovering Human Nature" by Nancy Hechinger, from *Human Nature,* January 1979. Copyright © 1978 by Human Nature, Inc. Used by permission of the publisher.

Stephen W. Hitchcock, "Can We Save Our Salt Marshes?" From National Geographic Society magazine, June 1972. Reprinted by permission of the National Geographic Society.

Fred Hoyle, "When Time Began," in the *Saturday Evening Post.*

James Joyce, "The Dead." From *Dubliners* by James Joyce. Copyright © 1967 by the Estate of James Joyce. All rights reserved. Reprinted by permission of The Viking Press. Passage from *Ulysses,* by James Joyce. Copyright © 1914, 1918 by Margaret Caroline Anderson and renewed 1942, 1946 by Nora Joseph Joyce. Reprinted by permission of Random House, Inc.

Agnes Newton Keith, "Bare Feet in the Palace." From *Bare Feet in the Palace* by Agnes Newton Keith. Copyright © 1955 by Agnes Newton Keith by permission of Little, Brown and Company in association with the Atlantic Monthly Press.

Michael Kernan, story/article from the *Arizona Republic,* May 8, 1977. Reprinted by permission of *The Washington Post.*

Kitchenaid Disposal advertisement. Reprinted by permission of Hobart Corporation.

Joseph Wood Krutch, *The Desert Year* © 1951, 1952 by the author. From *The Desert Year.* Published by Explorer Books. Reprinted by permission of William Morrow & Company, New York.

R. D. Laing, *The Politics of Experience.* From *The Politics of Experience.* Copyright © 1967 by R. D. Laing. Reprinted by permission of Penguin Books Ltd.

Lindsay Olive advertisement, from *Sunset,* December 1978. Reprinted by permission of Lindsay International Inc.

James Livingston, "Two Women." Reprinted by permission.

Kate Mangelsdorf, "How I Compose." Reprinted by permission.

Ralph Nader, "The Safe Car You Can't Buy." From *The Nation*, April 11, 1959.

Human Nature article, "Second Look: Maps and the Mind." From "Second Look: Maps and the Mind," from *Human Nature*, January 1979. Copyright © 1978 by Human Nature, Inc. "Why Americans Can't Write." From "Why Americans Can't Write" in *Human Nature*, August 1978. Copyright © 1978 by Human Nature, Inc. Both reprinted by permission of the publisher.

Maria Oparnica, "Personal Methods of Composition." Reprinted by permission.

Psychology Today article, "The State of the Apes." Reprinted from *Psychology Today* Magazine. Copyright © 1974 by Ziff-Davis Publishing Company. Reprinted by permission.

Marjorie Kinnan Rawlings, *The Yearling*. Copyright © 1938. Reprinted by permission of Charles Scribner's Sons.

The Saturday Review article, "The Innate Grammar of Baby Talk," March 18, 1972. Reprinted by permission.

Shirley Rish, "The Composing Process" and "Environmentalist, Preservationist, and Conservationist." Both reprinted by permission.

Harry Wolcott Robbins and Roscoe Edward Parker, *Advanced Exposition*. Copyright © 1935. By permission of Prentice-Hall, Inc.

Edwin Arlington Robinson, "Richard Cory." From *The Children of the Night* by Edwin Arlington Robinson. Reprinted by permission of Charles Scribner's Sons.

Albert Rosenfeld, "Interferon: Medicine for Cancer & the Common Cold?" from *Saturday Review*, November 1978. Reprinted by permission of Saturday Review, Inc.

Bertrand Russell, "What I Have Lived For." In the *Autobiography of Bertrand Russell: 1872–1914*. Copyright © 1951, 1952, 1953 by Bertrand Russell. Copyright © 1967 by George Allen and Unwin Ltd. By permission of Little, Brown & Company in association with the Atlantic Monthly Press. From *A History of Western Philosophy*, copyright © 1945 by Bertrand Russell. Reprinted by permission of Simon & Shuster, Inc., New York.

John Ruskin, "The Stones of Venice." From *The Stones of Venice*. Copyright © 1970 by John Ruskin. An Everyman's Library edition. Published in the United States by E. P. Dutton & Company, Inc., and reprinted with their permission.

Susan Schiefelbein, "Children and Cancer," from *Saturday Review*, April 1979. Reprinted by permission of the Saturday Review.

George Bernard Shaw, *Man and Superman*. From *The Collected Works of Bernard Shaw*, Ayot St. Lawrence Edition, 1930. Reprinted with permission of The Society of Authors on behalf of the Bernard Shaw Estate.

Irwin Shaw, "The Eighty Yard Run." From *Mixed Company*, Collected Stories of Irwin Shaw. Copyright © Random House, Inc., and reprinted with permission.

Snowdrift shortening advertisement. From *What Every Good Cook Knows* in Effective Advertising Copy by Merrill DeVoe and published in 1956 by Macmillan, Inc. Reprinted by permission of Hunt-Wesson Foods, Inc.

Spanish olive advertisement. "Spanish Olives. How to Tell the Original." Reprinted with permission of the Spanish Olive Commission.

Steinway piano advertisement. Reprinted by permission of Steinway & Sons.

John Steinbeck, "Chrysanthemums" and "Flight." Both from *The Long Valley* by John Steinbeck. Copyright © 1938 by John Steinbeck. Copyright © renewed 1966 by John Steinbeck. Reprinted by permission of the Viking Press.

John Stidworthy, "Snakes of the World." From "Snakes of the World" by John Stidworthy. Copyright © 1971, 1974 by Grosset & Dunlap, Inc. Copyright © 1969 by the Hamlyn Publishing Group Ltd. Reprinted by permission of Grosset & Dunlap, Inc.

Suntory Royal Whiskey advertisement, "Suntory Royal. Slightly East of Scotch." Reprinted by permission of Suntory International.

Arandas Tequila advertisement. Reprinted by permission of Maidstone Importers, Inc.

Texaco advertisement. This advertisement provided by courtesy of Texaco Inc.

Timberland boot advertisement. Reprinted by permission of Timberland Co.

Leonore Tiefer, "The Kiss." From *The Kiss* by Leonore Tiefer, from *Human Nature*, July 1978. Copyright © 1978 by Human Nature, Inc. Used by permission of the publisher.

Time Magazine article, "Faces in the Crowd," June 24, 1974; "Guns, Death, and Chaos," February 26, 1979; "The Price of Stormy Petrol," February 26, 1979; "A Matter of Night and Day," February 26, 1979; "Carter: Black and Blue," March 5, 1979; "Suck Them In and Outflank Them," March 12, 1979; "Close Encounters of A Kind," March 12, 1979; "Intimate Glimpses of a Giant," March 12, 1979; "Searching for the Right Response," March 12, 1979; "The Flick of Violence," March 19, 1979; "Windup of a No-Win War," March 19, 1979. Reprinted with permission from TIME, The Weekly News Magazine; Copyright TIME, Inc.

The Writing Process

Preliminary Considerations

Chapter 1

Preliminary Considerations

The Importance of Writing

Despite the claims of some students of communications that there is little need for people to learn to write in an electronic age, there is still an insistent and persistent cry for effective writing.

We are all becoming weary of brainlessness in public language: of bureaucrats who cannot express themselves clearly in writing, of business people who cannot write letters that are accurate and concise, of writers of legal contracts who cannot explain coverage in everyday language, of politicians who deceive with language, of doctors and lawyers who use jargon to impress or befuddle, of friends and acquaintances who can't say what they mean.

Even in an electronic age, you can scarcely hope to succeed unless you can express yourself in writing with some degree of effectiveness. Television announcers work from a script. Movie and TV writers depend in large part upon writing. People in many occupations and walks of life write memos, reports, business letters, personal letters, letters of complaint, sympathy notes, invitations, letters of congratulation, articles, essays, theses, examinations, ads, brochures, manuals, catalogs, captions for posters and photographs—the list is endless. Writing is more pervasive and more important than you sometimes think.

But even if writing were not as important for many public uses as it was in the past, it would still be valuable in education because it facilitates thought. Writing can help you to think critically. It can enable you to perceive relationships, to deepen perception, to solve problems, to give order to experience. It can help you to clarify your thoughts. Often you discover what you really think and feel about people, ideas, issues, and events only in the actual process of writing.

Cultural psychologists have found that nonliterate people lag far behind literate people in a variety of cognitive skills. Their studies support the conclusion that literacy, especially writing, promotes intellectual development. More specifically, they have discovered that literacy transforms a person's mental processes by replacing practical, situation-bound thinking with abstract, theoretical thinking. Whatever may be the value of concrete, situation-bound thinking in nonliterate cultures, in a technological society a person who cannot think abstractly is at a disadvantage. To learn to write, then, is to learn to think in a certain way.

Invention, Arrangement, Style

Writing is a form of thinking, but it is thinking for a particular audience, and for a particular occasion. One of your more important tasks as a writer is to master the principles of writing and thinking that will help you to achieve your goals. The most important of these principles are those of invention, arrangement, and style.

Invention is the process of discovering ideas for speaking or writing. Although for many writers the process is intuitive, you can learn to guide the process deliberately by using formal procedures for analyzing and searching.

Arrangement is the process of discovering ordering principles so that you can organize your ideas in such a way as to make them understandable and believable to your readers.

Style is the process of making choices about sentence structure and diction while in the act of writing. You can also make these choices consciously and deliberately when you review what you have written.

To divide the writing process into invention, arrangement, and style is merely a convenience. Invention, arrangement, and style may occur or recur in all three stages. Try thinking, for example, about a movie that you have recently seen. If you begin to write down these thoughts, in the process of thinking about what you want to say, you cannot help but put your ideas into some kind of larger pattern and at the same time into sentences and words.

You may have heard various writers make exclusive claims for each of these processes: discovering ideas is the most important part of the writing process; the organization of ideas is all important; style is everything in a piece of writing. Writers can make these claims because there is a sense in which each claim is correct. Invention is everything because it includes arrangement and style. Arrangement is everything because it includes invention and style. Style is everything because it includes invention and arrangement. All are parts of a single, ongoing, mental process. (We shall take up these matters more fully in subsequent chapters.)

Finding a Subject

Why is it that some people who are such good conversationalists have so much trouble putting their thoughts into writing? To some people, writing a letter is a difficult task. Yet ask those same people to talk about a personal experience or give you an opinion about some social or political issue, and they can talk articulately for hours. Every time you make a telephone call, purchase something at the local supermarket, ask directions of a stranger, talk amiably with a neighbor, argue heatedly with a friend, you are putting thoughts together and expressing them in words. No matter how unconscious the process may be, you are engaging in oral composition.

Some people are never at a loss for something to *say*, yet when you ask them to *write* about a personal experience, or about current events, they vehemently declare that they have nothing worthwhile to write about. If someone were to record one of your conversations on a tape recorder, you might be surprised to learn that your conversation is filled with interesting ideas, bits and pieces of gossip, vivid descriptions of people and places, and vigorous opinions about social and political issues, all delivered in a lively and pleasing style.

All of us experience and observe the world around us. Yet students often feel unable to write about it. One of my students wrote: "I have an enormous amount of trouble picking a topic or thinking of something to write about. Once a topic is *finally* chosen, I grope and stumble for words like a blindman searching for a pen." Another wrote:

Some people have a flair for writing—others don't. And unfortunately I am one of those people who doesn't have a talent for writing. Picture a one-hundred-and-twenty pound man, anemic, pale, his skin hanging to his bones, trying to lift a weight of several hundred pounds, and you'll get some idea of the effort it takes me to write a good sentence. Words should come to my pen like rain, a gentle rain, steady, falling from a still blue sky, or better yet like a violent rain from a cloudburst, exploding, bursting out of the clouds and flooding the earth. But I'm lucky if I can force a drop out of a faucet, turned on as far as it will go, my fingers wrenching it 'til it can be forced no further, my fingers hurting and aching from trying.

Neither student realized how easily and beautifully each was using analogies to write eloquently about the difficulty of writing.

Personal Experiences

What to write about? Finding a general subject is easy enough. The possibilities for a given writer are almost unlimited, although some people have a wider variety of experiences to draw upon than others. The place to begin obviously is with your own *personal experiences*, your thoughts, feelings, and observations.

Every experience has within it the seeds for a potential flowering of significant ideas. No subject is intrinsically better than another. It all depends on the insights and the depth of perception you bring to the subject. Even much maligned subjects such as "What I did last summer" can be handled by some writers with sensitivity, skill, and wit.

College life offers some first-rate material for subject matter. One student who was taking a lecture class at the university wrote a paper based on a careful observation of his instructor. Another conveyed in very vivid language an experience she had while working in the university library. A third student gave a very humorous description of his last zoology lab.

Job experiences offer a source from which good writing can come. Almost all of you have a certain background of job experiences, whether these experiences be summer jobs, part-time jobs after school, or chores around the house. The familiar stuff of everyday experience can be made interesting for others to read about. Everyday experience, I'm sure, is a very common topic of conversation in your home and among your friends. The problem, however, is to find some point of view or some angle of vision with which to see your subject.

One student had a summer job working in a mortuary. He described his experience with concrete and vivid details, and with a curious detachment:

Someone Has To Do It

Working for a mortuary was a new experience for me. The job supplemented my summer earnings for tuition and also provided me with a free room. It was a good job—someone has to do it—and it helped me out considerably.

We kept the mortuary open in the evenings from 5:30 to 10:00 P.M., conducting people, relatives, and friends to the respective parlors where they would pay their last respects to their departed, dear ones.

In the evening and early mornings we answered death calls, coming in from hospitals, private residences, and old folks or convalescence homes. Then we would telephone a mortician, giving him the required information about the deceased.

The next step was the preparation of the one-man cot—two white sheets and pillow slips, locked beneath restraining belts, covered over by a silver-gray coverall. This we placed in the hearse, and then we drove to our destination, usually meeting the mortician or funeral director there.

We would wrap the last remains in sheets and head back to the mortuary where we would unload the corpse on a white porcelain table, all prepared for embalming.

The coolness of the milk-white flesh and the stench from uncontrolled sphincter muscles will long remain in my memory. Yet it was a good job—someone has to do it.

—Bob

There are subjects from daily experience all around you: joyful, painful, pleasurable, distressing, sad, delightful, fascinating, rapturous, heartfelt. Good writers will give their personal impressions of particular subjects, telling honestly how the experiences affected them. It would be impossible to attempt to catalog all the possible subjects from personal experience that you could write about. But here are a few that some students have found worth considering:

descriptions of people, places, and things; reflections about life; job experiences; death; illness; embarrassing experiences; sex; love; dating; marriage; war; alienation; civil disobedience; drugs; race relations; fears; hopes; dreams.

Vicarious Experiences

A second source of subjects for writing is *vicarious experiences* from books, records, movies, and television. Often you will find that you have enough knowledge about a particular subject from courses you are taking, from books you have read, or from movies and television programs you have seen, so that extensive research is not necessary. You need merely to recall this information or to find ways of getting at it to make it the basis of an interesting paper.

The following paper discusses a bit of the plot of a movie its author saw as a young child, but the emphasis is on the lasting impression it made.

Movie Impressions

I hope that if and when I become a parent, I have enough sense to keep a strict eye on the entertainment my children watch. I know from my own recollection what damage a movie viewed at an impressionable age can do.

I was *very* young when I saw this particular film, but even now, parts of it are as vivid to me as when I ran screaming out of the theater. If I had only been a little older, it likely would have had no effect on me at all, but at that time I was impressionable.

The plot went something like this. A young man and his bride lived in a swank high-rise apartment. Every night a strange woman with long, black hair and flowing gown would appear, holding a music box that played high-pitched, eerie music. She would go to the young couple's bedroom and the music would cause the young bride to walk in a deep trance. Out they would float to the balcony, about ten stories up. Here the music really got strange, enticing the girl to lean way over the railing, almost sure to lose her balance. Just then her husband would be heard calling for her, the odd enchantress would disappear, and the girl would be safe, but she would awaken, confused and frightened. The next thing I remember about the story was that somebody was murdered and the police were doing a thorough investigation of the apartment. In the bedroom, suspense began to build as that eerie music started playing softly. It was deathly quiet as the police reached the closet and began feeling the walls for clues. Nobody talked! Only that creepy music was heard, causing my tension to build. Then—B-O-O-M!!! With a horrible crash, a body fell out of the ceiling when the police hit a secret panel. With a chorus of screams ringing in my ears, I lit out of that theater as fast as my fat little legs would go, and bawled . . . and bawled some more.

I'm sure my parents never knew that for months I was scared to death to go to bed with the closet doors open. My heart always pounded a little harder when I went over to shut them. I think I realized there wasn't a music-box woman hiding there, waiting for a chance to lure me to my doom, or a body hidden in the ceiling, ready to come crashing down if I touched a certain panel, but my fear wasn't something I could rationalize. It was imprinted deep in my consciousness, just as is the habit I still have of faithfully closing our closet doors before retiring every single night.

—Linda

Magazines, Books, Reference Sources

Obviously, much of the writing you do in your college career or in other writing situations will not be this personal. Sometimes you will be called upon to give a relatively detached account of something you have read, to give an objective rendering of a subject about which you know little. A third source of subjects for your writing then is *magazines, books,* and *reference sources,* in the library, on the newsstand, or in your home, which you deliberately go to because you want to write about a subject with which you have little familiarity.

You can find general subjects in every conceivable place. Look at the table of contents in magazines such as *Time* or *Newsweek.* You will find such general headings as the following:

The Nation	Business
The World	Religion

People	Milestones
The Law	Books
Behavior	The Theater
The Press	Music and Dance
Education	Show Business and Television
Sports	The Environment
Science	Medicine
The Economy	The Sexes

Surely this listing will afford you with at least a beginning.

Another obvious place to look is in the dictionary. Just casually follow the alphabetical listings, stopping at topics that seem to hold some interest for you, jotting these down as they strike your fancy:

acting	clothes
advertising	comic strips
abstract (art)	dreams
Academy Award	music
babble	slang
bullfighting	words (new)

A third place is the alphabetically arranged subject index or table of contents of a textbook or essay anthology. I compiled the following list in about ten or fifteen minutes by looking in several books on my desk:

African art	humor
astrology	illiteracy
blind dates	movies
civil disobedience	nursery rhymes
collective bargaining	Olympic games
dance	prisoners of war
death	reading
devil worship	rock lyrics
drugs	rockets
ESP	solar energy
fashions	superstitions
feminism	television
flying saucers	theft

The card catalog in the library is another source of general subjects. The subject heading is what you want. Behind each heading you will find a stack of cards with titles related to the subject you have chosen:

Surrealism
Surrealism and Film
Surrealism and Its Affinities
Surrealism and Painting
Surrealism and the Literary Imagination
Surrealism and the Novel
Surrealist Art
The Surrealist Movement in England
The History of Surrealist Painting
Surrealist Poetry in France

Periodical indexes such as the *New York Times Index* and the *Reader's Guide to Periodical Literature* offer an even more promising beginning than some of the other sources. To begin with, you need merely to go through the alphabetical listing of, say, the *Reader's Guide* to come up with an interesting list of topics to write about:

abstract expressionism   basketball
acupuncture   cathedrals
American Indian languages   climate
apocalyptic thoughts   cosmic rays
ballet   dancing

Occasionally, one of these general topics will have numerous subdivisions, each of which might be a suitable subject in itself:

Moving picture critics and criticisms
Moving picture festivals
Moving picture industry
Moving picture plays
    criticisms, plots, etc.
        single works
            Alien
            Amityville Horror

> *Dracula*
> *Gone with the Wind*
> *Invasion of the Body Snatchers*
> *Manhattan*
> *Rocky II*
> *Star Wars*
> *Superman*
> *Wedding, A*
> production and direction
Moving pictures
> animated cartoons
> art films
> audiences
> bibliography
> comedy
> dance films
> documentaries
> moral aspects
> rating
> science films
> social aspects
> special effects
> study and teaching
> themes

In addition to the list of general topics, each entry makes specific references to titles of articles and their sources, for further reading:

DEATH
> *See also*
> Children and death
> > Psychology
> Acceptance of the idea of mortality. Intellect 103:
> > 215–16 Ja '75
> Cold bright charms of immortality: study of death on
> > television. M. J. Arlen. New Yorker 50:73–8 Ja 27 '75
> Nobility in our gramp's decision to die: F. Turgend. M.
> > Jury. il pors Todays Health 53:18–23+ Ja '75

DEATH in literature
  Death. M. E. Stern. bibl Engl J 64:61–2 Ja '75
DEATH in Venice: opera. See Britten, B.
  —*Reader's Guide to Periodical Literature*, March 10, 1975

A final source is a good *encyclopedia.* If you know little about your general subject but you are interested in exploring it further, a useful first step would be to read the article to get an overview of it. The article itself would refer you to other books and articles. These in turn might have useful bibliographies you could pursue. Or you could look up the same subject in the *Reader's Guide to Periodical Literature* and read the articles related to it which are listed there.

Exercises

1. Write an essay in which you discuss which subjects would be most interesting to you if you had to write a personal experience paper.

2. Write an essay based on your personal experiences on *one* of the following general subjects: the death of someone near to you, an illness, a job experience, dating, love, marriage, an embarrassing experience, your fears and hopes, a dream (reverie, nightmare).

3. Draw up a list of subjects suggested by books you have recently read or by movies or TV shows you have seen.

4. Consult your dictionary or essay anthology. Compile a list of general subjects taken from these sources.

5. Consult the *Reader's Guide to Periodical Literature.* Go through the alphabetical listing and compile ten interesting topics to write about.

6. Consult a good encyclopedia. List ten topics from that source that interest you. Then read one or two articles in the encyclopedia to get an overview of your subject.

Limiting the Subject

Now that you have a general subject, do you just sit down and begin to write? Perhaps. If the subject is based on a personal experience, you might be able to do an interesting paper, exploring the subject as you go along, reducing it to manageable proportions. But more frequently, if the subject is a difficult one, or if it is a subject that needs focusing or demands a certain angle of vision, you need to be more methodical in how you go about handling it.

Sometimes in the very act of choosing a subject you can go a long way toward limiting it. For example, when looking for a general subject, instead of choosing a single-word subject from the table of contents or index of a book or magazine, choose the whole title or a portion of it. Although many of the topics are specific, others are general enough so that you can fill in your own content; or you may simply decide to handle the subject from your own point of view. The following are some typical subjects that are already partially limited:

> To drop out or not to drop out.
> This I remember.
> What _____'s second presidential term might be like.
> Why young people are giving up drugs.
> What are you scared of?
> What we must do about our junked-up landscape.
> How to put your trash to good use.
> What kind of person do you want to be?
> Women as sex objects in rock lyrics.

With just a little bit of thought, you could write about many of these topics. Further, the wording itself suggests a method of development. For example, the topic "To drop out or not to drop out" has the antithetical form of an argument. The title "This I remember" suggests a reminiscence. "What _____'s second presidential term might be like" is a hypothesis. The subject "Why young people are giving up drugs" can be developed by giving reasons. Other methods of development suggested by the remaining subjects are enumeration ("What are you scared of?"), problem/solution ("What we must do about our junked-up landscape"), process ("How to put your trash to good use"), and analysis ("What kind of person do you want to be?" and "Women as sex objects in rock lyrics").

I have said that in the act of choosing a subject you can go a long way toward limiting it. Suppose, however, that you have selected or been assigned a very broad topic such as the urban crisis, prejudice, the generation gap, or clothes. Obviously, there is so much that can be said about each of these subjects that you would hardly know how to begin. Most general subjects need to be divided into manageable parts. This can be done in two ways.

The first way is by *free association*—by *listing under the general heading anything that comes to your mind* regarding the subject:

Movies

The Poseidon Adventure
Earthquake
disaster films
Airport
The Towering Inferno
stereotyped plots
action
suspense
emphasis on plot

Generation Gap

values
life-styles
clothes
politics
religious beliefs
education
attitude toward race
music

Clothes

fashion
skin
communication
class distinctions
Pucci

unisex
uniforms
best-dressed women
best-dressed men
movie stars
like packages

As you can see, the topics in the subcategories are still too broad for a 500-word essay, but at least they are much more manageable.

The second method is to consider the various aspects of the general subject by asking a few basic questions:

1. *What is it?*
2. *What are its parts?*
3. *How may it be classified?*
4. *In what respect is it like or unlike something else?*
5. *What are some examples?*
6. *How does it work?*
7. *What are its causes or effects?*

You could add many more questions to these basic few, but at this point you are not being asked to explore the subject thoroughly. Your main concern at this moment is to reduce your subject to manageable proportions. The following are just a few examples of theme topics on the subject of prejudice suggested by using this probe:

1. What is prejudice?
2. Are all people prejudiced?
3. Examples of stereotypes about races and nationalities.
4. Kinds of prejudice.
5. How children learn prejudice.
6. A comparison of the attitudes of the prejudiced person with those of the unprejudiced person.
7. Are people born prejudiced?
8. Is prejudice innate?
9. Does education reduce prejudice?
10. Language as a source of prejudice.
11. Causes of prejudice.
12. Effects of prejudice.

13. How prejudices are formed.
14. Epithets, pejorative terms, and prejudice.

Although it is not absolutely necessary that you limit every subject in this way, there are many advantages to limiting a subject. A limited subject is a more unified subject. It helps you to eliminate unnecessary material. It tells the reader more precisely what you intend to cover. And it makes clearer your whole approach to the subject. Naturally, in selecting and limiting your subject you should always be guided by your audience and your purpose.

Exercises

1. Limit one of the following general subjects by asking these questions of it: What is it like? What are its parts? How may it be classified? In what respect is it like or unlike something else? What are some examples? How does it work? What are its causes or effects?

   a. jogging   f. smog
   b. censorship   g. war crimes
   c. jazz   h. rock music
   d. magic   i. sports
   e. generation gap j. feelings

2. Take one of the topics above and free-associate, putting down as much information about the subject as comes immediately to mind.

3. Take another topic from exercise 1 and use the journalist's questions (Who? What? When? Where? Why? How?) to explore it.

4. For this exercise, divide the class into groups of five or six. Then each group should list four or five specific essay subjects inherent in the following general subjects. Consider the audience appropriate for each subject and your purpose:

   a. music   d. bicycle racing
   b. values   e. theft
   c. fashions   f. noise

g. ethics   n. college education
h. childhood   o. taboos
i. shopping   p. prejudice
j. money   q. crime
k. superstitions   r. ecology
l. civil rights   s. TV
m. the cost of living   t. movies

5. What problems do you find with the following subjects for themes? Suggest ways to make each subject a suitable one:

a. nature   f. animals
b. proverbs   g. planets
c. Indians   h. machines
d. literature   i. sports
e. Arizona   j. studies

6. Examine the titles and headlines of articles in several current magazines and newspapers. Select a few general titles and then comment on how they can be narrowed in scope for purposes of composition.

The Writing Situation

As a writer, one of your tasks is to find something to say; but writing does not occur in a vacuum. It always occurs in some kind of context. In other words, a piece of writing comes into existence as the result of a response to a situation that often demands immediate attention. Let me illustrate this point with a particular example. You are away from home, attending a state university. The end of the semester is drawing near, and you discover that you are broke. You had enough money to last the entire semester, but recently you bought some record albums, a few books, and some clothing—things you could have done without, but they gave you satisfaction and pleasure. What to do? You decide to swallow your pride and to write to your parents, to a relative, or to a friend and ask for money. Your writing situation consists of the complex interrelations of persons, events, and objects which as a writer you must take into account in order to bring about a change in the situation.

A writing situation must take into account the **writer** (in this situation, the writer is you), the writer's **purpose** (the change you want to bring about in the reader), the **reader** or **audience** (your parents, relatives, or friends), and the **occasion** (the circumstances in which a particular event occurs, the time, the place, and the situation that demands immediate attention, the question that needs an answer, the problem that needs a solution, and so forth).

The Writer

Every writer puts something of himself or herself into a piece of writing. Even in so-called objective or impersonal writing, the writer appears as a certain kind of person. The writer takes on a certain role, and his or her writing takes on a corresponding tone. The doctor has a bedside manner, the lawyer has a business manner, the salesperson takes on a friendly tone, the judge sometimes appears stern. There is nothing negative about assuming a role or putting on a mask. When you are with your friends, you talk one way; when you are with your parents, you talk another way; at a job interview, you try to use your best speaking voice; when you tell a dialect joke, you assume another voice. The main idea of your essay may give the reader a hint about the role you are going to assume, but your whole text will reveal your attitude toward your subject.

Look at the following sentences and notice the difference in the writer's attitude toward the subject:

Crime in the streets is terrible; something must be done about it. Crime in the streets must end!

Crime in the streets is bad, but what can you expect when there is widespread unemployment?

Crime in the streets is no worse now than it ever was.

Crime in the streets is bad, but who cares? Live it up! Tomorrow we may all be dead from pollution or a nuclear war.

Obviously, a writer does not always write in an objective, dispassionate style. Sometimes he or she is angry, sometimes frustrated, sometimes hysterical. Other times the writer is reasonable or certain or skeptical or critical or joyful or ironic or dispassionate. Your attitude toward your subject is a part of your meaning, and discovering your attitude is an important step in the writing process.

Your attitude toward your subject, however, is not the only thing that you as a writer must keep in mind. Obviously, you ought to know your subject. And it is to be hoped that you will be interested in it. It is difficult to get your reader interested in your subject if you show no interest yourself. Finally, you need to consider whether your subject is appropriate to your readers. A good writer is knowledgeable, socially responsible, purposeful, and sensitive to the needs of his or her readers.

Exercises

1. Describe three writing situations in which you were involved as a writer. What was the occasion? What was the problem? Who was your reader? What was your purpose in writing?

2. Discuss in class some newspapers and magazines you read. What seem to be the predominant attitudes toward certain subjects in the editorials?

3. Write three sentences exemplifying in each one of the following attitudes: reasonable, angry, amused, frustrated, insensitive.

Audience

As a writer, you must not only choose an appropriate subject and determine your attitude toward that subject, but you must also determine your audience and your purpose. For example, if you were to write a paper for a classroom assignment, no matter how effectively you might construct a possible audience for your writing in your imagination, you know that one given is the instructor. He or she is the immediate audience for your writing. Another given is the other students in the class. Most writers for professional or popular journals have a pretty good idea of what the audiences are like, and their choices of subject matter, the main ideas of their essays, and their methods of developing their subjects usually reflect this knowledge.

Rather than simply assume your audience as given, however, you can determine the characteristics of your audience in a systematic way by asking certain basic questions:

What is the age of your readers?

What is their sex?

Where do they live?

What is their educational background?

What kinds of cultural interests do they have?

What are their social interests?

What do you know about their political beliefs?

What are their religious or philosophical beliefs?

What kinds of jobs do they hold? Are they professionals? White-collar workers? Blue-collar workers?

What kinds of leisure activities are they interested in? Movies? Sports? Reading? Jogging?

Is there anything not typical about this particular audience?

The result of asking these questions is that you will come up with a more complex picture of your audience.

In contrast to those who feel that writers should learn as much as possible about specific audiences and attempt to get views of their audiences that are as close as possible to reality are those who contend that writers *fictionalize* audiences, that is, they construct ideal audiences in their imaginations. According to Walter Ong, writers do not learn about their readers from daily life, but from other writers, who in turn have learned from still other writers the conventions of fictionalizing audiences. In fact, Ong argues, it might not be appropriate to talk about *audience* at all in relation to writing. Writers address *readers,* and readers do not form a collective audience in the same sense that an audience that goes to hear a speaker does. As the "readership" begins to read, it splits up into individual readers.

Ong has two things in mind when he says that the audience for writing is a fiction. First, in preparing to write, writers must assign some role to their imaginary audiences: concerned citizen, angry parent, intelligent layperson, belligerent redneck, alarmed voter, chagrined wife, disgusted consumer. Second, readers have to accept the role that writers have provided for them. When reading a work of fiction about some person in an exotic land, the reader must imaginatively project himself or herself into those surroundings. When reading an essay in a magazine about the dangers of pollution, he or she has to switch roles and become part of an audience that is concerned with pollution.

If we accept this point of view about the notion of audience, then it would seem that in the very act of formulating an idea or opinion we are choosing some roles for ourselves and assigning some roles to our audiences. For example, suppose you decide to write about religion and you use the thesis "My attitudes toward religion differ from those of my parents in a number of ways." The role you have chosen for yourself is that of a young adult who is struggling to come to grips with one of the most significant problems of the day. As a reader, I must accept the role of a concerned, older person who is honestly interested in your attitudes about religion and about the changing mores of the day. If you choose as a thesis "People tend to act out in life the things they see on television," then you are choosing the role of a concerned citizen who, because of recent newspaper accounts about adolescents acting out in real life the violence they watch on television, sees a cause-and-effect relationship between television shows and violence. As your reader, I must also assume the role of a concerned citizen.

Actually, these two views of how writers determine their audiences are complementary. Undoubtedly there are times when writers' audiences are so far removed in time and space that the writers must imagine their audiences. But there are other times when writers can with some assurance determine the actual characteristics of real audiences and can therefore proceed accordingly. Advertisers assuredly do more than imagine their audiences. They send out questionnaires, and as a result they can with amazing accuracy choose the appropriate audiences for their products.

Exercises

1. Using the questions enumerated in the section on audience, analyze an audience for whom you are planning to write.

2. You have been appointed fashion editor of a major magazine. As editor, your job is to write articles on some aspect of fashion or the clothing industry. Your boss has told you that your articles must go beyond a mere summary of what is in fashion. What subjects might you come up with if your readers were

   a. Women of limited income?   f. motorcycle riders?
   b. single men?   g. corporate executives?
   c. single women?   h. dry cleaners?
   d. weight watchers?   i. dog owners?
   e. travelers?

3. You have decided to write an essay on the influence of the blues on several rock groups. How will your strategies change for each of the following readers?

   a. a music professor
   b. a group of high-school students
   c. an all-black audience
   d. a group of rock fans
   e. a group of senior citizens

4. You have decided to write a letter to the editor of a local newspaper protesting the proposed building of a prison near your home. Your purpose is to encourage readers of the paper to join you in fighting the proposed building site. What arguments might you use to appeal to

   a. concerned parents?
   b. people who live near the site?

    c. politicians?
    d. students?
    e. taxpayers?

5. Bring to class two letters to the editor in the local newspaper or in a magazine. Be prepared to discuss the following questions:

    a. Who is the intended audience?
    b. Is there more than one potential audience?
    c. What is the purpose of each letter?
    d. Is the purpose explicitly stated in a sentence or two, or is it implied?

Purpose and Aim

Every kind of writing has some purpose, but these purposes are so numerous that for the less experienced writer it would be helpful if they could be reduced to a few categories:

To inform or instruct   (car owner's manual)

To convince or persuade   (advertisement)

To entertain or please,   (poem, joke)
by calling attention to
language and form

To express strong feelings   (diary, love letter)
and emotions

These categories, which are broad and general, I shall call the **aims** of writing to distinguish them from the numerous specific intentions that writers have. The writer's **intention** is the *response that he or she expects to get from the reader.* Over the years, writers have developed other terms to refer to these categories so that *writing that informs or instructs* is called **informative discourse.** *Writing that convinces or persuades* is called **persuasive discourse.** *Writing that entertains or pleases or has an aesthetic purpose* is called **literary discourse.** *Writing that expresses strong* *feelings and emotions* is called **expressive discourse.** Clearly, these aims overlap, and you could probably add some aims that are not included in the above list. But in most kinds of writing, one aim is dominant.

It ought to be obvious that as a writer you must first know your purpose before you can go about achieving it. Lawyers must develop strategies in relation to their aims if they expect to be successful in the courtroom. Contractors must know the purposes of the buildings that they are going to construct. If you formulate your purpose in terms of reader response, your writing will more likely be appropriate to your intended audience. The following scheme shows how the writer's purpose can be related to the desired response in the reader:

Writer's Purpose	*Reader's Response*
To inform or instruct	Understanding
To convince or persuade	Belief or action
To entertain or please	Aesthetic pleasure
To express strong feelings and emotions	Conduct or thought governed by emotion

Despite your good intentions, at times you might have difficulty keeping your dominant purpose in mind. One good strategy is to formulate a **purpose sentence.** This is a sentence that *explicitly sets forth your purpose in relation to your subject and to your audience.* Suppose, for example, you want to convince the director of freshman English that freshman English ought to be an elective. You might begin with an outline of the elements that will go into your purpose sentence:

Subject: Freshman English ought to be an elective.
Purpose: To persuade
Audience: The director of freshman English

Then you can easily combine the parts into a coherent whole:

Purpose Sentence: My purpose is to convince the director of freshman English that freshman English ought to be an elective.

The purpose sentence is not to be confused with your **thesis sentence**—one that *explicitly sets forth the main idea of your essay,* although it could be made into a thesis sentence:

Freshman English ought to be an elective.

The purpose sentence is designed to help you to keep your central idea in mind and to keep before you the response you expect to get from your reader. It can also be useful in helping you to plan your writing strategies.

Here are a few examples of purpose sentences related to the various aims:

My purpose is to get a friend who likes traditional art *to appreciate* a Jackson Pollock painting. (aesthetic aim)

My purpose is to get my parents *to understand* rock music. (informative aim)

My purpose is *to persuade* my uncle, who is a Democrat, to vote for a Republican governor. (persuasive aim)

My purpose is *to convince* my teacher to change the grade on my last essay. (persuasive aim)

My purpose is to help my sister *to understand* the basic sentence types of English grammar. (informative aim)

Notice that not all of these purpose sentences can easily be made into thesis sentences. Most are too formal and too general. Occasionally, you can take some of the wording of your purpose sentence and use it to compose a thesis sentence. ("You should vote for X for the following reasons.") But more often the purpose sentence serves mostly as a guide and as an attempt to make you self-conscious about the aims of writing in relation to your subject and to your reader.

Exercises

1. Using the following outline as a guide, fill in the content that might go into five purpose sentences:

   Subject: (fill in the subject)
   Purpose: (fill in the purpose)
   Audience: (fill in the audience)

2. Select a magazine advertisement and study it carefully. On a separate sheet of paper, answer the following questions:

   a. What is the purpose of the ad?
   b. Is there more than one purpose?
   c. Are some purposes immediate? Long-term? Hidden?
   d. In what way is the ad's purpose adapted to the audience?
   e. Who is the audience?
   f. Within the general readership of the magazine from which the ad was taken, how does the ad writer select out a more specific audience? By organizational strategies? By word choice? By the illustration?

3. Some writers would not agree that the writer's dominant purpose ought to be clearly indicated in a piece of writing. To some writers, writing is a process of discovering one's intention as one writes. Do you agree with this point of view? Are there certain kinds of writing, perhaps, that might lend themselves to one or another of these views.

4. What would you say would be the dominant aim of the following kinds of *discourse* (verbal expression in speech or writing)?

   a. a class lecture on black dialects
   b. a sermon
   c. an informal conversation with a friend
   d. a debate about nuclear power
   e. a patriotic speech on a national holiday
   f. an oral interpretation of a poem

Modes and Kinds of Discourse

After you have determined your subject, your purpose, and your audience, you must determine the manner of developing that subject and the kind of discourse. We will be looking at a variety of ways of developing ideas in subsequent chapters, but for the moment let's discuss briefly the general idea of modes.

A **mode** can refer both to *a way of getting ideas to write about* and to *the manner of developing those ideas.* These modes have labels that you are already familiar with, although you may have used different terms to refer to them. Perhaps you called them **techniques** or **processes.** As ways of developing paragraphs, they are sometimes referred to as **methods of development.** Some typical examples of these modes are the following: description, analysis, classification, definition, comparison, contrast, exemplification, narration, process, and cause and effect. Your choice of modes will necessarily be determined by your subject, your purpose, and your audience.

For example, imagine that you are a copywriter for an advertising firm and that your task is to write the copy for a food ad or a cosmetics ad. The subject matter seems to suggest that description would be the most appropriate mode. Suppose, on the other hand, that you are asked to write the copy for a stereo ad. Stereo buyers seem to like a listing of important features, so you would probably choose the mode of analysis, setting forth in much detail the outstanding features of the product. In much writing the modes are mixed. But in the beginning stages of learning to write, there is considerable value in isolating the modes and seeing them as simple.

The form or kind of discourse a writer chooses is usually the direct result of his or her purpose. For example, if your aim is to persuade, you might choose the form of a letter to the editor, a speech, a sermon, an ad, or a personal letter to convey your ideas. If your aim is to inform or instruct, you might write an expository essay, a book review, a movie review, a news article, a scientific essay, a literary critical essay, or an explanatory note. If your aim is to please or to entertain, you might tell a joke or write a poem, a limerick, a short story, a popular song, or a rock lyric. Finally, if your aim is self-expression, you might choose some form of personal or autobiographical writing, perhaps in a journal or diary.

At the beginning of the semester, you might find it useful to attach a cover sheet to your essays on which you list in outline form all of the elements that you must take into account in writing your essays. A typical outline for an assignment would look something like this:

General Subject: Automobiles
Purpose: To convince readers to buy a luxury car
Audience: Readers of *Esquire* magazine
Kind of Discourse: Magazine ad
Mode: Description

Exercises

1. Discuss in class: If you were writing advertising copy, what mode or modes might you choose to develop the following products?

   a. candy, gum, cookies, pastries
   b. drinks, staple foods, desserts
   c. perfumes, cosmetics, toilet articles
   d. men's suits, hats, stockings, dresses, shirts
   e. jewelry, silverware, watches
   f. moving pictures, novels, magazine subscriptions
   g. cars, tires, batteries, motor oil
   h. stereos, TV sets, radios, tape recorders

2. For what *readers* would you select any of the above-mentioned products?

3. It is often assumed in this age of mass media that writing is not as important as it used to be. Is this true? How could you verify this statement?

4. Interview the following people about the kinds of writing they do in their jobs: your mother or father; an uncle, aunt, cousin, brother, or sister; a friend; a celebrity. Then make a list and bring this list to class for discussion. Do not overlook even the seemingly most unimportant kinds of writing: a grocery list, a note, letters of various kinds, reports,

memos, invitations, and so forth. In compiling this information, use the familiar "who, what, when, where, why" questions of journalism. Who is doing the writing? What kind of writing is being done? For what purpose? When is it being done? Where?

Invention:

Probing the Subject

Chapter 2

Invention: Probing the Subject

Once you have decided upon a general subject and determined your attitude toward it, your purpose, and your audience, you are ready to explore your subject more fully.

To do this, you need a plan, a way to reach somehow into the recesses of your mind, to spin out of yourself, as a spider spins out a filament, a thread of thought that will develop into an orderly web. For invention is a thinking process. In its broadest sense, **invention** is *any mental activity that will bring to conscious awareness something previously unknown.* The process seems to have its origin deep within the human mind.

How Students Compose

Although many students are unsystematic in the way they go about getting ideas for writing and in the way they compose, the following student comments seem to indicate that there is a consistent pattern that some students follow in their prewriting and writing activities.

Maria

When I approach a writing project, I use very definite methods. I have not intentionally developed these methods. They have simply evolved over a period of years as habits which work well for me. They have proved to be consistently effective, and therefore I have retained them. They help me to achieve a certain balance and precision in my writing which I feel is essential to the validity of my work, and thus, if I were to discard even one of them, the quality of my writing would be diminished.

Invention

Before I begin the actual organization of my thoughts on paper, I usually research my subject for weeks, or even months, in advance. When I feel that I have done a sufficient amount of research and am satisfied that I know my subject well enough to begin writing,

Gestation Period

I then consciously try to stop thinking about the subject at all for several days, and instead occupy myself with very ordinary and usually rather quiet activities—long bicycle rides, evening walks, or perhaps some shopping I've been putting off. It is during this time that my thoughts begin to come together in my head, and when I feel

Readiness

that there is a flow, I begin to write. I cannot explain to the reader just exactly what this "flow" is. I don't understand it myself. I can only say that it is a sort of organic signal which tells me that I am ready—physically, emotionally, and spiritually—to begin putting thoughts into words.

When I finally sit down at the typewriter, it is always very late at night, for I have never been able to compose during the daylight hours. Usually I work for several nights like this, perhaps all through the night. But there is always a feeling of exhilaration the next morning—even if I have no sleep at all—because during those very quiet and private hours of the night before, I was able to reach out for a moment and touch . . . DELIGHT. And it is for that one moment that I write.

Conscious Composing

The most crucial period of the composition for me is the time I spend constructing my thesis or introductory paragraph. This may take hours to complete because it must convey to the reader, concisely and coherently, in just four or five sentences, the entire thought of the paper. Once this first paragraph is completed and I am satisfied with it, the rest of the words come relatively fast and almost seem to organize themselves. I always write in draft form. When this draft

Editing

is completed, I edit my work, usually making various changes and corrections in the text, then retype the paper in final form.

I don't know whether or not my methods of composition are very conventional. I suspect that they are not. But they are a very integral part of my writing and therefore an integral part of me.

Shirley

Often, when I sit down to do any kind of formal writing, I am reminded of Samuel Johnson's comment that anyone who writes except for money is a blockhead. I agree with Dr. Johnson's implication that writing is toil of the most arduous kind. Never, in my entire life, have I whipped out a paper. Hard work and mental anguish are always involved.

I have observed my husband's methodical composing process—note cards, outline, draft, final product—and tried to imitate it, hoping to lessen, if not the work, at least the anguish. For me, the result is guaranteed dullness. However, I do have a system for composing. Some processes are common to all my writing efforts.

Creative Tension

As soon as an assignment is given or I decide to produce a piece of writing, the project is rarely off my mind until I complete it. While driving a car, I must consciously and repeatedly haul my atten-

Indeterminacy

tion back onto the road. If I clear a cluttered room, I will later have no notion of the disposition of its contents. Theses, arguments, quotations in scattered, shotgun patterns flash through my mind. Opening (never closing) sentences are born and inspected. By the time I begin serious work, I have developed a rough, tentative thesis and some supporting thoughts. If the paper requires research, I assemble my

Conscious Composing

sources at this point, read, and make notes on sheets of lined paper. If no research is involved, I sit down and start writing. I often start half-a-dozen times. Sometimes a great opening sentence emerges in the middle of the second page, and so I begin again. Some of the thoughts incubated over a sinkful of dirty dishes are now coaxed, prodded, or wrenched into being.

Revising While Composing

I do not write rough drafts. Such efforts have never rendered me a satisfactory product. I labor over each sentence as I write, revising until I accept it, before moving to the next. If I leave a line less than finished, the spark that lit it dies forever. So I write slowly, painstakingly, and sometimes painfully, head throbbing and stomach churning.

Endings are my particular torment. Rarely does one simply suggest itself as other parts of the project might. I write, reject, and rewrite until something works.

Creative Satisfaction

I have considered whether I would be relieved to know I would never agonize through another piece of writing. The answer is an unqualified no. A finished piece is exhilarating. I anticipate that feeling throughout the work; it is part of my sustenance. Perhaps I just suffer from the old "because-it-feels-so-good-when-I-stop" syndrome.

Dinah

When the movie houselights came on after my first viewing of *2001: A Space Odyssey*, it was an unwelcome intrusion; I was mentally and emotionally transcending earthly bounds. I had to go home to my typewriter to continue my transcendency.

Occasion   It is this kind of emotional lather, following a concrete experience, that often precedes my making an effort to compose something in writing. These concrete experiences can be as simple as listening to a frog chorus after a rain, or as complex as contemplating the process of regeneration presented in Shakespeare's *Tempest*.

Indeterminacy   Sometimes while integrating a particular experience I perceive a concept forming in my mind. I don't think of the concept in words, but become aware of it in a process I characterize, in my own thinking, as the "split-second movie." It's difficult to explain. I "see" the concept, but it is such a fleeting entity, I can't hold it. It is the after-image of the "split-second movie" that I refer to as the perceived concept.

Composing   The hardest work of composing now begins. I organize random ideas, but in the most rudimentary fashion. I don't worry about an introduction; I just start at the point most interesting to me, and *Invention* write both ways. To generate material, I have imaginary conversations, starring myself and someone I'd like to impress. I dazzle this person with my profound insights, clever wording, and witty characterizations. The fun part is choosing only my best lines to build my written presentation.

      Next, I read what I have written, to see what I think. While I don't always know in exactly what direction to write, I do know if what I have written fits the perceived concept I am working toward. In art, there is a process called "rubbing." A special kind of paper is placed over an impression of a design, picture, or sometimes tombstone and rubbed over with the flat edge of a piece of granite or colored wax. The process by which I discover words for my concept is similar. I place my typewriter "against" the mystery mass of the concept and type until a clear image emerges.

Composing and Revising   Thus begins a tedious stretch of writing and revision—trial and error. I continue this process as long as I can stand it. Eventually, *Gestation* my ideas temporarily depleted, I leave the project for a period of time.

Unconscious
Invention

A few hours or days later, I begin writing again. At this stage, new ideas make their appearance rapidly, not in an orderly way, but crowding each other. The disorder of their appearance can be overwhelming. When this happens, I'm temporarily about as pleased as the Sorcerer was with his Apprentice. Ideas stumble in end-over-end, march, interrupt, and sometimes make so much noise I can hardly

Composing

write. I make an effort to classify at this point, but often settle for recording as quickly as possible—writing words, phrases, and incomplete sentences down randomly.

Arrangement
and
Revision

In the final process, I try to bring order. I sort, classify, fit, and revise for the finished work.

Kate

Because the process of writing has seldom been pleasant for me, I inevitably postpone composing a paper until the night before it's due (only, I add in defense, if it is fifty pages or less). When I finally

Gestation
Period

sit down with a pen and paper, I continue to procrastinate by listening to the radio or splitting the ends of my hair. However, at this time I am also fretting over what I will say and how I will say it, as well

Creative
Tension,
Invention

as whether or not I will finish before the deadline.

Only after I am nervous and tense do I start to write. At first I only scribble ideas as they come to me, as though I am trying to empty my head. At this early stage, I have a tremendous amount of energy and have to fight to write down the barrage of words.

Gestation
Period

After I have depleted my initial stock of ideas, though, I feel drained and usually have to procrastinate anywhere from fifteen minutes to three hours in order to feel sufficiently pressured to continue. However, I sense that while I am stalling, my subconscious is somehow

Conscious
Composing

still working on my paper.

The next stage of writing is more routine: I collect a thesis sentence from the ideas I previously wrote down and decide how to develop it. This is a systematic, logical process, and my energy level is much lower than before. After this, I write my first paragraph with care and deliberation before I allow myself more procrastinating,

Composing,
Gestation

for if I don't start to write now, I never will.

While actually composing the paper, I continue to alternate periods of wasting time with periods of writing. Wasting time appears to be as crucial as the actual writing, for besides allowing me an

Creative Tension — opportunity to rest and to clear my head, it increases my nervousness over not meeting the deadline. Consequently, my energy level is raised and my ability to concentrate increases. After I finally finish the paper (at three in the morning, to be precise), I hastily type it up (making numerous typographical errors), hand it in, go home, and sleep.

Robert

After long reflections on the question of how I compose, I have come to the conclusion that I am a masochist. When I am given a topic *Invention* for composition, for example, that requires research, I do extensive research. For me there is no speculation, no attempt to reduce the topic to manageable proportions. I simply walk to the library and check out every source on that topic that I can carry out in my arms, and return home to begin reading. Since I haven't even begun to limit my topic, the only aspects that I specifically look for are those that strike my interest. If I get halfway through a book and decide that I'm becoming too bored, I merely close the pages and open another book.

Inchoateness — After two or three weeks of such haphazard research, I feel as if I have enough ideas floating around in my mind to begin the writing process. Of course, this is usually a day or two before the assignment *Invention* is due, so that I have no choice but to attempt to make some sense *by* of all I have read. Like my research techniques, my initial efforts at *Brain-* organization are completely unmethodical. With my lucky silver pen *storming* in hand, I open a notebook and begin to jot down ideas and facts which I have found particularly interesting or truthful, along with thoughts about the subject which were formed as I read.

Conscious Composing — Once I have finished compiling this personal set of notes, I sit and stare at them. This is the only logical part of my composition, for I seek out various relationships and pursue lines of thought suggested by my notes. This is the point at which I begin the actual physical act of writing. I try to expand upon a certain relationship or set of relationships, or develop a line of thought, often writing several pages and then discovering that I've reached a dead end.

Gestation Period — It's about this time that I close my notebook and flip on the radio or go outside for a walk. The theme is still prominent in my mind, but at least I don't have all of my aborted attempts to deal with it staring me in the face. Somehow, as corny as it may sound, I get an inspiration. A definite thesis statement will pop into my head, and suddenly the chaotic jumble of ideas begins to sort itself out, each thought falling neatly into place. I hurry back to my notebook and begin to write, nonstop, the theme's organization logically suggested by my thesis and years of writing practice.

Illumination
Arrangement

In the writing that I do which doesn't require research, my methods are much the same, without the weeks of extensive reading. Again, I jot down fragments of ideas and make several unsuccessful starts until one of them seems to suggest a thesis and organization for the entire theme. It is a rare occasion that I know exactly what I want to say and how to say it from start to finish.

Invention

It has occurred to me as I have written this that I do have a method in my written composition, as unmethodical as it may seem. My processes are essentially the same for every composition I write, and they have always been successful.

I think it is clear from these student comments that *some* kind of systematic approach to writing is better than none at all. Those students who have a conscious awareness of what they are doing seem to have an easier time of putting their thoughts on paper. All of the students, however, use certain strategies that result in recognizable patterns.

The composing process begins with a kind of creative tension which, though it may be discomforting to the writer, seems necessary for the resolution of conflicts. In the beginning stage of invention, there is often a kind of indeterminacy, an inchoateness, a lack of clarity or precision. The process is dynamic. Ideas and images jostle one another. At this stage, there is also an order of sorts, a potentiality waiting to be realized, as the writer surrenders to an inner necessity. Sometimes even before he or she begins to write, the writer grasps the pattern to be developed in its full form. Sometimes the writer perceives a fragment of the whole, an image, a concept, but even at this stage, the part seems to contain the whole.

At some stage in the process, the writer must exert some conscious effort on the task at hand. In the prewriting stage, this might take the form of reading, taking notes, or thinking about the subject. In the writing stage, it consists of filling in details and making logical connections, giving to the writer's thought a determinate direction.

Often, this period of self-conscious activity is followed by a period in which the writer must while away the time or think about something else. Even in these moments of escape from the task at hand, the mind evidently continues to work, making connections, sorting out ideas. Some attention must also be paid to revision, either as one is writing or after the first draft is completed.

What also seems clear from these student comments is that seldom is the composing process strictly linear. A writer will gather ideas, think about these ideas, then procrastinate, gather more ideas, and begin to write, put the writing aside, try to think of other things, return to the writing with renewed vigor, write, revise while writing, reinvent, consciously follow a plan, unconsciously depart from that plan, make connections, revise again, and rewrite. Although the process is not strictly linear, it is useful to think of it as occurring in stages, even though these stages are idealized parts of what is really an organic and dynamic whole.

In my own writing, I follow a sequence of stages that can be described as prewriting, writing, and revision, even though there may be considerable overlapping in the stages. I gather ideas, consider my subject, my audience, and my purpose, and think hard about those ideas for weeks or months before I begin to write. The gestation period for me is at night, while I'm trying to go to sleep. Ideas jostle ideas as I make connections and perceive patterns. Sometimes the pattern for an entire essay will take shape in my head. When I begin to write, I continue to invent, but invention now means filling in details, giving examples, and so forth.

Exercises

1. How do you compose? Write a description of how you go about preparing for a writing assignment and how you actually do the inventing and writing.

2. Daydream! Deliberately put yourself into a situation that is pleasant and let your thoughts wander freely about the subject.

3. Imagine yourself in a strange new world. What do you see? What do you feel? What do you smell? What do you hear?

4. Think of a childhood memory, joyful or painful, happy or sad. Let the order of memory determine the process of invention.

5. Sit down in a room or outside under a tree. Write down freely what you see, hear, smell, touch, perceive.

Probing for Ideas

Although no two people would develop a general subject in exactly the same way, each of us to a certain extent must nevertheless, follow certain lines of development in our thinking because the mind is organized according to certain principles. It recognizes temporal, spatial, logical, and psychological principles and relationships in the universe.

Principles of composition such as analysis, classification, comparison and contrast, and cause and effect are *ways of thinking.* For example, not a day goes by that you don't analyze, classify, compare and contrast, or discover cause-and-effect relationships in the world around you. You see a tree and note the shape of its branches, the size of its trunk, or the color of its leaves. You classify it by naming it. You compare it to other trees. You observe it changing in time, notice that termites are causing it to decay or that it has been struck by lightning. When the tree is not in the immediate range of your vision, you substitute images or words to call it to mind, and these words or images facilitate your thinking about the tree. Every time you analyze, classify, exemplify, enumerate, compare, contrast, or discern cause-and-effect relationships, you are inventing ideas.

Compositional categories such as analysis, classification, and comparison and contrast, besides being principles of thought, are categories that suggest questions that can be used in exploring ideas for writing. These categories are sometimes called *topics*, a word that originally meant "places." (I have referred to them previously as *modes*.) The topics were literally conceived of as places in the mind or in books where ideas were stored, where one could go to get ideas. The term **topic** today is more frequently used to refer to the subject matter of a discussion or conversation. But I would like to use the term to refer to *categories that can be used to direct the search for ideas or the arrangement of these ideas into some orderly pattern.*

What I would like to propose is that in examining a subject to get ideas for writing, you use these topics or modes and the questions they suggest in a systematic way. To help you to do this, I have put these categories into a scheme to enable you to use them more efficiently:

Topics of Invention
A.
    Static
    1. Identification
    2. Analysis
       a. Partition
       b. Enumeration
    3. Description
    4. Classification
    5. Exemplification
    6. Definition
    7. Comparison and contrast
       a. Similarity
          (1) Literal
          (2) Figurative
       b. Difference
          (1) In kind
          (2) In degree

B. Progressive
    1. Narration
    2. Process
    3. Cause and effect

This visual scheme has two advantages. It shows you how the topics are related to one another, and it will enable you to remember them better for future use.

The static, logical topics are for the most part abstracted from time and space. Description, of course, is an exception, but what unites all of these topics is our ability to view them apart from their existence in time.

Obviously, many relationships exist among these categories. Probably all of the topics work together in the composing process, but for practical purposes you can separate them out. You can't classify without comparing or divide something into parts without noticing differences. All of these topics relate to dynamic processes in the human mind.

In order to use the topics to explore a subject, you need merely to move from one topic on the diagram to another, applying them to the subject at hand. You can start anywhere on the diagram that you like. Thus, you might begin by describing or defining your subject, dividing it into parts, classifying it, looking for significant examples, or comparing it to something else. Then you move on to the other topics, all the while obtaining a clearer idea of your subject as you apply each topic in turn. Once you have gone through the topics, you can repeat the procedure as often as you desire. The process is recursive. The result of applying these topics to a particular subject is that when you complete this procedure, you should have something to say, or at least you will be aware of the gaps in your knowledge and go on from there.

It may be that the topics may best be applied by putting them in the form of questions. The following are just a few of the many questions suggested by these topics:

Identification
Who or what is it?
Who or what is doing it or did it?
Who or what caused it to happen?
To whom did it happen?

Analysis
What are its pieces, parts, or sections?
How may they logically be divided?
What is the logical order?
What is the exact number?

Description
What are its constituent parts?
What are its features or physical characteristics?
How is it organized in space?

Classification
What are its common attributes?
What are its basic categories?

Exemplification
What are some representative instances, examples,
or illustrations?

Definition
What are its limits or boundaries?
What are its classes?
What are its common attributes?
What is its etymology?

Comparison
What is it like?
How is it similar to other things?
How does it differ from other things?

Narration
What happened?
What is happening?
What will happen?
When did it happen?
Where did it happen?

Process
How did it happen?
How does it work?
What are its stages or phases?
How do you make it or do it?

Cause and Effect
Why did it happen?
What are its causes?
What are its effects?
What is its purpose?
How is it related causally to something else?

Another plan is to put the topics in the form of statements and apply these directly to the topic you are exploring. The advantage of this procedure is that you will have fewer questions, statements, or topics to remember:

Identify the subject.
Describe it.
Divide it into parts.
Define it.
Classify it.
Give some examples.
Point out its similarities to or differences from something else.
Tell what happened, when it happened, and where.
Tell how it happened or how it is changing in time.
State its causes or effects.

In probing, clearly, you cannot apply all of the topics or questions to every subject. But merely by using some of them you will be able to get enough ideas to begin your writing.

To illustrate how the process of discovering ideas might work with an actual subject, let's take the general subject "automobiles" and explore it in a systematic way. I have chosen the subject of automobiles because it is one that is continually in our consciousness. (Perhaps you have recently bought a car or are about to buy a car, or someone in your family has bought a car, or a friend is about to buy one.) Automobiles are in our consciousness because of our concern with pollution, gasoline prices, traffic congestion, automobile accidents, and travel.

Identify the subject.

Cars of various makes and models. Chevrolets. Pontiacs. Cadillacs. Oldsmobiles. Buicks. Fords. Lincolns. Mercurys. Plymouths. Dodges. Chryslers. Hondas. Mazdas. Subarus. Toyotas. Volkswagens. Audis. Fiats. Datsuns. Subcompacts. Compacts. Large cars. Midsized cars. Luxury cars. Specialty cars. Gremlin. Opel. Skyhawk. Starfire. Sunbird. Chevette. Fiesta. Pinto. Arrow. Horizon. Rabbit. Malibu. Nova. Granada. Fairmont. Cutlass. Le Mans. Impala. Caprice. Cougar. Catalina.

Divide it into parts.

Noise-absorbing body mounts. Door and body seals. Vibration-dampening body mounts. Generous amounts of insulation. Acoustic-backed carpet and headliners. Smooth and quiet ride.

Wire wheel covers. Fiberglass-belted radial ply tires. White-wall radial tires. Surefooted grip in rain or snow. White-stripe glass-belted radials. Power windows. Side-window defoggers.

Electric clock. Courtesy lamp for ashtray. Reading lights on rear door. Two-tone paint treatment. Extensive corrosion-resisting treatment.

Power steering. Power brakes. Front disc brakes. Sport steering wheel. Custom leather-wrapped tilt steering wheel. Rack-and-pinion steering. Strong solid body. Tough frame. Body side molding. High-energy ignition system.

Four-cylinder engine. V-6 engine. V-8 engine. 98-cubic-inch engine. 134-cubic-inch. 231-cubic-inch. 260-cubic-inch. 305-cubic-inch. 1.6-litre engine. 1.7-litre. 2.2-litre. 3.8-litre. 4.3-litre. 5.0-litre. Four-cylinder, overhead cam engine.

Impressive space efficiency. Full-size room for six. Lots of room. Cramped. Too little elbow room. Fair comfort. Barely enough head room. Not enough leg room. More head room. More rear-seat leg room. Plenty of rear hip room. More usable trunk space. Twenty cubic feet of trunk space.

Five-speed manual transmission. Automatic transmission. Four-speed manual transmission. Crisp-shifting manual transmission.

Full carpeting. Color-keyed carpeting. Wall-to-wall carpeting. Cut-pile carpeting. Tufted seat backs. Notchback seats. Leather seating. Cloth fabrics. Vinyls. Vinyl upholstery. Reclining bucket seats. Corduroy bucket seats. Firm cushions.

Front-wheel drive. Four-wheel independent suspension. Electronic fuel injection. Battery that never needs refilling. Power sport mirrors. Instrument panel. AM/FM radio. Stereo. Cigarette lighter.

New fuel efficiency. High fuel economy. 21 mpg highway. 16 mpg city. 31, 32, 36, 40 mpg highway. 16, 20, 24, 25, 30 mpg city.

Describe the subject.
Great car. Beautiful. Ultimate in fashion and design. Remarkable design achievement. Elegant new luxury. Clean, functional lines. Clean and classic look. Luxurious comfort. Supple vinyls. Luxurious roominess. Comfortable. Elegant style. Handsomely detailed. Luxury and comfort. Color-keyed cut-pile carpeting. Elegantly tufted seat backs. Rich cloth fabrics. Sensationally smooth ride. Pleated and plush comfort.

Classify the subject.
General Motors (Chevrolet, Pontiac, Oldsmobile, Buick, Cadillac); *Ford* (Ford, Mercury, Lincoln); *Chrysler* (Plymouth, Dodge, Chrysler). *Chevrolet* (Monza, Chevette, Malibu, Nova, Impala, Caprice, Camaro, Monte Carlo); *Oldsmobile* (Starfire, Cutlass, Omega, Delta 88, 98, Toronado, Calais); *Buick* (Opel, Skyhawk, Century, Skylark, Le Sabre, Electra, Riviera, Regal); *Pontiac* (Sunbird, Le Mans, Phoenix, Catalina, Bonneville, Firebird, Grand Prix); *Cadillac* (Deville, Eldorado, Seville). *Ford* (Fiesta, Mustang II, Pinto, LTD, Thunderbird); *Mercury* (Bobcat, Monarch, Zephyr, Cougar, Marquis); *Lincoln* (Continental, Continental Mark IV, Versailles). *Plymouth* (Sapporo, Horizon, Omni, Arrow, Volare, Fury); *Dodge* (Colt, Diplomat, Monaco, Charger, Magnum XE); *Chrysler* (Le Baron, Newport, New Yorker, Cordoba).

Subcompact cars, compact cars, large cars, luxury cars, specialty cars.

Subcompact cars. AMC Gremlin, Buick Opel, Buick Skyhawk, Chevrolet Monza, Oldsmobile Starfire, Pontiac Sunbird, Chevrolet Chevette, Fiat 131, Ford Fiesta, Ford Pinto, Plymouth Arrow, Plymouth Horizon, Volkswagen Rabbit, Volkswagen Diesel, Datsun B210, Datsun F10, Dodge Challenger, Plymouth Sapporo, Dodge Colt, Dodge Omni, Honda Accord, Honda Civic, Mazda, Subaru, Toyota Corolla, Toyota Corona.

Compact cars. AMC Concord, Pacer, Audi Fox, Audi 5000, BMW 320, Buick Century, Buick Skylark, Chevrolet Malibu, Chevrolet Nova, Chrysler Le Baron, Dodge Diplomat, Datsun 810, Dodge Aspen, Plymouth Volare, Ford Granada, Ford Fairmont, Oldsmobile Cutlass, Oldsmobile Omega, Pontiac Le Mans, Pontiac Phoenix, Mercury Zephyr.

Large cars. Buick Le Sabre, Buick Electra, Chevrolet Impala, Chevrolet Caprice, Chrysler Newport, Chrysler New Yorker, Dodge Monaco, Plymouth Fury, Ford LTD, Mercury Marquis, Ford LTD II, Mercury Cougar, Oldsmobile Delta 88, Oldsmobile 98, Pontiac Catalina.

Luxury cars. Buick Riviera, Cadillac Deville, Cadillac Eldorado, Cadillac Seville, Lincoln Continental, Mark IV, Lincoln Versailles, Mercedes-Benz 2400, Mercedes-Benz 300D and 280SE, Oldsmobile Toronado.

Specialty cars. Buick Regal, Chevrolet Camaro, Pontiac Firebird, Chevrolet Monte Carlo, Chrysler Cordoba, Dodge Charger SE, Dodge Magnum, Ford Thunderbird, Oldsmobile Cutlass Supreme, Pontiac Grand Prix.

Define the subject.

A *subcompact* may be defined as a car that can accommodate four persons. It has a small four-cylinder engine. Although four-speed transmissions are common, some five-speeds are available. Automatic transmissions are also available in most models. Front-wheel drive is also becoming common in most subcompacts. Although a subcompact can usually accommodate four persons, the rear seat is often too cramped for adults.

A *compact* is a car about the size and weight of the Chevrolet Nova and some of the newly down-sized General Motors models such as the Buick Skylark and the Chevrolet Malibu. Most compacts are cars that have seating room for five or six persons. Most have automatic transmissions, but manual transmissions are also available in most models. Their engines range from the small four-cylinder to the large V-8.

Large cars are cars that tend to provide a quieter, more comfortable ride than do the domestic compact models. They are usually roomier inside. Large cars are often referred to as sedans. Included in this group defined as large cars are the old midsized models that haven't been down-sized yet and the new, so-called full-sized models.

According to automobile manufacturers, a *luxury car* is the best car that automakers can build. Luxury cars supposedly are cars with a truly superior ride, handling, and braking, but often they are no better than other good cars not defined as luxury cars. Unfortunately, the fuel economy of luxury cars is relatively low. The price of these cars is generally higher than that of other cars their size.

A *specialty car* has been defined by one automotive magazine as "basically a sedan showing off." Specialty cars have racy-looking coupe bodies in place of functional sedan bodies. The buyer of a specialty car gives up a little bit of practicality for style. Coupe lines result in a cramped seat. Some of the new, down-sized specialty cars offer fairly good gasoline mileage, but their overweight competitors have a relatively high fuel economy.

Consider the subject as a process.

Fuel-injected 89-cubic-inch four-cylinder engine starts and runs well. Not as peppy as last year. Standard four-speed manual transmission shifts crisply through forward gears. Downward push to engage reverse gear requires determined effort.

Ninety-eight-cubic-inch four-cylinder engine runs smoothly during warm-up. Starts fairly well from cold engine. Light acceleration in first and second gears produces annoying bucking and surging. Five-speed overdrive manual transmission shifts smoothly through first four gears. Fifth is often balky. Reverse requires firm downward push.

One-hundred-sixty-three-cubic-inch fuel-injected V-6 requires several seconds of cranking to start. Acceleration good. Car shudders during hard acceleration in first gear. Seats don't hold occupants well during hard cornering.

Engine runs smoothly and quietly. Automatic transmission stays in second gear for an annoyingly long time during gentle acceleration. Shift to third gear is abrupt during hard acceleration.

Two-hundred-cubic-inch V-6 stalls on cold start. Balky on partly warm starts. Once running, doesn't stall or hesitate. Stumbles and hesitates during warm-up driving. Runs reliably when fully warm.

Ride is somewhat stiff and always active. Motions fairly well controlled on average roads. Ride comfortable enough on expressways to prevent occupants from tiring on long trips. Ride deteriorates slightly when car carries its 725-pound capacity. Normal handling good. Accident-avoidance ability is very good.

Brakes are good. Regulating severity of stops somewhat difficult.

Ride is fair. Car jiggles constantly on almost all roads. Motions superficially cushioned on expressways and secondary roads. With recommended full load of 700 pounds, ride is a little worse. Normal handling good. Brakes shudder when hot.

Ride is good. Ride is firm, but well controlled on almost all types of road surface. Suspension soaks up most of harshness from broken pavement. Full 960-pound load actually improves the ride slightly. Normal handling is good. Brakes are good. Power brakes chatter and shake.

Ride is poor to fair. Car constantly snaps, jerks, and moves from side to side. Ride is tiring on expressways. Ride is painful on rough roads. Manual steering requires effort during parking in hard turns. Steering feels heavy. Sharp bumps provoke jolts. Rear suspension occasionally touches bottom when car is fully loaded. Rear end swings out on hard turns. Parallel ridges in the road diverts car from its straight course.

State some causes and effects.

Fuel tank is located under the floor and below the rear seat. Location protects it from crash damage. Fixed rearview mirror interferes with tall driver's view to the right front. Could cause accidents. Bumpers look sturdy. But one blow to the center of the front bumper and another to the center of the rear causes visible dents and bulges in both bumpers.

Seat belts are tight. Cause shoulder tension. Rear belts difficult to put on. Fuel tank safely positioned under the floor, below the rear seat. Well protected in a crash. Head restraint limits driver's view. Could cause accidents.

Head restraints prevent whiplash injury. Wipers leave upper corners of windshield unwiped. Sharp bumps cause suspension to bottom on the outer side. Effect is that the car skates outward from time to time. Fuel tank positioned on left side of car. Effect is that fuel tank is fairly vulnerable, more likely to be hit.

Front safety belts inconvenient and uncomfortable. Lap belt rides too high. Shoulder belt rubs against the neck. Head restraints provide whiplash protection for short persons only. Slight crash causes center of front and rear bumpers to bulge visibly.

Point out the subject's similarities to or differences from something else.

Car 1 has front-wheel drive. Car 2 does not. Car 1 has steel-belted radials. Car 2 has fiberglass-belted radials. Car 1 has rack-and-pinion steering. Car 2 does not. Car 1 takes regular gas. Car 2 takes unleaded.

Car A is a midengine car. Car B is not. Car A has 6 cylinders. Car B has 4. Car A has front-wheel disc brakes. Car B has front-wheel disc brakes. Both car A and car B have independent four-wheel suspension. Car A costs about $2000 less than car B.

Car X has a V-8 engine. Car Y has a V-8 engine. Car X has power windows. Car Y does not. Car X has side-window defoggers. Car Y does not. Car X has an electric clock. Car Y does not. Car X has a courtesy lamp for the ashtray. Car Y does not. Car X has reading lights on the rear door. Car Y does not. Car X has two-tone paint treatment. Car Y does not.

Car Y has extensive corrosion-resisting treatment. Car X does not. Car Y has a strong, solid body. So does car X. Car Y has a high-energy ignition system, but X does not. Car Y has a 260-cubic-inch V-8 engine. Car X has a 305-cubic-inch engine. Car Y has carpeting. Car X has color-keyed cut-pile carpeting. Car Y has 16 cubic feet of trunk space. Car X has 20 cubic feet of trunk space. Car Y has rich cloth fabrics. Car X has supple vinyls. Car Y has an AM/FM radio. Car X has a stereo/radio. Both cars have batteries that never need refilling. Car Y has no cigarette lighter, whereas car X does. Car Y gets 16 mpg in the city and 24 mpg on the highway. Car X gets 14 mpg in the city and 21 mpg on the highway.

Car 1 is a cat. A creature of fire and spirit. Car 2 is a classic piece of sculpture. Car 1 has catlike grace and surefootedness. Car 2 is sophisticated. The movement of car 1 is quick and agile. Car 2 is poetry in motion.

Now that we have compiled an undifferentiated body of material about the subject of automobiles, let's consider what we have done and where we go from here. We began systematically with some representative statements which the topics called to mind. We started with identification and ended with comparison. Actually, we could have begun at any point. You will notice that we didn't use all of the categories. The ones that we did use seemed to be the most appropriate for the subject. You will notice also that some categories generated a vast amount of material; others did not. This is to be expected. The amount of ideas generated by a particular topic will vary from subject to subject. Finally, you have probably observed that the ideas derived from exploring the subject are not too coherent. They seem to be more of a loose collection, a conglomeration, a catalog, a heap. This also is to be expected. When the ideas first come, you want to get them down on paper in any order, in sentences, in fragments, in catalog form, or whatever. Your primary purpose at this stage in the composing process is to "brainstorm" for ideas. The process is a little bit like that of free association, in which you jot down anything that comes to mind about a particular subject. It differs, however, in that the topics and the statements or questions they suggest give you a sense of direction often lacking in random associations.

Exercises

1. An important first step for many writers in inventing ideas is specifying the problem by putting the subject in the form of questions: What is pollution? What are the causes of pollution? Take one of the following general subjects and formulate as many questions about it as come freely to mind:

a.	flying saucers	k.	advertising
b.	rock lyrics	l.	prejudice
c.	death	m.	pollution
d.	escapism	n.	fashion
e.	energy crisis	o.	dance
f.	blind dates	p.	civil disobedience
g.	TV	q.	fantasy
h.	the generation gap	r.	materialism
i.	boxing	s.	acting
j.	humor	t.	religion

2. Now, in a more systematic way, take one of these same subjects and, using the probe outlined in this chapter, put the subject through the questions suggested by the topics of invention.

3. Putting the topics in the form of statements such as the following, probe one of the general subjects listed in question 2:

   a. Describe or define the subject.
   b. Divide it into parts.
   c. Classify it.
   d. Give some examples.
   e. Point out its similarities to or differences from something else.
   f. Tell what happened, when it happened, and where it happened.
   g. Tell how it happened or how it is changing in time.
   h. State its causes or effects.

4. Take a single topic, such as definition, division into parts, classification, exemplification, comparison, process, or cause and effect, and probe a general subject:

   a. nature   f. terrorism
   b. art   g. football
   c. slang   h. skyjacking
   d. music   i. fishing
   e. clothes   j. war

5. Take one of the following thesis statements and probe the main terms in the statement. Then write an essay, following the method of development suggested by the probe or the statement of the thesis:

   a. A liberal education is worthless in a recession.
   b. Love should (shouldn't) be the main reason for marrying someone.
   c. Suffering makes us better human beings.
   d. Love needs to be expressed in words.
   e. First impressions can be wrong.

From Subject to Thesis

Once you have put a general subject through a probe, your next step is to limit your subject. Some writers can do a good job of writing about a general subject. But for many, a general subject is often too broad to permit a significant handling of ideas. Therefore, instead of writing about the general subject of automobiles, you might instead want to limit the subject by adding qualifying words to it or formulating it as a title. For example:

How To Buy a Used Car.
Testing a New Car.
Why Buy a Specialty Car?
How To Save on a Car Loan.
Good Bets in Used Cars.

By narrowing your general subject to a more specific one, you have already gone a long way toward limiting it. But a subject is not a thesis. A **subject** is *the* **matter** *of a piece of writing, what it is about.* A **thesis,** however, is much more specific. It is *the* **working idea** *of a discourse, a theme, an assertion so clear-cut that the reader has no doubts whatsoever about what is to be discussed or proved.* "Daytime television" is a subject, but "Daytime television is of a very low quality" is a thesis. It is a proposition with a point of view. It makes readers nod their heads in agreement or disagreement. It has some kind of truth value. It can be the basis for a discussion.

A thesis underlies every kind of discourse. In poems or in stories, it is very seldom expressed explicitly, except in works inclined to teach or moralize too much, but with a little bit of effort it can be clearly expressed. For example, the theme of Nathaniel Hawthorne's short story "Young Goodman Brown" can be stated as "Evil exists in the hearts of all men." The theme of E. A. Robinson's poem "Richard Cory" may be expressed as "You can never judge a person's happiness from the outside." In literature, although the thesis may not be explicitly stated, there is a principle of unity, a concept, or a point of view that holds a story or the poem together. In an essay, the thesis usually appears in a clearly defined shape.

The thesis, then, is the main idea, the seed which contains in potentiality that which is necessary for the subsequent flowering of thought. If it were possible to summarize an essay in a single sentence, to reduce it to its most condensed form, then that form would be the thesis sentence. Formulating a thesis sentence is an important step in ordering your ideas.

Writers differ as to when they deduce their theses from the general subject. Should the thesis be formulated immediately after the determination of the general subject, or should it be formulated after the writer accumulates a body of ideas and explores them thoroughly? There is no simple answer to these questions. The thesis can either follow or precede the determination of the general subject or the exploration of ideas. Obviously, for many writers there is considerable overlapping in the process. In my own experience, more often than not I begin with a title or a controlling idea and then, by reading and note-taking or by some kind of mental probing of my subject, I gather sufficient material to get my writing under way. I have on occasion formulated my thesis in the process of writing, but even then, I usually have more than a general idea about what I am going to say. If you decide, however, to formulate your thesis before you explore your subject thoroughly, your thesis could give you a more definite direction in which to proceed in inventing ideas.

Naturally, in determining your thesis you will want to keep in mind your purpose and your audience. If your aim is to persuade, the wording of your thesis might be quite different than if your aim is to inform or instruct. Your purpose and your audience will also determine the kind of writing you choose. If you are a copywriter and your aim is to persuade, the kind of writing you choose to persuade your audience may be a magazine ad. If you're trying to convince a friend not to buy a certain kind of car, you might write him or her a letter.

So now you have a limited subject and you are ready to formulate your thesis. *State your thesis in a single declarative sentence.* Since the thesis is to be used primarily for your sake, state it in such a way that it clearly and precisely expresses your central idea. Then you can frequently return to it to get your bearings at every step of your writing. The thesis should be constantly in your mind as a point of reference. As the working idea of your writing, the thesis will also suggest the scope or limitations of your paper, and it can suggest ways of ordering your ideas.

The following are some typical examples of thesis sentences suggested by the subject of automobiles:

The automobile is the greatest single polluter of air.

Gas guzzlers not only waste fuel, they also waste money.

Few options are necessary for basic transportation, but some options do make sense.

In buying an automobile, there are two kinds of loans you should avoid: a consumer finance loan and a dealer's loan.

The new Plymouth Horizon gives you sporty features you'd pay extra for in many other cars.

Compare the features of the Chevrolet Citation with those of more expensive cars.

Down-sized spare tires can affect your car's performance.

Tax the gas guzzlers or ban them.

Buy yourself a Ford because it has the following outstanding features.

Here's how you can get a good deal on a new car.

You could easily have formulated thesis 1 ("The automobile is the greatest single polluter of air"). The wording of the thesis suggests that your plan of development would be to support the main idea with examples. This thesis could also be developed by cause and effect. Thesis 2 ("Gas guzzlers not only waste fuel, they also waste money") could be developed with examples. Thesis 3 ("Few options are necessary for basic transportation, but some options do make sense") can be developed by an enumeration of the options. Thesis 4 ("In buying an automobile, there are two kinds of loans you should avoid: a consumer finance loan and a dealer's loan") contains the kind of advice you might give to a friend. You could use a combination of enumeration and reasons to develop this thesis. Thesis 5 ("The new Plymouth Horizon gives you sporty features you'd pay extra for in many other cars") can be developed by an analysis of the car's features. The sixth thesis ("Compare the features of the Chevrolet Citation with those of more expensive cars") has the obvious structure of a comparison. Thesis 7 ("Down-sized spare tires can affect your car's performance") would be developed by causal analysis. Thesis 8 ("Tax the gas guzzlers or ban them") could be the title of a magazine article or the thesis of a persuasive essay. Thesis 9 ("Buy yourself a Ford because it has the following outstanding features") could be developed into an analysis essay or an ad that sets forth the features of the specific manufacturer's car. It is the only thesis composed of two sentences. Finally, thesis 10 ("Here's how you can get a good deal on a new car") can be the basis of a process essay, developed in terms of steps, or stages, or phases.

It is possible that after you have formulated your thesis, additional thinking or reading about your subject will force you to modify your original conception or to recast your thesis completely in another form. The invention of ideas is a process of thinking and rethinking a subject or a thesis, for the process of thought rarely goes on unchanged. The thesis, however, will give to your thought a particular direction.

Exercises

1. Using the information about automobiles derived from the probe in this chapter, formulate five thesis sentences. First include in outline form the necessary information to include in each thesis sentence: subject, purpose, audience.

2. Using one of the thesis sentences from question one, write an essay to support the thesis.

3. Formulate a thesis sentence for each of the following general subjects:

    a. prejudice   f. daytime TV
    b. world hunger   g. nuclear energy
    c. dreams   h. freedom
    d. blind dates   i. identity
    e. fears   j. marriage

4. From your own reading and experience, construct five thesis sentences.

5. Discuss the methods of development suggested by each of the following thesis sentences. What kind of support would you use to develop each?

    a. My family background has influenced my life in a number of ways.
    b. "Exploitation" can have a number of meanings.
    c. Frustration is beneficial for three reasons.
    d. TV has a deep influence on our lives.
    e. Making a home movie is easy to do.

There are many other useful approaches to generating ideas for writing. This one is particularly interesting because of the close relationship of the topics to mental processes. It must be extremely discomforting to find yourself in a situation where you're called upon to write something for a specific purpose or for a particular occasion, and you have only a vague notion of how to begin to get ideas. The method discussed in this chapter is one useful way to discover ideas. Obviously, the process, at least in the beginning stages, is somewhat artificial. The goal is to make the process habitual so that instead of having to probe every subject in a formal way, you so discipline your mind that it will automatically explore ideas systematically, by analyzing, classifying, comparing, or contrasting.

Summary Exercises

1. Analyze a picture, a magazine ad, a newspaper article, or a short poem. Be conscious of your mental processes as you are analyzing and inventing. As you are analyzing, put the ideas from your probe on paper in the

same order in which they come to mind. Then analyze your paper to see if you've put the ideas into any intelligible order.

2. Analyze some short articles or essays. What is the plan of development? What mental processes must the writer have gone through in order to arrive at that pattern?

3. Now put the full discovery procedure into play. Choose a general subject. Consider your attitude toward it. Consider your audience. Using one of the formal methods suggested in this chapter, probe the subject, limit it, and formulate a thesis sentence. Write the sentence in such a way that it indicates your plan of development. Then write an essay supporting the thesis.

4. The topics enumerated in this chapter can be stated in other ways than as questions. Choose one of the following formulations of the topics to probe the subject:

   a. Classify the dates you have had.
   b. Give directions to someone about how to make something or how to get someplace.
   c. Explain a scientific process.
   d. Trace the cause-and-effect pattern of an accident you witnessed.
   e. Compare any two things point by point.
   f. Compare something by analogy; for example, "love is like a fire," "love is like a raging torrent," "hate is like poison." Extend the comparison as far as you are able.
   g. Tell a story about something that happened to you.
   h. Describe a painting or a movie you have seen.
   i. Define some modern slang term with which you are familiar that doesn't have a dictionary definition.
   j. Summarize a story you have read recently.

5. Discuss the suitability or lack of suitability of each of the following proverbs as thesis statements:

   a. Thirty days hath September.
   b. After a storm comes a calm.
   c. Do not wear out your welcome.
   d. Variety is the spice of life.

e. There's no place like home.

f. Speech is silver; silence is golden.

6. Quotations can make good thesis statements. Collect at least five quotations and bring them to class for consideration as theme assignments.

Arrangement:

The Whole Theme

Chapter 3

Arrangement: The Whole Theme

Thus far, you have been following a sequence of logical steps in the composing process that might be described as follows:

Find a general subject (if you have not already been given one).

Limit the subject (unless you have been given a sufficiently narrow one).

Consider your attitude toward the subject.

Consider your audience and purpose.

Consider the mode or modes you might use and the kind of writing.

Probe for ideas.

Formulate a thesis sentence.

Beginning, Middle, End

What do you do now that you have probed your subject, collected your ideas, and formulated your thesis sentence? *Organize your ideas, giving them form.* As Thomas DeQuincy puts it, "The labor of composition begins when you have to put your separate threads of thought into the loom, to weave them into a continuous whole; to connect, to introduce them; to blow them out or expand them; to carry them to a close."

How is this done? By following a sequence of steps that can be outlined as follows:

In the beginning of your paper, perhaps in the first paragraph, indicate clearly what your general subject is, state your thesis, and indicate your plan of development.

In your middle paragraphs, take up the main ideas of your essay, allowing a paragraph or two for each main point.

In your final paragraph, conclude your essay, making sure that you leave your reader with a clear idea of what you have covered.

These three stages of development can be found in most kinds of writing. They are called simply the **beginning,** the **middle,** and the **end.**

The following student paper illustrates these stages nicely:

The Wasteful American

Beginning The economic slump is the biggest problem facing Americans today. Despite all the talk about deficit spending, oil prices, unemployment, and the impending depression, Americans continue to spend large sums of money on goods which are frivolous and damaging to the country.

Middle The economic boom in the fifties and sixties transformed Americans into the most wasteful people on earth. People in other parts of the world could live comfortably on our trash. Americans throw away disposable diapers, dishrags, and aprons. One company even developed disposable clothes. You wear them until they're dirty and then you throw them away. Americans also throw away paper plates, dishes, and cups and plastic knives, forks and spoons.

This tremendous waste also extends into other areas. While oil shortages increase, many Americans continue driving gas guzzling luxury cars. Younger Americans zoom around in their hot rods equipped with ridiculous devices which increase speed and power while diminishing gas mileage. While the price of paper products climbs, McDonald's continues to wrap a Big Mac in paper, put a cardboard strip around it, put it in a box, and then place it in a paper sack. While the prices for producing energy skyrockets, Americans continue to buy electric can openers, blankets, razors, knives, tooth brushes, and so forth. And while people starve all over the world, Americans buy tons of pet food to feed pets that range from aardvarks to zebras. I could go on and on with examples. Needless lights shine bright, tons of food go down garbage disposals, and litter covers the landscape. Yet for years little has been done. Wastefulness has become as American as apple pie.

End   The recent recession has prompted some changes though. Car pools have been formed, speed limits have been reduced, and recycling centers have been established. One newspaper even reported that garbage cans are not as full as they used to be. However, much remains to be done. America can no longer afford to waste its resources as it has done for the past twenty-five years. Perhaps the current recession will awaken Americans to the realities of a world that is overcrowded and running out of natural resources and force them to change their extravagant life styles.

—Reed

Exercises

1. Analyze fully the student essay titled "The Wasteful American." What is the thesis? What kind of details are used to support the thesis?

2. Poems have beginnings, middles, and ends too. Bring to class a poem that is organized in this way. Identify the three main parts and then discuss this three-part structure in terms of the ideas the poet is trying to convey.

Thesis and Support

In addition to organizing your ideas in three main parts, you want to break up the major divisions into a sequence of smaller steps that includes the statement of the **thesis** and the addition of **supporting details.**

The organizational plan of the following essay uses this method:

Beginning　　Despite the role that municipalities, industries, and agriculture play in polluting the environment, each of us is responsible in part *Thesis*　for trash pollution. Rather than blame someone else for the mess we're in or expect the government to begin massive cleanup programs, *there are a number of things that we can do to reduce trash pollution.*

Middle　　*The first thing we can do is to buy products in containers that disintegrate easily.* Plastic containers and aluminum cans, for *Supporting Details*　instance, are almost completely immune to biological decomposition. We should avoid, therefore, buying these. On the other hand, paper and cardboard products decompose fairly quickly. There is not much harm in purchasing these.

Supporting Details　*The second thing we can do is refuse to buy throw-away items.* We can refuse to purchase products that come in nonreturnable bottles. In planning for outings, we can forego styrofoam cups, plastic spoons and knives, and disposable plates. We can avoid using aluminum cans, plastic foil, and aluminum foil. On occasion, we can bring home unwrapped products, if the products are not perishable or if they won't soil easily, rather than have them wrapped in paper that will be discarded later.

Supporting Details　*The third thing we can do is to recycle throw-away items.* We can sell our old newspapers and magazines. We can give discarded clothing, furniture, and toys to charitable agencies for reuse. We can give our bottles and aluminum cans to agencies for recycling.

Supporting Details　*The final thing we can do is to avoid littering.* Instead of throwing plastic filter tips from cigarettes on the ground where they will not decompose, we should put them in the garbage. We should be careful not to discard gum wrappers, candy wrappers, and other trash on city streets and highways. We should carry litter bags in our cars and use them regularly.

End　　Each year we throw away tons of cans, bottles, bottle caps, paper, aluminum cans, cigarette packages, milk cartons, and cellophane wrappers and discard countless rubber tires, old automobiles, newspapers, and magazines. To add to the problem, we are running out of burial space in our city dumps, marshes, and wastelands. There is a need for each of us to realize that we are all responsible for pollution. *Clincher Sentence*　*These are just a few of the many things we can do to reduce trash pollution,* but we must do them now. Our goal is nothing less than a return to America the Beautiful.

The first paragraph introduces the essay. The second sentence of this paragraph states the thesis. The next four paragraphs add supporting details. The last paragraph concludes the essay.

Exercises

1. List some specific details that you might use to support one of the following statements:

   a. A casual encounter affected my life.
   b. People should be judged by what they do rather than by what they say.
   c. Anger can be beneficial.
   d. We need illusions to live by.
   e. A reasonable pride is justifiable.

2. Discuss the methods that you might use to develop one of the following sentences by thesis and support. Then choose one and write a thesis and support essay.

   a. There are two sides to every question.
   b. Opportunity seldom knocks twice.
   c. What's done cannot be undone.
   d. Absence makes the heart grow fonder.

Paradigms

Thinking of form in composition in such broad terms as beginning, middle, and end, or thesis and support can be useful to the beginning writer. But the approach to form in composition that I believe can be even more useful is one in which the writer conceives of form in terms of an underlying, abstract pattern. Quite obviously, in beginning a paper you cannot keep in mind all the specific details that go into making the finished paper. But you can envision a kind of core structure that bears the main burden of thought. Such a structure is called a paradigm.

A **paradigm** is *a kind of model or pattern that is abstract and general.* It is not to be confused with a traditional outline that is detailed and specific. Unlike a traditional outline, a paradigm is an **idealization,** a conception of a pattern in its absolute perfection. It represents the writer's **competence,** that is, *the writer's ability to use language.* But competence is always spilling over into performance so that it is possible to use these formalized patterns in your own writing. Because a traditional outline is so detailed, with its divisions and subdivisions, it can only be used for the specific piece of writing for which it is intended. A paradigm, however, represents a universal pattern that recurs from one essay to another. In other words, you can use the same paradigm and write completely different essays with it. A traditional outline is static. It represents a finished product. But a paradigm is dynamic. It represents *stages in thinking.*

The essay that we have just looked at is a good example of an essay that uses the paradigm as a principle of organization. The abstracted paradigm of that essay looks somewhat like this:

1. There are *a number of things* that we can do to reduce trash pollution.

2. *The first thing we can do* is to buy products in containers that disintegrate easily.

3. *The second thing we can do* is refuse to buy throw-away items.

4. *The third thing we can do* is to recycle throw-away items.

5. *The final thing we can do* is to avoid littering.

6. *These are just a few of the many things we can do* to reduce trash pollution.

Paradigmatic Structure

The value of paradigms is that they enable you to move your thinking in an orderly manner from the beginning of an essay to its conclusion.

For compositional purposes, you might best conceive of paradigms in relation to the topics of invention. You will recall that in the previous chapter we identified certain categories such as analysis, classification, comparison and contrast, and the like, and suggested that these categories symbolized corresponding thought processes, that is, that in the course of your everyday activities, you analyze, you classify, you compare, and you discover cause-and-effect relationships in the world around you. Further, these categories give rise to certain questions that enable you to explore a subject to get ideas for writing. Now I would like to make a related point: that the same categories that you use to probe a subject you can also use to arrange the details of that subject in an orderly pattern, that in fact the topics of invention are closely related to the patterns of arrangement. In other words, at the same time that you are probing a subject to get ideas, you are also arranging these ideas, putting them into some kind of intelligible form. Paradigms, at least the kind that we will be concerned with, represent *patterns of thought* that give your writing a sense of direction and provide you with a formal means of ordering your ideas.

What do these paradigms look like? The following are some typical examples of paradigms in their most abstract form:

Analysis Paradigm
Introduction (states the thesis)
Characteristic 1
Characteristic 2
Characteristic 3
Characteristics 4, 5, 6 . . .
Conclusion (restates the thesis, summarizes, and so forth)

Classification Paradigm
Introduction (states the thesis)
Type 1
Type 2

Type 3
Types 4, 5, 6 . . .
Conclusion (restates the thesis, summarizes, and so forth)

Exemplification Paradigm
Introduction (states the thesis)
Example 1
Example 2
Example 3
Examples 4, 5, 6 . . .
Conclusion (restates the thesis, summarizes, and so forth)

Cause-to-Effect Paradigm
Introduction (states the thesis)
Cause 1
Cause 2
Causes 3, 4, 5 . . .
Effect
Conclusion (restates the thesis, summarizes, and so forth)

Effect-to-Cause Paradigm
Introduction (states the thesis)
Effect 1
Effect 2
Effects 3, 4, 5 . . .
Cause
Conclusion (restates the thesis, summarizes, and so forth)

These patterns represent *stages in your thinking* as well as sections of an entire essay. You could, of course, write an essay consisting of five or six paragraphs if you were to follow each outline exactly, but it should be obvious that each of these paradigms can be shortened, lengthened, or modified to suit your own purposes. For example, in writing an analysis theme, you might decide to use several introductory paragraphs, rather than one. In addition, you might want to include qualifying or transitional paragraphs in key places in your essay. The result is that occasionally the abstract structure of your essay might look like this:

Analysis Paradigm
Paragraph 1 (introductory paragraph)
Paragraph 2 (a second introductory paragraph that includes the *thesis*)
Paragraph 3 (characteristic 1)
Paragraph 4 (qualification of paragraph 3)
Paragraph 5 (characteristic 2)
Paragraph 6 (qualification of paragraph 5)
Paragraph 7 (transitional paragraph)
Paragraph 8 (characteristic 3)
Paragraph 9 (conclusion)

In brief, what I am suggesting is that in composing an essay, in the process of discovering and arranging your ideas, you use paradigms to facilitate the movement of your thought. In subsequent chapters, I will be taking up the types of paradigms and discussing them at some length while relating them to the topics of invention and to underlying thought processes, but for the moment, let us consider in some detail specific ways of using paradigms to compose your own essays.

In the last chapter, we considered the general subject of automobiles. We probed it for ideas, using questions suggested by the categories of invention. Then we formulated some characteristic thesis sentences.

The thesis sentence not only gives direction to the composition as a whole, but it also suggests the kind of paradigm best suited to develop your ideas. Thus, if you select as your thesis "The new Plymouth Horizon gives you sporty features you'd pay extra for in many other cars," the word *features* suggests that you will develop your essay by means of analysis. If you select as an alternative thesis "Downsized spare tires can affect your car's performance," the word *affect* suggests a cause and effect pattern.

Composing an Essay

Let us take the process a step further and actually write an essay, using some of the ideas derived from the probe in the previous chapter. Naturally, in choosing a thesis you will want to keep in mind your subject, your audience, your purpose, the mode or modes of development, and the kind of writing. Not all of these elements, however, will be equally important in choosing your compositional strategies; at times, some will be relatively more important than others.

Consider now your choices. Your subject matter is given to you. You are going to write about automobiles. The kind of writing you choose will depend on the writing situation or on what the teacher tells you to choose. You can imagine yourself in any number of plausible situations in which you could write about cars. You could be writing an article in a popular magazine or a consumer magazine in which you give information about new cars to your readers. Or you might be writing a magazine ad in which you try to convince readers to buy a particular brand of automobile. Your writing could take the form of a letter to a friend in which you express satisfaction over the purchase of a new car. Each situation demands a different purpose: to inform, to persuade, or to express strong feelings.

What mode or modes might you use in developing your subject? If the car is a sporty car or a luxury car, you would probably decide to *describe* the sporty or luxurious interior. If it has safety features or gas-saving features you would probably choose the mode of *analysis*. If it has extra features or characteristics that its competitors do not have, you may decide to *compare* it to other cars.

What about considerations of audience? If your reader is a married couple with children, you might want to stress safety features or economy. If your reader is a mature man or woman with a large income, you might stress luxury. If your reader is a young college student, you might decide to emphasize sporty looks.

Suppose, after considering your subject, your audience, and your purpose, you choose as your thesis the statement "The Chevrolet Impala has the following outstanding features." This thesis suggests that you will be writing an analytic essay, perhaps supported by enumeration. If, however, you decide on the thesis "The new Thunderbird has sporty features you'd pay extra for in many other cars," your thesis would suggest either analysis or description. It would also suggest either an implicit comparison or an expressed comparison. Assuming that you decide to choose the first of these two theses, you can think of your overall compositional plan in terms of a kind of abstract pattern such as the following:

Introduction (states the thesis)
Feature 1

Feature 2
Feature 3
Feature 4
Conclusion (restates, summarizes, and so forth)

However, it is unlikely that you will confine yourself to discussing a single feature of the car in each paragraph. Instead, you would probably include a cluster of features or characteristics in each supporting paragraph. In that event, the paradigm would look like this:

Introduction (states the thesis)
Cluster of features
Cluster of features
Cluster of features
Cluster of features
Conclusion (restates, summarizes, and so forth)

Or you can employ a more detailed kind of paradigm in sentence form, as in the following scheme, keeping in mind that these patterns are not prior to but are the result of your thinking:

The Chevrolet Impala has the following outstanding features. . . .
The Impala has more space. . . .
The Impala has better fuel efficiency. . . .
The Impala has a number of luxury features. . . .
Chevrolet Impala is better than average. . . .

Then, using this sentence paradigm as the core structure of your thought, you write your essay.

You begin by putting your thesis sentence into your introductory paragraph. Then you put the supporting sentences of your paradigm into successive paragraphs. The resulting essay might end up looking something like this:

General Motors has done it again. They have come up with a new full-size car that is more efficient and more economical than full-sized cars used to be. This new car is the Chevrolet Impala. *It has the following outstanding features.*

The Impala has more space than the full-sized cars it has replaced. It has full-sized room for six passengers. It has plenty of head room, more rear-seat leg room, and plenty of hip room. It has more usable trunk space than ever before.

The Impala has better fuel efficiency. It has EPA mileage estimates of 21 miles per gallon on the highway and 16 miles per gallon in the city, and it gets this mileage with a 305-cubic-inch V-8 engine and an automatic transmission.

The Impala also has a number of luxury features. It has generous amounts of insulation and acoustic-backed carpet and headliners, for a smooth and quiet ride. It has wire wheel covers and whitewall radial tires. It has an electric clock, reading lights on the rear door, and a courtesy lamp for the ashtray.

Cars are shrinking. Almost all of the leading car manufacturers have down-sized their large cars. The best, however, among the large group of domestic models are the new General Motors cars. All get fairly good gas mileage and all give a fairly good performance. Of these cars, *the Chevrolet Impala is better than average.*

Suppose, however, that instead of using the essay form, you decide to write a magazine ad. Because of the mass audience your ad would have to appeal to and because of the contents of the magazine your ad would have to compete with, you would probably shorten your paragraphs and fragment your sentences to gain reader interest. The resultant copy might look like this:

The New Impala!
More Space Efficient, More Fuel Efficient,
More Luxurious Than Ever

General Motors has done it again!

They have come up with a new full-sized car that is more efficient. More economical.

The new Chevrolet Impala.

It has more space than older full-sized cars. Full-sized room for six passengers. Plenty of head room. And more usable trunk space than ever before.

It has better fuel efficiency. EPA mileage estimates of 21 mpg highway, 16 mpg city. With a 305-cu-inch V-8 engine and automatic transmission.

It also has generous amounts of insulation. Acoustic-backed carpet and headliners, for a smooth, quiet ride.

It has wire wheel covers and whitewall radial tires. An electric clock. Reading lights on the rear door, and a courtesy lamp for the ashtray.

Test drive a new Impala today! You won't go home without one.

In using paradigms to organize your writing, you need not follow the same kind of rigid order that was followed in the writing of the expository essay. The magazine ad above uses a paradigm. But the paradigm is less obvious than the one in the preceding essay, because the paragraphs and sentences have been broken down into smaller units and because some connecting links have been omitted. Ultimately, it is more important for you to understand *the principles that underlie these paradigms* than the paradigms themselves. Then, when you begin to write, you will automatically begin to think in terms of stages, or phases, or steps, or progressions of some kind.

Paradigms can be used with a great deal of flexibility as the following piece of professional writing illustrates:

The life of the ocean is divided into distinct realms. Each has its own group of creatures that feed upon each other and depend on each other in different ways.

There is, first of all, the tidal zone. Here land and sea meet. Then comes the realm of the shallow seas around the continents, which goes down to about 500 feet. It is in these two zones that the vast majority of all marine life occurs.

The deep ocean adds two regions, the zone of light and the zone of perpetual darkness. In the clear waters of the western Pacific, light could still be seen at a depth of 1,000 feet through the portholes of the *Trieste* on its seven-mile dive. But for practical purposes the zone of light ends at about 600 feet.

Below that level there is too little light to support the growth of the "grass" of the sea—the tiny single-celled green plants whose ability to form sugar and starch with the aid of sunlight makes them the base of the great food pyramid of the ocean.

—from *The Sea*, Life Nature Library

In this piece of writing, the paradigm is there, but it is not as formal or rigid as the paradigm in the previous essay. The opening sentence states the idea that the ocean is "divided into distinct realms." The next paragraph discusses two of these divisions. The third and fourth paragraphs discuss two more. But the divisions are not presented in lockstep fashion (e.g., the first, the second, the third). Numbers are used as signaling devices, but they are used flexibly. Synonyms are also used to help the reader follow the divisions.

You can easily pick out the key words that make up the paradigm, so that the resultant pattern looks like this:

1. The life of the ocean is *divided* into *distinct realms.*

2. There is, *first of all*, the *tidal zone.*

3. *Then* comes the *realm of the shallow seas.*

4. It is in *these two zones* that the vast majority of all marine life occurs.

5. The *deep ocean* adds *two regions*, the *zone of light* and the *zone of perpetual darkness.*

Notice that the key sentences that make up the paradigm are scattered in various places in the essay. The first sentence of the paradigm is the opening sentence of the essay. The second sentence of the paradigm is the first sentence of the second paragraph. The third sentence of the paradigm is also the third sentence of the second paragraph. The fourth sentence of the paradigm is the fourth sentence of the second paragraph. The fifth sentence of the paradigm is the first sentence of the third paragraph. It is obvious that the organization of this essay could have been quite different. For example, almost every sentence of the abstracted paradigm could have been used to start a new paragraph. But the writer decided to use this less formal pattern for his own particular purposes.

Exercises

1. Construct a paradigm in which you include a thesis sentence and supporting sentences in the form of steps, characteristics, types, details, or whatever.

2. Go back to chapter 2. There is more than enough material derived from the probe on automobiles for you to write several essays. Using this material, decide on the kind of essay you will write, your purpose, your audience, and your mode. Set this information up in outline form to be handed in on a separate sheet of paper, and then write your essay based on this information.

   The following is the format for the cover sheet:

   Subject:
   Aim or specific purpose:
   Audience:
   Kind of writing:
   Mode or modes:
   Thesis:

   Here is the same outline, with one possible handling of the material:

   Subject: automobiles
   Aim: persuasion
   Audience: college students
   Kind of writing: magazine article
   Mode: description

Form Consciousness

Although you impose order in the process of arranging your ideas in writing, you can also discover order in the writings of others. Research reveals that the best writers are those who can perceive form in their own writing and in the writing of others.

Following the processes of thought in the writing of others is analogous to recreating the processes of composition in your own mind.

In our discussion of the writing process up to this point, I have maintained that **formal principles of thinking are embodied in writing.** I have identified some of these principles as analysis, classification, comparison and contrast, and the like. They manifest themselves in the essay as principles of invention and patterns of arrangement. For example, comparison can be a means of probing a subject or of organizing an essay. If these principles are embodied in thinking as well as in writing, then you can get at them deductively, by moving through the stages of discovering ideas and arranging them in your writing, or inductively, by abstracting them from the writing of others and then using them in different subject matter. Thus, you can move from examining and describing principles and patterns of organization in the writing of others to using these principles and patterns in your own writing.

In order to get at these formal principles and patterns, I would like to suggest two methods of analysis. The first is *a type of structural analysis that follows the linear or chronological order of ideas from one sentence to another and from one paragraph to another.* I call this kind of analysis the **linear analysis** of a text. The second is *a type of analysis in which the paradigm is abstracted and placed in a formal scheme or pattern.* I call this kind of analysis the **paradigmatic analysis** of a text.

Exercises

1. Are you conscious of form in your own writing? In your sentences? In your paragraphs? In your essays? How do you organize your ideas in writing? Do you have a plan?

2. Look up the words *form, shape, structure, figure, outline, contour, configuration, profile, mold, design,* and *pattern* in your dictionary. Are there differences in the literal meanings? In suggested meanings?

3. What is meant by *form consciousness?*

4. Are you conscious of form in your own life? In your dancing? In your singing? In playing a game? In your speech? In thinking? Discuss.

Linear Analysis

To analyze the structure of an essay using linear methods, consider the essay as a kind of extended paragraph in which all the sentences are related to each other by coordination and subordination. Then, using a system of numbering and indenting the sentences to depict graphically the overall structure of the essay, go from sentence to sentence, considering the logical progression of ideas.

Begin with the opening sentence and label it number 1. Then go through each successive sentence carefully, searching for evidence of coordination and subordination. If the second sentence in the essay is like the first (is parallel in sentence structure or ideas), consider it as coordinate, label it number 1 also, and put it right under sentence 1. If the second sentence differs from the first (gives evidence of subordination of structure or ideas), give it the number 2 and indent it under sentence 1 as subordinate.

Do the same with the remaining sentences. As you consider each sentence in turn, indent it as subordinate or set it down as coordinate, and assign it an appropriate number. When you come to the last sentence in each paragraph, leave a space after this sentence and before the first sentence of the next paragraph, so that the paragraph divisions of the essay are obvious. Remember that even though you leave spaces between paragraphs, when you come to the first sentence of each paragraph, you disregard, for the moment, the part that these sentences play in their respective paragraphs and consider only their relationships to the last sentences of the previous paragraphs. Is the first sentence of the new paragraph subordinate to the last sentence of the previous paragraph? Then give it the next number and indent it. Is it coordinate to that sentence? Then give it the same number and set it down in parallel fashion.

The method of determining coordination and subordination between sentences in the essay is relatively simple. There are two kinds of subordination between sentences: grammatical subordination and meaning subordination. Some typical examples of grammatical subordination are the use of a pronoun in one sentence to refer to a noun or pronoun in a previous sentence; the use of transitional markers, such as *thus*, *therefore*, and *nevertheless*, to tie sentences together; the repetition of a word or a part of a word in a sentence to link it to a similar word in the previous sentence; and the use of a synonym to refer to an equivalent word in a previous sentence. Meaning relationships are much more difficult to determine, but in general, if a sentence gives an example, a fact, a detail, a reason, a qualification, or support of any kind, then consider it to be subordinate to a more general statement that precedes it.

Coordination, like subordination, can be based on grammatical structure or meaning. One of the clearest signs of grammatical coordination is parallel structure. Quite often, grammatical coordination will also contain meaning coordination. But if grammatical clues are not present or if they are difficult to discover, then look for groupings of examples, reasons, details, and consider sentences that contain these groupings as coordinate.

The following analysis of the introduction to Bertrand Russell's *Autobiography* is a good example of this kind of approach to form in composition:

What I Have Lived For

1

1. Three passions, simple but overwhelmingly strong, have governed my life: the longing for love, the search for knowledge, and unbearable pity for the suffering of mankind.

2. These passions, like great winds, have blown me hither and thither, in a wayward course, over a deep ocean of anguish, reaching to the very verge of despair.

2

3. I have sought love, first, because it brings ecstasy—ecstasy so great that I would often have sacrificed all the rest of life for a few hours of this joy.
3. I have sought it, next, because it relieves loneliness—that terrible loneliness in which one shivering consciousness looks over the rim of the world into the cold unfathomable lifeless abyss.
3. I have sought it, finally, because in the union of love I have seen, in a mystic miniature, the prefiguring vision of the heaven that saints and poets have imagined.
    4. This is what I sought, and though it might seem too good for human life, this is what—at last—I have found.

3

3. With equal passion I have sought knowledge.
    4. I have wished to understand the hearts of men.
    4. I have wished to know why the stars shine.
    4. And I have tried to apprehend the Pythagorean power by which number holds sway above the flux.
        5. A little of this, but not much, I have achieved.

4

3. Love and knowledge, so far as they were possible, led upward toward the heavens.
3. But always pity brought me back to earth.
    4. Echoes of cries of pain reverberate in my heart.
        5. Children in famine, victims tortured by oppressors, helpless old people, a hated burden to their sons, and the whole world of loneliness, poverty, and pain make a mockery of what human life should be.
            6. I long to alleviate the evil, but I cannot, and I too suffer.

5

1. This has been my life.
   2. I have found it worth living, and gladly would live it again if the chance were offered me.

This essay consists of five paragraphs. Paragraph 1 constitutes the beginning, paragraphs 2, 3, and 4 make up the body of the essay, and paragraph 5 constitutes the ending.

The first paragraph contains the *thesis* sentence:

Thesis   Three passions, simple but overwhelmingly strong, have governed my life:
the longing for love,
the search for knowledge, and
unbearable pity for the suffering of mankind.

(I have indented the sentence levels so that you can see the logical divisions more clearly.) The second sentence is subordinate to the first. It qualifies the statement in the first sentence. The phrase "these passions" in the sentence ties in with the phrase "three passions" in the first sentence.

In paragraph 2, the first sentence (beginning "I have sought love") picks up the first idea in the thesis sentence ("the longing for love") and comments on it. It is subordinate to the two previous sentences because it narrows down the general idea of love and begins to give reasons for Bertrand Russell's seeking it. The specific tie-in with sentence 1 is the repetition of the word *love,* and with sentence 2, the reference of the word *love* to the word *passions.*

The second sentence in this paragraph gives a second reason Russell has sought love. It also has a similar grammatical structure and thus is coordinate to the first sentence:

I have sought love, first, because . . .
I have sought it, next, because . . .

The third sentence in this paragraph gives a third reason for Russell's seeking love. It is parallel in structure to the two preceding sentences:

I have sought love, first, because . . .
I have sought it, next, because . . .
I have sought it, finally, because . . .

The last sentence ("This is what I sought . . .") summarizes the ideas in the other three sentences. The word *this* refers back specifically to the words *love, it,* and *it* in sentences 3, 4, and 5, and more generally to the ideas about love in these sentences.

In paragraph 3, the first sentence is grammatically parallel to the first three sentences of paragraph 2. It is also parallel in meaning because it is an enumeration of one of the three passions Russell mentions in his thesis—love, knowledge, and pity:

I have sought *love* . . .
I have sought it . . .
I have sought it . . .

    With equal passion
I have sought *knowledge* . . .

The next three sentences are subordinate to the first sentence of paragraph 3 and coordinate to each other:

I have wished to understand . . .
I have wished to know . . .
I have tried to apprehend . . .

Each sentence gives a specific example of the kind of knowledge sought:

. . . to understand the hearts of men
. . . to know why the stars shine
. . . to apprehend the Pythagorean power by which number holds sway above the flux

The last sentence in this paragraph ("A little of this, but not much, I have achieved") summarizes the author's achievement of knowledge. The phrase "a little of this" ties this sentence to the three previous sentences.

In the fourth paragraph, the first two sentences are coordinate to each other:

> Love and knowledge, so far as they were possible, led upward toward the heavens.
> But always pity brought me back to earth.

The connecting word *but* points to the basis of the parallel ideas: love, knowledge, and pity. There is also a basic antithesis that links these two sentences together:

> Love and knowledge . . . *led upward toward the heavens.*
> But always pity brought me *back to earth.*

The third sentence is subordinate to the previous sentence. The whole sentence, "echoes of cries of pain reverberate in my heart," is a synonym for the word *pity*. It qualifies the idea in the preceding sentence and organizes the ideas in the last two sentences.

The next sentence ("Children in famine, victims tortured by oppressors, helpless old people . . .") gives specific examples of the "cries of pain" of the previous sentence and is subordinate to it.

The last sentence ("I long to alleviate the evil, but I cannot, and I too suffer") comments on the idea of evil and pain in the previous sentence and is subordinate to that sentence.

Finally, the first sentence of paragraph 5 ("This has been my life") summarizes the thought of the whole essay. It is parallel to sentence 1 at the beginning of the essay. These two sentences act as a kind of frame device for the entire essay:

> *Three passions . . .* have governed *my life.*
> *This* has been *my life.*

The last sentence of the essay ("I have found it worth living, and would gladly live it again if the chance were offered me") qualifies the ideas contained in the previous sentence and comments on them and on the ideas contained in the whole essay. The word *it* ties in to the word *life* in the previous sentence.

Exercises

1. Do a linear analysis of a magazine ad or a short news story, using the methods outlined in this chapter.

2. In class, do a linear analysis of one of the student essays in this chapter or of one of your own essays.

3. Select a short, well-organized article or essay from a magazine or from your own reader and do a linear analysis of it.

Paradigmatic Analysis

A linear analysis is a necessary first step in any kind of rhetorical analysis. It takes into account every sentence in the essay. The purpose of a linear analysis is to allow you to follow the logical progression of ideas in an essay to see what goes with what, to see how every sentence in an essay is related to every other sentence.

The purpose of a paradigmatic analysis is to allow you to abstract the underlying organizational pattern of the entire essay and to use this pattern to produce your own essays. The kinds of patterns we will be particularly interested in abstracting are those related to the topics of invention and the patterns of arrangement that were discussed earlier in this chapter: analysis, classification, comparison and contrast, and the like. These patterns represent *dynamic organizational processes*. In the act of composing, *our minds think along these lines.*

How do you get at these underlying patterns? Once you make your linear analysis, go back over the essay and read it carefully. Then proceed, sentence by sentence, through the essay, looking for instances of repetition (word, phrase, clause, or meaning repetition that relate to the pattern under consideration. For example, in classification themes, key words, and phrases, such as *types, parts, categories, classes, basic kinds of, fundamental kinds, divided into* ___ *classes*, and the like will recur with enough frequency that the pattern will be unmistakable.) Then abstract the sentences and phrases that relate to the pattern under consideration and put them into a paradigm. In the first stages, you might want to use as much of the original wording of the text as possible. But quite often, you may need to *regularize* the text for the sake of revealing the underlying pattern more clearly. You can do this by using a sentence paraphrase, recasting the sentences in simpler form. The paraphrase need not be exactly equivalent to the text, but it must be equivalent in meaning. The resultant pattern represents the principle by which your essay moves from beginning to end.

Many essays are so regular that it is fairly easy to detect the underlying pattern. The Bertrand Russell essay has a clear-cut organizational structure, so that the process of abstracting the pattern should be easy enough to do. In the first stage of your analysis, you should keep as close as possible to the original sentences of the text.

To begin our analysis, notice, first of all, that the opening sentence of the essay is the *thesis* sentence, the sentence that states the main idea. It is also the sentence that indicates the plan of development. The word *three* in the thesis suggests that a pattern of enumeration will follow. And the word *passions* coupled with the word *three* indicates a complementary pattern of classification. The first sentence is an *analytic thesis sentence.* It not only indicates that the writer is going to talk about three things, but it also enumerates what these three things are, then picks them up again in paragraphs 2, 3, and 4. A conventional thesis sentence would have this structure:

> Three passions . . . have governed my life.

But an analytic thesis sentence breaks the statement into parts and indicates the plan of development, like this:

> 1. Three passions . . . have governed my life:
>   the longing for love,

> the search for knowledge, and
> unbearable pity for the suffering of mankind.

This thesis gives us a clue, a hint of what is to follow.

The second sentence in this paragraph qualifies and expands the idea of passions in the first sentence. The explicit tie-in is the repetition of the word *passions:*

> These passions, like great winds, have blown me hither and thither, in a wayward course, over a deep ocean of anguish, reaching to the very verge of despair.

You will note that in paragraph 2, no one sentence advances the pattern. There is, for example, no topic sentence. Instead, the first three sentences advance the pattern by giving the reasons why the author sought love. So you provide a sentence that can serve as the top sentence of the paradigm and add to it those sentences or phrases that constitute its support. The result is the following pattern:

> I have sought love . . .
>   I have sought love, first, because it brings ecstasy. . . .
>   I have sought it, next, because it relieves loneliness. . . .
>   I have sought it, finally, because . . . I have seen . . . the prefiguring vision of the heaven that saints and poets have imagined. . . .

The first sentence of the next paragraph unmistakably advances the pattern. It enumerates the second of Bertrand Russell's passions, knowledge:

> With equal passion I have sought knowledge.

And the subsequent sentences in that paragraph form the support structure:

> With equal passion I have sought knowledge.
>   I have wished to understand the hearts of men.

I have wished to know why the stars shine. . . . And
I have tried to apprehend the Pythagorean power by which number
holds sway above the flux.

The first sentence of the third paragraph repeats the words *love*
and *knowledge* of the two previous paragraphs and continues the
main idea. It is a transitional sentence. The second sentence of that
paragraph advances the overall pattern by enumerating the third passion that has governed Bertrand Russell's life. So use this sentence
and add to it the supporting details, but this time regularize the
support pattern to make it parallel the structure of the support patterns
of the previous paragraphs:

But always pity brought me back to earth.
[I have pitied] children in famine . . .
[I have pitied] victims tortured by oppressors . . .
[I have pitied] helpless old people, a hated burden to their
sons . . .
[I have pitied] the whole world of loneliness, poverty, and
pain. . . .

Finally, the first sentence of the last paragraph completes the
pattern, and coupled with the first sentence of the essay, it acts as
a *frame device* for the entire paradigm:

This has been my life.

If you put the various stages of the paradigm together, taking
just a few more liberties with the phrasing, you get this overall pattern:

1. Three passions . . . have governed my life: the longing for
   love, the search for knowledge, and unbearable pity for the
   suffering of mankind.

2. I have sought love.
   I have sought love . . . because it brings ecstasy. . . .
   I have sought it . . . because it relieves loneliness. . . .

I have sought it . . . because [. . . it contains] a vision of the heavens that saints and poets have imagined.

3. I have sought knowledge.
    I have wished to understand the hearts of men.
    I have wished to know why the stars shine.
    I have tried to apprehend the Pythagorean power by which number holds sway above the flux.

4. [I have sought pity.]
    [I have pitied] children in famine. . . .
    [I have pitied] victims tortured by oppressors. . . .
    [I have pitied] helpless old people. . . .
    [I have pitied] the whole world of loneliness, poverty, and pain.

5. This has been my life.

This pattern represents the organizational structure of the entire essay. The first unit states the main idea. Russell is going to talk about the three passions that have governed his life. The next unit enumerates the first passion, *love*, then supports it with the reasons why the author sought love. The next unit enumerates the second passion, *knowledge*, and supports it with an explanation of the kinds of knowledge Russell sought. The fourth unit names the last passion, *pity*, and the supporting details tell whom it is the author pities. The last unit concludes the pattern and returns to the beginning.

It is obvious that although the overall organizational pattern is *classification* (what is being classified is kinds or types of passions) reinforced by *enumeration*, the structure of the supporting paragraphs could have differed. For example, paragraph 3 could just as easily have been supported by reasons as by an explanation and enumeration of the kinds of knowledge that Bertrand Russell sought. This leads us to conclude that the main plan of the essay is carried by the underlying patterns of classification and enumeration. This is the pattern that represents the working idea of the essay and the principle of forward motion. If you normalize the text again, reducing it to its essential structure, you get a pattern that is more workable for compositional purposes:

> Three passions have governed my life.
> The first passion is the longing for love.
> The second passion is the search for knowledge.
> The third passion is the pity for the suffering of mankind.
> These are the passions that have governed my life.

For compositional purposes, you can abstract even more from the original pattern. You can then take the resultant pattern and put your own subject matter into it.

> Three passions have governed my life.
> The first passion is . . .
> The second passion is . . .
> The third passion is . . .
> These are the passions that have governed my life.

You can also vary the pattern by substitution:

> Three (four, five) things (passions, emotions, events) have governed my life.
> The first thing is . . .
> The second thing is . . .
> The third thing is . . .
> The fourth thing is . . .
> The last thing is . . .
> These are the things that have governed my life.

Or you can abstract even more, reducing the underlying pattern (or patterns) to a single abstract pattern:

> Introduction (states the thesis)
> Type 1 (or Characteristic 1)
> Type 2 (or Characteristic 2)
> Type 3 (or Characteristic 3)
> Type 4 (or Characteristic 4)

Types 5, 6, 7 . . . (or Characteristics 5, 6, 7 . . .)
Conclusion (restates the thesis, summarizes, and so forth).

Not every essay is as clearly organized as Russell's essay. Not every essay will have the paragraphs arranged in such a convenient order. Some essays may have several introductory paragraphs. The thesis, rather than being the first sentence of the essay, may be embedded in the second or third paragraph. In addition to containing the support paragraphs for the thesis, some essays may contain numerous transitional paragraphs or even paragraphs that digress from the main idea. Nevertheless, with enough practice and skill in analyzing, you should be able to abstract the underlying paradigm and make it generative in your own writing. In subsequent chapters, we will be looking at a large number of these patterns.

You should realize that the parts of the abstracted pattern do not necessarily bear a one-to-one relationship to corresponding paragraphs. The divisions represent ''sections'' of the essay. These sections could be paragraph divisions, or they could be larger thought units, as the following scheme indicates:

Paragraph 1 (Introduction)
Paragraph 2 (Statement of the Thesis)
Paragraph 3 (Characteristic 1)
Paragraph 4 (Qualification of Paragraph 3)
Paragraph 5 (Characteristic 2)
Paragraph 6 (Digression)
Paragraph 7 (Transitional Paragraph)
Paragraph 8 (Characteristic 3)
Paragraph 9 (Conclusion)

Exercises

1. Using the analysis of the Bertrand Russell essay as a model, select an essay from your reader or from a magazine and do a paradigmatic analysis.

2. Do a paradigmatic analysis of one of your own essays.

3. Using the paradigm from the Bertrand Russell essay, write an essay of your own in which you discuss passions or emotions or events that have governed your life. Try to follow the structure of Bertrand Russell's essay closely.

In subsequent chapters, I will be asking you to use paradigms of this sort in your own writing until you feel that you have such a firm grasp of compositional form that you can dispense with them. However, even more sophisticated writers use them in their writing. The idea is to *internalize the principles* upon which these patterns are based so that when you use them, they become intuitive rather than self-conscious. In this way, you will have acquired an invaluable resource to which you can return again and again.

Summary Exercises

1. Discuss some of the formal patterns that exist in nature, for example, the cycle of a storm, the change in seasons, the rhythmic movement of waves, the gradation of a sunrise, the ripening of crops, the beat of the heart, the rhythm of breathing.

2. Discuss some of the formal patterns that exist in art: plots, themes, motifs, refrains, climaxes, balance, hierarchies, rhythm, melody, movement, subordination, coordination, figure and ground, symmetry, genre.

3. Do dreams have a structure? Reveries? Daydreams? Trances? Hallucinations? Rituals? Incantations? Discuss.

4. Discuss the structure of a movie you have seen recently. Did it have a clearly laid-out plot? A thematic structure (for example, the themes of justice and honor in *The Godfather*)? A pattern of images? A central metaphor (life is a *Cabaret*)? A symbolic structure? A motif structure

(the hands in *The Pawnbroker, David and Lisa,* and *A Man and a Woman*)?

5. Did you know that there is a structure in the auditory memory? Try memorizing these telephone numbers: 9376532, 2357326, 5498514. Now memorize these: 9376-532, 235-7326, 54-985-14. Verbal structuring, as well as mathematical structuring, can help you to remember. It can also help you to reason.

6. Complete these opening phrases:

>   a. Once upon a time _____.
>   b. Long ago _____.
>   c. There once was a _____.
>   d. In the long and far-off times _____.
>   e. It was an early spring morning when _____.

7. Consider the following quotations for possible thesis topics. What kind of pattern of development would you follow in writing about one of these statements?

>   a. Character is higher than intellect.—Emerson
>
>   b. A little learning is a dangerous thing.—Pope
>
>   c. Sweet are the uses of adversity.—Shakespeare
>
>   d. Reading maketh a full man, conference a ready man, writing an exact man.—Bacon
>
>   e. Man is probably nearer the essential truth in his superstitions than in his science.—Thoreau
>
>   f. Fear always springs from ignorance.—Thoreau
>
>   g. Man is least himself when he talks in his own person. Give him a mask and he will tell the truth.—Oscar Wilde
>
>   h. A man's worst difficulties begin when he is able to do as he likes.— T. H. Huxley

i. The course of true anything never does run smooth.—Samuel Butler

j. Understand that a man is worth just so much as the things are worth about which he busies himself.—Marcus Aurelius

Patterns of Thought:

Analysis and Description

Chapter 4

Patterns of Thought:
Analysis and Description

It would seem to be a valid statement that *for every process, there must be a corresponding system.* The topics of invention and the patterns of arrangement represent an unbroken line of development from process to system. Paradigms seem to mediate between the processes of discovering ideas and arranging these ideas into an orderly pattern. Thus, **paradigms** are on the one hand *patterns of thought* that give to your writing a determinate direction, and on the other hand *formal patterns* that help you to order your ideas.

To learn to compose, however, is not simply to memorize a set of paradigms. It is rather *to master the system of principles that will make it possible for you to understand and to produce discourse.* A paradigm is the result of paradigmatic thinking and should be considered as a means to an end, not an end in itself.

In the next few chapters, you will be looking at a number of these compositional principles, in their paradigmatic form as well as in their larger patterns in the composition as a whole. The following are some of the most important of these compositional principles:

Analysis/Description
Classification/Exemplification/Definition
Comparison/Contrast/Analogy
Narration/Process/Cause and Effect

Analysis

Most of your day-to-day analyses are informal and intuitive. As you walk along the street, you may notice a tree, look at one of its branches, and discern its size or the texture of the bark or the shape and color of the leaves. After you see a movie, you may talk about the plot, isolate an exciting moment, or discuss a suspenseful scene. Every day, in almost everything you do, you analyze, dissect, differentiate, and trace things to their sources. Analysis is not only an important principle in your everyday thinking, it is also an important compositional principle.

Analysis is *the process of dividing anything complex into simple elements or components.* It is also the exact determination of those elements. It is the systematic separation of a whole into parts, pieces, or sections. Ideally, in the act of analyzing, you trace things back to their underlying principles.

Anything taken as a whole can be analyzed: a landscape, a seascape, a configuration of buildings in a city square, a painting, a picture, a poem, an argument, a philosophical system, a movie, a day in your life, an idea of any sort. In a *physical analysis*, you separate an object in space and break it into its components. In a *conceptual analysis*, you divide an idea into other ideas.

Purpose, Audience, Kinds of Discourse

Analysis can be found in almost any kind of writing, and it can be a means of achieving any of the broader aims of discourse: to inform or instruct, to convince or persuade, to entertain or please, and to express strong feelings and emotions. Your intention in analyzing is especially important because it will become the informing principle that shapes your perception of the whole. Unless you keep your intention constantly in view, your analyses will become mere classroom exercises.

To avoid making your analyses sterile exercises, you might ask yourself a number of questions about the purpose of your analysis in relation to your subject, your audience, and the kind of writing best suited to your needs:

1. What *subject* am I going to analyze? A physical object? A political issue? An institution? A current event? An idea? A work of art?

2. What *specific problems* might I encounter in analyzing this particular subject?

3. What is my *purpose* in making the analysis?

4. For what *audience* is the analysis intended? What features of my analysis might I include for one kind of reader but exclude for another?

5. How will my reader use the *results* of my analysis?

6. What is the most appropriate *kind of writing* in which to put my analysis? A scientific essay? A report? A printed brochure? A news story? A magazine article? An advertisement?

Invention and Analysis

What is the thought process like? In the process of analyzing anything, you begin with a general impression of the whole, keeping in mind the response you want to get from your reader. Then you have to abstract some feature or features from the whole to support your general impression, and focus your attention upon them. Next you have to hold these features in your mind as the object of your immediate thought in order to remember them later. After this, you have to attend to other features, noticing the connection among them and their relationship to other parts of the whole. Then, in order to understand the object of your analysis, you have to pull all of these features together, to see them as a whole. Finally, you have to come to some kind of conclusion about your analysis. Your conclusion will depend in part on your purpose and may be a comment on your analysis or a summary of your main points. All of this is a part of what I mean by invention by analysis.

If you decide to generalize from your experience and put the results of the process of analysis into the form of questions for subsequent invention, you will get something like the following questions: What are its pieces, parts, or sections? How may they logically be divided? What is the logical order? What is the relationship of the parts to the whole? You can then ask these questions of any new subject that you want to analyze.

Let me illustrate the process by analyzing with you the following familiar poem by E. A. Robinson:

Richard Cory

Whenever Richard Cory went down town,
We people on the pavement looked at him:
He was a gentleman from sole to crown,
Clean favored, and imperially slim.

And he was always quietly arrayed,
And he was always human when he talked;
But still he fluttered pulses when he said,
"Good morning," and he glittered when he walked.

And he was rich—yes, richer than a king—
And admirably schooled in every grace:
In fine, we thought that he was everything
To make us wish that we were in his place.

So on we worked, and waited for the light,
And went without the meat, and cursed the bread,
And Richard Cory, one calm summer night,
Went home and put a bullet through his head.

After several close readings of this poem, you begin to notice that there is an interesting pattern of imagery in the poem relating to royalty and another relating to bearing or upbringing, and you begin to isolate and to examine words and phrases that seem to make up these patterns.

You notice that there are patterns of words related to royalty, and you associate certain meanings with these:

Word	Associated Meanings
Richard Cory	Richard Coeur de Lion
crown	king's crown
imperially	like an emperor
arrayed	dressed like a king
glittered	gold and kingship
grace	an attribute of a good king

Then you notice that there is an overlapping pattern of words related to bearing or upbringing:

Word	*Associated Meanings*
gentleman	polite, gracious, and considerate
clean favored	complete, free from alterations
quietly arrayed	not showy, impressively orderly
always human	kind and courteous
admirably schooled in every grace	effortless charm and refinement

With additional readings and close analysis, you notice other features of the poem. Each of the first three stanzas is divided between a description of Richard Cory and the reaction of the people to him. The last stanza describes the people's attitude toward life and Richard Cory's denunciation of it.

The specific lines relating to the people's increasing degree of reaction to Cory can be abstracted from the poem and presented in a systematic way as follows:

Stanza 1: We people . . . *looked* at him
Stanza 2: he *fluttered* pulses
Stanza 3: we thought that he was *everything*
Stanza 4: our reaction (implicit in the stanza) when he shot himself was to be horrified

You will notice in the process so far that you have followed most of the steps needed to make a competent analysis: a careful reading of the lines, a critical examination of the parts, the separation of the parts from the whole.

Your final step is to try to determine the nature of the whole. You can do this by trying to abstract from the elements and from the poem as a whole what you take to be its theme or main idea. The theme unifies the whole and helps to order the parts.

Several statements of the theme are possible:

You can never judge a person's happiness from the outside.
Things are not always what they seem to be.
All that glitters is not gold.
Appearances are deceiving.

Putting the parts together, you arrive at a conclusion about the *meaning* of the poem, which goes something like this. Richard Cory was a man whom people looked up to. He seemed to have many excellent qualities. He was regal in bearing, well dressed, polite, gracious, and considerate. He had effortless charm and refinement. Less fortunate people, who seemed not to have his attainments and certainly not his money, envied him and cursed their own status in life. Yet evidently something in Cory was lacking. Perhaps he was more superficial than people thought. Perhaps the *glitter* was just that, a kind of surface glamour with no real depth of feeling. There is a hint of this in the phrase "admirably schooled in every grace." The word *schooled* suggests that Cory's gracious and charming manner was not natural. The theme suggested by all these details, then, seems to be "that appearances are deceiving, that you cannot always judge people by their external appearance."

Exercises

1. Probe a subject using the questions related to the topic of analysis (What are its pieces, parts, or sections? How may they logically be divided? What is the logical order? What is the relationship of the parts to the whole?).

2. Analyze one of the following general topics in class and list the subdivisions revealed by analysis:

   a. a painting
   b. a picture
   c. a movie
   d. a television show
   e. a day in your life

   f. a sentence
   g. the layout of a supermarket
   h. a magazine ad
   i. an idea
   j. a poem

The Structure of Analysis

After you have made your analysis, your next step is to put your ideas into some kind of pattern. (Once you have mastered paradigmatic thinking, the process will be less artificial. *As you are analyzing, your ideas will naturally fall into an appropriate pattern.*) The paradigmatic structure of many analytic essays has a pattern somewhat like the following:

> *Analysis Pattern 1*
> Introduction (includes thesis)
> Characteristic 1 (or part 1)
> Characteristic 2 (or part 2)
> Characteristic 3 (or part 3)
> Characteristic 4 (or part 4)
> Characteristic 5, 6, 7 (or part 5, 6, 7) . . .
> Conclusion (summary, return to beginning)

The following pattern is less idealized, and probably more like the kinds of paradigms you will find in your everyday reading:

> *Analysis Pattern 2*
> Introduction (includes thesis)
> Cluster of features
> Cluster of features
> Cluster of features
> Cluster of features
> Cluster of features
> Conclusion (comment, summary, etc.)

If these paradigms seem too abstract to work with, you can supplement them with a checklist such as the following:

Checklist
1. *Identify the subject to be analyzed.*
2. *Give the basis or bases you will use to divide it into parts.*
3. *State your reasons for the divisions.*
4. *Point out the purpose these divisions might serve.*
5. *List the features, divisions, or subdivisions.*
6. *Discuss each feature as you go along or at appropriate points in your analysis.*
7. *Present these features to your reader in the best possible order, depending on your purpose.*

8. *Close with the final point, with a comment on the analysis, or with a summary of the main points.*

Remember that the checklist is a reminder of the kinds of things that might go into your essay, not an outline to be followed in the exact order in which the items are presented.

Analysis patterns can be either inductive or deductive. If you begin with the parts and then show how these are related to the whole, you are proceeding inductively. If, in your writing, you begin with the whole and then move to narrower elements, you are proceeding deductively, unless the process is one of inverse induction. But whether you proceed inductively or deductively, you should keep in mind the purpose of your analysis. The features you decide to write about will depend on your purpose and your own interests. You are not analyzing simply for the sake of analyzing, but for the sake of some special point you want to make. In analyzing "Richard Cory," for example, I picked out only those structural features of the poem that seemed to reinforce the theme of appearance versus reality.

The following professional essay is a good illustration of a well-organized piece of writing that uses an analysis paradigm. I have indented and numbered the sentence levels so that the pattern stands out clearly:

The Frontier Disappears

1

Introduction   1. The United States of today is the product of a variety of forces: its European origins, the continuing impact of ideas from abroad, the constant mingling of peoples, and the changes wrought by the Industrial Revolution.

    2. Yet none of these forces was more significant than the frontier in endowing the Americans with the traits that distinguish them from other peoples of the world.

      3. Down to the present time many of our basic attitudes toward society and the world around us reflect that pioneer background.

2

Thesis

4. What are the characteristics that are traceable to this unique feature of our inheritance?

3

*Character-
istic 1*

5. We are a mobile people, constantly on the move, and but lightly bound to home or community.
    6. If you were to ask any group of Americans today how many live in the homes where they were born, only a handful would reply in the affirmative.
    6. If you asked that same question of a group of Englishmen or Frenchmen or Italians, an opposite answer would be given.
        7. Like our frontier ancestors, who shifted about so regularly that mobility became a habit, we are always ready for any change that promises to better our lives.

4

*Character-
istic 2*

5. We are a wasteful people, unaccustomed to thrift or saving.
    6. The frontiersmen established that pattern, for nature's resources were so plentiful that no one could envisage their exhaustion.
        7. Within a few years of the first Virginia settlement, for example, pioneers burned down their houses when they were ready to move west; thus they were allowed to retrieve nails, and none gave thought to the priceless hardwoods that went up in smoke.
    6. As a people we still destroy much that others would save.
        7. I had this driven home to me when, during a year's residence in England, I received a letter from one of that nation's largest banks, enclosed in a second-hand envelope that had been readdressed to me.
            8. Such saving would be unthinkable in the United States, where even the most

insignificant bank would never address a
client save on elaborately engraved
stationery, usually with the names of all
twenty-eight vice presidents parading down
one side of the page.

5

5. We are a practical, inventive people on whom the
   weight of tradition rests but lightly.
   6. In many lands of the world, people confronted with
      an unpleasant situation will quietly adjust
      themselves; in the United States, a man's first
      impulse is to change things for the better.
      7. This willingness to experiment came naturally
         to the pioneers who had no precedents on which
         to build.
         8. It has remained a trait of the industrial
            pioneers, whose ability to adapt and change
            has laid the basis for America's supremacy
            as a manufacturing nation.

6

5. We are individualistic people, deeply resentful of any
   intrusion into our affairs by government or society,
   also a basic attitude among frontiersmen.
   6. Aware that they were living in a land where
      resources were so abundant that only their own
      energies were necessary for success, they wanted
      to be left alone above all else.
      7. This trait persisted in American thought, even
         though the passing of the frontier has forced
         the government to adopt a more positive social
         role.
         8. Even today such activity is more resented in
            the United States than elsewhere; and this
            resentment also helps explain the almost
            fanatical American hatred of political systems
            such as facism or communism that are based
            on the subjugation of the individual.

7

Character-
istic 5

5. We are a democratic people.

6. Our pioneering forefathers originated neither the theory nor the practice of democracy; the western world was well on its way to political equalitarianism when the continent was settled.

7. But conditions in frontier communities vastly stimulated the trend.

8. There nature reduced men to equality by dimming the importance of wealth, or hereditary privilege.

8. There poverty served as a great leveler.

8. There the demand for self-rule was particularly strong, for frontiersmen knew that their problems were unique and must be solved locally.

9. And so on the frontier the democratic tradition was strengthened, until it became a part of the American creed.

10. The undying hatred of the United States for all forms of totalitarianism only mirrors the strength of this faith.

8

Conclusion

2. Thus has the frontier placed its stamp on America and its people.

3. In the continuing rebirth of civilization during the three centuries required to settle the continent, nature modified the characteristics of its conquerors, even in the midst of their conquest.

4. There emerged a new people, robust and strong, with an unwavering faith in the merits of the individual and an unswerving allegiance to the principles of democracy.

5. The frontier is no more, but its heritage remains to give a strength as well as individuality to the civilization of the United States.

—Ray Allen Billington, "The Frontier Disappears"

This essay has a very clear-cut pattern. Its structure can also be illustrated by the abstracted paradigm:

What are the characteristics that are traceable to this unique feature of our inheritance?

We are a mobile people, constantly on the move, and but lightly bound to home or community.

We are a wasteful people, unaccustomed to thrift or saving.

We are a practical, inventive people on whom the weight of tradition rests but lightly.

We are individualistic people, deeply resentful of any intrusion into our affairs by government or society, also a basic attitude among frontiersmen.

We are a democratic people.

Thus has the frontier placed its stamp on America and its people.

In an analysis essay, in addition to the characteristic paradigm, you come to expect words and phrases like the following:

characteristic	member	trait
feature	component	particular
aspect	constituent	division into parts
part	portion	subdivision
section	fraction	unit
sector	fragment	piece
segment	particle	detail
element	entity	ingredient

whole	analyze
totality	resolve
entirety	separate
collectiveness	dissect
unity	break up
embodiment	constitute
aggregate	compose
sum	embody
bulk	partition
mass	distinguish

These words and phrases provide meaningful clues that will enable your reader to follow the patterning of your ideas with less difficulty.

In your writing, it is more important for you to understand the principles of paradigmatic thinking and the principles of analysis than it is to follow these patterns exactly. At first, if you are having problems organizing your ideas, you might want to follow these patterns closely, until the kind of thinking that they represent becomes habitual. Later on, you will be able to use these patterns with a great deal of flexibility, as the following student paper illustrates:

A Diamond Is Forever

Rolling Stone magazine has never been a publication to concern itself with mushy, love-story-type themes. Most often, one finds articles on rock-and-roll music and the hazards of nuclear energy in the magazine. And yet, in the February 22, 1979, issue there is one full page of sentimental mush at its best (or worst). An advertisement for diamonds—specifically, what a diamond ring means to a young couple's budding romance—is nestled between an article on New Wave rock group Devo and a tongue-in-cheek ad suggesting a Valentine's Day gift of a Ted Nugent album. Has the diamond industry made a horrendous mistake? Probably. Not only is their ad laughably romantic and aimed at the wrong audience, but it is also poorly written.

A headline over the most prominent part of the diamond advertisement—a picture of a young couple enjoying a quiet moment together in a soda shop—starts the ad off in the wrong direction. It reads: "Our diamond means we now have the best of both worlds. Yours and mine." The phrase "yours and mine" takes up a separate line below the opening sentence and is centered between the tilted heads of the adoring couple in the picture. Now, *Rolling Stone* readers are *not* going to buy the premise of the opening sentence. A couple in love cannot miraculously attain a mixture of the best of their respective worlds simply by slipping a diamond ring onto a finger. What happens to the worst parts of their worlds when the ring goes on? Do his belching and her gum-cracking cease when the nineteen-hundred-dollar stone is purchased? *Rolling Stone* readers will, inevitably, ask these probing questions.

Next in line for rebuke is the centerpiece of the ad. The hairstyles and the clothing of the young couple in the picture seem to be right out of the late fifties or early sixties. The soft vignette of a young couple in an ice-cream parlor begs for criticism. A handsome male, not unlike Ryan O'Neal in appearance, leans over his dreamy-eyed, smiling gal to sip on an old-fashioned soda. The whipped topping of the soda appears about ready to topple onto the counter, and the moment is captured as if it were a candid snapshot. Sharing a soda with Sally went out with the Beach Boys. Injecting nostalgia into the ad is not going to sell diamond rings to readers of *Rolling Stone.*

The narrative form in which the ad is written continues below the ice-cream-parlor picture. The copy is written in the first person. The young woman, one would assume, does the narrating. "I still remember the day," she says, "you made this near-sighted musician see how exciting a game of football could be." She then goes on to reminisce about the time her boyfriend "sat through a concert without falling asleep." These recollections of times past are set apart in separate sentences so that the reader forms mental images of the events. Each mental image seems to pop into the frame occupied by the soda-fountain scene, so that the effect is like that of leafing through a photo album with the mind. This is a clever bit of psychology on the part of the advertisers, but it doesn't work for this audience. The reader that the diamond industry is reaching in *Rolling Stone* magazine is not one that is especially enthralled with football games and sitting through concerts. The type of concert implied in the ad is a classical concert. Just sitting through anything other than a rock concert would be almost unthinkable to most *Rolling Stone* readers.

A final point about the ad concerns the wording of the sentence "Being in love means we want to know what each other's all about." The wording here is awkward, if not grammatically incorrect. The phrase "each other's all about" in the sentence seems to be a shortening (decapitation might be a better word) of "each other's worlds are all about," but the omission of the two words leads the sentence, headed for sentimentality, into a brick wall of laughter and confusion. Because the reader must read the sentence again, this merely adds emphasis to the absurdity of the line.

The diamond industry would do better to include this kind of advertisement in a magazine whose readers are less apt to criticize and belittle established values. The ice-cream-parlor sweetness of this ad is laughable in almost any context, but buried within the pages of *Glamour* or *Seventeen* magazine, the absurdity would be less obvious.

—Ben

This is a well-written student essay. The student's purpose is to show how the magazine ad "A Diamond Is Forever" fails in relation to its intended audience. The features of the analysis are used as evidence to support his thesis. But these features are not presented without comment. The student writer sifts through the facts of the ad as he goes along, explaining and evaluating them and reaching conclusions about them.

In the professional essay entitled "The Frontier Disappears," the writer chooses to abstract the features of his analysis and present each one in a separate paragraph. In each paragraph, he expands on the particular characteristic by qualifying it, amplifying it, or commenting on it in some way.

In the student essay, the student writer, rather than devoting each supporting paragraph to a single characteristic of the ad, uses a cluster analysis as a way of presenting his ideas. In the first paragraph, he identifies his subject, provides the context for the reader's understanding of his discussion, and then states his thesis: "Not only is their ad laughably romantic and aimed at the wrong audience, but it is also poorly written." Then, in subsequent paragraphs, to support his thesis, he presents the results of his analysis in a cluster of features.

To achieve coherence, he organizes each cluster around a central idea. In paragraph 2, for example, he analyzes the headline and comments on its inadequacies. In paragraph 3, he criticizes the illustration. In paragraph 4, he discusses the narrative form of the copy. In the next paragraph, he isolates a particular phrase and comments on it. Finally, he concludes with a comment about "the ice-cream-parlor sweetness" of the ad and its inappropriateness in a magazine such as *Rolling Stone*. His concluding paragraph actually is a restatement of his thesis, a kind of return to the beginning. This is a suitable ending for his essay because he has been evaluating aspects of the ad in the supporting paragraphs.

These two essays are excellent examples of how the mode of analysis can be used in different kinds of writing, for different aims. The professional essay is a good example of historical exposition. The student paper is a good example of a critical essay, whose purpose may be to inform or persuade.

Here is one last example, an example of scientific writing, which uses the mode of analysis to inform or instruct:

The Anatomy of a Mollusk

Mollusks have a solid, unsegmented body which can be divided into four main parts unless greatly modified.

First is the head, bearing tentacles, eyes, and other sense organs. The mouth opens close to the anterior end and is often armed with teeth. The brain, or cerebral ganglia, is internal and is highly developed in the cephalopods.

The visceral sac is the next distinct part and it houses the gut, heart, and reproductive organs.

The foot is a muscular structure used for locomotion and burrowing and is developed into tentacles in the cephalopods.

The mantle is the fourth region of the body and is a fold of skin which develops from the posterior part and folds over, enveloping the visceral mass and separating it from the shell, thus forming a cavity between the shell and the rest of the body. The anus and excretory ducts open into the mantle cavity inside which the gills develop. The shell is secreted by the edge of the mantle and consists of an outer horny layer, with an internal pearly or nacreous layer of calcium carbonate.

—adapted from *The Animal Kingdom*

This is a good example of scientific analysis: The opening paragraph identifies the subject ("molusks") and sets up the division into "four main parts" ("head," "visceral sac," "foot," and "mantle"), then goes immediately into the analysis: The subsequent paragraphs each take up one of the divisions and extend the analysis initiated in the opening paragraph. The diction is Latinate and scientific ("anterior," "cerebral ganglia," "cephalopods," "visceral sac," "posterior," "nacreous," and "calcium carbonate") with some use of metaphorical language ("armed with teeth," "houses the gut, heart . . ."). Compared to the language of the student's critical essay which combines facts with evaluation, the language of this piece of writing is fairly objective.

Enumeration

Enumeration may be considered to be *a kind of informal analysis,* a subdivision of the topic of analysis. As a topic of invention, it answers such questions as What is the exact number? What is the logical order? How is it constituted? Like analysis, enumeration considers aspects or features of things as separate units. The mental process is concerned with *the sequential arrangement of successive things*: a group of objects, or events, or ideas, generally following each other in the order of time. Number can be thought of as a kind of abstract order, but when it is tied to time, it is related to narration, process, and cause and effect.

As a pattern of arrangement, enumeration presents ideas in numerical order so that there is a distinct separation of the elements of a group. Each part of the series reveals a definite pattern of advance. The numerical order reveals a recurrent causal or logical pattern. However, sometimes you may want to use an enumeration pattern in an essay to hold together parts of a subject that do not ordinarily lend themselves to a more logical form of organization. For example, if you are asked to give a speech, and you cannot think of a more logical way to present your ideas, at the very least you can announce to your audience that you are going to talk about three things or five things or some determinate number. This numbering will not only aid you in recalling the parts of your speech, but it will also give your audience a logical pattern to follow. There are times when you have some "things to say" about a subject, but the best you can do is to put them into some reasonable order. You could probably say more about the subject, but you limit yourself to a representative number, and this order at least serves your purpose.

Since enumeration is such a basic principle, it will often be found reinforcing other patterns such as partition, classification, process, and cause and effect. Whether you use it as a basic organizational pattern or in combination with other patterns, you will want to make clear to the reader your purpose and the basis of the enumeration. Usually your thesis will indicate your purpose and your plan of development.

Because we will be looking at a number of essays that use enumeration as a major or subordinate pattern of development, I will not present any special examples of the type at this time. But it is quite obvious that the paradigm will contain number words like *first, second*, and *next*, as the following scheme illustrates:

Enumeration Pattern
Introduction (includes thesis)

First (the first, one) . . .
Second (the second, two) . . .
Third (the third, three) . . .
Fourth (the next, four) . . .
Fifth, sixth, seventh (another, five) . . .
Finally (the final, six) . . .
Conclusion (summary, return to beginning)

Enumeration themes, like analysis themes, have a characteristic vocabulary. The following are a few representative words and phrases that can be found in enumeration themes:

number	string	list	to count
order	chain	item	to catalog
series	set	catalog	to number
succession	sequel	tally	to enumerate
progression	sequence	analysis	to itemize

Enumeration is probably the simplest kind of organizational pattern. Its simplicity, however, should not deceive you about its relative importance. In chemistry, in physics, in mathematics, number is of fundamental importance. In your everyday activities, numbering is so basic that you may sometimes forget its importance. You compute your grocery bills, number the pages of your letters, call the roll, catalog, count, list, tally, add, score, calculate, and itemize. Like time and space, number is an important principle in the universe.

Exercises

1. Write an analytic essay based on one of the following subjects. Be sure to consider your audience and your purpose for making the analysis. In this and in subsequent assignments, use a cover sheet, similar to the one suggested in chapter 3, that will include subject, purpose, audience, kind of writing, and mode.

   a. pop music
   b. a rock lyric

   c. a short poem
   d. a reproduction of a painting
   e. a life-style
   f. a political or social issue
   g. a magazine ad

2. Bring to class Xerox copies of a magazine ad. Distribute these to members of the class. Then analyze the headline, the picture, and the copy of the ad. Discuss these in relation to the purpose of the ad and the intended audience. Is the ad effective in achieving its purpose?

3. Analyze in class a movie or TV show the class has recently seen.

4. You are called upon to give a talk about the values college students hold. Write a speech in which you analyze these values and come to some kind of conclusion about them. (You can also use this topic for classroom discussion.)

5. Write a scientific analysis of a subject that interests you.

6. Select a newspaper article, a magazine article, or a short essay from your reader about a controversial issue (for example, nuclear power plants). Then do an analysis of the issues:

   a. Read the article carefully.
   b. Pick out all of the important *general statements*.
   c. Identify the *qualifying words: all, many, most, some, several, a few, always, sometimes, usually, never, seldom, occasionally*.
   d. Consider the *supporting evidence* for the general statements: examples, facts, statistics, details, descriptions.
   e. Look closely at the *connections* among ideas. Is the writer adding something new, qualifying, contrasting, or evaluating?
   f. Identify the *main idea*.
   g. Identify the writer's *conclusions*.

Description

Description is a mental process, a way of perceiving objects in space and time. It is really a mode of analysis. Like analysis, it is a process of dividing anything complex into simple elements. Like analysis, it deals with its subject as a whole and in its parts. And like analysis, it is more than an enumeration of the parts or qualities of an object. Unlike analysis, however, it deals with its subject more concretely. It relies heavily on sense impressions. Often, it depends for its effects on comparison and association. These are not absolute but relative distinctions, of course. As it pertains to composition, **description** is *a way of picturing images verbally in speech or writing and of arranging those images in some kind of logical or associational pattern.*

Embedded in the word *description* are two words: *scribere,* meaning "to write," and *de,* meaning "down" or "about." There is a hint in the etymology of the word *description* that something is being traced or drawn, that in describing you will follow the outline of an object visually and then write it down or "draw" it in words. The word *draw* is not an accidental association. Many writers have likened the process of describing to that of painting.

Purpose, Audience, Kinds of Discourse

Description can be found in almost any kind of writing, but it is frequently found in books of travel, history books, guidebooks, geography books, scientific articles, magazine ads, brochures for art galleries, books on architecture, magazine articles, descriptive poems, character sketches, novels, and short stories. Although it may be found in almost pure form, as in some magazine advertisements, description is usually mixed with the other modes.

Perhaps your most important prewriting consideration in describing a person, an object, or a scene is purpose, for your purpose will determine the nature of your description. For example, informative description will enable your reader accurately to identify the object you are describing. Persuasive description will enable you to appeal to the senses of your reader in such a way as to induce action. Evocative description will enable your reader to experience a mood or an emotion.

But to say that someone is describing something is immediately to give rise to the question To whom? The very act of describing implies an audience. Purpose and audience operate in the same fashion for description as they do for analysis.

Invention and Description

In getting ideas for writing a description, you might proceed exactly as a painter might. That is, whether you are looking at a landscape, a person, or an arrangement of fruit, you would tend to ask yourself certain questions that would make the process of invention easier. What does the object or objects look like, or feel like, or smell like? How would you group them logically or artistically? Would you follow the natural lines of the object or scene to be described? Is the object linear, angular, or circular? In describing an object or a scene, would you begin from left to right, from right to left, from bottom to top, or from top to bottom? Is the object or scene near or far away? If far away, would you depict it in the same way as if it were near? What is your point of view? What is the dominant impression of the object or scene? Does the scene evoke a mood or stir your feelings? How best can you convey sense impressions? Notice how easily questions like these come to mind when you are dealing with a particular pattern of thought. In answering these questions, you are inventing.

But you are a painter using words, not pigments. Instead of putting down your impressions on canvas, you will be putting them down on paper. But your task is very similar to that of the painter: to put into some kind of formal pattern the results of your mental perceptions. Like the painter, you will be concerned with form, position, color, light, sound, taste, touch, odor. Like the painter, you will be dealing with the particular and the concrete, with individuals of a class, not with generalized classes. You are not just interested in dogs, but in hounds, pups, whelps, curs, mutts, Saint Bernards, German shepherds, and collies. You are not just interested in birds, but in larks, starlings, robins, sparrows, canaries, finches, nightingales, and mockingbirds.

In the process of writing, you must select particular details and group them. At that time, other questions come to mind. Do you stress contours or outlines, definite lines, colors, or shapes? Do you stress masses and volumes of things? Do you see planes or successions of planes parallel to the picture plane? Do the forms recede—in and out, forward and backward? Are the forms confined in closed space, or are the representations of space infinite? Is there unity, balance, rhythm? Is the order intellectually formal or biomorphic, that is, developing in a natural way? Are the forms fantastic, never seen or imagined before, or seen perhaps only in dreams, myths, hallucinations?

At the moment, I am simply putting into words many of the things you do intuitively. Your mind is constantly questioning, inventing, probing, but I want you to make the process of invention and arrangement more self-conscious.

Exercises

1. Using questions such as those suggested (What is it? What are its constituent parts? How are the parts organized in space? What shape does the thing to be described have? What is its color, taste, feel, smell, sound?), examine a subject such as a landscape, a painting, a piece of fruit, a person's face, for a possible writing assignment.

2. Study a natural landscape, a cluster of buildings, a city scene, or a marketplace. Observe the choice of details, the arrangement of space, the landscaping.

3. Study some paintings, reproductions, or artistic photographs of a landscape, a still life, or a portrait. What is the central feature of the picture? How are the objects or figures grouped? What choices of details has the painter or photographer made? What kind of balance is there in the picture? What is the dominant impression? The point of view?

4. Compare a modern painting with a traditional painting. What is the difference in the handling of details, arrangement, point of view, and climax?

The Structure of Description

When you set out to describe a person, an object, or a scene, you have to decide at the outset your point of view, the choice of appropriate details, and the way you are going to arrange the details.

In description, *point of view* usually refers to physical location. But it may also refer to the mental angle from which you consider your subject. Occasionally, in describing, you may be able to *sense* your physical position in relation to the object. But it is usually better to determine your point of view in advance of your writing. In this way, your description will be more unified.

When moviemakers want to get several different views of a particular scene, they will move the camera from place to place. If they want to get a more general view of an object or scene, they will move the camera further away. If they want a more detailed view, they will move in close. Similarly, in describing, you may find it necessary to move from one point to another or from one scene to another.

Sometimes your point of view will determine your choice of details and the order of their arrangement. Sometimes the natural contours of the objects themselves will suggest a way of proceeding. But often you will have to impose some sort of order on your materials. The following selections illustrate a variety of patterns that you could follow:

Spatial Order: Depth

St. Mark's

And well may they fall back, for beyond those troops of ordered arches there rises a vision out of the earth, and all the great square seems to have opened from it in a kind of awe, that we may see it far away—a multitude of pillars and white domes, clustered into a long low pyramid of coloured light; a treasure-heap, it seems, partly of gold and partly of opal and mother-of-pearl, hollowed beneath into five great vaulted porches, ceiled with fair mosaic, and beset with sculpture of alabaster, clear as amber and delicate as ivory— sculpture fantastic and involved, of palm leaves and lilies, and grapes and pomegranates, and birds clinging and fluttering among the branches, all twined together into an endless network of buds and plumes; and, in the midst of it, the solemn forms of angels, sceptred, and robed to the feet, and leaning to each other across the gates, their figures indistinct among the gleaming of the golden ground through the leaves beside them, interrupted and dim, like the morning light as it faded back among the branches of Eden, when first its gates were angel-guarded long ago.

—John Ruskin, *The Stones of Venice*

Radiating Order: Moving Observer

A Tropical Landscape

On my right hand there were lines of fishing-stakes resembling a mysterious system of half-submerged bamboo fences, incomprehensible in its division of the domain of tropical fishes, and crazy of aspect as if abandoned forever by some nomad tribe of fishermen now gone to the other end of the ocean; for there was no sign of human habitation as far as the eye could reach. To the left a group of barren islets, suggesting ruins of stone walls, towers, and blockhouses, had its foundations set in a blue sea that itself looked solid, so still and stable did it lie below my feet; even the track of light from the westering sun shone smoothly, without that animated glitter which tells of an imperceptible ripple. And when I turned my head to take a parting glance at the tug which had just left us anchored outside the bar, I saw the straight line of the flat shore joined to the stable sea, edge to edge, with a perfect and unmarked closeness, in one levelled floor half-brown, half-blue under the enormous dome of the sky. Corresponding in their insignificance to the islets of the sea, two small clumps of trees, one on each side of the only fault in the impeccable joint, marked the mouth of the river Meinam we had just left on the preparatory stage of our homeward journey; and, far back on the inland level, a larger and loftier mass, the grove surrounding the great Paknam pagoda, was the only thing on which the eye could rest from the vain task of exploring the monotonous sweep of the horizon. Here and there gleams as of a few scattered pieces of silver marked the windings of the great river; and on the nearest of them, just within the bar, the tug steaming right into the land became lost to my sight, hull and funnel and masts, as though the impassive earth had swallowed her up without an effort, without a tremor. My eye followed the light cloud of her smoke, now here, now there, above the plain, according to the devious curves of the stream, but always fainter and farther

away, till I lost it at last behind the mitor-shaped hill of the great
pagoda. And then I was left alone with my ship, anchored at the
head of the Gulf of Siam.

—Joseph Conrad, The Secret Sharer

Dominant Image: Repetition

Fog

Fog everywhere. Fog up the river, where it flows among green aits
and meadows; fog down the river, where it rolls defiled among the
tiers of shipping, and the waterside pollutions of a great (and dirty)
city. Fog on the Essex marshes, fog on the Kentish heights. Fog
creeping into the cabooses of collier-brigs; fog lying out on the yards,
and hovering in the rigging of great ships; fog drooping on the
gunwales of barges and small boats. Fog in the eyes and throats of
ancient Greenwich pensioners, wheezing by the firesides of their
wards; fog in the stem and bowl of the afternoon pipe of the wrathful
skipper, down in his close cabin; fog cruelly pinching the toes and
fingers of his shivering little 'prentice boy on deck. Chance people
on the bridges peeping over the parapets into a nether sky of fog,
with fog all round them, as if they were up in a balloon, and hanging
in the misty clouds.

—Charles Dickens, Bleak House

Order of Memory: Fantasy

Night Town

The Mabbot street entrance of nighttown, before which stretches
an uncobbled tramsiding set with skeleton tracks, red and green will-
o'-the-wisps and danger signals. Rows of flimsy houses with gaping
doors. Rare lamps with faint rainbow-fans. Round Rabaiotti's halted
ice gondola stunted men and women squabble. They grab wafers
which are wedged lumps of coal and copper snow. Sucking, they
scatter slowly. Children. The swancomb of the gondola, highreared,
forges on through the murk, white and blue under a lighthouse.
Whistles call and answer.

—James Joyce, Ulysses

Order of Observations: Impressions

The Garden

I sat down in the middle of the garden, where snakes could scarcely approach unseen, and leaned my back against a warm yellow pumpkin. There were some ground-cherry bushes growing along the furrows, full of fruit. I turned back the papery sheaths that protected the berries and ate a few. All about me giant grasshoppers, twice as big as any I had ever seen, were doing acrobatic feats among the dried ground. There in the sheltered draw-bottom the wind did not blow very hard, but I could hear it singing its humming tune up on the level, and I could see the tall grasses wave. The earth was warm under me, and warm as I crumbled it through my fingers. Queer little red bugs came out and moved in slow squadrons around me. Their backs were polished vermilion, with black spots. I kept as still as I could. Nothing happened. I did not expect anything to happen. I was something that lay under the sun and felt it, like the pumpkins, and I did not want to be anything more. I was entirely happy. Perhaps we feel like that when we die and become part of something entire, whether it is sun and air, or goodness and knowledge. At any rate, this is happiness: to be dissolved into something complete and great. When it comes to one, it comes as naturally as sleep.

—Willa Cather, *My Antonia*

The first selection, by John Ruskin, displays an artistic grouping of details in space. The total effect is that of depth perception. In the Conrad selection, the observer first faces the sea and then turns completely around to face the shore. The effect is that of lines radiating from the observer to different parts of the picture. The Dickens selection uses a dominant image, the fog, as a way of organizing the description. The repetition of the word *fog* unifies the description and produces a dominant tone of dreariness. Quite obviously, not all descriptions are organized in space and time. The selection from *Ulysses* by James Joyce uses the order of memory, which is free from the confinements of space and time. It avoids logic. Memory, of course, is the voluntary calling to mind of past events. But this selection is further complicated by the fact that the mode of writing is a fantasy. The images therefore are bizarre, fanciful, hallucinatory, grotesque, whimsical, and unreal. In the absence of the objects of perception, the mind invents illusory images. Finally, the selection by Willa Cather uses no special order except that of reporting to the reader the random impressions received in the way in which they strike the observer.

The foregoing selections are specific examples of description, in all their concreteness.

The paradigmatic structure of description, however, may be illustrated as follows:

Paradigm 1: Vertical Order (bottom to top, top to bottom)
Paradigm 2: Horizontal Order (left to right, right to left)
Paradigm 3: Depth Order (inside, outside)
Paradigm 4: Circular Order (clockwise, counterclockwise)

A good example of horizontal order is this masterful description by James Joyce:

> A fat brown goose lay at one end of the table and at the other end, on a bed of creased paper strewn with sprigs of parsley, lay a great ham, stripped of its outer skin and peppered over with crust crumbs, a neat paper frill round its shin and beside this was a round of spiced beef. Between these rival ends ran parallel lines of side-dishes: two little minsters of jelly, red and yellow, a shallow dish full of blocks of blancmange and red jam, a large green leaf-shaped dish with a stalk-shaped handle, on which lay bunches of purple raisins and peeled almonds, a companion dish on which lay a solid rectangle of Smyrna figs, a dish of custard topped with grated nutmeg, a small bowl of chocolates and sweets wrapped in gold and silver papers and a glass vase in which stood some tall celery stalks. In the centre of the table there stood, as sentries to a fruit-stand which upheld a pyramid of oranges and American apples, two squat old-fashioned decanters of cut glass, one containing port and the other dark sherry.

—James Joyce, "The Dead"

Joyce uses a frame device to organize the details of this description. The opening sentence presents an image of both ends of the table, with the goose at one end and the ham at the other. The rest of the description is organized from these points in space. Sentence 2 shows the progression of objects from the ends of the table to the center. Sentence 3 focuses on the objects in the middle of the table, laden with food. The reader can visualize the scene very vividly and grasp the relationships of the objects on the table to one another. Not only is there a spatial movement from the ends to the center, but there is also a movement from meat to drink.

Within this larger pattern, there are smaller patterns that help to make up the whole. The sentences are loose or cumulative sentences. (The main idea is stated first, followed by subordinate ideas.) Each sentence furthers the spatial description while at the same time giving the reader a catalog of the food in all its concreteness. Joyce puts the burden of the spatial patterning on the prepositional phrases:

> at one end of the table
> at the other end of the table
> on a bed of creased paper
> round its shin
> beside this
> between rival ends
> on which lay bunches of purple raisins
> on which lay a solid rectangle of Smyrna figs
> in which stood some tall celery stalks
> in the centre of the table

These phrases are phrases of location and direction.

The verb choices are primarily static verbs, the verb "to be" and verbs of rest *(lay, stood, was)*. These reinforce the spatial pattern and contribute to the effect the reader gets that he or she is looking at a static picture, a still life. The point of view is that of an observer who is close to the scene he is describing.

The word choice is specific and concrete. Joyce appeals to almost all the senses. He uses words and phrases pertaining to shape and size, color, texture, and taste:

Shape and Size

great	solid	blocks
little	round	leaf-shaped
full	shallow	stalk-shaped
large	fat	rectangle
small	bunches	pyramid
tall	squat	parallel

Color

brown	purple	peppered
red	gold	dark sherry
yellow	silver	chocolates
green	oranges	

Texture

creased	frill	glass
sprigs	peeled	cut
stripped	grated	
peppered over	crust	

Taste
Fat brown goose
peppered over with crust crumbs
a round of *spiced* beef
grated nutmeg
chocolates and *sweets*

Joyce also uses a number of figures of speech to lend concreteness to the description:

Figures of Speech
a large green *leaf-shaped* dish
a *stalk-shaped* handle
blocks of blancmange and red jam
a solid *rectangle* of Smyrna figs
two decanters of cut glass . . . as *sentries* to a fruit-stand
a *pyramid* of oranges and American apples

Problems of Description

In this very small compass, Joyce manages to touch upon almost all
the aspects of description:

I. Methods of development
    A. Spatial (linear—left to right, right to left, bottom to top,
       top to bottom, clockwise, counterclockwise, and so forth)
    B. Repetition (same image repeated)
    C. Cataloging (accumulation of details and images)
II. Point of view
    A. Near or far
    B. Above or below
    C. Direct line
    D. Oblique
    E. Inside or outside
III. Imagery
    A. Literal
    B. Figurative
IV. Sense Appeal
    A. Sight
       1. color (red, orange, lilac)
       2. form (spiral, star-shaped, tubular)
    B. Touch
       1. thermal (hot, cold, sunny)
       2. simple (soft, hard, featherlike)
       3. pressure (squeeze, whizz)
    C. Taste
       1. sweet   6. rough
       2. salty   7. smooth
       3. sour   8. soft
       4. bitter   9. crisp
       5. corrosive   10. cool and warm
    D. Sound
       1. high (shrill, piercing, screech)
       2. low (moan, groan)
    E. Smell
       1. pungent (sharp, stinging, caustic)
       2. tart (sharp)

3. sour (acid)
4. rancid (rank)
5. camphoraceous

6. musky
7. floral
8. peppermintlike

Most of you will have little trouble with visual images. But you will find, as this list shows, that there are few terms to describe touch or taste or sound or smell. So you may have to have recourse to comparisons, to figures of speech.

On the surface, it would appear that there is nothing easier to do than to describe. But to describe is to do more than simply follow the natural contours of an object in space. It is also to be discriminating in selecting details and in grouping objects.

Imitation

One good way to learn to describe is to imitate. The following student paper is based on the Joyce model:

A Thanksgiving Table

A fat brown turkey lay at one end of the table and at the other end, on a silver platter covered with waxen paper, strewn with sprigs of parsley and bits of onions, lay a great duck, stripped of its feathers and outer skin and drenched in pools of cranberry sauce, encircled by thick clusters of dressing and beside this was a platter of spiced rolls. Between these rival ends were concave lines of side-dishes: two tiny cuplets of jelly, purple and red, a large silver bowl filled with billowy mounds of white potatoes, a small pear-shaped dish with a stem-shaped handle on which lay clusters of pitted grapes and crushed walnuts, a companion dish on which lay a quivering rectangle of fruit-laden salad, a dish of chocolate pudding dotted with whipped cream, a small bowl full of almonds and peanuts and a glass vase in which stood freshly cut stalks of garden onions and green celery. In the center of the table there stood, like majestic pillars, two graceful, ornate containers of spun glass, one containing pink wine and the other bubbly champagne, flanking a fruit bowl, upholding a pyramid of oranges and apples, mixed with freshly picked cherries and grapes.

—Jim

If you feel too constrained doing a strict imitation, you might try a loose one like the following:

A Wedding Table

In the center of the long lace-covered table towered a white cake, six layers high and decorated with delicate, sugary, pink roses set against light green leaves. Silver dishes containing creamy mints molded into roses and tinted in pink and green lay to the right of the cake. On the other side of the mints were two deep silver bowls filled with a mixture of salted nuts. To the left of the wedding cake were the forks, their prongs gleaming, arranged in three perfectly even rows. Beside the forks were the napkins, snowy white with fine silver engraving, placed in a diamondlike pattern on the tablecloth. Steaming urns of black coffee stood at one end of the table together with glass cups, delicately etched in silvery swirls. A small pitcher of cream, thick and golden, and a bowl of sugar that was perfectly molded into cubes were close by. At the opposite end of the table sat a large cut-glass punch bowl containing a sweet ruby-red juice and bulky chunks of glittering ice. The tall and slender candles, flaming on each side of the cake, created a soft glow over the entire table.

—Donna

Exercises

1. Analyze one of the descriptions by Ruskin, Conrad, Dickens, Joyce, or Cather in class. Then, using one of these models, do an imitation, following the order of development indicated.

2. Using the Joyce selection as a model, describe a holiday table laden with food, using a frame device. Use specific concrete details and figures of speech.

3. Describe a person, a bowl of fruit, a floral arrangement, or some other grouping by the still-life method.

4. Using one of the four spatial patterns outlined in this chapter, describe one of the following:

a. a seascape   f. a junkyard
b. a desert scene   g. a supermarket
c. a spring morning   h. a street in the winter
d. a graveyard   i. a garden
e. an antique shop   j. a room

5. Describe a painting or an artistic photograph.

People, Places, and Things

Description is concerned mostly with people, places, and things. The student papers reprinted below give you a variety of models to follow, based on these topics.

You might wish to describe a roommate, a close friend, a parent, a child, a niece or nephew, a teacher, a landlord, a rock star, or a celebrity.

John

Of all my neighbors, the one that I find most interesting is John. He stands about six feet and one inch tall, lanky and thin, narrow in the hips and shoulders. He has one of those protruding Adam's apples that a person can get fascinated with as he watches it bob up and down. John's face is one of the most unique I've ever seen. His chin is square with a small cleft in the center. He's got a very thin mouth that is almost like a single pencil line, always turned up into a smile. Hanging over his top lip is a thick orange-brown mustache, extending from one corner of his mouth to the other, thick toward the middle and tapering at the ends. His long nose is thin and turns under a bit, off center, just above the mustache. His small hazel eyes are set deep into his head, forming two deep canyons on either side of his nose. His thick, black, horned-rimmed glasses make his eyes look even smaller, like two brown dots on flesh-colored paper. His eyebrows are thick and bushy, rising just above his glasses. His short hair is curly and wiry, like a poodle's, forming what looks like a cap upon his head. His whole structure is bowed and when he walks he takes long easy steps swinging his arms back and forth. All in all John looks like a curly-headed Ichabod Crane.

—Kris

Or you might want to describe a scene you know well.

An Afternoon in the Woods

As I sit here under this grotesque spreading oak which displays partial death in its upper limbs, my eyes squint from the raging brightness of the afternoon sun. Moving my eyes across a level plain, I see a descending cow path, twisting and turning until it abruptly comes to a granite ledge where the trail zigzags down a steep slope to a clear running spring. Loose sandstone and clay have been churned up by the cattle and deer which have quenched their thirst from the sweet water at the bottom of the slope. The cold water pours over a small ledge of red, orange-brown, and conglomerated rocks, resembling peanut brittle, making a plunging, gurgling rhythm like a public water fountain in Paris continuously flowing. Dark green moss grows along the banks, and a few ferns sprout between shales on the steep slope. The scoldings of the bluejays spread from treetop to treetop as they voice their disapproval of my visit, accompanied by the sounds of a sorrel-colored squirrel sitting on a low branch of a large oak tree on the other side of the stream, eating last year's nuts, while a mother pheasant and her ten young chicks ramble across the small level plain to a farmer's field that has not yet been plowed, hoping to find a few kernels of last year's corn. A rain crow demands another shower, but the sky promises no rain. A soft breeze gently rocks the tops of the aspens, maples, oaks, honey locusts, and weeping willows, whispering forest gossip to the trees in the next valley, and the sweet fragrance of blooming sweet clover drifts into the valley from a nearby field. No sounds of speeding cars on hot pavement or screaming jets enter this peaceful spot. Soon, shadows cross the green valley floor, darkening the once sunlit area, while unrecognizable forms of tree stumps appear as miniature men in the partial shadows.

—Mary

The Elegant Creation

On the table before me is a container, a simple, clear, transparent glass vessel, tall and slender, with the top edge flaring out. It curves inward toward the bottom, forming a short, thin neck, supported by a round base, just a little smaller than the circle formed by the top edge. This container, however, is merely the complement to the delicacy which lies within. A scoop of French vanilla ice cream is the first ingredient, slightly melting and cold, conforming to the roundness of the vessel's bottom. Another scoop, balanced on the first, is topped by spoonfuls of rich, thick, butterscotch syrup, dripping down the sides of the ice cream and oozing to the bottom in wavy, golden ribbons. Whipped cream, light and fragrant, is heaped on plentifully in soft puffs of wispy white clouds. Crunchy, toasty nuts rest temptingly on the delicate blanket of whipped whiteness. A perfectly formed, bright red maraschino cherry perches precariously on top of the creation, adding just the right touch of color and elegance. A small indentation in the cherry, where the cherry's stem had once been, is slightly visible, winking like the eye of a demon temptress, luring me on to enjoy the butterscotch sundae.

—Dorothy

These are just a few of the many subjects suggested by the topic of description.

Although description is generally conceived of as a static pattern of discourse, more often than not it is mixed with narration. It makes sense, nevertheless, in learning the characteristics of description to see description as being static.

Scientific Description

Description is sometimes divided into two kinds: scientific description and literary or artistic description.

Scientific description is sometimes called *technical* or *objective description. Objective description* attempts to *represent the object as accurately as possible.* It adheres strictly to a part-by-part analysis, exact measurement, and enumeration of details. It is factual, detached, and impersonal, uninfluenced by emotion or personal involvement. It is usually written in the third person singular, with the agent of the action omitted. There is seldom any hint that a person is involved in describing. The focus is on the subject standing apart, known in and of itself.

The following is a good example of scientific description:

The Emerald Tree Boa

The Emerald Tree Boa *(Boa canina)* is found in tropical South America. As its name suggests, it is arboreal and it has an extremely prehensile tail. It feeds mainly on birds and squirrels and also on iguana lizards. It possesses front teeth that are highly developed, probably proportionately larger than those of any other nonvenomous snake. Tree boas grow to about six feet.

When adult, emerald tree boas are a bright emerald green with creamy or white spots. These boas rest in a characteristically coiled position on the top of branches, with the front of the body above and inside the outer rings, looking a little like a bunch of green bananas. The color, posture, and the light spots break up the outline of the snake's body, leaving them almost impossible to detect at rest in the trees. Although the adults are this uniform and striking color, the young specimens are more variable and differ from their parents. They are yellowish, or even pink, with white markings edged with dark purple or green. As they become mature, the markings change to the adult pattern. In captivity, emerald tree boas are usually quiet and can be handled without attempting to bite.

—From *Snakes of the World.*

This selection has most of the characteristics of a good scientific description: specific details, comparisons, and precise diction. The writer combines a description of the behavior of the boas ("It feeds mainly on birds and squirrels and also on iguana lizards," "In captivity, emerald tree boas are usually quiet. . . .") with a concrete and specific description of its physical dimensions and characteristics. He describes the size of their teeth ("proportionately larger than those of any other nonvenomous snake"), by means of a literal comparison, and the size of their bodies ("about six feet"). He then describes the color, posture, and markings of the adults of the species ("a bright emerald green with creamy or white spots," "characteristically coiled position") and of the young specimens ("yellowish, or even pink, with white markings edged with dark purple or green"). In addition to color nouns and adjectives to describe the boas, the writer uses a metaphorical comparison ("looking a little like a bunch of green bananas") and a literal comparison (they are "more variable and differ from their parents"). Besides precise diction dealing with size, color, posture, and markings, the writer also uses formal and scientific diction for descriptive purposes ("arboreal," "prehensile tail," *"Boa canina,"* "specimens"), yet the total description is not difficult to understand, written as it is for the general reader.

Literary Description

Literary description is *artistic description.* It is sometimes called **subjective** or **impressionistic description.** The *writer's aim* in this kind of description is not to give accurate, factual information, but to *create a mood, a feeling, or an impression by the use of imaginative language.* What is described is colored by the writer's subjective reactions to the object perceived. The style of literary description is characterized by colorful, suggestive, and vivid language and the artistic grouping of details. The selection from James Joyce's "The Dead" is a good example of literary description. Literary description is not confined to imaginative literature, however. Artistic description can be found in magazine ads where the aim is persuasion, in personal letters, in informal essays, and the like.

This selection from *The Red Badge of Courage*, by Stephen Crane, is an excellent example of literary description:

> The column that had butted stoutly at the obstacles in the roadway was barely out of the youth's sight before he saw dark waves of men come sweeping out of the woods and down through the fields. He knew at once that the steel fibers had been washed from their hearts. They were bursting from their coats and their equipments as from entanglements. They charged down upon him like terrified buffaloes.

Behind them blue smoke curled and clouded above the treetops, and through the thickets he could sometimes see a distant pink glare. The voices of the cannon were clamoring in interminable chorus.

The youth was horror stricken. He stared in agony and amazement. He forgot that he was engaged in combating the universe. He threw aside his mental pamphlets on the philosophy of the retreat and rules for the guidance of the damned.

The fight was lost. The dragons were coming with unvincible strides. The army, helpless in the matted thickets and blinded by the overhanging night, was going to be swallowed. War, the red animal, war, the blood-swollen god, would have bloated fill.

—Stephen Crane, *The Red Badge of Courage*

This passage describes a young soldier's panic and that of his fellow soldiers as they retreat in his direction. The action is seen from the young man's point of view. His horror is expressed by an extensive use of figurative language.

In the first paragraph, the retreating soldiers are viewed impressionistically by the youth as "dark waves of men . . . sweeping out of the woods and down through the fields." The wave metaphor is then replaced by a simile that describes the horror-stricken men as charging on the youth "like terrified buffaloes." The cannon's roar is personified as sounding like a chorus of human voices "in interminable chorus." In the last paragraph, the enemy soldiers are described as "dragons . . . coming with invincible strides." Finally, war itself is described as "the red animal" which would soon "have bloated fill." Crane's purpose in this passage is not to give a factual, objective picture of retreating soldiers, but to give us some insight into the young soldier's feelings. The description is dominated by a single mood—horror.

Exercises

1. Write a technical description of one of the following subjects. Aim for precision of diction, accuracy, and objectivity.

a. a stereo
b. a solar invention
c. a new engine
d. a plant
e. a bird or an animal

f. a part of the body
g. a kitchen utensil
h. a tool
i. a mechanism
j. a felt-tip pen

2. Cut a picture from a magazine. Describe the picture as accurately and as objectively as possible. Attach the picture to your description when you hand it in.

3. Describe a city scene, a marketplace, a landscape, or a similar subject from an objective point of view. Then write an impressionistic description of the same scene.

4. Describe some scene in fair weather. Then describe the same scene in fog, rain, or snow. Change the season, or time, or activity, or whatever.

5. Describe a strange or exotic landscape, perhaps on an unknown planet. Describe the plant life, the animal life, or the terrain.

6. One interesting kind of literary description is *expressionism*. Expressionism is the distortion of reality to communicate feelings and emotions. It is antirealistic, not being concerned with objective accuracy.

   Analyze the following excerpt from Poe's "The Fall of the House of Usher." How does the language of description contribute to the ominous atmosphere? Consider the impressionistic diction, the surrealistic images, the sound devices, and the narrator's comments.

   > During the whole of a dull, dark, and soundless day in the autumn of the year, when the clouds hung oppressively low in the heavens, I had been passing alone, on horseback, through a singularly dreary track of country; and at length found myself, as the shades of the evening drew on, within view of the melancholy House of Usher. I know not how it was—but, with the first glimpse of the building, a sense of insufferable gloom pervaded my spirit. I say insufferable; for the feeling was unrelieved by any of that half pleasurable, because poetic, sentiment, with which the mind usually receives even the sternest natural images of the desolate or terrible. I looked upon the scene before me—upon the mere house, and the simple landscape features of the domain—upon the bleak walls—upon the vacant eye-like windows—upon a few rank sedges—and upon a few trunks of decayed trees—with an utter depression of soul which I can compare to no earthly sensation more properly than to the after dream of

the reveler upon opium—the bitter lapse into everyday life—the hideous dropping off of the veil. There was an iciness, a sinking, a sickening of the heart—an unredeemed dreariness of thought which no goading of the imagination could torture into aught of the sublime. What was it—I paused to think—what was it that so unnerved me in the contemplation of the House of Usher?

—Edgar Allan Poe, *The Fall of the House of Usher*

Patterns of Thought:

Classification, Exemplification, Definition

Chapter 5

Patterns of Thought:
Classification, Exemplification, Definition

Classification

Pick up the classified advertising section of your local newspaper and you will find broad categories such as the following: rentals, automotive, miscellaneous, livestock and produce, business and finance, business services, personals and services, educational, employment, and announcements. Then look at the subcategories of any of these broad categories and you will notice subdivisions such as these:

Automotive

Autos for Rent	Sports Cars
Autos for Sale	Trucks
Station Wagons	Autos
Convertibles	Imported Autos

Livestock and Produce

Dogs	Livestock
Cats	Poultry
Birds, Fish	Fruits
Pets	

Or go into a drugstore or a supermarket and look at the greeting cards. Some cards are classified according to official American holidays:

American Holidays

Christmas	Father's Day
New Year's	Independence Day

Valentine's Day   Thanksgiving
Easter   Halloween
Mother's Day

Others are classified under a miscellaneous category:

Miscellaneous
Formal   Birthday
Traditional   Death
Contemporary   Sickness
Humorous   Wedding
Floral   Anniversary
Cute   Sympathy

These are not very elegant ways of classifying things, but for special purposes it is sometimes convenient to group things together in a rough way, even though some of the categories may seem to be arbitrary. These examples illustrate that classifying is a familiar, everyday activity. Things may be classified; events may be classified; ideas may be classified.

Classifying is an important part of thinking. Yet the process as it develops in the child is a gradual one. In the first stage of concept formation, given an assortment of blocks or objects, a child will put them together at random, without any logical basis, because they appear together in time and space. But the objects have no intrinsic bonds according to the child's thinking. In the second phase of concept formation, the child puts objects together on the basis of bonds that actually exist between these objects. To be sure, the child's subjective impressions play some role in his or her thinking, but he or she no longer mistakes these impressions for connections between things. Instead, he or she groups objects on the basis of color, shape, or size. In the last phase of concept formation, the child is able to abstract and isolate elements and to view them apart from "the concrete experience in which they are embedded."

Is classification merely the process of giving a common name to things, or is it the discovery of universal properties that things have in common? Anthropological linguists have postulated a kind of linguistic and cultural relativity for classifying. The Hopi Indians, for example, have one class word that includes everything that flies except birds. Thus airplane pilots, airplanes, and insects all belong to the same class. The Eskimos have numerous names for snow: *wind-driven snow, snow on the ground, slushy snow, icy snow, hard-packed snow, falling snow.* Color classification varies in different cultures. The Shona, a tribe in Rhodesia, have three class names for colors. Other tribes have two. Botanists divide flower colors into blue (cyanic) and yellow (xanthic).

Purpose, Audience, Kind of Discourse

Classification is used constantly by people in hundreds of professions and occupations—by scientists, teachers, doctors, lawyers, historians, librarians, grocery clerks, and insurance agents. One of the simplest purposes to which classification can be put is the simple physical process of sorting. Consider the amount of sorting you do in your everyday life. You sort your clothes, your books, your record collection, stamps, coins, important papers of various kinds. In brief, one of your most important aims in classifying is to put experience in order.

Although classification can be found in many kinds of writing and used for a variety of purposes, one of the most important aims of classification is to inform or instruct. Therefore, you are more likely to find classification in expository than in persuasive or literary writing. Some typical examples of kinds of writing that use classification are articles and textbooks on botany, chemistry, biology, political science, anatomy, anthropology, psychology, and sociology, and library classification, scientific essays, magazine articles, museum catalogs, and classified ads.

Naturally, your audience will be an important factor in making your classification. If your audience has a specialized knowledge of your subject, your classification will tend to be formal or scientific. If your audience has little or no knowledge of your subject, your classification will probably be informal. In scientific classification, your focus will be on the subject itself, and your classification will tend to be exhaustive. But informal classification is more audience-centered. In informal classification, you may classify the same subject in any number of ways, depending on your purpose and on your reader's knowledge, interests, level of understanding, and so forth.

Invention and Classification

Classifying is a basic mental activity. It is *the process of grouping similar ideas or objects, the systematic arrangement of things into classes on the basis of shared characteristics.* As a topic of invention, it is related to definition (to define is to put the thing to be defined into a class); analysis (to classify is to divide into parts or categories); enumeration (to classify is to enumerate members of a class); and comparison (to classify is to group similar things). The topic of classification suggests questions that you can ask of any subject, such as How may an object or an idea be classified? What are its common attributes? What are its basic categories? What is the basis of the classification? What is the purpose of the classification?

Any group of individuals or objects possessing something in common can be classified. But you should not confuse classification with analysis. When you analyze, you begin with one object or idea and divide it into parts on the basis of differences. When you classify, you begin with many things and group them according to similarities. The term in an analysis is always singular: *a painting, a movie, the human body, an apple, a poem, a sentence, a house.* The term in a classification is always plural: *cars, jobs, popular songs, drugs, blind dates, clothing styles.*

When you classify, you should first determine the basis of classification, the common feature or quality that unites all the elements of the group. If, for example, you are classifying apples, you can classify them by color:

or you can classify them by taste:

When you classify, always keep in mind the purpose of your classification. Your purpose should be clearly defined.

The principles of classification are similar in many respects to those of analysis:

> *There can be no classification unless the things to be classified are considered similar to each other in some respect.*

> *Only one principle of division may be applied at each level of classification.*

> *At each level, the classes must be mutually exclusive.*

> *In a scientific classification, the classes at each level must cover the whole field.*

To follow the principles of classification in your thinking is to participate in one of the most fundamental acts of the human mind.

Ludwig Wittgenstein gives some of the best practical advice about classifying for compositional purposes. Look at those events or proceedings, he says, that we call games: "I mean board-games, card-games, ball-games, Olympic games, and so on. What is common to them all?—Don't say: 'There *must* be something common or they would not be called *games*'—but *look and see* whether there is anything common to all."

Exercises

1. Probe one of the following subjects by using questions suggested by the topic of classification (How may it be classified? What are its common attributes? What are its basic categories? What is the basis of the classification? What is the purpose of the classification?).

a. drugs	f. days
b. drinks	g. movies
c. useful things	h. voters
d. cars	i. tables
e. school	j. crimes

2. Discuss in class the ways in which you are viewed (that is, classified) by different people.

3. Discuss national, racial, and other kinds of stereotypes as exemplified by the following:

   a. Athletes are dumb.
   b. Blacks have rhythm.
   c. Italians are amorous.
   d. Germans are stubborn.
   e. Irish are hot-tempered.
   f. Americans are materialistic people.

The Structure of Classification

The paradigmatic structure of classification essays has a pattern that may be depicted as follows:

Classification Pattern
Introduction (includes thesis and class words)
Type 1 (or subclass 1)
Type 2 (or subclass 2)
Type 3 (or subclass 3)
Type 4 (or subclass 4)
Type 5, 6, 7 (or subclass 5, 6, 7)
Conclusion (summary, return to beginning)

In addition to their basic paradigmatic structure, classification essays have a basic vocabulary that enables the reader to follow the logical progression of ideas:

kinds	categories	classify
sorts	sources	compile
types	orders	assemble
classes	clusters	string together
varieties	groups	collect

Put into the form of *suggestive statements*, the process of organizing classification essays may be described as follows:

Keep in mind your purpose before you begin to write.

In your thesis sentence, provide a clear statement of the basis of your classification.

In your introduction, supply a list of the types or classes into which you will group your subject.

In subsequent paragraphs, take up each type or class, defining or explaining each one and giving examples.

The essay that follows, taken from *Time* magazine of June 26, 1974, is a good example of an informative article that uses the steps outlined above.

Faces in the Crowd

Introduction   Who's playing at the local rock palace? One way to find out is to look at the marquee. Another, says California promoter Steve Wolf, is to watch the crowd strolling—or floating, in the case of heavy grass consumers—through the door. "Audiences resemble the groups they come to see," says Wolf. Those words are reckless understatements.

No one who has ever mixed with a San Francisco psychedelic-style concert crowd is likely to forget the experience. Going to see Boz Scaggs, Grace Slick, or Hot Tuna? Better take earmuffs and a flak jacket. Psychedelic rock crowds can be hostile collections of spacy Vietvets still suffering from post-Viet Nam syndrome, pimply feminists in granny glasses, and young high school dropouts. Bottles and firecrackers spin through the air. At a Grateful Dead concert, usually a four- or five-hour affair, the typical freak is a blend of drug hunger, male lonerism, and musical knowledgeability. He will attend somnolently to the music (probably after swilling a bottle of wine), sway ecstatically forward toward the performers. In contrast, the audience for balladeer James Taylor, or the country-rock group Poco, whose music has crisp pattern and infectious surfaces, has a well-scrubbed look and an enraptured response to the music.

Of course, when hallowed groups like the Rolling Stones, the Who, or Bob Dylan make one of their infrequent appearances, categor-

Thesis ies crumble; everybody comes, just like the World Series. Still, it is possible to define five general types of audience on the basis of dress, manner, consumption, age, and music taste. The catetories:

Type 1 *Heavy Metal.* So named because of the massive banks of amplifiers, drums, and loudspeakers employed by Grand Funk, Led Zeppelin, Black Sabbath, and Blue Oyster Cult. The music is pure buzz—heavy, simplistic blues played at maximum volume and wallowed in mostly by young teen-agers, just experimenting with marijuana, the lingua franca of rock, and perhaps hard drugs too.

This audience can be trouble for concert-hall managers. Says Cleveland promoter Jules Belkin, "They are up on the seats boogieing and running around the hall." Dress ranges from scruffy jeans to $200 velveteen jackets. The girls may come in couples to ogle, say, at topless Mark Farner of Grand Funk. Then there are the brassy groupies with their stevedore vocabularies who haughtily flaunt their backstage passes. The boys come in gangs and do what gangs do— fling lighted matches, fight the bouncers, sometimes toss empty wine bottles. Vomiting from too much beer or wine is a status symbol. If these kids do not have tickets, they break in. A heavy security force, sometimes including local police, is *de rigueur* at most rock concerts.

Type 2 *The Listeners.* Performing groups that attract this crowd include the Moody Blues, Yes, Weather Report, and The Eleventh House. The music is predominantly classical or jazz rock. The Listeners tend to be Heavy Metal graduates—youths ranging in age into the early 20's, who know and care about musicianship. Sedated by grass, Seconals, and Quaaludes, they tend to applaud rather than scream their approval.

Type 3 *Squeaky Cleans.* A description used by singer Bette Midler to characterize fans of the soft, often poetic songs of such bards as Cat Stevens, James Taylor, Joni Mitchell, Melanie. This is an orderly dating crowd in its late teens and early 20's who are interested in love songs. Girls generally outnumber the boys by 2 to 1. Melanie's ethereal fans tend to invade the stage, only to sit quietly at her feet, perhaps lighting candles. Mitchell's following emulates her. "Since Joni started wearing gowns," says Wolf, "the girls have started wearing dresses and makeup."

Type 4 *Glitter Trippers.* Glitter stars do not seem so much to have created their fandom as to have been created by it. The fastest-growing audience in rock dotes on the finery of such brocade-, sequin-, mascara-, and rouge-wearing performers as Todd Rundgren, Suzi Quatro, Alice Cooper, and the New York Dolls. Occasionally a glitter singer like England's bisexual David Bowie is actually good. Mostly, though, admits the Dolls' David Johansen, "the whole glitter trip is just jive." A concert can also be simply an excuse for youngsters to come out for a reasonably harmless masquerade party. The kids go on parade to show off their white tuxedos and top hats, feather boas, and of course glitter, lavishly applied to face and body.

Type 5   *The Evening-Outers.* These are the young married, who, says one New York promoter, "are dressed to the nines, and smoke where they're supposed to." As mellowed graduates of the 1960's rock revolution, they will naturally show up to hear the Stones or Dylan, but mostly they turn out for the Carpenters, or the Fifth Dimension. Promoters like the Evening-Outers because they spend money generously at the concession bars.

Conclusion   Begun by the Beatles a decade ago, the rock revolution succeeded beyond everyone's wildest dreams. Rock defined an emerging segment of America, financed a counterculture, and spawned a $2 billion industry. Its principal gift to those who were young in the 1960's was to provide a common means of expression—a common music, a common language, even a kind of cathartic theater in which a Janis Joplin assumed almost mythic dimensions as a tragic heroine and Dylan strolled the stage like an Orpheus. It is no secret that rock's classic era is gone forever, along with the social bonds that nurtured it. The current fragmentation of the rock audience certifies that. In fairness, it must be added that it also signifies a diversity of personal taste and music style unknown previously in American pop music. If rock can be described as being in a somewhat self-expressive romantic era, can its neoclassic period—or a pop Stravinsky—be far behind?

The first two paragraphs introduce the essay. Paragraph 3 states the thesis and helps to organize the classification pattern in the remainder of the essay ("It is possible to define five general types of audience on the basis of dress, manner, consumption, age, and music taste"). The next six paragraphs define the types of audiences (Heavy Metal, The Listeners, Squeaky Cleans, Glitter Trippers, and The Evening-Outers) and give specific examples of the types. And the final paragraph concludes the essay.

The following classification selection is less formal than the *Time*

magazine essay, yet in many ways the classification scheme is more
rigorous. In this passage, the author describes the Philippine marketplace as it existed in 1953:

The Philippine Marketplace

1

1. Today, under the long skylit roofs of the market sheds, the long
   trestle tables are spread with miles of food.
   2. There is meat on the meat stalls now—carabao, pork, and beef
      in long, red, gluteal rivers—and entrails, organs, and tripe in
      slithering mounds.
   2. There are great mountains of cabbages, greens, beans,
      cucumbers, lettuce, white radishes, leeks, and squash, and of
      breadfruit, pineapple, mango, lansone, guava, blimbing, and
      durian in semiquarantine and smelling like cheese.
      3. One entire row of tables and stalls deals in nothing but
         blazing bananas, golden fingers clutched in clumps and
         clusters, yellow masses piled high, great green claws hanging
         down, and golden crowns swirling like blazing haloes as they
         hang on strings, and the air is alive with the gold of bananas
         and the smell of their ferment.

2

2. But more important than anything else, for it is the manna
   of the Philippines, there are fish in the fishmarket.
   3. I walk between hills of scales down aisles of opalescent sheen,
      and see fish with flattened gills shimmering and slithering,
      smelling of salt and sea and covered with slime; fish of every
      color, shape, and feel, soft, hard, red, yellow, black, blue,
      purple, jade, and green.
      4. Here are crustacea like round ribbon rosettes, like flowers
         just opening, like pools in surf-drenched rock; crab,
         crayfish, mussels, oysters, and clams.
      4. There are octopuses like wet black rubber tubing, and
         like dark purple bruises.
      4. There are fish like whales and fish like midgets, like balls
         and those like swords, fish wide and flat, tall and thin,

round and star-shaped, spiked and spindly, and fishes
not at all like fishes.

5. All these are fresh, but their like may be found
shriveled, dried, salted, cured, and stinking high
and loud, in all sizes, from minnow-size bait in
countless hordes to huge cross-cuts of whale-like tunas
and dried octopus hanging from strings overhead.
—Agnes Newton Keith, *Bare Feet in the Palace*

The marketplace being described is a tropical market filled with
exotic sights and smells. The point of view is close up, with the
observer moving among the tables and stalls. Although the observer
is moving, the scene itself is static.

The initial sentence organizes the discourse: "Today, under the
long skylit roofs of the market sheds, the long trestle tables are spread
with miles of food." The general notion of the marketplace is introduced by the phrase "market sheds." Then you get a picture of the
trestle tables under the "roofs of the market sheds." Finally, you
are presented with the idea of a great quantity of food ("miles of
food") to be found in this marketplace. Subsequent sentences in
this paragraph and in the following paragraph add specific details
to the initial general statement and classify and describe the kinds
of food found in the marketplace.

The following scheme graphically depicts the relationships that
exist among the classes:

I. Food
  A. Meat
    1. carabao   3. beef
    2. pork
  B. Entrails
    1. organs   2. tripe
  C. (Vegetables)
    1. cabbages   5. lettuce
    2. greens   6. white radishes
    3. beans   7. leeks
    4. cucumbers 8. squash

D. (Fruit)
   1. breadfruit   5. guava
   2. pineapple   6. blimbing
   3. mango   7. durian
   4. lansone   8. bananas
E. Fish
   1. fish of every color, shape, and feel
   2. crustacea
   3. crab
   4. crayfish
F. (Mollusks)
   1. mussels
   2. oysters
   3. clams
   4. octopuses
G. Fish of various shapes and sizes
   1. minnow-size bait
   2. whale-like tunas

   This graphic outline reveals the following things. First, there
is a movement from explicit (food, meat, entrails) to implicit labeling
(vegetables, fruit, mollusks). (I have put the implicit class concepts
in parentheses in the above outline.) Second, the classification technique is that provided by the use of ordinary language, since this is
not a strict scientific classification. (For example, were this a scientific
classification, the fish would have been described as "vertebrate, cold-
blooded craniate animals with permanent gills, belonging to the super-
class Pisces in the phylum Cordata.") Finally, the classification becomes less formal and precise and almost disappears in the second
paragraph, as the bountifulness of the fish seems to overwhelm an
orderly perspective. The classification pattern, then, helps to organize
the wealth of specific images relating to the copiousness and luxuri-
ousness of the Philippine marketplace.
   I think that the preceding examples and discussion make abundantly clear that classification is the normal way in which our minds
perceive almost anything. But when you go to put the ideas received
from your classifying into patterns for writing, perhaps it is best to
follow some basic plan of organization, rather than to rely strictly
on the order of your impressions.

Exercises

1. Write an essay in which you classify the audiences you have seen at a rock concert or at some other public affair.

2. Analyze a classification essay from your reader.

3. Write a classification essay based on one of the following topics:

   a. blind dates
   b. people
   c. clothing styles
   d. television shows
   e. popular songs
   f. kinds of art
   g. jobs
   h. people's voices
   i. vacations
   j. dreamers

4. Classify for a possible theme topic one of the following:

   a. your favorite movies
   b. the worst movies you have seen
   c. your favorite television programs
   d. your favorite songs
   e. the worst words you know
   f. the names of people you admire

5. Classify the students on your campus. Consider carefully the basis of classification (for instance, Catholic, Methodist, hippie, yippie, jock, cowboy, longhair, middle class, upper class, English, German, Armenian, freshman, sophomore, and so forth).

Exemplification

Exemplification is *the process of illustrating a general principle, statement, or law by citing specific examples.* It is the act of showing or illustrating by using examples.

Thinking by means of examples is one of the most important ways of making your ideas clear. Concrete ideas are almost always easier to understand than abstract ideas. How often in your own conversations have you paused after making a general statement and added, "for instance," "for example"? A significant and interesting example can lend much needed support and validity to your arguments.

Purpose, Audience, Kind of Discourse

Exemplification is generally found in those kinds of writing whose aim is to inform and persuade. Exemplification can be found in magazine articles; essays; critical reviews; legal writing, in which the example might serve as a precedent; scientific writing, in which examples serve as illustrations of laws or general principles; textbook writing, which uses the example to instruct; argumentative writing, where the example is used as proof; short narratives such as the fable and exemplum that point up a general truth; news articles; advertising, and manuals of various kinds.

By their very nature, examples seem to be audience-centered. If you supply your readers with appropriate examples to support a general statement in an expository essay or the proposition in an argument, you will be helping them to grasp your ideas in a way that a page of abstract exposition will not. But a mere enumeration of examples is not enough. You want to give your readers examples close to their own experiences, and insure their understanding of these examples by means of a short conclusion. In sum, examples can have both expository and persuasive force.

Invention and Exemplification

As a topic of invention, exemplification is closely related to classification (each example is a member of a group or class of persons or things); analysis (examples are parts of wholes); and definition (giving examples is one way of supporting definitions). Exemplification answers such questions as What are some representative instances, examples, or illustrations? What is the supporting evidence?

Exemplification almost always accompanies generalization. **Generalization** is *the process of forming general concepts on the basis of observing particular instances or examples.* When you generalize, you extract the common element from a number of particular experiences. The process is often intuitive, but it is easy enough to test the validity of a generalization by reviewing a sufficiently large number of examples in your mind.

A generalization must contain at least one general term:

All men are created equal.
Some politicians are dishonest.
Many citizens are fed up with white-collar crime.
Political writing is generally bad writing.
Most humor is basically sadistic.

In formulating generalizations, you might want to keep a few points in mind. *First, a generalization is an inductive conclusion. Be certain, therefore, that you can support your generalizations with a reasonable number of examples. Second, the general terms in a general statement may be unnecessarily broad. Qualify, when necessary, your general terms. Suppose, for example, you make a statement that "politicians are dishonest." Do you mean that "all politicians are dishonest," "most politicians are dishonest," "some politicians are dishonest," or "a few politicians are dishonest"? Finally, general statements may be statements of fact, statements of opinion, or statements of inference. Be sure that you are clear in your own mind about the differences and that you convey these differences to your reader:*

The price of gasoline is rising. (statement of fact)

It is unfortunate that the price of gasoline is rising. (statement of opinion)

The price of gasoline will go up after the first of the year. (inference)

Exercises

1. Formulate a general statement and be prepared to probe it in class and support it with specific examples.

2. Give some examples of a successful person, a happy person. What makes a person happy or successful?

3. Give in class some examples of movies that present an optimistic view of life, a pessimistic view of life. Then discuss.

The Structure of Exemplification

The process of organizing an exemplification essay is generally very simple. In its most abstract form, the paradigm looks like this:

Exemplification Pattern
Introduction (includes the generalization)
Example 1
Example 2
Example 3
Example 4
Example 5, 6, 7 . . .
Conclusion

Sometimes, instead of supporting your generalization by a series of examples in successive paragraphs, you might want to use a single extended example that you amplify over the course of several paragraphs. Or you may give several examples in the same paragraph.

Like classification themes, exemplification themes have a characteristic vocabulary:

example	typical	cite
instance	exemplary	quote
sample	to illustrate	as follows
case	commonplace	for one thing
specimen	as proof	generally
quotation	as a matter of course	on the whole

In writing an exemplification theme, you might want to keep these things in mind: *First, state your generalization in a single declarative sentence. If, however, your generalization needs qualification, add as many qualifying statements as you think necessary. Second, begin your first supporting paragraph with an expression such as "for example," "for instance," "one example," and so forth. Although this might seem a bit formal, it will force you to keep in mind the pattern you are following. Third, choose examples that are related to your experience. Fourth, arrange your ideas in order of importance.*

The following student paper uses a very simple exemplification pattern. The first paragraph states the thesis and qualifies it. The next four paragraphs give positive examples to support the thesis. The sixth paragraph gives a negative example. The next paragraph qualifies the idea in this one by analogy. And the final paragraph gives another negative example and concludes the essay.

Be a Touchable

Is American society full of untouchables? From my own experiences, I would say no. In fact, it never even occurred to me that some people might be repelled by a friendly pat on the shoulder. But after our discussion about this in class the other day, I did some visiting with several friends on the matter. My family and I seem to be somewhat in the minority.

For example, my family, while not being made up of the greatest cheek-kissers, has always been very generous with the hugs, hand squeezes, arm-in-arm walks, and comforting shoulder pats. All of this is spontaneous. Nobody has ever said to me, "Now, Linda, go kiss your Aunt Ada." It just so happened I thought enough of my Aunt Ada to *want* to kiss her now and then when she had been especially nice. When Dad introduces me to anyone, he always has that big protective arm right around my shoulders that tells me he is proud of me far better than his words could.

I wouldn't think of walking into Grandma's house without grabbing both of her hands in a tight squeeze and smiling into her eyes so that she can get a good look at her granddaughter.

My husband and I went bowling with my cousin and his wife the other night, and he often threw his arm around my shoulders or Virg's as we visited. I didn't think that was queer at all. In fact, I thought it was very sweet the way he has accepted Virg in the family.

How comforting it was to have my aunt's arm around me after my Grandpa's funeral! She knew how very close we were, and her words could never have been as warm and understanding as that arm was.

Several of the people I talked to about this had different thoughts. One lady I work with said she didn't like people "pawing" her. A girlfriend said she had no reservations about kissing her husband, but couldn't kiss her parents, although she wished she could.

My answer to that would be for heaven's sake TRY!!! Don't regret it later that you didn't. I was uneasy about going into a swimming pool for the first time, and even after that first step was taken, it was a long time before I felt comfortable in my role as a swimmer. Now I love to swim and I think what a loss it would have been if I had been afraid to try, then follow through. I think the analogy holds for life. If you *want* to be more affectionate with your loved ones, just try, and keep at it. Soon it may become so natural you will wonder what all the fuss was about.

Don't be like my cousin Jo, who loved her father dearly but just couldn't show it. When she was 18, she finally brought herself to kiss him, but it was too late; he was in his coffin, unable to feel the delightful sense of touch the living have to share, if we only will.

—Linda

The student paper reprinted below uses the same basic pattern, but is even simpler in form. The first paragraph states the thesis ("Professional athletes in a number of fields are making more money than ever before"). The next four paragraphs cite specific examples from different professional sports (golf, basketball, baseball, and football). And the final paragraph concludes the essay.

Playing for Pay

Recent years have been golden ones for professional athletes. Professional athletes in a number of fields are making more money than ever before.

For example, in golf there have been three professional golfers who topped the one-million-dollar mark in lifetime earnings.

In basketball, one player recently negotiated a contract providing him with an annual income of $200,000. And within the past year, several college All-Americans signed basketball contracts which made them millionaires overnight. Today the least amount that a pro basketball player can receive annually is in excess of $13,000.

Baseball's rosters contain a number of stars who receive $100,000 or more to play for a single season. Six-figure bonuses are commonplace.

The same is true in football. College stars sign contracts which guarantee them financial security before they have proven themselves on the field as professionals. Well-established players receive salaries comparable to the stars in the other sports.

All of the big names in the major sports profit handsomely from product endorsements, personal appearances, speaking engagements, and business opportunities made available to them. It all adds up to a highly lucrative business to those who possess the ability to participate.

—Bruce

Exercises

1. Write an exemplification essay on one of the following general subjects:

   a. local place-names
   b. peculiar personal names
   c. nicknames
   d. current fads

2. Formulate five general statements that can be supported by examples.

3. Support one of the following generalizations by means of examples:

   a. People are judged by their language.
   b. A person's early experiences with members of other races or nationalities determine his or her prejudice or lack of it.

c. People conform to what they think are the conventions of their own group.

4. Give examples of how slang may be effective in certain situations.

5. You have probably heard the expressions "The best things in life are free" and "The best things in life cost money." Write an essay in which you support one of these statements with examples from your experience. Begin your first supporting paragraph with a signaling device such as "for example" or "for instance."

6. Select one of the following proverbs and write a short paper in which you support the proverb with examples.

   a. Love is blind.
   b. Truth is stranger than fiction.
   c. Discontent is the first step in progress.
   d. We are all slaves of opinion.
   e. Everyone has his or her price.

Definition

Definition is closely related to classification. As such, it is *a way of thinking in classes.* But it is also *a way of thinking in differences.* Thus, definition is related to comparison and contrast. Definition and description are also closely related; definition is a kind of abstract description. Definition most resembles description when it restricts or sets boundaries to a thing, when it tries to tell exactly what a thing is. To **define,** then, is to *set bounds or limits to a thing, to state its essential nature.*

Purpose, Audience, Kind of Discourse

Definition has a number of purposes in your writing: to explain things to your readers, to make clear the key points in an argument, to make yourself understood in everyday affairs, to specify, particularize, itemize, individualize, and characterize.

Almost all expository or persuasive writing contains definitions. Definition often appears at the beginning of an expository or persuasive essay to explain unfamiliar terms or to make clear a specialized use of a word. It often combines with classification to limit class words. In analysis, it is used to characterize the parts that are separated from the whole.

Definition can be found in scientific essays, textbooks, dictionaries, books of reference, expository essays, magazine articles, encyclopedia articles, news stories, research reports, manuals, and government publications.

Invention and Definition

As a way of probing a subject, definition is closely related to both description and classification. It answers the questions What is it? What are its limits or boundaries? What is its genus? What are its species? When someone asks you what something is, if it is a concrete object, you will have a tendency to describe it; if it is an abstract entity, you will tend to define it. Of course, concrete objects can be both described and defined. Defining is such a natural mental process that it is difficult to keep a person from defining. But although the process is intuitive, not everyone defines effectively, and some conscious attention to the process can be helpful.

The idea that the process is a natural one is constantly being reinforced by the conversations I hear every day. Some time ago, I was watching the "Good Night, America" program on television. Geraldo Rivera was interviewing one of the leaders of the Hell's Angels. Rivera commented that when he tried to take some unauthorized pictures of the Hell's Angels, he was almost "thumped." *Thumping*, he explained, is "beating someone to within an inch of their lives." More recently, I was reading an interview between a local reviewer and a rock-music promoter. During the interview, the term *roadie* came up. "Roadies," the promoter was explaining, "are the male equivalent of groupies. They tag along with the band taking care of the equipment and doing odd jobs. They are attracted to the glamour surrounding the rock world. They only make $150 a week. They live on beer, chicks, and coke [cocaine]. Give them $150 a week and a motel room and they'll mutter, 'Hey, man, far out.'"

Although definition is a process that you use unconsciously almost every day of your life, in writing it has more formal uses. One use, quite obviously, is to clarify difficult or obscure terms in such a way that you will have no problem being understood.

Every discipline has its jargon. Linguists, for example, use terms such as *morpheme, phoneme, tagmeme, functional shift, clipping, blending,* and the like. Clearly, these terms need to be explained to a general audience. So if you are using a difficult or unfamiliar term in your writing, you should attempt to explain it before you go on to other ideas.

New terms also need to be defined. Within the past few years, you have absorbed, without any self-consciousness, hundreds of new words from newspapers, magazines, movies, and television, words such as *trashing, fragging, gig, grody, grunt, groupie, go-kart, granny glasses, mod, maxi, light show, jock, nerd, feelie, dove, hawk, dawk, Day-Glo, cop-out, acid trip, zizzi, zonked, tank tops, New Left, acid head, freak.* Granted that you know in general what these words mean; you want to be precise in your writing, and precision often means definition.

Sometimes you may want to define a word whose meaning is so broad that it needs to be restricted. *Free world* is one of those terms. In the so-called *free world,* there are dictatorships such as those in some Central and South American countries, whereas beyond the *Iron Curtain* there are countries such as Yugoslavia and Bulgaria that have shown remarkable independence. What do you mean by the word *free* in your definition?

A final use of definition is to make fine distinctions between terms. For example, some people often use the words *love* and *sex* as synonyms. Do they in fact mean the same thing? What is the difference between love and sex? Love and affection? Love and devotion? Love and infatuation?

How to Define
Logical Definitions

To define a word using **logical** or **formal definition,** *put the word to be defined into a class and then differentiate it from other members of the same class:*

Term	Class	Differentiation
To frag	is to kill or injure a superior officer	by using a fragmentation grenade.
Overkill	is the ability to destroy an enemy	several times over.
A granny dress	is a loose dress similar to those worn by grandmothers	which reaches from the neck to the ankles.
A freebie	is anything gotten	free of charge.
The mini	is a short dress	two to four inches above the knee.

In putting a definition into a single sentence, use the same part of speech for the term to be defined as for the class term. Define a noun with a noun, an infinitive with an infinitive, and so forth. Keep the class word restricted. The larger the class, the more distinguishing characteristics you will have to add in order to separate the word from other members of the class.

Sometimes definitions can be used for humorous or satirical purposes. The following graffiti use the definition form (sometimes without the verb *be*) for just these purposes:

Hit and run means never having to say you're sorry.
Love means saying I'm sorry every five minutes.
Happiness is a warm poppy.
Life is a hereditary disease.

Most of these definitions actually do not follow the strict logical form of the formal definition; they are rather closer to definition by synonym. Here are a few that define by **negation:**

Bacteria is not the back entrance to a cafeteria.
Free is not equal, is not free.
Graffiti is not the Italian defense minister.

And here are a few that define by apposition:

> Reincarnation: a split infinity
> Picnic: a meadow lark
> Oleo Acres: one of the cheaper spreads

Synonyms

To define a word using **synonyms,** simply *substitute for a word or phrase an equivalent word or phrase.* Although definition by synonym is not as exact as other methods of defining, it is a very common and useful method of defining words, because if you substitute a better-known or less difficult word for one that is difficult or obscure, your reader will at least have a partial understanding of your intended meaning:

> *Lewd* means lustful.
> A *gnu* is an African antelope.
> The word *cockamamie* means absurd or foolish.
> To *cop out* is to withdraw.
> *Grotty* means miserable.

Etymology

To define a word **etymologically,** *trace the origin and historical development of the word, including any changes in its form or meaning.* For example, suppose you use the word *lucid* in a conversation and somebody says, "What does the word *lucid* mean?" You might reply: "The word *lucid* comes from the Latin word *lux, lucis,* which means 'light.' If you shed light on something, you make it clear. Hence the word *lucid* means 'clear.' "

These are the three main methods of defining. Some writers add definition by examples, by comparison, by description, or by repetition, but these latter seem more properly to be aids to definition rather than ways of defining.

Dictionary Definitions

A **dictionary definition** is not a special method of defining. It includes, rather, most of the methods that we have been discussing:

logical or formal definitions, synonyms, and etymologies. Let us look at a typical dictionary entry:

> **suburb** (sub′ərb) n. abbr. *sub.* **1.** a usually residential area or community outlying a city. **2.** *Plural.* The perimeter of country around a major city; environs. Used with *the.* [Middle English, from Old French *suburbe,* from Latin *suburbum: sub-,* near + *urbs,* city (see **urban**).]

The entry contains the word itself, the pronunciation of the word, the part of speech, and either (or both) a formal definition or a definition by synonym, followed by the etymology of the word. In defining a word, you need not be bound by the dictionary definition of the word, but you will find it useful to take it into consideration.

Exercises

1. Write a one-sentence logical definition of five of the following words:

   a. Afro
   b. charisma
   c. bummer
   d. jock

   e. macho
   f. superstar
   g. subcompact
   h. honky

2. Define one of the following terms in a single paragraph by tracing its etymology:

   a. raccoon
   b. butcher
   c. colossal
   d. cockroach
   e. steward

   f. bunk
   g. boycott
   h. Tabasco
   i. zombie
   j. dandelion

3. Coin a word and then define it in as many ways as you are able.

4. You are an advertiser with a new product. Invent a name for the product. Then define it and discuss it in a single paragraph. Think of some product names to get you started (*Tide* washes away dirt; *Duz* does everything).

5. Discuss in class the meaning of these terms:

a. boredom e. physical attractiveness
b. morality f. progress
c. responsibility g. individualism
d. good taste h. sportsmanship

6. Define one of the following, using the methods discussed in this chapter:

a. the perfect woman (man) e. a good bargain
b. an ideal gift f. soul food
c. the perfect date g. acid rock
d. soul music h. a great athlete

Patterns of Definition

How do you use definitions in your writing? Often at the beginning of an essay, you may need to explain key words necessary for understanding the meaning of what is to follow. Or you may want to explain a term that may be unfamiliar to the reader. In an argument, you would certainly want to make clear the terms of the argument. Definition is invaluable here.

Definition is seldom the length of an entire theme, although in some books or articles in which the author is trying to come to grips with the essence of a thing, it can be of essay length. More frequently, however, a definition goes on for a sentence or two or for the length of a paragraph. In the following selection from *The Theater of the Absurd*, Martin Esslin uses a variety of ways of defining:

> "Absurd" originally meant "out of harmony" in a musical context. Hence its dictionary definition: "out of harmony with reason or propriety: incongruous, unreasonable, illogical." In common usage in the English-speaking world, "absurd" may simply mean "ridiculous." But this is not the sense in which Camus uses the word, and in which it is used when we speak of the Theater of the Absurd. In an essay on Kafka, Ionesco defined his understanding of the term as follows: "Absurd is that which is devoid of purpose. . . .

Cut off from his religious, metaphysical, and transcendental roots, man is lost; all his actions become senseless, absurd, useless."

The first sentence defines by etymology. The word there that gives the reader a clue is the word *originally*. The second sentence is the "dictionary definition." It gives a string of synonyms. The third sentence defines by giving another synonym. The next sentence merely states, but does not define, Camus's stipulative use of the word. The last sentence is a logical definition, which is also stipulative; that is, Ionesco specifies the way he is going to use the term in an essay on Kafka.

In the next selection, E. M. Forster distinguishes between a story and a plot by first defining each term logically, then adding examples, and finally, toward the end, defining by function:

> Let us define a plot. We have defined a story as a narrative of events arranged in their time-sequence. A plot is also a narrative of events, the emphasis falling on causality. "The king died and then the queen died" is a story. "The king died, and then the queen died of grief" is a plot. The time-sequence is preserved, but the sense of causality overshadows it. Or again: "The queen died, no one knew why, until it was discovered that it was through grief at the death of the king." This is a plot with a mystery in it, a form capable of high development. It suspends the time-sequence, it moves as far away from the story as its limitations will allow. Consider the death of the queen. If it is in a story we say, "and then?" If it is in a plot we ask, "why?" That is the fundamental difference between these two aspects of the novel. A plot cannot be told to a gaping audience of cave-men or to a tyrannical sultan or to their modern descendant the movie-public. They can only be kept wide awake by "and then—and then—." They can only supply curiosity. But a plot demands intelligence and memory also.
>
> —E. M. Forster, *Aspects of the Novel*

The Structure of Extended Definition

How is a definition extended? One way is to begin with a logical definition, use it as a thesis sentence, and then expand the *class*

word and the *attributes* in subsequent parts of the paper. The resulting paradigm would look somewhat like this:

> *Extended Definition*
> Introduction (includes logical definition)
> Expansion of the genus
> Expansion of the differentia
> Conclusion (summary or restatement)

An alternative pattern might look something like the following:

> *Extended Definition*
> Introduction (includes sentence definition)
> Supporting details
> Supporting details
> Supporting details
> Supporting details
> Conclusion (summary or restatement)

If you follow this paradigm, you would expand your thesis with examples, additional kinds of definitions such as synonyms or etymologies,
comparisons, contrasts, analogies, explanations, quotations from authorities, and the like. The method of development is generally deductive, although an inductive order is possible.

The structure of the following professional essay by W. Nelson
Francis is a good example of an extended definition that reveals the
underlying paradigm very clearly. I have indented and numbered the
levels so that the pattern stands out.

Three Meanings of Grammar

1

1. A curious paradox exists in regard to grammar.
   2. On the one hand it is felt to be the dullest and driest of academic
      subjects, fit only for those in whose veins the red blood of
      life has long since turned to ink.
   2. On the other, it is a subject upon which people who would
      scorn to be professional grammarians hold very dogmatic
      opinions, which they will defend with considerable emotion.

3. Much of this prejudice stems from the usual sources of prejudice—ignorance and confusion.

4. Even highly educated people seldom have a clear idea of what grammarians do, and there is an unfortunate confusion about the meaning of the term "grammar" itself.

2

5. Hence it would be well to begin with definitions.

6. What do people mean when they use the word "grammar"?

7. Actually, the word is used to refer to three different things, and much of the emotional thinking about matters grammatical arises from confusion about these three different meanings.

3

8. The first thing we mean by "grammar" is "the set of formal patterns in which the words of a language are arranged in order to convey larger meanings."

9. It is not necessary that we be able to discuss these patterns selfconsciously in order to be able to use them.

10. In fact, all speakers of a language above the age of five or six know how to use its complex form of organization with considerable skill; in this sense of the word—call it "Grammar 1"— they are thoroughly familiar with its grammar.

4

8. The second meaning of "grammar"—call it "Grammar 2"—is "the branch of linguistic science which is concerned with the description, analysis, and formularization of formal language patterns."

9. Just as gravity was in full operation before Newton's apple fell, so grammar in
the first sense was in full operation before
anyone formulated the first rule that began
the history of grammar as a study.

5

8. The third sense in which people use the word
"grammar" is "linguistic etiquette."
9. This we may call "Grammar 3."
10. The word in this sense is often coupled
with a derogatory adjective: we say
that the expression "he ain't here" is
"bad grammar."
11. What we mean is that such an
expression is bad linguistic
manners in certain circles.
12. From the point of view of
"Grammar 1" it is faultless;
it conforms just as completely
to the structural patterns of
English as does "he isn't
here."
13. The trouble with it is like
the trouble with Prince
Hal in Shakespeare's
play—it is "bad," not in
itself, but in the company
it keeps.

6

7. As has already been suggested, much confusion
arises from mixing these meanings.
8. One hears a good deal of criticism of teachers
of English couched in such terms as "they
don't teach grammar any more."
9. Criticism of this sort is based on the
wholly unproved assumption that
teaching Grammar 2 will increase the

student's proficiency in Grammar 1 or
improve his manners in Grammar 3.

10. Actually the form of Grammar 2
which is usually taught is a very
inaccurate and misleading analysis of
the facts of Grammar 1; and it is
therefore of highly questionable value
in improving a person's ability to
handle the structural patterns of his
language.

11. It is hardly reasonable to expect
that teaching a person some
inaccurate grammatical analysis `
will either improve the
effectiveness of his assertions or
teach him what expressions are
acceptable to use in a given
context.

7

7. These, then, are the three meanings of
"grammar": Grammar 1, a form of behavior;
Grammar 2, a field of study, or science; and
Grammar 3, a branch of etiquette.
—W. Nelson Francis, "Revolution in Grammar"

The thesis sentence is the second sentence of the second paragraph: "What do people mean when they use the word 'grammar'?"
The word *grammar* is the key word which is to be defined. The
next sentence indicates the plan of development ("The word is used
to refer to three different things"). Then subsequent sentences and
paragraphs enumerate a different meaning of the word *grammar* ("the
first thing we mean . . . ," "the second meaning of 'grammar'. . . ,"
"the third sense in which people use the word 'grammar'. . .").

The abstracted underlying pattern has the following structure:

The word [*grammar*] is used to *refer* to *three different things*. . . .
The *first* [*meaning of grammar*] is "the set of formal patterns in

which the words of a language are arranged in order to convey larger meanings.''

The *second meaning* of ''grammar'' . . . is ''the branch of linguistic science which is concerned with the description, analysis, and formularization of formal language patterns.''

The *third* [*meaning* of *grammar*] is ''linguistic etiquette.''

These, then, are the *three meanings* of ''grammar'': . . . a form of behavior, . . . a field of study, or science, and . . . a branch of etiquette.

In writing your own extended definitions, you may choose to follow a formal pattern very closely, as in the Nelson Francis essay, or you may want to use a less formal approach, as in the following student paper:

Environmentalist, Preservationist, Conservationist: What's the Difference?

The word *environmentalist* has been bandied about so much that a person can't be sure in a given instance whether the word is complimentary or pejorative, whether it applies to someone favoring an automobile noise-abatement program or someone wishing to close Yellowstone Park and convert it to a pristine wilderness. Once very modish, the word is now almost useless as a conveyor of precise meaning.

Until the 1960s, environmentalists were simply people who were concerned about the environment, about litter, polluted streams, and endangered wildlife. The word *environmentalist* was not a household word. But in the sixties, the term became identified with the youth protest movement and with causes as diverse as vegetarianism and antiwar demonstrations. Through the late sixties and into the seventies, the meaning of the word came to depend increasingly on the point of view of the user. Thus, land developers labeled Environmental Protection Agency officials as *progress-blocking environmentalists*. Concerned citizens who demanded that air- and water-polluting industries ''clean up their act'' proudly identified themselves as *concerned environmentalists*.

Probably the most serious consequence of the loose definition of the word has been the blurring of the distinction between *preservationist* and *conservationist.* Both are now indiscriminately referred to as *environmentalists.* A preservationist who advocates closing a wilderness area to all public use is termed an environmentalist, as is the conservationist who urges moderation that will permit public use of an area while preventing depletion of its natural resources. The term is more likely to be interpreted as the *radical preservationist,* with sometimes serious consequences.

If one can derive a moral from all of this, it might be as follows: There is a need for precision in the definition of words that one uses. Imprecise diction, whether deliberate or not, is potentially as dangerous as outright misrepresentation.

—Shirley

Exercises

1. Discuss in class the student essay entitled "Environmentalist, Preservationist, Conservationist." What methods of defining does this essay use? Is it effective in achieving its purpose?

2. Write an extended definition, in the manner of the Nelson Francis essay, of one of the following:

   a. curiosity   e. skepticism
   b. jealousy   f. superstition
   c. culture   g. patriotism
   d. leadership   h. a well-rounded person

3. Write an essay in which you try to explain to a friend the differences among a liberal, a conservative, a radical, a moderate. Include logical definitions and give specific examples.

4. Write an essay in which you discuss the differences in connotation (suggested meaning) between *naked* and *nude, drinker* and *drunkard, old man* and *geezer, drifter* and *hobo, original* and *eccentric.*

5. Discuss in class, by defining the differences, these terms:

   a. open-minded, bigoted
   b. love, affection, devotion, fondness, infatuation
   c. generousness, selfishness
   d. clever, stupid
   e. aggressive, timid
   f. free speech, license
   g. demonstration, riot

6. Select one of the following words or phrases to define, analyze, and illustrate in context. Consider the following points: (a) denotation (literal meaning) and connotation (suggested meaning) of the word, (b) any technical or limited uses of the word, (c) your own reaction to the use of the word and your reasons, (d) a critical evaluation of the meaning and effectiveness of the word in general communication.

   a. academic freedom   e. sophistication
   b. open mind   f. adult
   c. progress   g. individualism
   d. modern   h. culture

7. According to chronological age, you probably are one who can be described as a teenager, a youth, an adolescent, a juvenile, a young adult, a guy or a gal, a stud or a chick. Write a short theme analyzing your personal responses to these words as they apply to you. Do you like them or dislike them? Why? What does each connote? Are there any other words that you prefer as self-description?

8. Examine your attitude toward abstractions such as honor, virtue, love, loyalty, brotherhood, and truth. Cite specific experiences of the use of these words, avoidance of them, and so forth.

Patterns of Thought:

Comparison and Analogy

Chapter 6

Patterns of Thought:
Comparison and Analogy

Comparison

Comparison is such a familiar everyday activity that it may be difficult for you to think of it as an important mental process. Yet without the ability to perceive similarities, you could not classify, define, or generalize. And without the ability to perceive differences, you could not analyze, define, or describe.

Comparison is *the process of examining two or more things in order to establish their similarities or differences.* Both the word *comparison* and the word *contrast* conjure up all sorts of interesting images in the imagination, images that reflect their widespread use in everyday thinking. The word *comparison* calls to mind words and expressions such as *twin, double, counterpart, brother and sister,* and *look-alikes.* The word *contrast* calls forth words and expressions such as *mismatched, nonconformity, a shade of difference,* and *this, that, or the other.*

Although comparison and contrast are closely related, they can be regarded as different mental processes. In examining any two things, you can mentally explore their similarities without necessarily exploring their differences, or you can mentally investigate their differences without investigating their similarities. In actuality, any relationship between two or more things will involve some degree of similarity as well as some degree of difference.

Purpose, Audience, Kind of Discourse

Of the rhetorical modes, comparison may well be the most important. The word itself suggests choices from among alternatives. Seldom a day goes by that you don't have to make important choices. You have to choose between two careers, two or more products, two political candidates, two goals, two courses of action. In making your choices, you use comparisons for every aim (informative, persuasive, expressive, and aesthetic) and for any kind of audience.

Comparisons underlie everything we do. Scientists use comparisons in their experiments. Logicians use them to draw conclusions. Politicians use them to formulate policies. Judges use them to render decisions. Ministers and priests teach and admonish us with comparisons.

Comparisons can be found in any kind of writing: magazine articles, advertising, essays, news articles, letters, editorials, textbooks, scientific writing, reports, political speeches, pamphlets, instruction manuals, poems, fables, and parables.

Invention and Comparison

The topics of similarity and difference, with their subtopics of literal and figurative similarity, difference in kind, and difference in degree, are perhaps the most fundamental topics in the inventive process, giving rise to such questions as What is it like? How is it similar to other things? How does it differ from other things?

Literal similarity is based on perceiving likenesses between subjects that belong to the same class, as in these examples:

> This table is square. That table is square.
> Both trees have drooping branches.

Figurative similarity is based on perceiving likenesses between subjects that belong to different classes:

> The skin around his eyes is pulled tight, like the skin of an onion.
> We were as naked as stone.

Difference in kind is based upon perceiving differences in common *traits* or *aspects* of a thing:

> This flower has bright, colorful blossoms.
> That flower has pale, faded blossoms.
> Lincoln was largely self-educated: Ford was not.

Difference in degree is based upon perceiving the *extent* to which a thing is unlike something else:

> *Crest* toothpaste is better than other toothpastes.
> The influence of television is greater than that of newspapers.

In exploring a subject by using the topic of comparison, you would probably follow a sequence of steps that might be described as follows:

> *Choose subjects that are interesting enough to challenge your imagination.*
>
> *Try, if you decide to compare two commonplace subjects, to look at them from a fresh point of view.*
>
> *Consider your purpose and your angle of vision. What particular point of view, what particular insight can you give your readers to make them see what you see?*
>
> *Be certain that there are enough aspects of the things to be compared to make a valid and interesting comparison. An aspect is a characteristic or feature of the thing to be compared, considered from one point of view.*
>
> *Choose only the most significant aspects of a subject to compare.*

Exercises

1. For purposes of class discussion and as an exercise in invention, compare or contrast

   a. two styles of clothing
   b. two movies
   c. two television shows
   d. two songs
   e. two talk-show hosts
   f. two ideas
   g. two kinds of music
   h. two dances
   i. two magazines
   j. two sports

2. Discuss, as an exercise in invention, some of the cultural differences that exist between any two nationalities, racial groups, special interest groups, or subcultural groups in the United States.

3. Write five sentences in which you point out the similarities between two things. Write five sentences in which you point out differences. Make five of the comparisons literal and five figurative. Then discuss these sentences in class.

4. Bring to class magazine ads that use comparisons to make a point, and discuss the effectiveness or lack of effectiveness of the comparisons.

The Structure of Comparison

Once you have explored your subject, you have got to decide upon an organizational plan. In developing your overall plan, in your introduction indicate the purpose of your comparison (your purpose, of course, could be implicit in your paper), give your reader some idea of the things to be compared, and indicate your plan of development. Then, in subsequent paragraphs, take up the points of the comparison.

In developing specific patterns, there are a number of basic paradigms that you can follow:

> *The Half-and-Half Pattern*
> Introduction (includes thesis, sets up comparison)
> Subject 1
>   Characteristic 1
>   Characteristic 2
>   Characteristic 3
>   Characteristic 4 . . .
> Subject 2
>   Characteristic 1
>   Characteristic 2
>   Characteristic 3
>   Characteristic 4 . . .
> Conclusion (summary, return to beginning)

The Characteristics Pattern

Introduction (includes thesis, sets up comparison)

Characteristic 1

   Subject 1

   Subject 2

Characteristic 2

   Subject 1

   Subject 2

Characteristic 3

   Subject 1

   Subject 2

Characteristic 4 . . .

   Subject 1

   Subject 2

Conclusion (summary, return to beginning)

The following student paper is a good example of the *half-and-half pattern.*

Myrtle and Peterbone

Thesis   In the days of my younger youth, the days of popsicle addicts and hula-hoop freaks, I had two great friends I divided my time with. Myrtle and Peterbone were both my friends, but that is the closest they ever came to having anything in common.

Subject 1   Myrtle was my childhood Doris Day. Her hair was so blonde that it would turn green from swimming in public pools, and the sunkissed freckles on her nose and knees was all the tan she ever got. Her nose was pug and turned up, and she always seemed to have her front teeth missing. She invariably wore that no-teeth smile together with a pink sunsuit to offset her aquamarine twinkling-star eyes.

Myrtle's parents were sort of hicks. They wore cowboy clothes and boots and someone was always cleaning catfish in the sink. Myrtle's mother must have been kind of quiet because all I remember of her are the swooshing and squeaking her levis and cowboy boots made as she did her Saturday housecleaning on Sunday morning. Myrtle's father is just as vague to me, but I think he wore flowered cowboy shirts and talked in kind of a twang whenever he wasn't engrossed in a beer can and the TV wrestling match. So while Myrtle's parents swooshed and squeaked and twanged, we would go off to see what new activities we could create for amusement.

The best thing Myrtle and I did together, aside from normal girlhood play, was tying strings onto locusts' wings and flying them around our heads like motordriven model airplanes. We never seemed to hurt them, as cruel as it may seem. We only did it in the summertime when the locusts drove everyone crazy with their noisy symphonies. The rest of the year we conjured up new species of paper dolls, tortuously hard games of jacks, or different schemes for not getting caught playing in the nearby irrigation ditch. When I would get tired of girlish pastimes, I would go over to Peterbone's.

Subject 2   Peterbone was Myrtle's opposite. He was a coffee-with-cream colored Catholic Mexican, with charcoal-black crewcut hair and the deepest ebony eyes I'd ever seen. No swimming pool could turn his near-bald head green, and if Peterbone ever had freckles, they were all run together into a tawny bronze. Peterbone had one front tooth missing, but no natural occurrence was responsible—it had been knocked out by a mean older brother. A white shirt and old jeans were what he wore the most, along with scuffed black shoes (untied) and two different kinds of socks.

Peterbone's parents were Mexican, but they nearly always spoke English, except when a family fight began. Then a tidal wave of Spanish words would crash into the air and I would, if present, stare dumbfounded as the deluge of Latin curses deafened my ears.

Choo-chee was Peterbone's mother. She wore red bandana scarves on her raven hair and yellow zoris on her size ten feet. She was very kind to her naughty boys and laughed with them lots of times when they got into trouble. She never kept a really neat house because she liked daytime soap operas, but her smiles and hot tortillas kept you from noticing. Peterbone's dad was a fireman. He didn't have much of an accent, but he wore white shirts too and liked boxing matches on Friday nights.

When Peterbone's parents were busy, we liked to stomp on caps in the driveway or sail boats down the ditch. That was only if Peterbone was in a good mood. If he wasn't, he would hold back my arms and get his brother Bobby to sock me in the face or stomach. One day I retaliated and punched Peterbone right in the nose. It bled all down his white shirt and I played with Myrtle for a long time after; but Peterbone's mean streak was what I liked the most.

As a Kool-Aid wino, I had a childhood full of locusts and caps and two strange friends as different as jellybeans and brussel sprouts. Myrtle and Peterbone were as different as night and day. Or perchance they were more like two different novels, but both shelved under the title of friend in my faded rose scrapbook of people I know.

—Linda

This student paper is beautifully organized, interestingly written, and sensitively handled. The basic comparison between the two friends is set up in the opening paragraph ("Myrtle and Peterbone were both my friends, but that is the closest they ever came to having anything in common"). In the next three paragraphs, Myrtle, Myrtle's parents, and the activities of Linda and Myrtle are described. Then, in the following four paragraphs, Peterbone, Peterbone's parents, and the activities of Linda and Peterbone are described. Finally, the last paragraph returns to the beginning.

If you find the half-and-half pattern a bit restrictive, you might want to try the *characteristics pattern*, in the manner of this student essay:

My Old Ford and My New Maverick

Only a few short weeks ago, I guided my trusty Ford Galaxie over to the car lot where I exchanged it (and a large check) for a new Maverick. I had decided that the time had come when I'd have to break down and trade in the Ford before the Ford went ahead and broke down itself. Besides, it really wasn't safe anymore and my friends were afraid to ride in it. Although I have only had the new car for a short time, already I can see many significant differences between the two cars.

As far as size and comfort are concerned, the Ford has the Maverick pretty much beat to hell. The Ford's massive trunk could accommodate eight large suitcases, twenty full potato sacks, or three huddled bodies at a drive-in movie gate. It could sleep two comfortably, three less comfortably, or two couples quite cozily. In fact, it could carry at once the whole of my earthly possessions, including my ironing board and my coffee table.

The Maverick's trunk is smaller than the Ford's. Its ten cubic feet include all sorts of weird angles and a spare tire secured in a position so that it is always in the way. It will accommodate eight large handbags, twenty full popcorn sacks, or three huddled chihuahuas. It can sleep one uncomfortably, two very uncomfortably, or three contortionists quite nicely. As for overall load capacity, I'm lucky to be able to stuff in my clothes, let alone my furniture. In fact, the Maverick would be a great family car for crowded cities—it would discourage large families.

Economy is another story. The Maverick goes for 430 miles on a tank of gas, long enough to find a parking place even at ASU. It burns no oil and requires no coolant. Perhaps most important, it is very unlikely to fall apart, and if it does, it has a warranty.

With an equivalent amount of gas, the Ford would go about half as far as the Maverick or about long enough to find a gas station before running out again. In fact, it uses as much oil as the new car uses gas, and it needs coolant regularly because regularly it boils over anyway.

As far as extra features are concerned, the two cars are about even. This is, however, more the case of off-setting penalties than one of equal virtues. The Maverick has no air conditioner, but the Ford has no heater. The Ford has no gauge lights, but the Maverick has so few gauges that it doesn't really matter. The new car's plastic floor looks cheap compared to the Ford's thick carpet, but it isn't bothered by mud and spills like the carpet in the Ford was.

For better or worse, I'm stuck with the Maverick. Even if it doesn't prove to be better than the Ford, at least it's different.

—Phil

The first paragraph of this essay sets up the basic comparison between the old car and the new ("Although I have only had the new car for a short time, already I can see many significant differences between the two cars"). The next two paragraphs take up the first characteristic of the two cars, size and comfort. Paragraphs four and five take up the second characteristic, economy. Paragraph six takes up the idea of extra features. And paragraph seven concludes the essay.

Both the half-and-half pattern and the characteristics pattern are fairly easy to follow. The *point-by-point pattern* is a variation

of the characteristics pattern, in which the features of the subjects
to be compared are presented in single sentences, using words like
both, each, also, and *too.* The following article, which appeared in
the *New York Times,* after John F. Kennedy's picture replaced that
of Franklin on the half dollar, uses a combination of the half-and-
half pattern and the point by point pattern:

Kennedy and Franklin

Benjamin Franklin, symbol of American enlightenment in the Age
of Reason, now steps aside for John Fitzerald Kennedy, champion
of reason in the Age of the Atom. Franklin, whose profile has graced
the United States fifty-cent coin since 1948 is being replaced by the
image of the thirty-fifth President. That Kennedy should occupy a
place held by Franklin is appropriate, for there are many parallels
in the lives, outlooks, and interests of the two American figures.
Points of likeness range from the coincidental to the philosophical.

Both men were born in the Boston area: Franklin on Milk Street
in the city proper and Kennedy in suburban Brookline. Both lived
in England for a time, Franklin as an agent for the colonial
Pennsylvania Assembly and Kennedy as the son of the American
ambassador.

While in England, Franklin once considered establishing a
swimming school. He was an excellent swimmer who one day covered
the distance on the Thames from Chelsea to Blackfriars—about three
miles. Kennedy's swimming ability saved his life when, as a young
naval officer in World War II, he swam from his rammed PT boat
to the safety of a lonely southwest Pacific islet. The distance was
about three miles. At Harvard, he was a member of the swimming
team.

Before entering public life both men were active journalists—
Franklin was publisher of the *Pennsylvania Gazette* and, earlier, of
his brother's *New England Courant;* Kennedy was a reporter for the
International News Service in 1945. Both were authors of popular
works in the field of biography: Franklin with his *Autobiography*
and Kennedy with his Pulitzer-prize-winning *Profiles in Courage.*

Interests in culture and the intellectual life were common
characteristics. Kennedy held his alma mater, Harvard University,
in special esteem and served on its Board of Overseers. Franklin helped

found the Academy of Philadelphia, which grew into the University of Pennsylvania.

Both were intensely concerned with science (Franklin was a scientist in his own right) and keenly aware of its value to mankind. In 1783 Franklin watched the first hydrogen balloon's ascension from Paris' Champ de Mars. To a sceptic who questioned the worth of the experiment Franklin replied: "What good is a newborn baby?" In February 1962 Kennedy was personally on hand at Cape Canaveral to honor Astronaut John H. Glenn on his return to the spaceport from America's first manned orbital flight. Kennedy devoted time and much effort to promote the nation's technological development.

—From *The New York Times*, Jan. 5, 1964

In using comparison patterns, you need not restrict yourself to these patterns exactly as outlined. Paradigms can be used with a great deal of skill and flexibility, as the following student paper illustrates.

Two Women

The Phoenix Art Museum exhibits approximately fifteen sculptures on its grounds, all by twentieth-century artists, ranging from jagged iron abstractions to strictly representational bronze castings. The most commanding of these, at least in terms of sheer bulk, is Paolo Soleri's *Flying Woman*. One of the least commanding, or so it seems at first, is Francisco Zuniga's *Woman at Siesta*. Each is situated in the grassy mall area between the Phoenix Library and the museum, the Soleri rising from the lawn abruptly, the Zuniga sleeping peacefully beneath a Palo Verde.

Soleri's woman is constructed of welded plates of iron-ox, a sheet iron developed for commercial use, whose surface rusts evenly, creating a superficial shield against deeper rusting. The Zuniga is of cast bronze and has developed the light turquoise patina associated with that more traditional material. The rust-orange color of the Soleri heightens its distinctiveness from its grassy surroundings, while the greenish hue of the Zuniga causes it to blend even more unobtrusively with the grass and the blue-green leaves of the Palo Verde beneath which it rests.

The Soleri sculpture consists of two stacked cubes that rise to an overall height of fifteen feet. The lower, much smaller block has sides of five feet in length, with exactly centered circular openings in each of the vertical sides that are each three feet in diameter. The upper block duplicates this pattern on a larger scale: the sides are nine feet in length for the cube, with circular openings measuring almost seven feet in diameter. Through these circular openings the angular woman flies, parallel to the ground, one arm stretched in front of her, the other behind, in a sort of side-straddle swim stroke through the air and the cube. Her angular face is centered in the opening that faces the main entrance, her legs outstretched side by side behind her.

The Zuniga drapes over a folding chair, her head reclined against the topmost slat. From ground level to the top of her head measures four-and-one-half feet.

Each sculpture is an exaggeration. The Soleri is far too angular. The Zuniga is far too round. Soleri's woman owes more to geometry than to flesh-and-blood women; Zuniga's woman owes her rounded form to too many tortillas. The lines of the Zuniga woman are exaggerations taken from life—the high cheekbones and narrow nose are common features among native Mexican Indians. Soleri's woman seems, on the other hand, to be an exaggeration of an abstract idea. No woman I've ever heard of has eleven distinct planes in her left thigh. This is not an indictment. Artists are free to illustrate abstract ideas no less than to represent or exaggerate nature, certainly.

But this *is* an indictment. Soleri's woman, represented as flying, is actually supported beneath her rib cage by struts, which anchor her to the bottom inside of the upper cube. Her (angular) hair, as though duplicating the famous oversight of the *Boy Removing Thorn From Foot,* hangs straight down rather than streaming behind, as Newton's second law of motion insists that hair propelled through space at the speed necessary to keep such an enormous bulk aloft would do. Thus, the sculpture defies a law of craftsmanship—that the supporting elements be incorporated into the functional elements—and it also defies the laws of gravity and inertia we all must live with.

There is a worse flaw. The *Flying Woman* is one-dimensional. She was created to be seen from the front. Viewing her from any of the other three sides, one cannot discern exactly what the jumble of metal is—neither her function, her gender, nor her species is apparent, except from the front. Sculpture, by definition, presents a three-dimensional object.

By contrast, Zuniga's woman sleeps peacefully, not aspiring to much, perhaps—but still patiently complying with the laws of physics, the demands of careful craftsmanship, and the aims of sculpture. Approached from any angle, she is obviously a woman asleep, supported from the earth by a folding chair. Thus, her support is a functional part of the sculpture. She is three-dimensional, and she does not demand that the viewer temporarily discount physics.

The Soleri sculpture seems to me to represent a lofty idea that is attractive but not possible, or both attractive *and* possible—but in a form different from the expression. In either case, the sculpture fails. The Zuniga seems to take on a much smaller aim. This woman will never leap beyond the bounds of geometry. Instead, when she wakes, she is likely to eat again and perhaps call her children to her side. Except that she will not awaken. She is sleeping. We all sleep. We all at one time took for our domains of sleep the soft, inviting body of a mother. The Zuniga seems full of that invitation. It accomplishes what it seems to propose. It is a successful sculpture.

—Jim

In this paper, the student uses a comparison paradigm, but avoids the rigidity of a strict half-and-half pattern or point-by-point pattern. His purpose is aesthetic appreciation through evaluation and interpretation. His audience is the other members of the class, although one can imagine a similar kind of essay appearing in a newspaper or magazine. The kind of writing is a critical essay, and the mode is contrast. The comparison paradigms help the student to think through his subject and to illuminate the features of each piece of sculpture through contrast.

The opening paragraph provides the reader with the situation at the Phoenix Art Museum and sets up the comparison. The second paragraph uses a point-by-point comparison. It deals primarily with the materials from which the two pieces of sculpture are constructed. The next paragraph describes the physical appearance of the Soleri sculpture. Paragraph four describes the Zuniga sculpture. The juxtaposition of the two descriptive paragraphs provides the contrast. The next paragraph returns to a point-by-point comparison, on the sentence level, of the exaggerated details of each sculpture. Sometimes the comparisons are made by juxtaposing sentences ("The Soleri is far too angular. The Zuniga is far too round"). Sometimes the comparisons are made within the same sentence ("Soleri's woman owes more to geometry than to flesh-and-blood women; Zuniga's woman owes her rounded form to too many tortillas''). Paragraphs 6 and 7, which point to the ostensible flaws in Soleri's conception, contrasts with paragraph 8, which praises Zuniga's craftsmanship in relation to his aim. The last paragraph furthers the interpretation and concludes with an evaluation.

Exercises

1. Analyze the preceding student essay. Does it use any of the traditional linking devices to achieve coherence in the comparison? If not, how does the essay achieve coherence?

2. Rewrite the essay using a half-and-half pattern throughout. Rewrite the essay using a point-by-point pattern throughout.

3. Write an essay, using one of the patterns discussed in this chapter, in which you compare and contrast

   a. two paintings   f. two magazine ads
   b. two art objects   g. two sports figures
   c. two poems   h. two celebrities
   d. two people   i. two writers
   e. two cities   j. two political parties

4. Compare and contrast the same place at two different times of the day, at two different seasons of the year, or at two different periods of your life.

5. Compare adolescence with childhood or adolescence with adulthood.

6. Get Xerox copies of reproductions of the statues of David by Michelangelo, Donatello, and Verrocchio. Then write a comparison-and-contrast essay based on these artworks.

7. Compare Botticelli's *Venus and Mars* with Veronese's *Mars and Venus United by Love.*

8. Compare Henri Matisse's *The Red Studio* (painting) with W. D. Snodgrass's poem "Matisse: *The Red Studio.*"

9. Compare Vincent Van Gogh's picture *The Starry Night* with Anne Sexton's poem, "The Starry Night."

10. Compare the lyrics of two popular songs.

11. There are many other interesting comparisons that can be made of artworks in the same medium (two paintings, two sculptures) and artworks in different mediums (painting and poem, painting and sculpture, sculpture and poem). If you are acquainted with any of these, you can use them for class discussion or for a writing assignment. The pictures of magazine ads, especially those that are artistically done, may also be worth using.

Analogy

An **analogy** is *an extended comparison*. It is a kind of logical inference based on the premise that if two things resemble each other in some respects, they will probably be alike in other respects. If you wish to explain a concept and you find that your readers may not be familiar with your subject or that your subject is difficult and complex, you can compare it point by point with something similar, but more familiar and less complex. The etymology of the word, from the Latin word *analogia* and the Greek *analogos*, meaning "proportion" or "equality of ratios," supports this notion of a point-by-point comparison with something else. The Latin and Greek sources suggest equivalence, correspondence, and likeness of relations.

It is difficult to imagine thinking without analogies. The process of discovering ideas using analogies is very similar to that of discovering ideas using comparisons. You explore your subject by comparing it point by point with something similar. Thinking in analogies is so ubiquitous that it is hard to see how we could get along without such thinking.

The Structure of Analogy

The organizational patterns of analogy are very similar to those of comparison and contrast. The point-by-point comparison pattern seems to be especially suitable to expressing ideas analogically. In organizing your ideas analogically, therefore, you might put them in a pattern somewhat like the following:

Point-by-Point Analogy Pattern
Introduction (sets up the analogy)
Subject 1 is similar to subject 2 in this respect
Subject 1 is similar to subject 2 in this respect
Subject 1 is similar to subject 2 in this respect
Subject 1 is similar to subject 2 in this respect . . .
Conclusion (therefore, subject 1 is similar to subject 2 in some respect known of one, but not known of the other)

In the following selection from *The Politics of Experience* by R. D. Laing, the author uses a pattern of organization that might be described as a point-by-point analogy pattern. In this passage, the analogy of a plane formation is used to point out that schizophrenia may be nothing more than a label that some people apply to others.

A revolution is currently going on in relation to sanity and madness, both inside and outside psychiatry. The clinical point of view is giving way before a point of view that is both existential and social.

From an ideal vantage point on the ground, a formation of planes may be observed in the air. One plane may be out of formation. But the whole formation may be off course. The plane that is "out of formation" may be abnormal, bad or "mad," from the point of view of the formation. But the formation itself may be bad or mad from the point of view of the ideal observer. The plane that is out of formation may also be more or less off course than the formation itself is.

The "out of formation" criterion is the clinical positivist criterion.

The "off course" criterion is the ontological. One needs to make two judgments along these different parameters. In particular, it is of fundamental importance not to confuse the person who may be "out of formation" by telling him he is "off course" if he is not. It is of fundamental importance not to make the positivist mistake of assuming that, because a group are "in formation," this means they are necessarily "on course." This is the Gadarene swine fallacy. Nor is it necessarily the case that the person who is "out of formation" is more "on course" than the formation. There is no need to idealize someone just because he is labeled "out of formation." Nor is there any need to persuade the person who is "out of formation" that cure consists in getting back into formation. The person who is "out of formation" is often full of hatred toward the formation and of fears about being the odd man out.

If the formation is itself off course, then the man who is really to get "on course" must leave the formation. But it is possible to do so, if one desires, without screeches and screams, and without terrorizing the already terrified formation that one has to leave.

Laing's main point is that many people are labeled schizophrenic because they are "out of formation" with society. But being "out of formation," he contends, is not necessarily the same thing as being "off course." Quite often, it is society and society's values that are "off course." "The perfectly adjusted bomber pilot may be a greater threat to species survival than the hospitalized schizophrenic deluded that the Bomb is inside him," argues Laing.

The points of the comparison may be illustrated as follows:

society = formation of planes
people = planes
"abnormal" person = "out of formation" plane
"normal" person = "in formation" plane
"abnormal" person = "off course" plane
"normal" person = "on course" plane

To many writers, an analogy is nothing more than an extended metaphor in which the comparison is put in terms of relationships. The following scientific analogy illustrates this process.

Observations indicate that the different clusters of galaxies are constantly moving apart from each other. To illustrate by a homely analogy, think of a raisin cake baking in an oven. Suppose the cake swells uniformly as it cooks, but the raisins themselves remain of the same size. Let each raisin represent a cluster of galaxies, and imagine yourself inside one of them. As the cake swells, you will observe that all the other raisins move away from you. Moreover, the farther away the raisin, the faster it will seem to move. When the cake has swollen to twice its initial dimensions, the distance between all the raisins will have doubled itself—two raisins that were a foot apart will have moved two feet apart. Since the entire action takes place within the same time interval, obviously the more distant raisins must move apart faster than those close at hand. So it happens with clusters of galaxies.

The analogy brings out another important point. No matter which raisin you happen to be inside, the others will always move away from you. Hence the fact that we observe all the other clusters of galaxies to be moving away from us *does not mean that we are situated at the center of the universe.* Indeed, it seems certain that the universe has no center. A cake may be said to have a center only because it has a boundary. We must imagine the cake to extend outward without any boundary, an infinite cake, so to speak, which means that however much cake we care to consider there is always more.

—Fred Hoyle, "When Time Began," *The Saturday Evening Post*

In this selection, the analogy is pretty straightforward. Hoyle wants to explain to the general reader a scientific concept: "that the different clusters of galaxies are constantly moving apart from each other." The basic metaphor he uses is that of a raisin cake baking in an oven. The cake is the universe, constantly expanding. Each raisin represents a cluster of galaxies. The raisin is one of the clusters of galaxies, and the observer is inside.

Not every analogy is a scientific analogy or an explanation of a complex subject. The following magazine ad uses an analogy as a way of selling a product.

Judgment From the Bench

Those who sit in judgment of a piano come from many branches of musical achievement. But they all look for the same signs of truth to emerge.

Responsiveness, for instance, is always called upon—especially when a new concerto is being tried.

Clarity must come forth—as in the case of enunciating vs. blurring the inner voices of Bach's fugues. Reliability, above all, will figure hard in the outcome of every rock concert.

To all these points, Yamaha pianos plead guilty as charged.

Judge one at your nearest Yamaha dealer. But whatever you do—

don't sentence yourself to life without a piano. In fact, we'd rather you buy another piano than no piano at all.

—ad for *Yamaha* piano

Exercises

1. Analyze the Yamaha ad in class. Set up a kind of outline or equation showing the points of the comparison. Does the analogy break down at any point? Is the ad effective? This ad was taken from *The New Yorker*, October 7, 1972. Discuss the ad in relation to its intended audience.

2. Write an essay, using one of the following analogies:

   a. Thinking is like exploring.
   b. Courting is like playing a game.
   c. Life is a river (stream, tributary, eternal sea).
   d. Life is a journey (hourglass, book, plant).
   e. My moods are like the seasons.
   f. _____ is like falling leaves (a dying fire, a shooting star).

3. Select one of the following as the basis of an analogy and then write an essay using the analogy to illustrate an idea:

   a. a merry-go-round   d. a clock
   b. a bridge   e. a puzzle
   c. a broken mirror   f. a wasp's nest

4. Use one of the following proverbs as the basis of an analogy paper:

   a. Time is like an arrow.
   b. Words are like bees: they have honey and a sting.
   c. Marriage is a lottery.
   d. Lost credit is like a broken mirror.
   e. Courage is fire; bullying is smoke.

5. Write a scientific analogy to explain an idea.

6. Write a persuasive essay in the manner of the Yamaha ad, using an extended analogy.

Patterns of Thought:

Narration, Process, Cause and Effect

Chapter 7

Patterns of Thought:
Narration, Process, Cause and Effect

Narration

Seldom a day goes by without friends or acquaintances coming up to you and telling you a joke, an interesting story, an incident that happened to them, or the plot of some movie or television show they have just seen. What happens to people in their work and in their leisure time constitutes the very pulse of life. Much of your conversation as well as much of your writing consists of narration.

Narration, as a pattern of thought, consists of *the act of following a sequence of actions or events in time*. It is *a recounting of the facts or particulars of some incident or experience*.

Purpose, Audience, Kind of Discourse

Narration can be used to achieve any aim: to inform or instruct, to convince or persuade, to entertain or please, or to express strong feelings and emotions. Narration as a process in and of itself does none of these, except perhaps in an indirect manner. It all depends on the uses to which you put your narration. Tell a story in one context, and it will be entertaining. Tell the same story in another context, and it may be instructive or persuasive.

Narration can be found in numerous kinds of writing: the narration of personal experiences, biographies, autobiographies, journals, diaries, memoirs, reminiscences, logs, records, genealogies, newspaper stories, magazine ads, short stories, novels, ballads, folk songs, movie scripts, travel accounts, chronicles, histories, anecdotes, obituaries, and sermons.

Many of these forms have their own distinctive pupuses, although the same narrative techniques and the same forms can be put to many different uses. Literary narratives such as the novel or short story usually have an aesthetic aim. Narration in sermons or magazine ads has a persuasive aim. Biography usually has an expository aim, which is to set forth a part or the whole of a person's life to explain his or her character, influence on others, or accomplishments. The aim of autobiography is similar to that of biography. Some obvious differences, of course, are that biography is an account of a person's life written by someone else, whereas autobiography is written by oneself. Biography is written in the third person; autobiography is written in the first person. Biography has a different aim from that of autobiography. Historical narratives, like biographies, have informative and instructive aims. In such writing, the author seeks to explain general trends, customs, worship, warfare, commerce, governments, and agriculture. Or the writer may seek to illuminate the characters of men and women, their wisdom or foolishness, intelligence or passions.

Whereas the autobiography puts its emphasis on introspection, journals and diaries, because they are so brief, are usually less introspective. They do, however, often give us personal impressions and fresh insights into experience. What they lack as connected narratives, they gain in vividness and immediacy. They are less structured than biographies and autobiographies and more anecdotal, containing brief observations, direct impressions of life, bits and pieces of information, personal reactions, and intimate thoughts.

Invention and Narration

As a method of invention, narration answers such questions as What happened? What is happening? What will happen? When did it happen? Where did it happen?

Because of its concern with time, narration is related to process and cause and effect:

Narration	*What* happened?
Process	*How* did it happen?
Cause and effect	*Why* did it happen?

In narration, however, the emphasis is on the *what* (although, for example, the elements in a plot are related by cause and effect). In process, the emphasis is on the *how*. And in cause and effect, the emphasis is on the *why*. To recount the particulars of an occurrence in time and space is to invent.

It is interesting to note that time is usually conceived of in terms of space. Events are conceived in relation to one another:

$$event_1 \qquad event_2 \qquad event_3 \qquad event_4$$

Yet your awareness of time comes not from space, but from some inner sense of the passage of events. Number is sometimes associated with time, and this helps to give you some notion of what is meant by a "time sense." An important synonym for *narrate* is *recount*. But an equally strong synonym, *relate,* brings you back to the spatial relation. Whether you think of time as sequence or relation, your feeling for time helps you to penetrate deeply into the nature of reality.

I have said that narration is a recounting of particulars in a temporal sequence. The word *recounting* suggests a self-contained series: "This happened, and then this happened, and then this happened." The word *particulars* assumes that narration will be concerned with the individual and the concrete. The basis of narration, the *what*, is concerned with the simplest kind of progression in time, contiguity. Particulars are related to each other because they occur in time. But in a plot or in a scientific process, they are also causally related.

In any event, to narrate is to invent. In the process of invention, you must come up with a succession of details, and shape and proportion each part. You must also keep in mind the end to be achieved. Each part must prepare for what is to follow.

Narration is a dynamic mode, for experience is dynamic and changing. The squirrel you looked at in the yard yesterday is no longer there. The tree you trimmed last summer has long since shed its leaves. You yourself are now probably taller, bigger, wider, or thinner than you were last year. When you go home for the Christmas holidays after a semester at school, you notice that everything seems strange or different. Your little brother or sister has grown an inch taller. Your father has another wrinkle. Your room seems different than you had imagined it, perhaps because your mother has moved the furniture around.

How do you express these changes in narration? By verbs, by prepositions, by adverbs. "It started snowing on Saturday night," wrote one student, "the wind whipping about the house, moaning low and then shrieking high and shrill like a banshee, whirling gusts of snow around, blotting out the black of the night sky." Another wrote: "The raindrops fell against my window, tapping rhythmically against the glass, then spattering in all directions from the middle, slithering lazily down the smooth surface, and finally dripping from the corners of the sill."

In narratives, you normally think of the verb as carrying the burden of the action. Action verbs are much more vivid than passive verbs: *glide, slide, ramble, stroll, amble, plod, tramp, strut, stride, toddle, spurt, sprint, scamper, dash, crawl, loiter, waddle, slouch, hobble, limp, jostle, clash, crash, smack, whack, jab.* Prepositions and adverbs help to convey action: *now, then, afterwards, later, since, therefore, after, from that time on, hereafter, today, tomorrow, eventually, while, early, slow, fast, till, by, in, at, from, to.* Narration, like the other modes, has a characteristic vocabulary that gives the reader a sense of the passage of time:

now	first	previously
then	second	every day
before	third	a long time ago
after	once	one of these days
earlier	former	last year
later	latter	up to this time
soon	prior to	on that occasion

Exercises

1. Using the questions suggested by the topics of invention, probe a narrative subject.

2. As a classroom exercise, relate to other members of the class some simple experience that actually happened to you.

3. Tell the plot of a movie or television show that has a strong narrative interest.

4. Reinvent! Take a plot from an old story and bring it up to date with a new setting and new characters.

The Structure of Narration

Because narration follows the laws of chronological succession, in writing your own narratives, you can follow a kind of abstract paradigm that might be depicted thus:

> *Narration Pattern*
> Introduction (time, place, persons, beginning of action)
> Event 1 . . .
> Event 2 . . .
> Event 3 . . .
> Events 4, 5, 6 (or incidents 4, 5, 6)
> Climax (point of intensity of action)
> Conclusion

Translated into more specific terms, the pattern might look like this, with, of course, considerable overlapping in the stages:

> Introduction
> Initial incident
> Rising action
> Suspense (foreshadowing, withholding information, surprise, and so forth)
> Turning point
> Falling action
> Climax
> Conclusion

The *introduction* sets the time and place of the action, introduces the characters, and shows their relationship to one another. The *initial incident* is the foundation of the plot. It brings the inciting force into action and moves the story forward. The *rising action* consists of a connected series of incidents or episodes which increase suspense. *Suspense* is that moment in the action that stirs excitement in the reader. It is an emotional appeal, making the reader fearful, or angry, or happy. *Foreshadowing* is a hint of something to come. *Withholding information* is one way of achieving suspense. Another way is to *surprise* the reader, to mislead deliberately. The *turning point* is that part of the narrative at which the conflicting forces of the story meet. The *falling action* is an intense series of events in which the writer begins "to tie the knot." The *climax* is the result of all of the elements of the story. It is the *resolution,* the point of highest intensity, and the place where the conflict rages fiercely. The *conclusion* is the logical ending of the story. It should be clear and satisfying and make sense. Not all of these elements of course will appear in a given narrative.

The *action* of a story may be *physical* or *mental.* Since a story involves people in action, there is usually some kind of *conflict* involved in the action. The main character is tested in some way and emerges victorious or defeated. Some familiar conflicts at the heart of most stories are the individual versus nature, the individual versus society, the individual versus God, the individual versus the supernatural, the individual versus other men or women, the individual versus himself or herself. When the conflict is internal or between an individual and another man or woman, the basis of the conflict is usually good or evil, virtues or vices: honesty/greed, hope/despair, courage/cowardice, generosity/selfishness, duty/lack of responsibility, forgiveness/revenge, chastity/lust, patience/impatience, compassion/lack of compassion, and so forth.

In many narratives, *character development* is more important than plot. The characters are the "actors in a story." Characterization can be developed by *personal action,* by *speech,* by *introspection,* by what *other people* tell us about a character, by the *author,* and by the *interests, tastes, possessions,* and *surroundings* of a character.

The *theme* of a story is its main point. It is an idea the writer wants to impress on his or her readers. It usually is expressed by means of character and incident.

In telling a story, a writer may use the *first person* or the *third person.* The first person is limited in that all of the events are seen through the eyes of one person. The third person allows the writer to portray the events from many angles.

Not all of the narratives that you write will have an extensive depiction of character or long, involved plots. Perhaps most will be merely a recounting of a series of events, as in personal narratives, reminiscences, and news stories. Autobiography and biography may or may not have plots. Journals, diaries, memoirs, and letters are usually too brief and too unconnected to allow for an extended treatment of plot.

The following narrative, taken from Willa Cather's *My Antonia*, is an excellent example of a literary narrative with an aesthetic aim. It follows very closely the pattern of a well-plotted narrative.

The Men Who Fed the Bride to the Wolves

When Pavel and Peter were young men, living at home in Russia, they were asked to be groomsmen for a friend who was to marry the belle of another village. It was in the dead of winter and the groom's party went over to the wedding in sledges. Peter and Pavel drove in the groom's sledge, and six sledges followed with all his relatives and friends.

After the ceremony at the church, the party went to a dinner given by the parents of the bride. The dinner lasted all afternoon; then it became a supper and continued far into the night. There was much dancing and drinking. At midnight the parents of the bride said goodbye to her and blessed her. The groom took her in his arms and carried her out to his sledge and tucked her under the blankets. He sprang in beside, and Pavel and Peter (our Pavel and Peter!) took the front seat. Pavel drove. The party set out with singing and the jingle of sleigh-bells, the groom's sledge going first. All the drivers were more or less the worse for merry-making, and the groom was absorbed in his bride.

The wolves were bad that winter, and everyone knew it, yet when they heard the first wolf-cry, the drivers were not much alarmed. They had too much good food and drink inside them. The first howls were taken up and echoed and with quickening repetitions. The wolves were coming together. There was no moon, but the starlight was clear on the snow. A black drove came up over the hill behind the wedding party. The wolves ran like streaks of shadow; they looked no bigger than dogs, but there were hundreds of them.

Something happened to the hindmost sledge; the driver lost

control—he was probably very drunk—the horses left the road, the sledge was caught in a clump of trees, and overturned. The occupants rolled out over the snow, and the fleetest of the wolves sprang upon them. The shrieks that followed made everybody sober. The drivers stood up and lashed their horses. The groom had the best team and his sledge was lightest—all the others carried from six to a dozen people.

Another driver lost control. The screams of the horses were more terrible to hear than the cries of the men and women. Nothing seemed to check the wolves. It was hard to tell what was happening in the rear; the people who were falling behind shrieked as piteously as those who were already lost. The little bride hid her face on the groom's shoulder and sobbed. Pavel sat still and watched his horses. The road was clear and white, the the groom's three blacks went like the wind. It was only necessary to be calm and to guide them carefully.

At length, as they breasted a long hill, Peter rose cautiously and looked back. "There are only three sledges left," he whispered.

"And the wolves?" Pavel asked.

"Enough! Enough for all of us."

Pavel reached the brow of the hill, but only two sledges followed him down the other side. In that moment on the hilltop they saw the whirling black group on the snow. Presently the groom screamed. He saw his father's sledge overturned, with his mother and sisters. He sprang up as if he meant to jump, but the girl shrieked and held him back. It was even then too late. The black ground-shadows were already crowding over the heap in the road, and one horse ran out across the fields, his harness hanging to him, wolves at his heels. But the groom's movement had given Pavel an idea.

They were within a few miles of their village now. The only sledge left out of the six was not very far behind them, and Pavel's middle horse was failing. Beside a frozen pond something happened to the other sledge; Peter saw it plainly. Three big wolves got abreast of the horses, and the horses went crazy. They tried to jump over each other, got tangled up in the harness, and overturned the sledge.

When the shrieking behind them died away, Pavel realized that he was alone upon the familiar road. "They still come?" he asked Peter.

"Yes."

"How many?"

"Twenty, thirty—enough."

Now his middle horse was being almost dragged by the other two. Pavel gave Peter the reins and stepped carefully into the back of the sledge. He called to the groom that they must lighten—and pointed to the bride. The young man cursed him and held her tighter. Pavel tried to drag her away. In the struggle, the groom rose. Pavel knocked him over the side of the sledge and threw the girl after him. He said he never remembered exactly how he did it, or what happened afterward. Peter, crouching in the front seat, saw nothing. The first thing either of them noticed was a new sound that broke into the clear air, louder than they had ever heard it before—the bell of the monastery of their own village, ringing for early prayers.

Pavel and Peter drove into the village alone, and they have been alone ever since. They were run out of their village. Pavel's own mother would not look at him. They went away to strange towns, but when people learned where they came from, they were always asked if they knew the two men who had fed the bride to the wolves. Wherever they went, the story followed them. . . .

The first two paragraphs set the scene in time and place (a wedding in a small village in Russia in the middle of winter); introduce the characters (two brothers, Peter and Pavel, the bride and groom, the wedding guests); and set forth the initial incident (the wedding party, after much dancing and drinking, setting out at midnight for the groom's village). Subsequent paragraphs then take up each incident in turn.

The narrative progression might be depicted as follows:

The wedding party sets out in sledges at midnight for the groom's village.

The wolves come together to attack the sledges.

The hindmost sledge is lost.

Another driver loses control.

The sledge of the groom's father overturns.

The horses panic, and the second-to-last sledge overturns.

Pavel knocks the groom over the side to lighten the sledge, then throws the bride after him.

Finally, Pavel and Peter drive into the village alone, with the "bell of the monastery of their own village, ringing for early prayers."

Of the sixteen paragraphs in this selection, the shortest are those with dialogue. Most of these consist of a single phrase or sentence. The longest paragraph is paragraph 15, the second-to-last paragraph, which contains the largest number of words (135) and the largest number of sentences (10). The length seems natural when you consider that this is the most action-packed and suspenseful part of the narrative, that climactic moment when Pavel throws the bride and groom to the wolves.

Most of the sentences are short, or give the appearance of being short due to extensive use of coordination. Most of the short sentences come in the chase scenes, to convey rapid action and increase the excitement and tension. The longest sentences come at the beginning of the story (to set the scene in time and place), at the beginning of the chase scene, at the end of the chase scene (with Pavel and Peter riding into the village), and at the end of the narrative.

The sense of passing of time and the action is conveyed by prepositional phrases:

after the ceremony
at midnight
over the hill
behind the wedding party
over the snow
at length
down the other side
in that moment
across the fields
at his heels
behind them
beside the frozen pond

abreast of the horses
over each other
into the village

adverbs and adverbial nouns:

over	too late
all afternoon	out
then	far
far	now
in	away
beside	alone
presently	ever since

and verbs:

sprang	breasted
drove	reached
set out	followed
were coming together	screamed
came up	overturned
ran	shrieked
left	ran
overturned	was failing
rolled out	got tangled up
sprang	overturned
stood up	must lighten
lashed	knocked
lost control	threw
were falling behind	drove
shrieked	run out
sobbed	went away
went	

In just sixteen paragraphs, Willa Cather is able to convey a wide range of human emotions: merriment, fear, tension, unspeakable horror, anger, and sadness. All the structural elements work together to produce a masterful narrative.

The following student paper has most of the characteristics of
a good narrative.

To Surf

I had been out all day. I had been too exhilarated by the huge, rolling
waves, the taste of saltwater, the sting of coral cuts to notice hunger
or fatigue.

For the first time in my life, I had body-surfed. I was excited
with my new knowledge. Wanting to show the natives of the islands
I could take any wave they could, I swam farther and farther out,
looking for a bigger wave, a higher crest.

I would swim out to where the waves rose the highest, wait
for just the right one to come swelling across the sea, time my start
to the exact moment, and ride the wave until it was nothing but a
ripple. Then I would repeat the process.

Often on my way back out I would come head on with a surfer.
But I had been taught just when to go under the board and how
long to stay under. The boards didn't scare me unless I became aware
that the rider was scared. These were the ones who tried to go around
you or ditch the board. You couldn't be sure when you were under
a "green rider" that he wouldn't bounce the board right over your
skull. But this too was a part of the game. This was one of the reasons
I had traveled so far from home.

I didn't even mind the coral cuts. They hurt like everything
when you suddenly find yourself thrown right into a bed of the
sharp, cutting animals. If you had time to think, you could tell by
the flow of water where these piles of deadly skeletons lay. But if
an unexpected wave caught you and carried you into it, you knew
you had to get out of the coral and get out of it fast. Because if
another sudden wave were to come beating down on you, you would
be crushed further into the sea's torture chamber. Even this I hadn't
minded earlier.

But now I was beginning to tire. I felt a hollow, heavy sensation
in my stomach. I had had nothing to eat since breakfast and it was
late in the afternoon. Most of the swimmers were already going home.
Boats were coming in. The waves were growing smaller and smaller
until now there were hardly any. My girlfriend Cindy had been lying
on the beach for well over an hour. Although I could not see her,

I imagined her resting, asleep in the last rays of the day's sun. I envied her as my muscles began to ache. My eyes burned from the salt. My skin was dry and would have been red from the sun except for the white, sticky layer of salt covering it. My swimsuit was full of sand and my legs and feet hurt from the tiny cuts. I started swimming back to shore. I had not realized I was so far out. In my attempt to catch the last dying waves I had swum far out past the breakwater. The water, fortunately, was not over my head and I thanked God for small favors. As my arms tired of swimming I decided to float in. It was then, with absolute terror, that I discovered that the tide was going out and going fast. That explained why the waves had diminished. The tide was reversing! The native swimmers had known this and had long since swum in. There were only a few stragglers left, inexperienced, dumb tourists like myself who had gone out looking for that last wave, that last thrill. In panic I started swimming madly. This lasted only a few minutes though. Reality told me to save my strength. If I could only get within calling distance of Cindy, I could yell to her. I stood up and walked now. It seemed with each step I took the water pulled me back three. The water was just below my shoulders now. I tried to think of anything but what was happening to me. This failed. All I could think of was calling out to Cindy. I must have been making progress. The water was at my waist.

I could now make out the people on the beach. I scanned each girl, looking for Cindy's familiar suit. My eye caught the flash of bright purple suit on dark-tanned skin. That was no mistake. That was Cindy. I was overjoyed. Then I realized she was with three guys. Probably servicemen on R and R. I was mad. REALLY MAD. Here I was nearly drowned, at the very brink of death, and she was lining up a date. With my anger I gained new strength. I walked the rest of the way in. The tide, although low, was getting stronger now, but in my fury, so was I. At last I had made it. I walked up onto the beach and picked up my beach mat. As I headed for the hotel Cindy called out to me. "How was your swim?" she asked. "Great," I bellowed back. With that, my remaining strength drained. My knees shook as I walked the half-block back to the hotel. In the elevator I thought I would collapse. I finally reached the fourteenth floor and practically crawled to the door. The door was locked! Cindy had the key. I sank to the floor. Covered with salt and sand, my skin burned, my hair tangled, I didn't want to go to the main lobby to get the other key. Besides I wasn't sure I could take another elevator ride. So I sat in front of my door.

—Vada

This story, with its irony, is very suggestive of the Stephen Crane short story "The Open Boat" in which four shipwrecked men in an open boat are distraught when they realize that some bathers they see on the beach are not even remotely aware of their plight. In the student's surfing story, the additional irony of being locked out of her room adds just the right final touch to the conclusion.

Not all narratives need to be this well plotted. Some instead may have a thematic unity, such as this student narrative based on a reminiscence:

Try to Remember . . .

Try to remember the kind of September
When life was slow
And oh so mellow
Try to remember the kind of September
When grass was green and grain was yellow
Try to remember the kind of September
When you were a tender and callow fellow
Try to remember, and if you remember,
Then follow . . .

That's such a lovely, lovely song. I have the entire album from the *Fantasticks*, but I always hover over the record player, catching the needle before it goes to the next song, and play "Try to Remember" over and over. Someday, that band will be worn out, and all the others will be like new.

I probably never would have even thought of it today, except that I received a call from grandfather's friend, who lives in Lincoln. My grandparents live in Iowa, and these people had gone to visit them, and get some apples from the orchard. My grandfather had asked them to drop off some apples for me, and so they did. A brown grocery bag full of red delicious, jonathans, and even a banana apple, and one yellow delicious. I looked at those apples and remembered. . . .

When I was a child, "tender and callow," we would go to my grandfather's and pick those apples ourselves. Mom would dress my sister and me, and my brother, who was too young to reach most of the branches then, in sturdy shoes, and jackets, and long jeans, to protect our little legs from the poison ivy that usually was already dead by then, anyway. But it was a ritual. We'd load my grandparents up in the car, and head for the orchards.

My grandfather had planted those trees by himself, when he was young. And my grandmother would herd the cows through the fields nearby. Now, my grandfather was nearly ninety, and he had been crippled for years. He could barely get into the car, let alone walk through his own orchard. And my grandmother was not too much better. She would get out of the car, and take quick little steps in her old-ladies' shoes, the weeds catching on her brown cotton stockings. Her back was kind of hunched now, and she had to breathe hard if she reached up too far over her head. But we, who were young, would run through those orchards, through the prickly thistles, through the tall grass, now yellow and dried, through the tangled vines of orange bittersweet, over the road with countless ruts left from the last rainstorm when the tractor came through in the mud. We would run from tree to tree, taking only the biggest and best apples, and comparing each other's baskets full to one another. Occasionally, we would stop, polish a particularly choice red apple, and bite into it, the juice dribbling down our chins, mixing with the brown dust already on it. Then we would toss the cores into the woods, as far as we could throw them, and listen for them to drop in a crackling pile of fallen leaves. It was usually very cold when we went to the orchards, or at least it always seemed so, and most often we would be picking apples while the sun set in a lovely pink, yellow, and blue autumn sky. The air was fresh and clean. And we ran and ran until our freedom was ended not by our choice, but by fatigue, and the falling darkness.

I slowly took each apple out of the brown grocery sack they had sent, and very nearly polished them with my tears along with a pink terry-cloth towel. I put them in an old metal pot that I had in the room, and they are sitting there gleaming at me now. They're picked now, but they grew in freedom all summer, on trees, in the calm country. Funny they should find their way into a stuffy, cramped college dorm room. Sometimes, I wonder that about me too.

—Laura

Here the emphasis is not on a rigid plot structure, but on the order of memory.

Sometimes, in writing a story, you may wish to make your theme explicit. The following student narrative follows an inductive pattern (from particular to general), with the narrative as a kind of extended example for the concluding generalization in the last paragraph.

The Promise That Grew

Some years ago, I was caught in a sudden, blinding snowstorm near Indiana, Pennsylvania. My car stalled at the edge of town. I floundered into town and into the nearest store. The proprietor phoned for help to get my car out of the snowdrift.

In a short time, a tall blond man showed up with a team of horses and pulled me out of the drift into town. I asked him how much I owed him for his trouble. He refused any pay, saying, "I will charge thee nothing but the promise that thee will help the next man thee finds in trouble." I thanked him and made the promise.

After he left, the storekeeper explained that my Good Samaritan was a Mennonite who considered it wrong to charge anyone for a service made necessary by an act of God.

Four years later, a friend and I were driving over flooded land south of St. Louis, Missouri. We crossed through water a foot deep without any trouble, but through my rearview mirror, I could see that the small car behind us stalled. I waded back while my companion reversed the car so I could hook up onto his bumper with tire chains.

We pulled the man out and waited until he got his engine started. Then he offered to pay me. I told him of my experience in Indiana, Pennsylvania, then repeated the Mennonite's words: "I will charge thee nothing but the promise that thee will help the next man thee finds in trouble." He promised, and we parted.

About one year later, my family and I were camping about one hundred miles from Aurora, Missouri, and we pitched our tents near the James River. We'd been told that it never flooded at that time of year, but the river evidently misread the calendar, for I awakened in the middle of the night with a very cold back from water deep enough to cover the canvas cot. We loaded our soggy equipment into our car, but we were unable to drive it to higher ground. I waded back to an inn some distance from our camping spot and asked the innkeeper if he could get help to pull us out.

In a short time, a farmer showed up with a tractor and a long rope and pulled us to safe ground. When I offered to pay him, he told me of a man who had helped him get his tractor out of the mud and then said: "I will charge thee nothing but the promise that thee will help the next man that thee finds in trouble." The quotation was identical to that of the man in Pennsylvania, although I know of no Mennonites or Quakers in that section of Missouri.

How far one man's act of kindness had traveled!

—Fred

In writing your own narratives, it is not necessary to develop long, involved plots. Unless you intend to become a novelist, most of your narratives will be of the kind found in the narration of personal experiences, anecdotes, autobiography, letters to friends, journals, diaries, and newspaper stories. Your stories may indeed have a built-in plot, but your main purpose will be to tell a compelling and interesting narrative based on personal experiences. Then the kind of concreteness that you can get only from firsthand experiences may carry into your more abstract writing.

Exercises

1. Analyze in class the student narratives titled "To Surf" and "The Promise That Grew," using the outline of traditional narrative techniques discussed earlier (introduction, setting, characters, initial incident, rising action, and so on).

2. Write a brief *autobiographical sketch* of your childhood or adolescence.

3. Write a *brief narrative* on one of the following general subjects:

   a. a job experience   f. a dream
   b. a date   g. a racial incident
   c. falling in love   h. a humorous experience
   d. a college experience   i. a death or illness
   e. an accident   j. a natural disaster

4. Write a *newspaper account* of a fire or some other incident.

5. Write a *character sketch* in the form of an obituary notice.

6. Someone interested in employing a friend of yours has asked you to give a frank summary of his character. Imagine the exact situation and write the letter.

7. Write a *biographical sketch* of someone you know well.

8. Recount some episode in the *history* of your county, parish, city, or state. Emphasize the people involved.

9. In the manner of the student narrative "To Surf," give a first-person account of one of the following: a narrow escape, a brave act, an embarrassing experience, a journey, a practical joke.

10. Write a short paper, based on a *reminiscence,* in the manner of the student paper "Try to Remember."

11. Expand one of the following into a full-length narrative:

    a. For one day, you will express all of your feelings about people truthfully, no matter whom you may hurt.

    b. You go to a party, only to discover that six people have on the same outfit as you do.

    c. You have been drinking, and you hit an old man or woman at a crossing while you are driving.

    d. You arrive at the air terminal just as your plane is departing.

    e. You are eating in a fancy restaurant, and when it is time to pay the bill, you discover that you have left your wallet at home.

12. The TV show *Roots* has reawakened our interest in genealogy, history, biography, and autobiography. Trace your genealogy or that of someone in your family. Write down all you know about your family, beginning with yourself, your parents, your grandparents, your great-grandparents. Include dates of births, marriages, and deaths, places of residences, and so forth. Interview your uncles, aunts, or grandparents. Check family records: old photo albums, letters, newspaper clippings, notes, diaries, journals, and other such sources of information.

Process

A **process** is *a series of actions, changes, functions, steps, or operations that bring about a particular end or result.* Like narration, process suggests ongoing movement and continuous action. The emphasis in a process theme, however, is on the *how*, rather than the *what*. These are relative rather than absolute differences, of course, since like narration, a process can be concerned with the *what*, and like cause and effect, it can be concerned with the *why*.

When you think of a process, you generally tend to think of slow, gradual changes and of a series of interlocking steps whereby an end is achieved. Some synonyms for the verb form of the word *process* are *change, alter, vary, modify, transform, convert,* and *transmute.* The word *change* is perhaps the most important synonym, suggesting as it does a transition from one state to another. A change alters the quality of a thing and modifies its form or appearance. Like the other topics and patterns with which you will be concerned, this one carries a train of rich images and expressions: *mutation, transformation, transfiguration, metamorphosis, transubstantiation, transmigration,* and *a kaleidoscope of colors.*

Purpose, Audience, Kind of Discourse

Process as a mode of developing a subject can be found in any kind of discourse that emphasizes a system of operations or steps in the production of something or a series of actions, changes, or phases that bring about an end or result. Although the primary aim of process exposition is to inform or instruct, it can also be used to persuade, as in certain magazine advertisements which outline the steps in the making of a product to convince the reader of the product's excellence.

Since process is by definition a sequence of actions, changes, or operations that brings about some desired end or result, then as a writer you can best appeal to your audience by logically presenting the connected series of actions that lead to the desired end.

Process can be most profitably employed in the following kinds of writing: scientific essays, instruction manuals, booklets, research reports, cookbooks, directions for doing something, natural history, biology, chemistry, explanations of a mechanism, explanations of a social process or a historical process, explanations of a natural process, explanations of a creative process, advertising, and argumentation.

Invention and Process

As a topic of invention, process answers basic questions such as How did it happen? How does it work? How do you make it or do it? What are the stages, phases, steps, or operations? To recount a series of changes, a sequence of steps, a particular method of doing something, an explanation of a scientific process, the steps in an argument, a course of action, a series of operations, a procedure, a function, or the alteration in the position, size, quantity, and quality of something is to invent.

Your awareness of process comes from a sense of some kind of change. You notice that the hands on your watch have changed position. You observe that the plants in your garden are changing in size and quantity. You change the quality of the water in your shower from hot to cold. You watch people, animals, and plants around you come into existence, mature, grow old, and die. You observe that the sky grows dark, it begins to rain, leaves fall from the trees, autumn comes, then winter, then spring, then summer. You notice the yellows in a sunset shade into the oranges, the oranges into the reds, and the reds into blues, purples, and greens. Life ebbs and flows, moves, pulsates, palpitates, throbs all around you.

Process analysis is a special form of exposition in which you present a step-by-step description of how some process takes place:

a natural process, a scientific process, a mechanical process, a historical process, a social process, a creative process. Process exposition is concerned with *how* topics: how flowers changed the world, how the universe was formed, how the American Revolution began, how LSD was discovered, how liquor is made, how to operate a car, how the heart works, how to eat crabs, how to bake a cake.

Because process is a kind of dynamic exposition, its characteristic vocabulary tends to emphasize change:

phase	state	inconstancy
occurrence	condition	inversion
step	conversion	permutation
change	displacement	modulation
alteration	transformation	qualification
mutation	fluctuation	metamorphosis

Some process terms are very similar to those of narration: *now, then, next, afterwards, later, thereafter, from, to.* Others are similar to those of enumeration: *first, second, third, one, another, a third.* The verb tenses in a process may be present (if you are giving directions) or past (if you are explaining something that has already taken place). The voice may be active or passive (generally used in scientific descriptions). The person may be first (in an informal account), second (in giving directions), or third (in an objective description of a process).

Exercises

1. Using the questions suggested by the topics of invention, probe a process subject.

2. In class, for purposes of invention, analyze a natural process, a scientific process, a mechanical process, a historical process, a political process, a social process, or a creative process.

3. Explain in class how one of the following works:

    a. an eggbeater
    b. a bicycle
    c. a razor
    d. a rifle
    e. an engine

4. Play the game of "Charades" in class. Choose sides and take turns acting out a process.

5. Explain to someone in class how to

    a. swim   f. sell something
    b. box   g. put down someone
    c. skate   h. make coffee
    d. lie   i. play a musical instrument
    e. tell jokes   j. clean a rug

The Structure of Process

The rhetorical structure of a process may be conveyed by a very simple paradigm:

Process Pattern
Introduction (thesis)
Step 1 (phase 1) . . .
Step 2 (phase 2) . . .
Step 3 (phase 3) . . .
Step 4 (phase 4) . . .
Step 5, 6, 7 (phase 5, 6, 7) . . .
Conclusion (summary and so forth)

In writing process themes, you want to divide your subject into stages, phases, or operations. If the process you want to explain involves giving directions or making something, your introduction will usually contain a description of the material and the tools or implements or materials to be used. If it does not involve directions, as in the explanation of a natural process, your introduction may contain an explanation of the principles involved, but the primary emphasis will be on the chronological order, on the *what, how,* and *when* of the process.

The following student description of the process of making candleholders is an excellent example of the directions-for-doing-something theme. It follows the process paradigm fairly closely, but without using the enumeration pattern throughout.

The Process in Making Candleholders

If you are stuck for a gift but short of time and money, beautiful, stained-glass candleholders, which sell in candle shops for five dollars each, are relatively easy and inexpensive to make. These candleholders take about ten hours to complete, but the process is fun and easy.

Before beginning, you must have the needed materials. These consist of a wide-mouthed drinking glass about five inches high, an old windshield, glass stain, tile grout, glue, and black acrylic paint. With these materials you can make up to fifteen candleholders (if you have that many glasses).

The first step is breaking and staining the windshield. To break the windshield, wrap it in an old blanket and hit it several times with a hammer. The glass will shatter, but not separate. After this is done, break off small pieces of various shapes and sizes, and stain them any color. The stain will dry almost immediately.

While the pieces are drying, cover the drinking glass with a thin coat of glue. This will give the shattered, stained pieces of glass something to hold on to.

When the pieces have dried, attach them to the drinking glass. This is done by gluing each piece separately to the drinking glass, as close to each other as possible. It is important to remember that the stained side of the pieces must be glued toward the inside of the glass. If this is not done, the stain will wash or peel off the candleholder.

Once the drinking glass is completely covered with the brightly colored pieces, it is time to grout the candleholder. To do this, fill the spaces between the stained glass with grout, forming a smooth, rounded edge around the mouth of the glass, and then cover the bottom of the glass with a smooth layer of grout. Allow the grout to dry the amount of time specified by the instructions on the package of grout.

With a damp rag, remove any grout which covers the stained glass after the grout has dried. After removing the excess grout, smooth out the grout with a piece of sandpaper.

Now it is time to paint. Carefully paint the grout with black acrylic paint. Do not be concerned if the paint covers parts of the glass since acrylic is a water-base paint and washes off easily. After the paint dries, use a damp cloth to remove any paint on the glass.

If you follow these directions carefully, you can finish a candleholder in a matter of a few hours. Candleholders cost approximately one dollar apiece, and they are very beautiful to own or to give as gifts.

—Ina

Because process themes are relatively easy to write, you may be turned off by a straightforward account. Instead, you might want to try your hand at a humorous approach to writing a process theme, in the manner of the following student essay:

Lobe-Botomy

The first thing you need for a do-it-yourself-pierce-your-ears kit is a sadistic friend. Then you need lots of ice, a sharp sewing needle, and a good bottle of booze.

Obtaining the sadistic friend was no problem for me. In fact, Linda had been "needling" me all semester to let her do the job. She had had her lobes gored since high school "and it looked so easy anybody could do it," she said, eager eyes fastened on my little lobes. My ears are tiny anyway and my earlobes are attached like a button-down shirt. This gave Linda momentary doubts because she remembered something about a nerve in the upper lobe that, if punctured, would paralyze that side of the body. This gave me more than momentary doubts, but she assured me that the story was just a rumor. Besides, the surgical tray and anesthesia were all ready.

It was the night before my last final exam, first semester, freshman year. The next morning I was to take my seventh test. Since I had been gorging my head with knowledge for two solid weeks, I was so out of it I didn't even require the friendly Southern Comfort winking at me from the table.

The lobe-botomy operation took place at Linda's apartment, which was abundantly stocked with ice cubes. There I sat limply in a cushiony old chair watching detachedly the frantic activity around me. First, Linda banged the ice tray against the sink, trying to chip a few hunks from the frozen mass in which she had forgotten to place the cube divider. Then, with a caldron of boiling water popping on the stove (you'd think I was having a baby), she scrounged through a drawer full of thread, paper clips, bottle openers, wire, plastic bags, thumbtacks, ashtrays, and Elmer's glue for a big-enough knitting needle.

While Linda sterilized the needle, only slightly smaller than a whaling harpoon, I held a two-pound ice chunk in a washcloth to my right earlobe. After about fifteen minutes it was deadened enough so that I couldn't feel a pinch. Meanwhile much of the ice had trickled down my sleeve. After fifteen more minutes both patient and doctor were ready. I closed my eyes as Linda walked over to me, smiling, her hands behind her back. A few seconds later she plucked my ear away from my head and I felt the needle's searing jab. In the first place she had forgotten to let it cool, and secondly it hurt like hell. I yelped and at the same instant heard cartilage crushing inside my head. "My God! She missed," was my first thought, confirmed by blood trickling down my neck. But no, Linda had been only slightly off target due to my sudden jerk. But my scream and the blood had scared her, along with the difficulty she had getting the needle through my lobe. "I should have had a thimble," she berated herself. "Why not a hammer," I said tearfully.

That made her mad. "Ungrateful," she muttered. "You can just go around with a hole in one of your ears like a goddam pirate," she sniffed. I apologized and soothed and convinced Linda to take up the knife again because, no matter how much it hurt, I wasn't going to go around unbalanced. So this time I held the ice to my ear a whole hour and didn't feel the penetration nearly as much as before. But the blood—and especially the sound of popping cartilage— I'll never forget.

That was three and a half years ago. Since then my sadistic friend has kept her ears clean and abandoned the ear-bobbing business. And I've developed an allergy to gold and can't wear my much-suffered-for earrings.

—Carol

The pattern in this essay is less formal than that of the preceding student essay, but the puns, the concrete description, and the wit make this a delightful model to emulate.

Descriptions of processes in the natural sciences are very easy to come by. Although this example is taken from a book, it is not unlike the more popular kinds of scientific writing you might find in magazines. Its aim is to explain and inform:

How Snakes Shed Their Skins

When a snake has grown a new epidermis and is about to shed its skin, it secretes a thin layer of fluid between the old and new skin (which are no longer touching), giving the snake a clouded milky appearance. This can be seen especially at the eyes, for the milky fluid covers the pupils and makes the snake almost, if not completely, blind. This condition may last for as much as a week; during this period, snakes normally remain in hiding.

A day or two after the cloudiness has cleared, the snake will shed its skin. This is accomplished by opening and stretching the mouth and rubbing it on surrounding objects until the old skin at the edges of the lips begins to split. Rubbing continually, the snake starts to wriggle out of its skin. This is usually sloughed off in one piece from head to tail, turned inside out in the process by the emerging snake. Sometimes the skin will break up, however, and come off in pieces, as during the shedding of lizards.

The sloughed-off skin is a perfect cast of the snake. The large belly scales, the pattern of scales on the back, the eye spectacle and even casts of facial pits can all be seen. It is completely devoid of color as the pigment cells remain in the dermis, which is never shed. The shed skin is transparent with a white tinge. After it has been detached from the snake for a while, it usually becomes brittle. The sloughed-off skin is not especially attractive, but the newly emerged snake is seen at its best. Most species show their best bright colors in the days immediately following molting; as the upper skin gets older, the colors do not show through as well.

—From *Snakes of the World*

If you are asked to write a description of a scientific process, you may want to use the third person rather than the second, and make the tone more impersonal and objective.

Industrial Alcohol

Industrial alcohol is produced by a process known as fermentation. Fermentation is the process of producing alcohol and carbon dioxide from simple sugars such as glucose (a colorless, yellowish syrupy mixture) and fructose (a very sweet sugar that occurs in fruit and honey). The chemical change that occurs is brought about by the catalytic action of ferments (or enzymes).

The chief ingredient for the production of industrial alcohol is molasses, either cane-sugar molasses or beet-sugar molasses.

In the process of making industrial alcohol, the molasses is first diluted with water. It is then made slightly acid to promote the growth of yeast and to retard the growth of bacteria. Afterwards it is heated to 70 degrees Fahrenheit and to it is added a yeast culture. The yeast secretes an enzyme known as invertase which converts the sucrose in the molasses to glucose and fructose. The concentration of the alcohol can then be increased by distillation.

In addition to using cane-sugar or beet-sugar to produce alcohol, manufacturers use corn, potatoes, various kinds of grain, and other substances containing starch. When starch-containing substances are used, the starch is converted to sugar in the preliminary stages.

Although descriptions of scientific, mechanical, or natural processes tend to be impersonal and objective, you can make them less impersonal, if you wish, by basing them on personal experiences. The following student theme describes the process of canning pineapple with great accuracy, without sacrificing the personal element.

How to Can Pineapple

Two summers ago, our family flew to Hawaii. When we arrived at the hotel, the Royal Hawaiian proved how it had acquired its "royal" reputation. At five o'clock the evening of our arrival, a handsome, dark-skinned Hawaiian boy knocked on our door and presented us with a large, boat-shaped pineapple shell. It was filled with bright, juicy chunks of pineapple. This welcome became a daily ritual which we all looked forward to. The Dole Pineapple Cannery was on our list of places to visit. It proved educational as well as lots of fun!

The pineapple is a sweet, yellow fruit, especially thirst-quenching when eaten in the warm, humid climate of the Hawaiian Islands. It is grown on large plantations. The luscious fruit is produced in slices, chunks, tidbits, spears, and crushed form. How is this done? The process may be described as follows:

After the ripe pineapples arrive at the cannery in specially designed bins or trucks, and are unloaded mechanically for their long, rapid trip through the cannery, they are washed and sorted according to size. Then they enter the "ginaca" machine which removes the shell, cuts off both ends of the fruit, punches out the core, and leaves each fruit a golden cylinder. It even scrapes the shell, leaving the husk nearly dry, ready to be made into bran.

Next, the trimming tables receive the pineapple cylinders at the rate of fifty to one hundred a minute. Here women in white caps, aprons, and rubber gloves pick up each cylinder and trim away any eyes, bits of shells, or overripe portions left on the fruit.

The trimmer then puts the clean cylinder on a moving, stainless-steel conveyor which takes it through a cold-water spray to the slicer where guarded knives cut it into uniform slices. Then other white-capped workers select perfectly matched slices and place them in cans according to grades.

After the cans are filled with slices, chunks, or whatever size fruit is being processed, they move on to syrupers and through vacuum seamers where covers are attached and sealed. Still moving fast and steadily, they come to cookers where they are sterilized and heated at 200 degrees Fahrenheit, for five to fifteen minutes, depending upon the size of the can and the kind of product.

The fruit, of course, is now very hot, so without pausing a second the cans move through water coolers. The cans of crushed fruit go through a cold-water spray device aptly called a "hula cooler" which shakes as it sprays, getting the contents cool in the center as well as on the outside.

The cans are then placed in cases, and the cases are stored in warehouses, where they leave the state as a finished product under many competitive brand names.

I'll always remember my first taste of fresh Hawaiian pineapple. I can still see the rows and rows of pineapples growing in the fields. I can hear the roar of the giant machines in the plant and the workers efficiently handling the fruit. I know now why Hawaii supplies 80% of the world's pineapple.

—Jackie

Like narration and the other temporal modes, process exposition is not simply the recounting of a sequence of actions or events. To be effective, a process theme must involve the idea of purpose. Here is a sequence of events, but what holds them together? A random sequence of events will make neither an interesting narrative nor a successful process theme. But if you keep in mind the question "What is it for?" you will be well on your way to writing a successful process theme.

Exercises

1. Analyze in class the scientific essay "How Snakes Shed Their Skins." Outline the steps in the process. Discuss the language. Is it formal or informal? Does it use scientific diction or popular diction? Pick out the figures of speech. How are they used to support the writer's purpose?

2. Discuss in class a process that you have observed in a factory or in some other place.

3. Write an analysis of a natural process such as the cycle of the seasons; the beat of a heart; the composition of an essay, a painting, or a piece of music, a thought process; a learning process.

4. Write a scientific essay in the manner of "How Snakes Shed Their Skins."

5. Write on one of the following topics:

    a. How _____ was formed.
    b. How to play a certain game.
    c. How to cook a certain dish.
    d. How to make a particular drink.
    e. How to perform a particular operation.
    f. How _____ was discovered.
    g. How to control a crowd at a rock concert.
    h. How _____ works.

6. Write a humorous process theme in the manner of "Lobe-Botomy."

7. Write on one of the following:

a. How to produce _____.   e. How to sell _____.
b. How to extract _____.   f. How to eat _____.
c. How to make _____.   g. How to build _____.
d. How to prepare _____.   h. How to plan _____.

Cause and Effect

Why does the wind blow? What causes it to rain? Why does the sun shine? Where does the rainbow come from? Why is the sky blue? Where do babies come from? How did the elephant get his trunk?

Almost all these questions a child would be likely to ask, but the questions should not be dismissed lightly for this reason. Scientists such as Sir James Jeans have written articles explaining why the sky is blue. Doctors have prepared manuals for parents and children explaining where babies come from. And Rudyard Kipling wrote a beautiful tale of causation in which he gave a fanciful explanation of how the elephant got his trunk. All these questions and their answers are related to the rhetorical process that we call cause and effect.

A **cause** is *a force or influence that produces an effect. It is an agency or operation responsible for bringing about an action, event, condition, or result.* The word calls to mind other words and expressions such as *origin, source, first principle, author, producer, agent, instrument, ground of being, prime mover, foundation, support, influence, font, genesis, rationale, intention,* and *the straw that broke the camel's back.*

An **effect** is *anything that has been caused. It is the result of a force or an action.* Another meaning of the word **effect** is *something worked out, accomplished, or produced.* The word *effect* calls to mind such related words and expressions as *consequence, result, derivation, end, outcome, denouement, development, production, performance, offshoot, creation, handiwork, outgrowth, harvest, emanation,* and *issue.*

Cause and effect are correlative terms. The one always implies the other. If a tire on your car blows out and your car hits a lightpole, there is a correlation between the blowout and the accident. We say that one *causes* the other.

Cause-and-effect relationships are embedded in our language:

> February brings the rain
> Thaws the frozen lake again.
>
> March winds and April showers
> Bring forth May flowers.
>
> If in October you do marry,
> Love will come, but riches tarry.
>
> When December snows fall fast,
> Marry, and true love will last.

But in dealing with cause-and-effect relationships, you want to go beyond language, since language encodes relationships that are already operating in the universe.

What is it that you do when you discern cause-and-effect relationships? You notice that a particular cause or combination of causes is followed by a particular effect, or that a combination of effects follows from a particular cause or causes. A man lights a match near a leaking gas pipe. The man is subsequently killed by a gas explosion. The coroner concludes that the man's carelessness is the cause of his death. Actually, the juxtaposition of the flame and the gas caused the accident.

Another man is driving down the highway in the middle of the winter. It has been snowing, and the road is now covered with ice. The car hits a slick spot in the road, and the man swerves the car in such a way that the car skids and runs off the road, causing the car to overturn. Who or what caused the accident? Philosophers and scientists would say that any causal explanation should take into account not only the *immediate cause* of an effect, but also the *necessary conditions*. The immediate cause was the poor handling of the car by the driver. The necessary conditions were that it had snowed, the snow had turned to ice, and the ice had made the road slippery.

According to scientists, no effect is ever the product of a single cause. A cause is the sum total of all the conditions that help to bring about an effect. It is the combination that constitutes causality. Thus, in strict scientific terms, it would be inaccurate to say that "B is the cause of A" or "A is followed by B." It would be more accurate to state that events A, B, C, D, E in combination caused an event: X. But in everyday matters, it is usually sufficient to pick out one or two of the most conspicuous events and maintain that these produced a particular result. In such cases, you accept the necessary conditions as given.

A familiar old nursery rhyme illustrates this chain of causality beautifully:

> For want of a nail the shoe was lost,
> For want of a shoe the horse was lost,
> For want of a horse the rider was lost,
> For want of a rider the battle was lost,
> For want of a battle the kingdom was lost,
> And all for the want of a horseshoe nail.

It is customary to compare causal events to the links in a chain. But causal events are not merely links in an observable chain. They are part of complex conceptual patterns. Causes *are* connected to effects, but this is because you tie them together through experience and reflection. Consider an accident in which one car goes through a red light and plows into another. According to the police, the driver of the first car caused the accident by negligence. The driver claims that his brakes did not hold, yet he just had new brake shoes put on the car. The automobile mechanic blames the failure on faulty construction by the maker of the brake shoes. The brake-shoe manufacturer blames the foreman, who in turn blames the workman, who in turn blames faulty equipment. When you discern cause-and-effect relationships, then, you bring to your understanding of causality certain assumptions and presuppositions. Otherwise you would not be able to explain anything. For compositional purposes, however, you would not be expected to take into account the total cause, including all the necessary conditions of an event. You are expected to be as careful as possible in your causal analyses.

Purpose, Audience, Kind of Discourse

Cause-and-effect thinking can be found in any kind of writing, for any purpose. Ordinarily, you associate cause-and-effect thinking with scientific writing. But it can be found in everyday reasoning, formal arguments, reports, magazine articles, textbooks, historical explanations, scientific explanations, news articles, proposals, manuals, accident reports, political analyses, TV commentaries, and magazine ads.

Cause and effect can be used for any of the writer's purposes: to justify or condemn some action; to prove or disprove an idea, belief, or assertion; to explain; to give an account of something; to produce a feeling; to investigate; to draw conclusions.

Insofar as your readers are logical beings, they will be looking for reasons in your writing, especially when you want to inform them or ask them to accept or reject a course of action.

Invention and Cause and Effect

As a topic of invention, cause and effect answers such fundamental questions as Why did it happen? What are its causes? What are its effects? What is its purpose? How is it related causally to something else? In inventing, you follow a sequence of events in time, notice the transference of a force or condition from one thing to another, and attempt to explain these relationships.

Cause and effect is related to narration and to process because all three are concerned with chronological progression. But in cause and effect, you are more interested in the *why* than in the *what* or the *how*.

Cause-and-effect exposition is a special form of exposition that presents a step-by-step description of *associated* sequences of events. Something more than just contiguity is involved in the process. Even though frequently all that you observe is two or more events following each other in time, you reason from your knowledge of other kinds of causal connections that there is some kind of bond holding these events together, and you imagine what this connection might be. Experience teaches you that certain events are always followed by other events, and you ascribe to the sequence the idea of cause and effect.

The average person understands how to use the word *cause*. Ask her or him what a cause is, and the reply will probably be, "Something that makes something else happen." Cause-and-effect themes have a commonsense vocabulary to convey logical relationships that even the average person will have no trouble with:

cause	in	as a result of
effect	by	for this reason
bring about	of	therefore
produce	so	consequently
give reasons for	thus	accordingly
accomplish	since	on account of
originate	due to	owing to
follow from	because	by the agency of
make possible	if	by means of
result from	then	in effect

In addition to characteristic words and phrases, sentences that convey action imply cause-and-effect relationships:

The intruder was killed by a bullet.
Robert smashed the window with a rock.
The wind lifted the edge of the roof and sent it crashing to the ground.
Amy kicked George in the leg.
The leaves changed from a dark green to a bright orange.

In your sentences, you usually attribute some cause to an agent, an instrument, or some agency.

Exercises

1. Probe a cause-and-effect subject by using the questions in this chapter suggested by the topics of invention.

2. Write five thesis sentences for a causal analysis.

3. Discuss in class the cause of an accident which you witnessed or in which you were involved. Discuss the effects of the same accident.

4. Discuss in class your most embarrassing (happiest, saddest, maddest) moment. What caused this embarrassment? What were the effects?

5. Discuss the effects of

   a. watching television late on a school night
   b. no breakfast before school
   c. no meal before heavy drinking
   d. staying outdoors on a freezing night

6. Discuss the causes of a solar eclipse, a rainbow, a flood, bird migration.

The Structure of Cause and Effect

Causal essays tend to fall into two basic types: those in which you proceed from cause to effect and those in which you move from effect to cause.

Cause-and-effect sequences fall into relatively simple paradigms:

Cause-to-Effect Pattern
Introduction (includes thesis)
Cause 1 . . .
Cause 2 . . .
Cause 3 . . .
Cause 4, 5, 6 . . .

Effect . . .
Conclusion (summary and so forth)

Introduction (includes thesis)
Cause . . .
Effect 1 . . .
Effect 2 . . .
Effect 3 . . .
Effect 4, 5, 6 . . .
Conclusion (summary and so forth)

Keep in mind that the numbers of the paradigms refer to sections of the paper and not necessarily to paragraph divisions.

Effect-to-Cause Pattern
Introduction (includes thesis)
Effect 1 . . .
Effect 2 . . .
Effect 3 . . .
Effect 4, 5, 6 . . .
Cause . . .
Conclusion (summary and so forth)

Introduction (includes thesis)
Effect . . .
Cause 1 . . .
Cause 2 . . .
Cause 3 . . .
Cause 4, 5, 6 . . .
Conclusion (summary and so forth)

In composing cause-and-effect essays, you divide an event into the number of *necessary* conditions involved in the event. Naturally, the particular elements you abstract from an event will be determined by your purpose and your interest. If, for example, an adolescent dies from an overdose of drugs, the doctor may rule that the OD was the cause of death. The police, on the other hand, may blame the drug pusher. And parents will search their hearts to see if there was something in their own behavior to contribute to the cause of death. In ascribing a certain cause to an effect, be aware that your purpose determines the way you interpret the effect.

The following cause-and-effect essay, based on an Associated Press news story, is a good example of an essay that moves from cause to effect.

Liquor Prices Could Go Down

Introduction   A few years ago, the United States sold millions of bushels of corn and wheat to the Soviet Union. At that time, some critics advocated that Americans should drink less in order to make more grain available for food. That idea went over like a lead balloon with the liquor industry. They argued that only a small amount of grain, comparatively speaking, goes into the production of hard liquor. Eliminating booze production, they maintained, would make very little difference in the food supply. Now, a few years later, prospects for a record grain production are so good that these critics have been silenced, and liquor consumers may look forward to some relief from the higher prices.

Cause   The Agriculture Department estimates the 1975 corn crop will yield a record 6.05 billion bushels. Farmers are delighted at what they expect to be a record harvest. Already over 177 million bushels of corn have been sold to the Soviet Union, and the Agriculture Department expects corn exports to exceed 1 billion bushels.

Effect 1   One effect of this projected record harvest is expected to be lower prices for whiskey drinkers and drinkers of other kinds of alcoholic spirits, although one industry liquor spokesman maintains that a record grain crop would have a negligible effect on whiskey prices. It would, however, keep prices from going up.

Effect 2   Another effect of a bumper corn crop would be that the cost of livestock grain would go down, thus resulting in lower prices for milk, meat, and poultry.

Conclusion   Whiskey imbibers are being warned, however, not to cheer too soon. Some critics are complaining that the recent grain deal with Russia could send prices skyrocketing again.

This news story is based on a very simple cause-and-effect pattern. The opening paragraph provides the introduction, giving the reader some background concerning fluctuating prices for grain and liquor. The second paragraph states the cause for a possible reduction in liquor and food prices. Paragraphs 3 and 4 give the effects of a bumper grain harvest: lower liquor prices and lower food prices. And the last paragraph concludes with a warning.

Many news stories contain cause-and-effect patterns embedded in the narrative. Headlines such as "Driver is killed as auto overturns and hits an embankment," "Yastrzemski drives in two runs to beat the Detroit Tigers," and "Gunman takes $2 million in gems from London safe-deposit center" are based on cause-and-effect relationships. Many books and magazines present cause-and-effect articles about the dangers of taking heroin, speed, alcohol, or some other drug.

The student paper that follows uses a cause-to-effect pattern of development.

Why Preventative Detention Is Wrong

I recently read that President Nixon and Attorney General John Mitchell had sent a piece of legislation to Congress, modeled after their infamous "D.C. Crime Bill," which would permit the federal government to hold suspects in jail for up to sixty days pending trial. The plan is to prevent crime by incarcerating presumably dangerous criminals, rather than allowing them freedom on bail. In actuality, this measure would thwart justice, not crime, if enacted, through the perversion of our Constitution and some of our most basic legal principles which have long been the hallmark of our system of jurisprudence.

The most flagrant effect which would result from adopting the President's bill would be a major deterioration of the presumption of innocence which has guided criminal proceedings ever since the Star Chamber Court was abolished in the 17th century. Imagine locking a man behind bars for a period of two months *before he has even had a trial!* Whatever happened to the Constitution which guarantees the right to a speedy trial? Or what about the Eighth Amendment which assures the suspect of his right to reasonable bail?

This matter of bail is one long entrenched in our constitutional history. And without exception, the Supreme Court has held time and time again that the only purpose for bail is to assure the appearance of a defendant at trial. In a case where the suspect owns a home in the community, has a job, and appears to be a sound risk in terms of showing up for trial, then a low bail, or none at all, is called for. Where the suspect is likely to run, then a high bail is required. But there is *no* provision in the Constitution for *pre-trial* punishment. We have traditionally believed that it is wiser to see if the accused is *guilty* before inflicting a sentence.

President Nixon would have us believe that with the present backlog of criminal cases on the docket it is dangerous to permit certain people to roam the streets after they have been accused. The obvious answer to this argument is to hire more judges, more court personnel, more prosecuting attorneys in order to speed up the trial progress. It is not at all uncommon for a case to be delayed for several years due to the volume of cases. In comparison, sixty days may not be very long, but for something which has not yet been proven in court, it can well be sixty days too many. We must speed up the process, not file the cases away behind iron bars. The old adage "Justice delayed is justice denied" is all the more critical if someone is rotting in jail.

—Barry

The student paper reprinted below moves in the other direction, from effect to cause.

No one familiar with the four televised Kennedy-Nixon debates during the presidential race in 1960 can deny the effect of television on American politics. The charisma of a candidate has become as important a factor as his political program, thanks to the mass exposure he gets through the medium of television. Nixon, for example, could not compete with John F. Kennedy's charm, dry wit, and warm smile, as they debated on nationwide television in the autumn of Kennedy's presidential victory. Viewers responded to the style of the young Democrat—of the estimated 120,000 Americans who had seen at least one of the four debates, an opinion poll showed that seventy-five percent of those whose vote had been swayed by the television confrontation were influenced in favor of the charismatic senator from Massachusetts. Television had truly come into its own as a major factor in American politics as it exposed the public not only to the political facts but also to the political personalities in a way no other medium could.

Politics is not the only area of American life in which television has had a significant effect. Family life, too, has changed as a result of television. Conversation is a virtually nonexistent form of meaningful communication in many American households, for the family gathers only to eat and to cluster in front of the twenty-six-inch, full-color screen in what is called the living room. Often, even meals are eaten in front of a TV program that is too good to miss, and the evening dinner, traditionally a family gathering accompanied by a discussion of the day's events, is turned into an exercise in futility, as forks grope for nutritious food while eyes remain glued to the screen. Family games, outings, songfests, and reading are abandoned in favor of prime-time fare. Sometimes the only verbal communication two family members will have in a day is an argument over which TV program will reign on the evening's agenda, although the popularity of a second or even third television set is wiping out even this meager contact.

Social customs have also been affected by television. TV dates are common, eliminating the need for any involved verbal contact between those who date, and guests in a household are frequently invited to join the host in viewing a particular show, rather than in socializing by pleasant talk or by some more active form of entertainment such as a game. Indeed, much socializing has been eliminated by television, for it is much easier to sit at home and be amused than to force yourself to get up, make yourself attractive, and go out and amuse others.

Television has affected many varied and seemingly separate areas of American life, from politics to the dinner hour, from education to the crime rate. In 1938, E. B. White wrote, "I believe TV is going to be the test of our modern world. . . . We shall stand or fall by TV—of that I am quite sure." The boob tube, the living room babysitter, the electronic pacifier, whatever you call it, this 20th-century invention has affected the lives of virtually every modern American. It is now up to the American public to realize the significance of these effects and to channel them into more positive currents in American life.

—Sandra

Exercises

1. Select a brief cause-and-effect essay or magazine or newspaper article and do both a linear and a paradigmatic analysis of the essay.

2. Analyze the picture of a magazine ad for cause-and-effect relationships.

3. Write on one of the following:

   a. the causes of inflation
   b. the effects of inflation
   c. the effects of smoking
   d. the effects of taking some drug or hard liquor
   e. the causes of _____
   f. the effects of _____

4. Describe in detail the effects of your first smoke (drink, kiss, lie, or the like).

5. Write an essay on one of the following topics:

   a. likely effects of early marriages
   b. short-term effects of the energy crisis
   c. effects of movie censorship
   d. causes of your attitude toward sex (God, religion, politics, education, or other controversial subject)
   e. moral standards

6. You are a mad scientist. Describe the effects of a diabolical experiment on one of your enemies.

7. Discuss the effects of air (noise, visual) pollution in a place you know well.

8. Discuss the effects that certain television programs (or movies) might have on children.

Persuasion as an Aim:

Induction and Deduction

Chapter 8

Persuasion as an Aim:
Induction and Deduction

In the preceding chapters, you have been asked to use a variety of modes of invention and organization in your writing and to consider a variety of aims: informative, persuasive, aesthetic, and expressive. Because persuasion is such an important aim, in this chapter and in the next I want to focus on the kinds of thinking and compositional techniques appropriate to this aim.

Actually, all of the compositional strategies you have learned so far can be used in the service of persuasion. Modes of invention and organization such as analysis, description, exemplification, narration, comparison, analogy, and cause and effect can be used for any of the writer's aims, for any audience, and for any kind of discourse. Traditionally, however, the kinds of logical thinking that go into the making of arguments have been given the names *induction* and *deduction.*

Every day you encounter numerous situations that depend upon persuasion. Advertisers try to get you to buy their products. Politicians solicit your vote. Priests and ministers try to lead you on the path to salvation. Newspaper editorial writers attempt to convince you to vote for or against nuclear power plants. Your friends and neighbors argue with you about anything and everything—religion, politics, nuclear energy, the oil crisis. . . . And you argue back—sometimes convincingly, sometimes ineffectively, usually un-selfconsciously. In your writing, however, a selfconscious attention to the process can be helpful.

Public issues must necessarily be resolved by influencing the beliefs and actions of other people. Skill in argumentation and persuasion can be a means to help you get things done and to combat the evils of doublespeak and propaganda. You might think that all you have to do to get your point across is to be forceful and sincere, but to be persuasive, your arguments have to be presented effectively.

Argumentation is *the giving of reasons to support the truth or falsity of a proposition.* A **proposition** is *a statement upon which an argument is based or from which a conclusion is drawn.* It is a sentence phrased in such a way that it can be the basis of a discussion. It is the thesis of an argument. Think, for a moment, of what such a statement might contain: an opinion, an authoritative decision, a judgment, a sentiment, a conviction, an attitude, a belief, a criticism, an impression.

To write an argument, then, you begin with a proposition. Next you add other sentences to it, and other sentences to these sentences, and you depict the relationships among these sentences in such a way as to lead your readers to accept your conclusions and perhaps to act on them. Your proposition, in other words, must be supported by reasoning and evidence. Otherwise, it stands as an unsupported generalization. **Reasoning** is *thinking in a connected, logical manner by induction or deduction.* It is the drawing of conclusions from observations, facts, or hypotheses. **Evidence** is *the material used to prove your point—facts, ideas, statistics, examples, testimony, and so forth.*

Reasoning by Induction

When you reason inductively, you begin with particular bits and pieces of evidence and then draw a conclusion from this evidence. **Induction** is *reasoning from the particular to the general.* It is coming to a conclusion about all members of a class from examining only a few members of the class. Because the evidence is incomplete and the facts limited, you must "leap" from these facts to a general conclusion.

Induction tells you what to expect. If you reach into a basket of tomatoes and pick out six or seven that are rotten, you might conclude that the rest of the tomatoes are rotten, too. You might be right or you might be wrong. Your conclusion would be *probable*, but the only way you could be certain would be to examine every tomato.

Many of our conclusions are based on an *inductive leap*. We believe that aspirin cures headaches because we've taken aspirin in the past, and indeed aspirin did cure our headaches. Therefore, it is reasonable to believe that aspirin will cure our headaches in the future.

In its logical form, an inductive reasoning process looks like this:

Aspirin cured my headache a year ago.
Aspirin cured my headache six months ago.
Aspirin cured my headache last month.
Aspirin cured my headache two weeks ago.
Therefore, aspirin cures headaches.

Reasoning by Deduction

When you reason deductively, you begin with a general statement as a premise, apply it to a particular instance, and then draw a conclusion from it. **Deduction** is *reasoning from the general to the specific*. It proceeds through steps that comprise what is called a syllogism. A **syllogism** consists of three sentences or propositions. The first two sentences are called premises. The last sentence is called the conclusion. In its traditional form, the syllogism looks like this:

All women enjoy dancing.
Joan is a woman.
Therefore, Joan enjoys dancing.

The conclusion is valid because the reasoning is sound. But it may not necessarily be true. If the premises (sentences 1 and 2) are true, then the conclusion (sentence 3) is true. But a moment's thought will reveal that the major premise ("all women enjoy dancing") is not necessarily true. Therefore, the conclusion may be false.

Inductive reasoning generally takes the form of examples, testimony, analogy, and cause and effect. Deductive reasoning often takes the form of the syllogism and the enthymeme (the sentence form of the syllogism). However, even though you reason to a conclusion inductively, in your writing you can state your conclusion first and then supply reasons for supporting it.

Because of the close relationship that exists between induction and deduction, in this chapter we shall be moving back and forth between the two kinds of thinking. But we will also be looking at a wider range of categories than is ordinarily dealt with in discussions of argumentation. Besides the usual methods of reasoning by induction (examples, testimony, analogy, cause and effect), we will be examining categories such as analysis, description, narration, and comparison, usually associated with expository or literary writing. In the next chapter, we will be dealing almost exclusively with deduction as it relates to the syllogism and the enthymeme.

Arguing by Analysis

In chapter 4, you learned that **analysis** is *the process of dividing anything complex into simple parts.* Besides being a thought process, analysis is also a method of getting ideas as well as a way of organizing those ideas. Although analysis can be used for any of the writer's aims and in any kind of writing, most of the analyses you have looked at thus far have been examples of informative writing. Yet analysis is also an important mode of developing arguments.

In writing an argument, giving features or characteristics or details amplifies the central idea. In using analysis for persuasive purposes, you divide a whole into its component parts. But in writing expository essays, you proceed in much the same manner. Wherein lies the difference? The most obvious difference is in the writer's intention. In persuasive writing, your purpose is to secure conviction or action. In expository writing, your purpose is to inform or instruct. In expository writing, all you have to do to achieve your purpose is to convince your readers of the soundness of your thinking. But in persuasive writing, you must also provide your readers with motives and reasons for believing your assertions. If you want your readers to do something, you've got to ask them to do it: to get out and vote, to fill in a questionnaire, to buy a particular product, to travel to a mountain resort, to fly to Hawaii.

How is this done? Not only by logical reasoning and evidence, but also by *direct command,* by *invitation,* and by *suggestion.* The most effective arguments extend the call for action throughout the text, embedded in the reasoning process, but many persuasive essays get action by calling for it near the end of the discourse. Here are some examples:

The Command
See and drive this great new car today.
Vote for _____.
Ban nuclear energy!
Impeach_____.

And in a more humorous vein:

Repeal inhibition.
Fight air pollution—inhale.
Be alert—the world needs more lerts.
Get high on helium; it's a gas.

The Invitation
We invite you to join us at the Holiday Inn.
We hope you'll make your next cake with Swans Down
Cake Mix.
Please try our coffee today.

The Suggestion
Why not give minorities job preferences?
Your girl will be impressed if you say it with flowers.
You will look so much better if you buy an Arrow shirt.

The direct command makes an urgent appeal to the reader. It uses exhortation to get action. The invitation employs polite and courteous language. It sometimes resembles a social invitation. The suggestion uses implication and inference. Like the invitation, it is courteous, but in addition it makes use of coaxing, flattery, and pleading.

In arguing by analysis, you can use both inductive and deductive thinking. In an inductive analysis, you proceed from the parts to the whole. In a deductive analysis, you go from broader to narrower elements.

The paradigmatic structure of analytic arguments is very similar to that of expository essays, except that the thesis is a proposition to be argued:

Analysis Pattern 1
Introduction (includes proposition to be argued)
Feature 1 (or detail 1)
Feature 2 (or detail 2)
Feature 3 (or detail 3)
Feature 4 (or detail 4)
Feature 5, 6, 7 (or detail 5, 6, 7) . . .
Conclusion (includes call for action)

Analysis Pattern 2
Introduction (includes proposition to be argued)
Cluster of features (as evidence)
Cluster of features
Cluster of features
Cluster of features
Conclusion (includes call for action)

An inductive pattern is also possible. Here is an example of an inductive pattern in a slightly less abstract form:

Analysis Pattern 3
This political candidate has this qualification.
This political candidate has this qualification.
This political candidate has this qualification.
This political candidate has this qualification.
This political candidate has outstanding qualifications.
Vote for him/her.

The following is a good example of a persuasive essay that uses inductive reasoning toward a conclusion:

If you've never driven a car with front-wheel drive before, you're in for a new and rewarding experience. GM's new Chevrolet Citation, Pontiac Phoenix, Oldsmobile Omega, and Buick Skylark are front-wheel-drive cars that will be GM's frontrunners for the '80s.

They all have *transverse-mounted engines.* Because the engine sits sideways, overall length is reduced, yet each car has plenty of room for passengers and luggage. A 4-cylinder engine is standard, but a V-6 is also available.

Each car has a *MacPherson Strut front suspension* that helps create a roomier passenger compartment.

Each has *rack-and-pinion steering* for quick, easy response.

All have *front disc brakes* with a new low-drag design with audible wear indicators.

All have *radial tires* in a new design, with a special rubber compound to lower rolling resistance even more than conventional radials.

Each has a maintenance-free *Delco Freedom battery* that never needs water.

Each has maintenance-free *wheel bearing assemblies*, completely sealed, preset for precise clearance, and lubed for life.

These are just some of the *outstanding standard features* that you get on these exciting new front-wheel-drive cars. Drive one at your GM dealers today and draw your own conclusions.

—adapted from a General Motors ad

This essay uses an inductive chain of reasoning very much like that exemplified in analysis pattern 3. Each paragraph highlights a feature of the new GM front-wheel-drive cars. As the evidence mounts, paragraph by paragraph, the reader is led into *(induced)* the generalization in the final paragraph. The essay concludes with a call to action.

Advertisers make extensive use of the mode of analysis to convince their readers of the relative superiority of their products. In an inductive arrangement, the ad opens with attributes of the product, with features, facts, or other proof, and then shows how these selling points are beneficial to the reader. This inductive sequence gains conviction because it piles up facts about a product, explains its qualities, and then leads the reader to conclude that the product has benefits from which he or she can profit.

Arguing by Description

Description is *a mode of analysis,* and like analysis it can be found in any kind of writing, to achieve any of the writer's aims. In literary writing, where there may be long stretches of description, it tends to follow a spatial pattern. Often, however, it is subordinate to the mode of narration. But in persuasive writing, descriptive elements and details are arranged largely in the order of observation.

A good example of descriptive reasoning for persuasive purposes can be found in magazine advertising. As in magazine ads that use a kind of abstract analysis of features to win conviction, magazine ads that use concrete sensory details present descriptive material in the form of product attributes or benefits. Advertisers present this material in such a way as to differentiate their brand from competitive brands and to convince their readers that the quality of their merchandise is consistent with the price.

In advertising, descriptive copy is often called human-interest copy because it appeals primarily to the senses and the emotions, and the reader's response to it is instinctive. Consequently, persuasive writing that uses description relies heavily on suggestion rather than deliberation. If all of our actions were based on deliberate choices, there would be little place in persuasive writing for description. But human beings are not always logical. They are also moved by instincts and feelings of hunger, anger, fear, and desire.

Writers who use description for persuasive purposes often give conflicting advice about the kinds of techniques best suited to win conviction from their readers. According to some writers, vague, general words such as *beautiful, magnificent,* and *luxurious* have little human-interest value. They claim that the best descriptions individualize the person or object to be described. Therefore, the writer should fill his or her writing with concrete and vivid sensations of sight, smell, taste, and touch. Other writers claim that description need not always be concrete and specific to be good. Sometimes certain objects are difficult to describe precisely. Other times, it seems better to give the observer's reactions to the perceived object than to give a precise description of the object. Whatever may be true in other kinds of writing, in persuasive writing a combination of suggestive and concrete description can be effective.

Here is an example of a magazine ad that uses a combination of concrete and suggestive description to achieve its purpose:

Caramel-Vanilla: A Golden Merger of Two of Nature's Richest Flavors

We've blended the taste of luscious vanilla with creamy caramel and now have a deliciously mellow cordial with a rich flavor that's more than equal to its parts. Sip it straight, blend it half-and-half with fresh cold milk, or be creative and experiment. It's delicious fun.

And its name, Caramella, is as soft and mellow as its taste. Look for the distinctive white bottle from Arrow.

The headline serves the function of a thesis sentence: "Caramel-Vanilla [is] a golden merger of two of nature's richest flavors." This sentence organizes the descriptive details that follow by repeating the idea of the blending of ingredients in successive sentences. The word *caramel-vanilla* in the headline, which is a compound, introduces this idea, and then the idea is repeated in the words *merger, two, blended, Caramella, more than equal to its parts,* and *blend.*

Within this framework, the ad uses a combination of concrete and suggestive details to convince the reader to buy the product. The concrete details appeal directly to the senses: *mellow* ("soft, sweet, juicy, full-flavored"), *creamy* ("rich in cream"), *caramella* ("caramel and vanilla"). The suggestive details direct the reader to feel a certain way about the product: *delicious* ("pleasing, enjoyable"), *luscious* ("pleasant"), *rich* ("excessive proportion of pleasing ingredients"), *distinctive.* There is also an effective use of sound devices to reinforce the idea that Caramella is a pleasant experience: *creamy caramel, deliciously mellow, Caramella,* soft and *mellow.* There is no direct call for action at the end of the ad. Instead, the act of description, with its appeal to the reader's sensations and feelings, makes an effective selling appeal.

Although magazine advertising may seem to be a specialized kind of persuasive writing, politicians, businessmen and -women, and religious organizations have borrowed techniques from copywriters to sell ideas, goods, and services. You can learn much from ad writers about how to use description for persuasive purposes.

Exercises

1. Bring to class a magazine ad that uses the mode of analysis to secure conviction (for example, car ads, stereo ads, ads for soap, and so on). Discuss the chain of reasoning. Is it inductive or deductive? Is the argument convincing?

2. Bring to class for discussion a food ad, a perfume ad, a cosmetic ad, a clothing ad, or a jewelry ad that uses description for persuasive purposes. What is the method of organization: inductive? deductive? What is the order of impressions? What is the diction like? Is the selling appeal explicit or implicit?

3. Describe your home in such a way that you make it appealing for someone who wants to swap homes for a summer vacation. The form of writing can be a letter or an ad.

4. You work for Japan Air Lines. Write an ad to get people to take a trip to the Orient.

5. Write an ad describing a Las Vegas holiday for two.

6. Describe the benefits of a pleasure cruise to South America or Europe.

7. Using the mode of description, write a persuasive essay to get your reader to do one of the following: see an exhibit; visit a special place; reevaluate a song, a painting, or another work of art; visit a place of historical interest; avoid a certain place.

Arguing From Example

Reasoning by example is *the typical inductive form of reasoning.* When using this method of developing ideas in persuasive writing, you cite a series of particular examples, all of which display a certain relationship to one another, and then draw a general conclusion from them.

The following ad for Coach Leatherware uses this process effectively. The illustration is simple. It consists of four pictures of leather bags or purses, arranged in a rectangular shape, two pictures at the top and two at the bottom. The text reads as follows:

Example 1: This is a Coach bag. You can get it at Goldwater's.
Example 2: This is a Coach bag. You can get it at Bonwit Teller.
Example 3: This is a Coach bag. You can get it at Dayton's Oval Room.

Example 4:   This is a Coach bag. You can get it at Garfinckel's.
Conclusion: Coach bags are sold in the nicest stores.

Here is an ad for Aetna Life and Casualty that uses a similar chain of reasoning:

> A truck without brake lights is hit from behind. For "psychic damages" to the driver, because his pride was hurt when his wife had to work, *a jury awards $480,000 above and beyond his medical bills and wage losses.*
>
> A 67-year old factory worker loses an arm on the job. His lawyer argues that he should receive wages for all the remaining years of his life expectancy. He had been earning about $10,000 a year. The jury awards him a sum equal to almost $89,000 a year.
>
> Then there's the one . . . but *you* can probably provide the next example. Most of us know hair-raising stories of windfall awards won in court. Justified claims should be compensated, of course. Aetna's point is that it is time to look hard at what windfall awards are costing.
>
> What can we do? Several things:
>
> We can stop assessing "liability" where there really *was* no fault—and express our sympathy for victims through other means.
>
> We can ask juries to take into account a victim's *own* responsibility for his losses. And we can urge that awards realistically reflect the actual loss suffered—that they be a fair *compensation,* but not a reward.
>
> Insurers, lawyers, judges—each of us shares some blame for this mess. But it is you, the public, who can best begin to clean it up. Don't underestimate your own influence. Use it, as we are trying to use ours.
>
> Aetna wants insurance to be affordable.

Although reasoning by example is generally inductive, for purposes of writing persuasive essays you can present your conclusion in the beginning of your essay and then follow it up with representative examples to support your conclusions.

This ad for Texaco uses a single extended example to make its point:

> Texaco is working to get more than oil out of the ground.
> Texaco doesn't just look for new sources of oil, it also looks for new ways to conserve the oil we already have.

For example, Texaco has developed a way to produce one of the raw materials for making chemical fertilizer. This method, which is a coal gasification process, uses coal instead of natural gas or petroleum liquids.

Recently, Texaco's coal gasification process was selected by the Tennessee Valley Authority for use in its National Fertilizer Development Center in Alabama.

In the future, this process may be widely used and America will be able to save some of the natural gas and petroleum liquids which it so desperately needs.

This coal gasification process is just one example of how Texaco puts its resources to work for you.

In reasoning by example, try to avoid common weaknesses by keeping in mind the following advice:

1. *Cite a reasonable number of examples.* In arguments using examples, there is a danger of generalizing from too few examples. It is difficult, however, to determine how many examples are necessary to lend force to an argument. Sometimes a single long example can be effective.
2. *Cite typical examples.* If you select examples that are unusual or exceptional, you might draw misleading conclusions from them. Your examples should be representative.
3. *Account for negative examples.* In generalizing from examples, you might come across negative examples that do not support your conclusion. Nevertheless, you must account for these negative instances, perhaps by showing that they are not significant or that they are exceptions.

Hasty Generalization

A **hasty generalization** is *one that is based on insufficient evidence.* The problem arises when the writer tries to extend his or her conclusion beyond the examples on which it is based. All arguments of this kind leap from the known to the unknown. But the difficulty lies in justifying this leap with too few examples, with the lack of typical examples, or with the failure to account for negative examples. Is it true, for instance, that "Americans are the most waste-ful people on earth"?

Sweeping Generalization

A **sweeping generalization** is *one that needs to be qualified* by words and phrases such as *some, a few, many, most, usually,* and *sometimes.* Advertisers use sweeping generalizations extensively to make claims of exclusivity (note my use of the sweeping word *extensively*), as in the following examples:

> No other product lets you bake so many things so quickly.
> Nothing performs like a Saab.
> Did you know that no leading oil tastes lighter than Mazola 100% corn oil?

In your own writing, you will be more effective if your generalizations are less sweeping:

> All politicians are dishonest. (sweeping)
> *Most* politicians are dishonest. (still too sweeping)
> *Many* politicians are dishonest. (less sweeping)
> *A few* politicians are dishonest. (you're on safer ground)

Exercises

1. Analyze the Aetna ad. Besides the inductive use of examples, the ad uses other methods of development. What are they? Are they effective?

2. Write an inductive argument supported by examples.

3. Evaluate these generalizations:

   a. Children who read are not dropouts.

b. The best American-made movies are the ones the major studios have absolutely no part in making.

c. All Democrats are liberal.

d. Most Republicans are conservative.

e. Nothing can be perfectly safe. Should we ban automobiles, cigarettes, and bathtubs? The biggest danger of nuclear power is that we won't have enough.

f. Most women are conceited.

g. You mean you wear contact lenses, too? You're the fourth person with blue eyes I've met recently who wears contact lenses. Blue-eyed people must have weak eyes.

h. Dan had his wallet stolen downtown. Carol lost her purse. If I go downtown, I'll be robbed.

i. I asked everyone in class if he or she smoked grass. Not one said yes. Marijuana is not used in this school.

j. This morning I got a flat tire. An hour later I got a speeding ticket. On the way home I got into an accident. Today sure was a lousy day.

Critical Review

The **critical review** makes widespread use of all of the kinds of reasoning we have discussed thus far, in the form of features, characteristics, particulars, and examples. The writer studies a movie, a TV show, a book, a record album, a painting, or a piece of sculpture and comes to a conclusion about it. In the review, the writer cites particular passages from a book in the form of examples, or the descriptive features of a movie or a painting, and uses them as evidence for the conclusion.

The chain of reasoning in the critical review can be inductive or deductive. If you begin with particular features that account for your conclusion, then the pattern is inductive. If, however, you begin with a judgment about the work and then support your judgment with evidence, then the pattern is deductive. The details of the analysis constitute the body of the review.

Here is one pattern that you might find useful in writing a critical review:

1. In the opening paragraph, *identify the work you are reviewing* (title, genre, name of artist, singer, director, writer, and so on). For example: *"Youth Terror: The View from Behind the Gun* is a disturbing TV documentary on teenage crime"; *"The Stories of John Cheever,* published by Knopf, is a collection of sixty-one short stories dating from 1947."

2. In the same paragraph, in a sentence or two, *give an overall evaluation of the work.* (*"Last Embrace* is a film in which a stylish director and a superb cast . . . do their best to triumph over a script that lacks witty writing and genuinely suspenseful substance.")

3. If necessary, in the first or second paragraph, *give your reader any background information necessary for understanding your review.*

4. *Give a brief summary of the contents of the work you are reviewing,* as objectively and as accurately as you can.

5. *Cite evidence, in the form of details, to support your earlier judgment* of the work. Point out specific strengths and weaknesses.

6. *End* your review *by restating your earlier evaluation, by making a recommendation* to your reader, or *by coming to a significant conclusion* about the work.

The review that follows uses most of the steps outlined above:

Norma Rae is a warm-hearted story about the realities of working and living in a small Southern town in America. This film was directed by Martin Ritt. The screenplay was written by Irving Ravetch and Harriet Frank.

Norma Rae is an account of a young Southern woman (played by Sally Field) who has little education and a routine job at a local cotton mill. She has two children and no husband. Her life changes when an educated union organizer (Ron Leibman) comes to the mill from New York to unionize the workers. He breaks through her suspicions and convinces her to help him organize a union in a union-busting mill. She gets into trouble at the mill, and when it appears that her children might hear about her sexual past, she confides in them and in her new husband (Beau Bridges), who feels she is neglecting him and the children because of union work.

The strengths of this movie are considerable. Sally Field plays a tough, vulnerable, and high-spirited woman with a somewhat questionable sexual past. Yet she has a moral spirit that is awakened by Reuben's friendship and their attempt to organize the workers. Ron Leibman, as Reuben, is a New York intellectual who wins out over small-town suspicion and prejudice. He reveals himself in his dealings with Norma Rae and the mill workers to be sensitive, witty and human.

As the story of a woman who copes with adversity and who realizes her moral potential, the film is a success. Its weaknesses are the result of a plot that is somewhat stereotyped and didactic (Norma Rae causing the machines in the mill to stop, company goons to the attack, the mill workers rallying round, the triumph of justice) and a story that takes too long to get going. The moviegoer is not quite sure if the main interest is to be in the possible romantic attraction between Norma Rae and Reuben (left undeveloped) or in the ordinary lives of the mill workers.

If the story is weak, the acting of Sally Field and Ron Leibman, and the characters they portray, make this a movie worth seeing. We need more movies that depict the everyday trials and tribulations of real people.

Exercises

1. Although the above review follows a logical plan of development, at times it makes generalizations about the movie without sufficient support. For class discussion, isolate all of the general assertions and then determine if there is enough evidence to support these assertions.

2. For discussion, bring to class a review of a movie you have recently seen. Do you like the review? Do you agree with the conclusions? Does the reviewer offer evidence for the evaluation?

3. Compare two reviews of the same movie, record album, play, TV show, or novel.

4. Write a review of a movie, a TV show, a book, a painting, a record album, a new building that has distinctive architectural features, a play, or a poem.

5. Reviews can be about a variety of subjects. Bring to class, for discussion, several of the following: a book review, a movie review, an art review, a TV review, a music review, a dance review, a theater review, a cuisine review, or a travel review.

Arguing by Narration

In **arguing by narration,** *you present your narrative in such a way that it serves as an inductive example to support your conclusion.* Narration as a mode of developing ideas has great human-interest appeal for readers. The narrative mode is intensely dramatic and dynamic. Because it is filled with action, it leads naturally to inducing action in others.

In using this mode of persuasion, you try to get your readers to identify with the characters in the narrative or with the situation being dramatized. This attempt to get your readers to identify with the characters or the situation is an important part of the persuasive appeal.

Narratives in argumentation can be of various kinds: factual narratives, fictional narratives, monologues, or dialogues. **Factual narratives** are *based on actual events,* and even when some liberty is taken with the names and places, the situation must be recognized as one that could take place in everyday life. **Fictional narratives** are *invented stories whose content is largely produced by the imagination.* However, a part of the content may be based on fact.

The following ad is a good example of a fictional narrative. The illustration depicts a man looking wistfully through a store window at a Steinway piano:

The Man Who Thought He Couldn't Own a Steinway

To him it had always been "the only piano."

Yet a little voice in the back of his head kept whispering, "You can't afford it."

Then one day he sharpened a pencil, quieted the voice in the back of his head, and did some serious figuring.

To his surprise, he discovered that the Steinway was not too much more expensive than the piano he'd been considering. Which didn't have the tone of a Steinway. Or the Steinway touch. It didn't have Steinway's Hexagrip Wrestplank. Or Steinway's Diaphramatic Soundboard. Or any of the exclusive features that makes a Steinway feel and sound like a Steinway.

"I'm being penny-wise but pound-foolish," he cried. So he bought the Steinway he's always wanted, which he and his wife and family are all enjoying.

He has only one regret. "I should have done it years ago," he says.

For more information, please write to John H. Steinway, 109 West 57th Street, New York 10019.

Monologues are *narratives in which the talk is by a single person.* The advantage of using a monologue instead of a fully developed story is that it allows a single character to act as a spokesperson for the writer. It is important in this kind of writing that the speaker talk with a believable voice.

The following ad for Timberland boots uses monologue copy very effectively. The illustration depicts an old man from the country sitting in the cab of his truck, with his feet extended from the cab. Naturally, he has on Timberland boots.

> "It was two of those fellers from the city come up the road in a big green car, asked me if I wanted some new boots. I didn't. Already had boots, had 'em for seven years. But they talked and we drank some, and then we looked at the boots some, and I tried 'em on. Now, I have to say, they did seem to have my size. So I walked 'em about for maybe a week, and once I went over and stood in Orville Wade's creek, just to see if they were waterproof, which they were. When those boys came back from the city, this is what I said. One, I said thank you for the fine boots, which are warm and dry as a hen's bottom. Two, I'd like a pair of 13 wides for Cousin Luther, double wide on the left foot where the tractor run it over."

> TIMBERLAND.   A whole line of fine leather boots that cost plenty, and should.

Dialogues are *narratives that have at least two speakers.* In writing dialogues, use dialogue tags such as "said he" and "she said" sparingly to avoid monotony.

The dialogue reprinted below, taken from a Whirlpool ad, moves inductively from the telephone conversation to the conclusion and selling appeal at the end of the ad:

How One Family Got Their Laundry Done Over the Phone (Based on an Actual Call)

(telephone rings)
Cool-Line Consultant: Whirlpool Cool-Line. May I help you?
Man: I certainly hope so. I rush home from work, gobble down dinner, pack the kids in the wagon, and head out to pick up our new Whirlpool washer. Then back home, hook it all up, and . . . nothing.
Consultant: Nothing?
Man: Absolutely zotz. Our four-year-old can make the door open and close, but that's all. So now, the store's closed, my wife's really steamed, and I'm not too thrilled myself. Now what are you gonna do about it?
Consultant: Our Cool-Line service is here to help get things working

for you. Let's run through a quick checklist. First—now, don't get mad—did you plug it in?

Man: We're not that dense.

Consultant: Both water lines hooked up and the water turned on?

Man: Of course.

Consultant: And you set the dial to regular wash and pulled out the control knob?

Man: Look, the washer really doesn't work! Might take the repairman a whole day to fix it.

Consultant: Might take just a few minutes. You see, Whirlpool appliances are designed to make servicing as quick and easy as possible. But before you call for service, let me ask you one more question.

Man: Shoot.

Consultant: Why did you buy a new washer? What was wrong with the old one?

Man: It was really on the fritz. Blowing fuses and stuff. The service guy said it was hopeless.

Consultant: Is there any chance that old washer blew a fuse one last time without your knowing it? Will you check?

Man: Oh my aching. . . . hang on. *(minutes later)* This is embarrassing. All we needed was a new fuse. I'm sorry I hassled you.

Consultant: Sorry you had trouble. Glad we could help.

Man: Hey, thanks again.

This is the kind of two-way communication we've been having on our Whirlpool Cool-Line service for the past eleven years. It's just one example of the continuing concern we have for our customers who purchase Whirlpool appliances.

If you ever have a question or problem with your Whirlpool appliance, call our toll-free 24-hour Cool-Line service at 800–253–1301.

Appeal to Pity

The **appeal to pity** is *an emotional appeal,* often using the mode of narration combined with description, *in which the writer attempts to persuade his or her readers to accept a conclusion on the basis* *of pity or sympathy.* A good example of the appeal to pity is the ever-recurring situation in which a student asks a teacher to change a grade, saying that he or she will flunk out of school or lose a scholarship unless a higher grade is given.

An appeal to pity is not necessarily a logical fallacy. A relevant appeal is one that addresses an issue which *by its nature* arouses sympathy. If, for example, a charitable organization makes a plea for money in order to aid needy children and shows a picture of a starving, wretched child, this strategy is bound to evoke an emotional response in the reader. The child's wretched condition *is* the issue. Therefore, the emotional appeal is appropriate. If, however, the appeal to pity fails to touch on the issue, as in the case of the student who receives low grades because of poor performance, then the appeal is irrelevant.

Here is an appeal designed to get sponsors for needy children in India, Brazil, Taiwan (Formosa), Mexico, and the Philippines, which appeared in *Time* magazine several years ago:

She Needs Your Love

Little Mie-Wen in Formosa already knows many things . . . the gnawing of hunger . . . the shivering of fear . . . the misery of being unwanted.

But she has never known love. Her mother died when she was born. Her father was poor—and didn't want a girl child. So Mie-Wen has spent her baby years without the affection and security every child craves.

Your love can give Mie-Wen, and children just as needy, the privileges you would wish for your own child.

Through Christian Children's Fund you can sponsor one of these youngsters. We use the word *sponsor* to symbolize the bond of love that exists between you and the child.

The cost? Only $12 a month. Your love is demonstrated in a practical way because your money helps with nourishing meals . . . medical care . . . warm clothing . . . education . . . understanding housemothers. . . .

Little Mie-Wen and children like her need your love—won't you help? Today?

Exercises

1. The Steinway piano ad appeared in *Harper's* in 1977. Discuss the relation to the intended audience. Is there a conflict in the story? Who are the characters? What is the diction like? How does the persuasive appeal work?

2. Does the voice of the speaker in the Timberland ad seem believable? Examine the ad closely. What is the language like? Pick out dialect features, words and phrases, or other stylistic devices that characterize the speaker. Is the ad convincing?

3. How would you characterize the customer in the Whirlpool ad? What is his language like? Does the language of the consultant seem as if it were part of the conversation of the actual telephone call? Is this ad persuasive?

4. Bring to class examples of writing that use narration for persuasive purposes. Try to find examples of each type: factual narratives, fictional narratives, monologues, and dialogues. Then discuss how the narrative mode is used in the service of persuasion.

5. Write an argument, using the mode of narration.

6. Write an essay in which you use an appeal to pity as the basis of your argument.

Arguing From Authority

When you argue from **authority,** you include in your argument *statements from an expert in some particular field.* A mere assertion, such as "Everybody knows that . . . ," is not enough. You should name the authority, quote his or her exact words, or paraphrase them.

The statement of the authority may take the form of a letter of recommendation, a quotation, a testimonial, an opinion poll, a best-seller list, a critical statement about a book or a movie, or the testimony of a witness at a trial. The logical structure of an argument by authority consists simply of repeating the words of the expert. A more sophisticated form of argument by authority is that in which the statement of the expert becomes the premise of a deductive form of reasoning.

You must often rely on the opinions of others because you don't have firsthand evidence yourself, or because such evidence is difficult to obtain. You also draw on these opinions because the experts who offer them have special training and experience in a particular field and are thus more qualified to make judgments in that field than is the average person.

Authorities can be of various kinds. There is the *prestige authority,* whose fame is known to the audience. He or she may or may not be an expert. There is the *expert authority,* who has special knowledge and experience. There is the *nonexpert authority,* who has had no special training or experience. There is the *lay authority,* the common man or woman who constitutes the majority of people, whose opinion is solicited *because it is typical.*

The **testimonial** is *an effective form of arguing from authority in which a real person gives a sincere statement about a product or service.* The people are real in the sense that they are not fictitious, but they may be professional models rather than actual users of the product.

Here is a testimonial, in the form of a monologue, of a Head and Shoulders shampoo ad. The speaker is a young woman, seated in a chair, with a magazine opened before her and a bottle of Head and Shoulders dandruff shampoo prominently displayed in the foreground. The ad appeared in *Mademoiselle* magazine in March 1977. The text reads as follows:

> I never tried a dandruff shampoo. I just sort of ignored my occasional itches and flakes. After all, my hair had bounce and shine and was very delicate. And since I washed my hair an awful lot, I really wanted a mild shampoo.
>
> Then my best friend (who has gorgeous hair, by the way) told me about Head & Shoulders. She said I'd love the fresh smell, the thick, rich lather. And it would leave even my baby fine hair soft and shiny, while controlling dandruff at the same time. She told me Head & Shoulders was the only shampoo she used.
>
> I sure am glad I listened to her. Head & Shoulders is everything she said it was. You can see for yourself how wonderfully shiny

my hair is. And not a worry about those itches and flakes. Now I wouldn't trust my hair to any shampoo but Head & Shoulders.

It is difficult to determine the age of the young woman in the illustration. She could either be a high school student, perhaps a senior, or a college student. Not only is she young looking, but also she uses characteristic phrases such as *sort of, awful lot*, and *sure am glad* that a teenager might use.

It is also difficult to tell if the young woman in the ad is an actual user of the product or if she is a model. She is not identified by name, nor are her words included in quotations. Perhaps we would be justified in accepting this testimonial as a fictional narrative.

Many testimonials use *celebrities* to endorse products. People like to look at pictures of celebrities in magazine ads and to read about them. The extent to which testimonials from celebrities are effective is in direct proportion to the extent to which the reader believes the endorser actually has knowledge of the product he or she is credited with using.

The following testimonial by Carol Lawrence for General Foods International Coffees is a good example of the type.

Carol Lawrence Presents Orange Cappuccino

"I love Italy. I love oranges. I love coffee. I suppose that's why I love everything about Orange Cappuccino.

"Of all the countries I've visited, I've always had a special affection for Italy, land of good food, good art, and lots of my good relatives.

"So it wasn't surprising how much I enjoyed Orange Cappuccino. This flavor from General Foods International Coffees, inspired by Italian Cappuccino, is a delightful treat.

"It has a creamy brown color and a delicate aroma. Yet it's a wonderfully full-bodied coffee with an extra note of flavor: the enticing taste and bouquet of lively orange.

"Orange Cappuccino has such a satisfying flavor I drink it the way the Italians drink their own Cappuccino—in a relaxed and unhurried way. As you know, Rome wasn't built in a day."

Argument from authority frequently takes the form of *massed evidence* or *group authority*. **Massed evidence** is *a large collection of facts or quotations of the same kind, with little explanation or comment.* Massed evidence is used in magazine advertisements, on book jackets, and in movie ads. One ad for Woody Allen's film *Manhattan* consisted entirely of quotations such as these:

> "*Manhattan* is inspired! One of Allen's most brilliant movies!"—Gene Shalit *(Today)*, NBC–TV
>
> "*Manhattan* deserves a stream of bravos! I can't urge you strongly enough to see *Manhattan.*"—Rona Barrett, ABC–TV
>
> "A masterpiece! A perfect blend of style, substance, humor, and humanity!"—Richard Schickel, *Time*

Recently, while I was flying to Colorado on Frontier Airlines, I happened to run across these massed quotations in a Frontier Airlines magazine:

Frontier. For the Long Stretch

"You allow an amount of legroom that I thought had disappeared years ago."—B. W. McPherson, Huntsville

"I especially enjoyed the roominess offered in your seating arrangement."—J. W. Moeller, Wichita

"Thanks, Frontier, for your legroom, good food, and friendly service—don't change it."—C. Schuld, Ft. Collins

"We wish to compliment you on the roominess of the aircraft."—Mr. & Mrs. R. O. Zincke, St. Louis

"Frontier is definitely far superior to other airlines. Thank you for being you."—K. Bolles, Denver

FRONTIER AIRLINES: First-class comfort at coach prices.

Although there is a sense in which testimonials prove nothing, they have great psychological appeal. First, they present the point of view of the user of a product or service. Second, people tend to believe a statement if it comes from an authority. Third, people want to associate themselves with others whom they like or admire.

Fallacious Appeals to Authority

In the writing of arguments, the fallacious appeal to authority can take several forms: citing an authority in one field (for instance, Reggie Jackson in baseball) when deciding a question in a completely different field (automobiles); citing an all-inclusive or vague authority ("Experts agree," "Everyone knows"); citing authorities that may be outdated (such as quoting from an old science book); citing authorities that are biased; citing authorities who may have been paid for their testimony.

Here are some questions that you might ask to determine if the appeal to authority is valid:

1. *Is the argument you are preparing really a matter for authority?*

2. *Is the authority an expert on this subject (rather than on some other subject)?*

3. *Is the authority prestigious? What positions does he or she hold? What kind of training and degrees does he or she have? Publications, awards, or grants?*

4. *Is the authority reliable?*

5. *Is the authority prejudiced? Is he or she influenced by self-interest? Does he or she represent a special interest group?*

Exercises

1. Over the past few years, cigarette advertisers have switched from the green-world archetype, where the Salem smoker takes his girl, to testimonials. Bring to class a group of ads for Vantage, Salem, or Winston cigarettes, and discuss the effectiveness or lack of effectiveness of the testimonials. Does the endorsement come from real people? How can you tell? Is the voice authentic? Compare the language of the various ads. Is the language similar?

2. Bring to class for discussion ads that use celebrities to sell a product.

3. In celebrity ads, there ought to be some kind of association between the celebrity and the product. Consider the following: Elizabeth Ashley for Je Suis skin fragrance, Redd Foxx for Teachers Scotch, Reggie Jackson and Wilt Chamberlain for Volkswagen, Farrah Fawcett-Majors for Wella Balsam shampoo, Catherine Deneuve for Chanel, Yul Brynner for Lauder's Scotch, Lola Falana for Hanes pantyhose, Florence Henderson for Wesson oil. If possible, bring to class the original ads. Are the ads convincing? Is the voice of the celebrity authentic? Is there a proper association between celebrity and product? Is any of the celebrities an authority for the product?

4. Bring to class some examples of massed evidence or group authority for discussion.

5. Bring to class examples of best-seller lists, best popular albums, and so forth. Discuss their use as arguments from authority.

6. Proverbs, maxims, and wise sayings are a form of argument from authority. Discuss their uses to win arguments in everyday life. For example, did your parents ever use them on you? Have you ever heard politicians use them?

7. A friend is applying for a job and has given your name as a reference. Write a complimentary letter of recommendation for that friend. Now imagine that the friend has personal habits that would make you hesitate in writing a letter. Write the letter anyway, but qualify it in such a way as to point out the friend's shortcomings, but without jeopardizing the friend's chance for a job.

8. Write an argument, using some form of authority to support your argument. It can be in the form of an essay, a letter to the editor, or a magazine ad.

Arguing by Comparison

In **reasoning by comparison,** *you state a resemblance between two things and then draw a conclusion from that resemblance.* When you argue by comparison, you present two units of thought to your reader and then point out how one is different from, or superior to, or more desirable than, the other:

Spanish Olives: How To Tell the Original From the Reproduction

The olive on the left is a true-blue Spanish green olive. The olive on the right just looks like one.

The olive on the left was grown in Spain, where the dry climate and mineral-rich soil help an olive ripen to its tangiest best. There's no telling where the olive on the right was grown.

The olive on the left was treated with meticulous care. By people who learned long ago that a bruised olive hurts business. As for the olive on the right, you really can't be sure how it was treated.

How do you tell them apart? Simple. Just read the label.

The olive on the left comes in a jar with the Spanish Olive Man symbol on it. The olive on the right doesn't.

So now you can be sure of the green olive you're getting, before you lay down your hard-earned green for it.

This ad for Spanish olives was taken from *McCall's* magazine, October 1977. Because there are so many ads in magazines, a successful ad has to grab the reader's attention immediately and then attempt to gain conviction. The illustration is the means of getting attention in this ad. It consists of a picture of two green olives, juxtaposed against a background of dark blue shading into royal blue and then gray.

The writer of this ad uses a simple point-by-point comparison pattern. Never mind that this paradigm has been used repeatedly. It is effective *because* it is conventional. The very shape of the comparison pattern has persuasive force. I am convinced that when the reader finishes this ad, he or she is persuaded of the relative superiority of one product over the other on the basis of the reasoning process alone, for if you look carefully at the evidence within the process, you come away with the impression that there are very few facts on which to base a buying decision. Isolated from their context, the "facts" look like this:

The Olive on the Left	*The Olive on the Right*
true-blue Spanish green olive grown in Spain	looks like one no telling where the olive on the right was grown
treated with meticulous care	can't be sure how it was treated
comes in a jar with the Spanish Olive Man symbol on it	doesn't [come in a jar with the Spanish Olive Man symbol on it]

In using comparison as a mode in developing arguments, many writers find it natural to consider *both sides of a question.* Is the subject under discussion good or bad, desirable or undesirable? Use the **pro-and-con method of comparison** to present a balanced view of a subject. The process allows you to move from a narrow or one-sided view of a subject to a larger perspective. You begin by stating one side of the question, then contrast this view with a counterstatement, moving back and forth until you come to a conclusion.

You can see the process at work in the following article by Isaac Asimov, taken from the *TV Guide* of December 14, 1974:

UFOs: Are They Visitors From Space—or Unreliable False Observations?

When most people think about flying saucers or, as they are more austerely called, "unidentified flying objects" (UFOs), they think of them as spaceships coming from outside Earth, and manned by intelligent beings.

Is there any chance of this? Do the "little green men" really exist? There are arguments pro and con.

Pro.   There is, according to the best astronomical thinking today, a strong chance that life is very common in the universe. Our own galaxy, containing over a hundred billion stars, is only one of perhaps a hundred billion galaxies.

Current theories about how stars are formed make it seem likely that planets are formed also, so that every star may have planets about it. Surely some of those planets would be like Earth in chemistry and temperature.

Current theories about how life got its start make it seem that any planet with something like Earth's chemistry and temperature would be sure to develop life. One reasonable estimate advanced by an astronomer was that there might be as many as 640,000,000 planets in our galaxy alone that are Earth-like and that bear life.

But on how many of these planets is there intelligent life? We can't say, but suppose that only one of a million life-bearing planets develops intelligent life forms and that only one out of 10 of these develops a technological civilization more advanced than our own. There might still be as many as 100 different advanced civilizations in our galaxy, and perhaps a hundred more in every other galaxy. Why shouldn't some of them have reached us?

Con.   Assuming there are 100 advanced civilizations in our own galaxy and that they are evenly spread throughout the galaxy, the nearest one would be about 10,000 light-years away. Even assuming coverage of that distance at the fastest speed we know of—the speed of light—the trip would take at least 10,000 years. Why should anyone make such long journeys just to poke around curiously?

Pro.   It is wrong to try to estimate the abilities of a far-advanced civilization, or their motives either. For one thing, the situation may not be average. The nearest advanced civilization may just happen to be only 100 light-years away, rather than 10,000.

Furthermore, because we know of no practical way of traveling faster than light doesn't mean an advanced civilization may not know of one. To an advanced civilization, a distance of 100 light-years or even 10,000 light-years may be very little. They may be delighted to explore over long distances just for the sake of exploring.

Con.   But even if that were the case, it would make no sense to send so many spaceships so often (judging by the many UFO reports). Surely we are not that interesting. And if we are interesting, why not land and greet us? Or communicate without landing? They can't be afraid of us, since if they are so far advanced beyond us, they can surely defend themselves against any puny threats we can offer.

On the other hand, if they went to be merely observers, and not interfere with the development of our civilization in any way, they could surely so handle their observations that we would not be continually aware of them.

Pro.   Again, we can't try to guess what the motives of these explorers might be. What might seem logical to us might not seem so logical to them. They may not care if we see them, and they also may not care to say hello. Besides, there are many reports of people who have seen the ships and have even been aboard. Surely some of these reports must have something to them.

Con.   Eyewitness reports of actual spaceships and actual extraterrestrials are, in themselves, totally unreliable. There have been innumerable eyewitness reports of almost everything that most rational people do not care to accept—of ghosts, angels, levitation, zombies, werewolves, and so on.

What we really want, in this case, is something material; some object or artifact that is clearly not of human manufacture or Earthly origin. These people who claim to have seen or entered a spaceship never end up with any button, rag, or other object that would substantiate their story.

Pro.   But how else can you account for all the UFO reports? Even after you exclude the mistaken, the gags and hoaxes—there remain many sightings that can't be explained by scientists within the present limits of knowledge. Aren't we forced to suppose these sightings are extraterrestrial spaceships?

Con.   No, because we don't know that the extraterrestrial spaceship is the only remaining explanation. If we can't think of any other, that may simply be a defect in our imagination. If any answer is unknown, then it is simply unknown. An Unidentified Flying Object is just that—unidentified.

The most serious and levelheaded investigator of UFOs I know is J. Allen Hynek, a logical astronomer who is convinced that some UFO reports are worth serious investigation. He doesn't think they represent extraterrestrial spaceships, but he does suggest that they represent phenomena that lie outside the present structure of science, and that understanding them will help us expand our knowledge and build a greatly enlarged structure of science.

The trouble is that whatever the UFO phenomenon is, it comes and goes unexpectedly. There is no way of examining it systematically. It appears suddenly and accidentally, is partially seen, and then is more or less inaccurately reported. We remain dependent on occasional anecdotal accounts.

Dr. Hynek, after a quarter of a century of devoted and honest research, so far ends with nothing. He not only has no solution, but he has no real idea of any possible solution. He has only his belief that when the solution comes, it will be important.

He may be right, but there are at least equal grounds for believing that the solution may never come, or that when it comes, it will be unimportant.

The organizational pattern of this article is very pronounced. Asimov sets up his thesis in the second paragraph ("Do the 'little green men' really exist?"), and then uses the last sentence in that paragraph to organize the essay ("There are arguments pro and con"). Then, in subsequent paragraphs, he takes up one point at a time, explores it thoroughly, and then considers a contrasting point of view. The resultant pattern is pro/con, pro/con, pro/con, pro/con, followed by a conclusion. The following scheme reveals the basic paradigm:

Introduction (includes thesis)
Pro (for)
Con (against)
Pro (for)
Con (against)
Pro (for)
Con (against)
Pro (for)
Con (against)
Conclusion

In this article, Asimov dispassionately analyzes the question as to whether life exists on other planets. He presents evidence and logical reasoning, refuting each argument point by point, but he does this within the framework of a comparison paradigm. He tries to convince his audience intellectually, by conviction, rather than by emotional appeal, and each step in the process is clearly formulated. Conviction is the logical part of argument that avoids the shaky emotional basis of some persuasive arguments.

Faulty Comparison

In reasoning by comparison, try to avoid the following errors in reasoning. These are most commonly found in advertising writing, but the principles are applicable to any kind of writing that uses the mode of comparison.

Avoid the **floating comparison.** This is *a comparison in which one half of the comparison is missing, so that the comparison seems to be floating in the air.* One tire company claims to have a new tire that lasts "20 percent longer." 20 percent longer than what? Last year's tire? A competitor's tire? A food manufacturer advertises an all-vegetable shortening that "is lighter, creamier, and more digestible." Lighter, creamier, and more digestible than what? Than it was before? Than all other brands? Than any brand of all-vegetable shortening? Than any brand that sells for the same price? What is missing, of course, is reference to the other product. The comparison is made to things that don't even exist.

Avoid **excessive use of superlatives.** When every medicine ad promises the "fastest" relief, every soap powder gives the "whitest" wash, every toothpaste the "fewest" cavities, every cigarette the "mildest" smoke, then you've got to believe that these claims are idle boasts. The test is whether or not a superlative claim is *factually* true. Can the claim be verified by objective standards? Quite often, the language is not clear enough or believable enough to be meaningful.

Superlative claims can also be made by using such words as *the, only,* and *exclusive.* This strategy is often used when it is difficult to determine significant differences between products. It's *"the* car of the decade," one advertisement reads. "It's the *only* tire made with. . . ." reads another.

Arguing by Analogy

An **analogy** is an *extended comparison.* It is *a process of reasoning based on similarity.* When you reason by analogy, you go from one particular case to another, basing your conclusion on similarities between two sets of circumstances. In arguing by analogy, you argue that if two things resemble one another in certain respects, they also resemble one another in other respects.

Analogies are often confused with metaphors. Both are based on similarity, but an analogy *argues from those similarities.*

An analogy may be literal or figurative. A **literal analogy** is *based on the same class of objects.* A **figurative analogy** is *based on different classes of objects.* Thus, if you compare a Buick with a Ford, that's a literal analogy. If you compare a Ford with a mustang, that's a figurative analogy.

Here is an example of a figurative analogy that appeared in *The New Yorker* on October 7, 1972:

Do You Have an Unfaithful Watch?

At first you tell yourself, "What's a few minutes off?"

But when you catch your watch cheating on you time and time again, when you're forced to turn to the wrist of some stranger . . .

That's when you wish you had an Accutron watch. Accutron by Bulova. The true-blue tuning-fork watch.

Its tuning-fork movement is guaranteed to keep it faithful to within a minute a month.

It can't be led astray, like others can, by an unbalanced balance wheel.

And it's so loyal that even if you deserted it for months, it would do nothing but lie there and count the seconds until you returned.

Testing the Analogy

Test all arguments from analogy to determine if the reasoning is valid. Determine what the main issues are. Figure out precisely what is being compared. Determine if the similarities and differences are relevant. Extend the analogy. Attack half of the comparison. Attack the whole analogy.

Faulty Analogy

It has become a cliché to state that analogies never prove anything. Yet they do have persuasive force. An analogy is faulty if the points being compared *are not alike in all essential respects;* if there are *negative instances;* and if there is a *single comparison* on which to support the conclusion, rather than an extended series of comparisons.

Exercises

1. Evaluate the following comparisons and analogies:

   a. Try Handle With Care on *your* summer washables. You'll say it really does more.

   b. Smooth some Balm Barr [cocoa butter] on your skin and see why it's better.

   c. Nothing performs like a Saab.

   d. Reach toothbrush. Designed like a dental instrument.

   e. Rise is thicker than the leading foam.

   f. The Three Mile Island "event" will do for nuclear power what the Hindenburg did for zeppelins.

   g. After the Three Mile Island accident, I intend to vote against any politicians who say "Maybe" to nuclear power, regardless of their opinions on all other matters. What good is a chicken in every pot if the broth is radioactive?

   h. Strengthening the CIA is a step in the right direction. If we're so intent on being the world's babysitter, we need to know what the kids are doing.

   i. Wake up to an ocean-fresh shave. Old Spice makes every shave smooth sailing.

   j. Unless we are careful, the computer may soon warp our thinking abilities as a nation, just as the automobile has withered our walking ability.

2. Analyze and evaluate the Accutron watch ad.

3. Bring to class for discussion an ad that uses comparison or analogy for persuasive purposes.

4. Write a comparison paper, using one of the following, in which you argue the superiority of one over the other:

   a. two songs
   b. two political candidates
   c. two similar movies
   d. two talk-show hosts
   e. two paintings

   f. two cars
   g. two sports commentators
   h. two magazines
   i. two products
   j. two TV shows

5. Discuss in class how the analogies in the following proverbs might be extended for a persuasive essay:

   a. Anger is a stone cast at a wasp's nest.
   b. Courage is fire; bullying is smoke.
   c. Confidence is a plant of slow growth.
   d. Lost credit is like a broken mirror.
   e. Gratitude is a heavy burden.

6. Write an argument, using a pro-and-con format, on one of the following topics:

   a. abolition of capital punishment
   b. motion-picture censorship
   c. federal control of the oil industry
   d. state or federal ownership of all utilities
   e. strict wage and price controls on gasoline
   f. nuclear power plants
   g. keeping or doing away with the 55 mph speed limit

7. You marry young. Your spouse is critically injured shortly after in an automobile accident. On his or her deathbed, your spouse asks you to promise not to remarry. Less than a year later, you fall in love again. Give arguments (reasons) for and against having to honor your promise.

Arguing From Cause and Effect

When you reason from **cause to effect** or from **effect to cause,** you note that certain actions produce certain effects and that certain effects are produced by certain causes. If, in writing an argument, you start off with causes and move to effects, you advance ideas deductively. The following public-service message that appeared in a local newspaper uses this method of development.

Shoplifting Is a Crime

Cause Shoplifting a 20¢ candy bar or a $1 lipstick doesn't sound like a serious crime. But if the shoplifter is caught, it will add up to more than $1.20. Storeowners are no longer giving a "second chance"—not even for a candy bar, and *an arrest for shoplifting can follow you the rest of your life.*

Effects Convicted shoplifters are denied admission into many colleges and are barred from holding government or bonded jobs. Professions that require special licensing, like law or insurance, are closed to them. They can't even get a mortgage, loan, or credit card. What can be even more tragic than the jail sentence or fine is the teenager delivered in a police car to his home or the business executive earning $25,000 a year who has to explain to his family why he shoplifted a couple of ties.

No matter how little the item costs, shoplifting is stealing.

If you first describe certain effects, results, or consequences in writing an argument, and then move to the causes or agents that produced them, you advance ideas inductively. This ad by Caterpillar Tractor Company, which appeared in *Time* magazine on July 3, 1978, proceeds from effect to cause:

The Arizona Floods Cost Less Than the Copper Depression!

The March 1978 floods, dangerous and overwhelming as they were, caused a statewide property loss of 24 million dollars. But there is a copper industry depression in Arizona that caused far greater losses.

Effects One effect of the copper industry depression is the loss of more than 46 million dollars in wages last year alone. Another is that Arizona businesses lost more than 39 million dollars in copper industry purchases. A third is that state and local governments lost more than 9 million dollars in taxes. A fourth effect is that one out of every four Arizona copper workers is unemployed. And there is no end in sight.

Causes   There are two main causes of the depression. The first is that foreign copper is cheaper than Arizona copper because of lower wages and lower environmental standards. American industry is buying copper from Chile, Peru, and other nations. An environmental tariff is one solution. A second cause is our own governmental policy. America should maintain a copper stockpile for defense purposes. It is not doing so. Yet its purchases would help.

Here's something you can do. Our statistics for Arizona's copper depression are verified. They are likely new to you. We suggest you send them to your state legislator. They may be new to him, too.

Faulty Causal Reasoning

Faulty causal reasoning, sometimes called by its Latin name, *post hoc, ergo propter hoc* ("after this, therefore because of this"), consists in *assuming that because one event comes before another in time, the first event is the cause of the other.* It is true that causes come before effects, but it does not follow that because one occurrence precedes another, there is necessarily a causal relation between them.

This form of reasoning is sometimes found in political arguments. It goes something like this: "After the Carter Administration came into power, the country suffered an energy shortage. Therefore, the policies of the Carter Administration are responsible for the energy crisis."

Superstitions are based on faulty causal reasoning. "Pretty soon," said Huckleberry Finn, "a spider went crawling up my shoulder, and I flipped it off and it lit in the candle; and before I could budge, it was all shriveled up. I didn't need anybody to tell me that that was an awful bad sign and would fetch me some bad luck, so I was scared and 'most shook the clothes off of me."

Exercises

1. Evaluate these causal arguments:

   a. Smoking causes cancer. Don't smoke.

   b. You take away gasoline and you destroy the family.

   c. Antiscience and anti-intellectual activity is much more widespread than even a few years ago. There are ten times as many American college students enrolled in astrology courses as in astrophysics courses.

   d. If thousands of Catholics are turning to Pentecostalism, it is because they miss the ecstasy and mysticism of the old Mass.

   e. Last Saturday there were more people in line for confession than I have seen in years. Your story must have scared the hell out of them.

   f. We figure if we can make driving safe for these people, we'll be making driving safe for everybody.

   g. Like anyone who has been in party politics for a long time, our senator is tainted with ideological impurity.

   h. Your hair is a mess, and your face is as red as a beet. You must have gotten drunk last night.

   i. Listerine antienzyme toothpaste offers you continuous protection against tooth decay.

   j. Those students who type their themes get better grades than those who do not.

2. Bring to class several magazine ads that use cause-and-effect arguments for persuasive purposes, and discuss their effectiveness.

3. Write an essay, using cause-and-effect reasoning, in which you argue that television shows which depict physical violence cause violence in everyday life.

4. Imagine that because of an Arab boycott of oil in the Middle East or because of a dwindling supply of gasoline, Congress has voted to limit drastically the private ownership or use of cars to conserve energy. Write an argument in which you discuss the effects of such a policy.

5. Write an essay in which you argue against teenage marriages, citing harmful effects of early marriages.

6. Write a letter to your campus newspaper, in which you argue that doing away with final examinations will have beneficial (or negative) effects.

7. Write a persuasive essay, using a topic of your own choice, in which you argue from cause to effect or from effect to cause.

Persuasion as an Aim:

The Syllogism and the Enthymeme

Chapter 9

Persuasion as an Aim:
The Syllogism and the Enthymeme

If a superstitious friend comes up to you and says, "I shall be unlucky today, because today is Friday the thirteenth," you might be amused at his superstitious beliefs, but you can't fault his logic. He has been engaged in a process called deductive thinking. The superstition is, of course, arrived at inductively. But the superstitious friend is applying that superstition to a particular case, and so is reasoning deductively. **Deductive thinking** is *the process of reasoning from a general statement to a logical conclusion.* The syllogism is one form that deductive thinking takes.

The Categorical Syllogism

The **syllogism** is a *mode of thinking in which you reason from two statements, or propositions, called premises, to a third statement, or proposition, called the conclusion.* A **premise** is *a statement that serves as the basis of an argument.* An argument, in the form of a syllogism, looks like this:

> All people are basically honest.
> Joan is a person.
> Therefore, Joan is basically honest.

The first sentence is called the **major premise.** In an argument, the major premise is usually drawn from experience or assumed to be self-evident. The second sentence is called the **minor premise.** The minor premise states a new idea. It is a particular instance of the previously stated general idea. It needs to be supported with evidence. The third sentence is the **conclusion.** The conclusion follows logically from the two premises.

There are four kinds of statements that enter into a syllogism:

1. A *universal affirmative* statement (All people are basically honest. Everyone watches television.)

2. A *universal negative* statement (No person is basically honest. Not everyone watches television.)

3. A *particular affirmative* statement (Some people are basically honest. Some people watch television.)

4. A *particular negative* statement (Some people are not basically honest. Some people do not watch television.)

You can recognize a universal statement because it contains words such as *all, every, everyone,* and *everybody.* A particular statement will have words such as *some, many,* and *a few* in it. A negative statement uses words such as *no, not, not any, never, nothing,* and the like. An affirmative statement is one in which the predicate asserts that something is true of the subject

The simplest form of a statement that goes into a syllogism is the **categorical proposition.** (The *categorical syllogism* is so called because its major premise is a categorical proposition.) It consists of a subject, a copula (a form of the verb *to be*), and a predicate term. It has the following form:

Subject Term	Copula	Predicate Term
All women	are	beautiful.
No woman	is	beautiful.

Logicians use variations of this form, with the verb *to be,* because it is easy to spot the terms. The wording of the proposition below is found more in speech and writing. But because it contains no linking verb, it is harder to pick out the terms:

All Europeans appreciate jazz.

If you rewrite the sentence, however, to include a form of the verb *to be*, the terms are easier to pick out:

All Europeans   are   people who appreciate jazz.

In addition to having three sentences, a syllogism contains three terms: a major term, a middle term, and a minor term. In the following syllogism, the **major term** is the predicate term in the major premise and in the conclusion *(appreciate jazz)*. The **middle term** is the common term in each of the premises *(all Europeans, European)*. The **minor term** *(Marcello)* appears in the minor premise, and it is the subject term of the conclusion:

All Europeans appreciate jazz.
Marcello is a European.
Therefore, Marcello appreciates jazz.

A syllogism is **valid** if the relationship among the terms is logical and if it follows certain set rules. In the above syllogism, there is a common term in each of the first two sentences *(all Europeans, European)* which allows us to connect the ideas in each sentence:

All Europeans appreciate jazz.
Marcello is a European.

This term drops out in the conclusion, and the remaining terms combine to form a sentence:

Marcello appreciates jazz.

If the major premise had read *"Most Europeans appreciate jazz,"* you would have had to qualify your conclusion with a word such as *probably:*

Most Europeans appreciate jazz.
Marcello is a European.
Therefore, Marcello *probably* appreciates jazz.

Here is another valid syllogism, with a negative major premise:

No Europeans appreciate jazz.
Marcello is a European.
Therefore, Marcello does not appreciate jazz.

Rules for a Valid Syllogism

1. You can have only *three terms* in a valid syllogism. The following syllogism is not valid because it contains four terms:

   All women are *independent creatures.*
   No girls are *servile.*
   Therefore, no girls are independent creatures.

   Because there are four terms *(all women, independent creatures, no girls, servile),* there are no logical links to allow the writer to go from one sentence to another.

2. You must be sure to distribute the middle term at least once. A middle term is distributed if it refers to all or most of the individuals in a class *(all, every, most, no, not any).* A middle term is undistributed if it refers to particular individuals in a class *(some, a few, many).* The following syllogism is not valid because the middle term *(some women, woman)* is not distributed at least once. What is true of some women is not necessarily true of Joan:

   Some women are vain creatures.
   Joan is a *woman.*
   Therefore, Joan is a vain creature.

3. You cannot extend a term in the conclusion if it has not already been extended in the premise:

   All men are vain creatures.
   Some Arizonans are men.
   Therefore, *most Arizonans* are vain creatures.

   In the above syllogism, the term *most Arizonans* in the conclusion is an extension of the term *some Arizonans* in the minor premise. Therefore, the syllogism is not valid.

4. You cannot draw a conclusion from two particular premises. The following syllogism is not valid because the major and minor premises are particular statements:

Some women are vain.
Some Arizonans are women.
Therefore, some Arizonans are vain.

5. You cannot draw a conclusion from two negative premises. The syllogism that follows is not valid because the conclusion follows from two negative premises:

No men are vain.
No Arizonans are men.
Therefore, no Arizonans are vain.

6. Finally, if one of your premises is negative, then your conclusion must be negative. The syllogism below is not valid because the major premise is negative, but the conclusion is affirmative:

All women are *not* vain.
Joan is a woman.
Therefore, Joan is vain.

A syllogism is **valid,** then, if the form is such that you can logically deduce a conclusion from the premises. A syllogism is **true** if certain facts and evidence make the statements true.

In deducing conclusions, sometimes you can go immediately from one proposition to another, without a middle term. Common sense should help you in doing this. For example, what's true of the universal must be true of the particular. If it is true that all people are basically honest, then it must be true that some people are basically honest. If it is true that no people are basically honest, then it must be true that some people are not basically honest.

Similarly, contradictory statements cannot both be true. If it is true that all people are basically honest, then the contradictory statements, some people are not basically honest, must be false. If it is true that no people are basically honest, then the contradictory statement, some people are basically honest, must be false.

Contrary statements cannot both be true. If it is true that all men are basically good, then it can't be true that no men are basically good. If it is true that some men are basically good, no deduction can be made about the statement that some men are not basically good.

The Hypothetical Syllogism

The **hypothetical syllogism** has a conditional proposition (a sentence containing an *if* clause) as its major premise. This premise expresses a hypothetical (*uncertain* or *conjectural*) relationship of causation or resemblance:

If the rain continues, the bridge will be lost.

In a conditional proposition, the *if* clause is called the **antecedent.** The second clause (the clause to which the "condition" is applied) is called the **consequent.**

The hypothetical syllogism, like the categorical syllogism, consists of three propositions: the major premise containing the *if* clause, the minor premise, and the conclusion:

If the rain continues, the bridge will be lost.
The rain will continue.
Therefore, the bridge will be lost.

Rules for the Hypothetical Syllogism

1. If you affirm the truth of the antecedent (the *if* clause) with the minor premise, then the consequent (stated in the main clause) necessarily follows, and your conclusion is valid:

   If you inject heroin, you will die.
   You inject heroin.
   Therefore, you will die.

2. If you affirm the truth of the consequent, it does not necessarily follow that the antecedent is true, and your conclusion is invalid:

If you inject heroin, you will die.
You will die.
Therefore, you inject heroin.

3. If you deny the consequent, you may draw a valid conclusion. But be certain to make both the minor premise and the conclusion negative statements:

If you inject heroin, you will die.
You will not die.
Therefore, you do not inject heroin.

4. If you deny the antecedent, then your conclusion is not valid:

If you inject heroin, you will die.
You do not inject heroin.
Therefore, you will not die.

The Disjunctive Syllogism

The **disjunctive syllogism** has a disjunctive proposition (one that gives alternatives, such as *either . . . or . . .*) as its major premise. A disjunctive statement is one that sets forth alternative possibilities:

Either you are mortal, or you are immortal.

Like both the categorical syllogism and the hypothetical syllogism, the disjunctive syllogism contains three sentences: the major premise (which has the words *either, or*), the minor premise, and the conclusion:

Either you are mortal, or you are immortal.
You are not immortal.
Therefore, you are mortal.

In speech and in writing, the conclusion of a disjunctive syllogism is sometimes omitted:

Either you are coming, or you are not.
You are not coming?

Rules for the Disjunctive Syllogism

1. When formulating a disjunctive proposition, be careful to set up alternatives that are mutually exclusive and therefore contradictory. In the following example, the alternatives are not mutually exclusive:

   Either she is a singer or a dancer.
   She is not a singer.
   Therefore, she must be a dancer.

   Actually, she could be both a singer and a dancer, or she could be a musician or an actress. But if you recast the major premise to read

   Either she is a singer, or she is not a singer,

   then the alternatives are mutually exclusive.

2. Be sure to include all of the possibilities in a disjunctive syllogism. Failure to do so destroys its validity, as in the following example:

   Either excessive heat or excessive moisture killed her roses.
   Excessive heat did not kill her roses.
   Therefore, it must have been excessive moisture.

   All that is needed to destroy this conclusion is to show that other causes, such as insects, heavy winds, frost, or hail, might have been responsible for killing the roses.

Exercises

1. Analyze the following syllogisms and comment on their validity or lack of validity:

   a. Those who succeed in life work hard.
      Everyone is anxious to succeed in life.
      Everyone works hard.

b. All X is Y.
   Some Y is Z.
   Therefore, some Z is X.

c. No fish are mammals.
   No fish are birds.
   No birds are mammals.

d. Some soldiers get killed in battle.
   Some civilians get killed in battle.
   Some civilians are soldiers.

e. Some X is Y.
   All Y is Z.
   Some Z is X.

f. All lawyers are articulate people.
   Some doctors are not articulate people.
   Lawyers are not doctors.

g. Because some people are honest,
   and honest people want to avoid jail,
   some people want to avoid jail.

h. No sensible people are smokers.
   Some Americans are sensible people.
   Some Americans are smokers.

i. All left-wing liberals are radicals.
   All radicals are communist.
   Therefore, all left-wing liberals are communist.

j. Switzerland loves freedom.
   I love freedom.
   Therefore, I am Switzerland.

k. All Martians are green.
   Jeffrey is not green.
   Therefore, Jeffrey is not a Martian.

l. No Chinese are North Americans.
   All Americans are North Americans.
   All Americans are Chinese.

m. All drunken drivers are potentially dangerous.
No thinking person is a drunken driver.
No thinking person is potentially dangerous.

n. All price-fixing is immoral.
Some immoral actions are illegal.
Some price-fixing is illegal.

o. Since only lunatics want to go to the moon,
this man cannot be a lunatic,
because he wants to stay here on Earth.

p. If it rains, I will get wet.
It rains,
Therefore, I will get wet.

q. Unless you stop, I will get mad.
You will not stop.
Therefore, I will get mad.

r. Either Hitler is dead or he is hiding in Argentina.
He is not hiding in Argentina.
Therefore, he must be dead.

s. Either his shoes are Italian-made or they are British-made.
They are Italian-made.
Therefore, they are not British-made.

t. Obviously, whales have warm blood.
They are mammals.

The Enthymeme

The **enthymeme** is *a shortened form of the syllogism in which one of the premises or the conclusion is missing.* It is the form usually encountered in speech or writing.

Here is an enthymeme in which the major premise is missing:

The price of meat will go up
because of the poor corn crop.

The conclusion is stated in the main clause: "The price of meat will go up." The minor premise is stated in the *because* clause: "because of the poor corn crop." The major premise, which is missing, can easily be supplied:

> The price of meat will go up whenever the corn crop is poor.
> The corn crop is poor.
> Therefore, the price of meat will go up.

Here is an enthymeme in which the conclusion is missing:

> Either Chris Evert or Virginia Wade will win the match.
> Chris Evert's chances were lost when she sprained her ankle.

The conclusion of this enthymeme, like the major premise of the previous enthymeme, can easily be supplied:

> Therefore, Virginia Wade will win the match.

In writing, enthymemes take various forms. They may take the form of a complex sentence with a *because* or *since* clause; a compound sentence joined by words such as *therefore, consequently, so,* and *for* ("The corn crop is poor; therefore, the price of meat will go up"); or two sentences placed together ("The corn crop is poor. The price of meat will go up.").

Enthymemes, like the syllogisms they replace, can be categorical, hypothetical, or disjunctive. A good example of a hypothetical enthymeme in a recent ad for Kent cigarettes depicts two cigarette packages with the following text:

> Come for the filter.
> You'll stay for the taste.

If you reword the sentences slightly, you get this conditional enthymeme:

> If you come for the filter,
> you'll stay for the taste.

Presumably, the reader will affirm the antecedent and be led to accept the inevitable conclusion.

A recent ad for Texaco oil company uses a similar strategy. The illustration pictures an oil rig in the Gulf of Mexico with this caption:

> If we don't go into deep water,
> we'll all be in hot water.

Besides the argument embedded in the enthymeme, there is a larger argument implicit in the entire ad: Drilling in deep water costs money. We are in hot water because we're dependent on imported oil. We will be less dependent on imported oil if we explore more offshore sites. But leasing costs and expenses are higher for offshore wells than they are on land. Nevertheless, Texaco is continuing to drill deeper wells, literally getting into deep water. Of course, the ad doesn't say that the costs will be passed on to the consumer, but the argument is clearly designed to placate customers who are concerned over the increasing cost of gasoline and the high profits of the oil companies.

The disjunctive enthymeme, like the hypothetical enthymeme, can be found in many magazine ads, where it is used very effectively. Whatever one may think about the validity of the enthymeme in the following ad for True cigarettes, there is no doubt about its effectiveness. The picture depicts a man sitting on a log with his bare feet in the sand, holding a True cigarette. The text reads as follows:

> After kicking around everything I'd heard about smoking,
> I decided to either quit or smoke True.
> I smoke True.

It's pretty obvious that the alternatives are not mutually exclusive. Yet the smoker seems to be given only two choices: quitting or smoking True. If he decides to smoke (what he has heard, of course, is that smoking is dangerous to his health), then he could smoke any kind of cigarette, not just True. But the alternatives are set up in such a way that if he decides to smoke, he must smoke True. The complete argument, reconstructed, goes something like this: "I've considered seriously everything I've heard about the dangers of smoking, but I enjoy smoking, so I've decided to continue. True cigarettes have the lowest tar and nicotine content. That's why I smoke True."

To test the validity of an enthymeme, simply rewrite it, putting it into the form of a syllogism. Then follow the same procedures you would follow to determine if a syllogism is valid.

One of the most important errors to guard against in using enthymemes is *hasty generalization in the major premise*. Ordinarily, in a syllogism, the major premise is there to be examined and evaluated. But in an enthymeme, the major premise must be assumed by the reader or listener.

The following is an example of a statement attributed to the Republican senator from California, S. I. Hayakawa, in the early summer of 1979, when long lines began to form at the gas pumps and some Congressmen began to cry for decontrol of gas prices:

"Let gas go to $1.50, even $2.00 per gallon.
A lot of the poor don't need gas because they are not working."

Needless to say, Senator Hayakawa's remarks were greeted with public indignation. What is missing from this statement is the major premise:

Major Premise:
Minor Premise: They are not working.
Conclusion: A lot of the poor don't need gas.

Reconstructed, the chain of reasoning goes something like this: "Anyone who is not working does not need gas. The poor are not working. Therefore, the poor don't need gas." The argument is valid, but not true because the assumed premise is faulty. The poor may need gas so they can obtain jobs. And, of course, all of us need gas for reasons other than to go to work: to go to the grocery, to visit friends, to run errands, perhaps to make an emergency trip to the hospital, and so on.

Exercises

1. Supply the missing proposition in each of the following enthymemes. Then determine if each is valid or not.

a. If you're Spanish or Italian, you may as well resign yourself to being emotional.

b. When we were in New Orleans, we went to the French Quarter. All of the architecture there is excellent.

c. Most of Fellini's pictures are offbeat, so *Amarcord* is probably offbeat too.

d. Smith must be crooked; all of those politicians are.

e. These new clothes are really expensive, so I refuse to buy at Frederick's Department Store, because all their clothes are expensive.

f. If you read about it in the local paper, don't believe it.

g. There is no sense in paying high prices for coffee, since it is well known that coffee has no nutritional value.

h. Because they are gas guzzlers, most large cars are not very economical.

2. Convert the following categorical syllogisms into enthymemes:

a. All criminals ought to be prosecuted.
   Price fixers are criminals.
   Therefore, price fixers ought to be prosecuted.

b. All nutritional foods are healthy.
   Sugar is not a nutritional food.
   Sugar is not healthy.

c. All excellent movies are works of art.
   No Westerns are works of art.
   No Westerns are excellent movies.

d. Most hard drugs are habit-forming.
   Heroin is a hard drug.
   Heroin is habit-forming.

e. No man wants to be untruthful.
   Michael is a man.
   Michael wants to be truthful.

3. Bring to class magazine ads that use enthymemes, hypothetical syllogisms, or disjunctive syllogisms to sell a product or make a point. Then analyze the arguments in class.

Planning an Argument

You seldom state arguments in complete syllogisms, although recently I have come across an ad for Snowdrift shortening that uses the deductive sequence of a syllogism to make its selling point:

What Every Good Cook Knows

Just a little difference in ingredients makes a big difference in cooking results. Snowdrift is just a little lighter than ordinary shortening— and that can make the big difference in giving your family lighter, more digestible foods.

The major premise offers benefits that have a general appeal to the reader. ("Just a little difference in ingredients makes a big difference in cooking results"). The minor premise—the proof part—gives supporting details in the form of product attributes ("Snowdrift is just a little lighter than ordinary shortening"). The proof part is flexible. You can use it to enumerate several product attributes or, as in this ad, one or two. The conclusion applies directly to the reader ("and that can make the big difference in giving your family lighter, more digestible foods").

The advantage of the deductive sequence is that it enables the writer to analyze the proposition carefully and to pick out the facts that will be most effective with the reader. The deductive order gives the major premise or assertion first and then backs it up with evidence, explanations, and logical reasoning.

Most arguments, however, are based on the enthymeme rather than the syllogism. *The logical structure of an argument consists of a series of enthymemes that exhibit the framework of the chain of reasoning and the evidence upon which the argument is based.*

To write an argument based on the enthymeme, begin with the conclusion of the syllogism as your thesis. Then add the minor premise to it in the form of a *because* clause. The minor premise is the proof part of your argument. You must support it with the kinds of evidence considered in the previous chapter: facts, personal opinions, attributes, descriptive details, examples, statistics, testimony and other evidence from authority, narrative examples, comparisons, analogies, causes, and effects.

The following example, adapted from a public declaration by musicians and celebrities such as John Denver, Art Garfunkel, Mia Farrow, Israel Horovitz, John Simon, Stevie Wonder, and Howard Johnson, who oppose nuclear power plants, is a good example of a thesis in the form of an enthymeme:

> Nuclear power should be banned
> because it represents a grave threat to life on this planet.

In this thesis statement, the *main clause* states the conclusion of the enthymeme ("Nuclear power should be banned") and the *because* clause states the minor premise. Put into the form of an incomplete syllogism, the statement reads:

Major Premise:
Minor Premise: Nuclear power represents a grave threat to life on this planet.
Conclusion: Nuclear power should be banned.

Taking the process one step further, you can easily supply a major premise so that the syllogism is complete:

Major Premise: Any form of power that represents a grave threat to life on this planet should be banned.
Minor Premise: Nuclear power represents a grave threat to life on this planet.
Conclusion: Therefore, nuclear power should be banned.

Why not write an argument in the form of a syllogism, you might ask at this point? Well, you could write an argument in this way if you so desired. But in many arguments, you don't need to state the major premise, because the major premise usually contains assumptions that you already share with your reader. It is the common ground from which your argument starts. You don't need to prove the statement that "any form of power that represents a grave threat to life on this planet should be banned." Common sense and the law of self-preservation will tell you that none of us wants to endanger our lives. More important than explicitly stating the major premise in this argument is setting forth the conclusion that you want your readers to accept. And they will more readily accept your conclusion if your reasoning is sound and your evidence is substantial.

Stating your thesis in enthymeme form will spell out for your reader your specific intention. Second, it will help you as a writer to keep your intention clearly in mind. Third, it will help you to organize the sections of your essay more effectively.

You can expand the enthymeme which constitutes your thesis statement in a number of ways. One way is to state your proposition and its proof (the conclusion and the minor premise in the form of a *because* clause) and then add to your main reason *subordinate reasons* in the form of additional *because* clauses or phrases. These subordinate ideas will be the proof of the main idea, and each subordinate idea must be supported with evidence (facts, examples, testimony of witnesses, opinions of authorities, and so forth). The resulting paradigm for the proposition on nuclear power would look something like this:

Thesis:	Nuclear power should be banned
Main Reason:	because it represents a grave threat to life on this planet,
Sub. Reason:	because of the unresolved question of nuclear-waste storage,
Sub. Reason:	because of the failure of the emergency core-cooling system in tests,
Sub. Reason:	because of the danger of theft or accident during the transportation of nuclear materials, and
Sub. Reason:	because of the continuing rise in incidence of cancer, leukemia, and genetic disease, which are known to be radiation-related.

This paradigm is in the shape of a single sentence, but for purposes of writing an argument, the thesis and the main reason could go together to form your thesis statement ("Nuclear power should be banned because it represents a grave threat to life on this planet"). Then each subordinate reason could be put into sentence form, each sentence marking a division of your essay. Naturally, each of the subordinate propositions has to be supported by evidence of some kind. So the thesis and the main reason (the enthymeme) constitute the proposition to be proved, and the supporting reasons constitute the proof of your argument. A more idealized version of the paradigm would look like this:

Introduction (includes thesis and main reason)
Reason 1 (plus supporting evidence)
Reason 2 (plus supporting evidence)
Reason 3 (plus supporting evidence)
Reason 4 (plus supporting evidence)
Reason 5, 6, 7 . . . (plus supporting evidence)
Conclusion (application of above to reader)

Another way to expand an enthymeme for organizational purposes is to state your thesis in a single sentence. Then, instead of adding to it a single main reason, which has to be supported by subordinate reasons, you add a series of parallel reasons—all of which, presumably, are main reasons to support your assertion.

Here is an example of a thesis statement, taken from a recent article in *Esquire* magazine about an attempt to abolish the fraternity system at Dartmouth College. Incensed by what he believed to be immoral and uncivilized behavior on the part of some fraternity brothers, English professor James Epperson made a stirring speech to the Dartmouth faculty on November 6, 1978, in which he urged the college's board of trustees to ban fraternities from the campus. The outline of his argument goes something like this:

Fraternities should be abolished
    because they are racist,
    because they encourage destructive behavior,
    because they are anti-intellectual,
    because they encourage drunkenness, and
    because they are sexist.

What looks like a single enthymeme here is really a series of connected enthymemes, with the independent clause ("Fraternities should be abolished") serving as the conclusion of each enthymeme and each *because* clause serving as a minor premise:

Minor Premise: Fraternities are racist.
Conclusion: Therefore, they should be abolished.

Minor Premise: Fraternities encourage destructive behavior.
Conclusion: Therefore, they should be abolished.

Minor Premise: Fraternities are anti-intellectual.
Conclusion: Therefore, they should be abolished.

Minor Premise: Fraternities encourage drunkenness.
Conclusion: Therefore, they should be abolished.

Minor Premise: Fraternities are sexist.
Conclusion: Therefore, they should be abolished.

If you put these enthymemes into an outline, you get the following paradigm:

Thesis: Fraternities should be abolished.
Reason: They are racist.
Reason: They encourage destructive behavior.
Reason: They are anti-intellectual.
Reason: They encourage drunkenness.
Reason: They are sexist.

In its more abstract form, the paradigm would look like this:

Introduction (includes the thesis or proposition to be proved)
Reason 1 (plus supporting evidence)
Reason 2 (plus supporting evidence)
Reason 3 (plus supporting evidence)
Reason 4 (plus supporting evidence)
Reason 5 (plus supporting evidence)
Conclusion (application of above to reader)

The paradigm can then be used as the basis of the essay:

Fraternities should be abolished because they are racist, they encourage destructive behavior, they are anti-intellectual, they encourage drunkenness, and they are sexist.

Fraternities are racist. They do not encourage blacks and other minorities to join.

Fraternities encourage destructive behavior. Their members are uncivilized. Theft and vandalism are frequent among their members.

Fraternities are anti-intellectual. Their members go to college to have a good time and to make social connections rather than to enrich their minds. Those who do study are scorned.

Fraternities encourage drunkenness. Heavy drinking is the norm. Then, when fraternity brothers get drunk, their drunkenness is used to justify vandalism and other forms of offensive behavior.

Finally, fraternities are sexist. Almost all of them exclude women from being members. But even worse, they are actively and aggressively sexist. Women who walk along Fraternity Row at night must put up with obscene proposals. At fraternity parties, some women are scorned, ridiculed, and physically intimidated. Fraternity brothers who "make out" are frequently required to give detailed descriptions of what went on.

For these reasons, fraternities should be abolished.

This is not a complete argument, to be sure. The argument needs a more suitable introduction and a conclusion, and each of the reasons in the respective paragraphs needs more supporting details as proof of the argument. But the model does show how the enthymeme can be used to construct effective arguments.

In the beginning stages of learning to write deductive arguments, you might want to follow these paradigms closely. Ultimately, however, what is more important is that you make the process of deductive thinking habitual, so that in your written arguments, the paradigms will be a direct result of your thought processes.

I said earlier that arguments are seldom stated in complete syllogisms because the major premise usually contains assumptions that you share with your reader, and therefore they need not be stated explicitly. But what if your reader does not share the assumptions in your major premise? They you might want to use the syllogism rather than the enthymeme to present your argument. In that case, you would want to present supporting evidence for both your major and your minor premise.

The following syllogism is one formulation of a very traditional argument for the existence of God:

Major Premise: Anything that displays design, order, and harmony must have some intelligence directing it.

Minor Premise: The world displays design, order, and harmony.

Conclusion: Therefore, the world is the work of an intelligent being in the universe.

It can be embedded in the larger patterning of an essay to produce the following argument:

The Argument From Design

The idea that the universe exhibits an orderly design and that this design is proof of a purposeful intelligence in the universe is exemplified by the psalmist who sang, "The heavens declare the glory of God, and the firmament showeth his handywork." Yet modern men and women, in an atmosphere of technical accomplishments and what might be called the new hedonism, often have doubts about the existence of God. To many modern thinkers, the existence of God has become the central religious problem of the twentieth century. In view of modern people's skepticism, is there any evidence that God exists? To many thinkers, proofs of God's existence have always been available, and many of these proofs are just as relevant today as they were in years gone by. One of the most popular of these proofs is the argument from design. The argument goes like this.

Anything that displays design, order, and harmony must have some intelligence directing it. Can there be a design without a designer? If you were asked to give an account of anything man-made, such as a car, a building, or a machine, you could not give a complete account if you omitted the maker. Similarly, if you were to try to give an account of the workings of the universe, of its organic regularities and its orderly structures and processes, you would have to conclude that the principle of order is an intelligence operating and directing it for some purpose toward some intelligible goal.

Order itself must have a cause. A work of art does not produce itself, but is the result of the intentions of an artist. Language is a formal creation in which a writer imposes form on his or her materials. A pool player striking a ball can be said to be operating with a purpose. Everything has a purpose. Why are there doors and windows at regular intervals in the walls of a house? Why are the streets of cities laid out in orderly designs? Why is the produce in supermarkets arranged in such an orderly fashion? What is the probability of an orderly structure in the universe coming into existence by chance? An intelligent order in the universe is the work of an intelligent being.

Everywhere, *the world displays design, order, and harmony.* The planets revolve around the sun in the same plane. The simplest molecules contain several thousand atoms, all intricately organized. The universe is an intricate and orderly balance of rhythms, forces, and processes. Numbers, scales, times, crystal forms, symbolic forms, sentences, and languages of all kinds reveal order and complexity. Order is a necessary condition for anything in the universe to function: the human body, plants, machines, athletic teams. Recurrent features in the world repeat themselves over and over again: the patterns of leaves, the colors in sunsets, the symmetry of plants and flowers, the shapes of birds, the odor of roses, the rhythm of waves.

When things in the universe show orderly progression, design, and harmony, they cannot be said to do so of their own nature. It follows, therefore, that this order is a matter either of chance or of design. But as you have seen from numerous examples, whatever comes about in this world is not the result of accident. *Therefore, the world is the work of an intelligent being in the universe.*

Let us assume, now, that your readers do share the assumptions in your major premise. In that case, you turn your syllogism into an enthymeme:

> The world must be the work of an intelligent being in the universe because it displays design, order, and harmony.

Then you use the enthymeme as the thesis in your argument and add the supporting evidence. But this time, let us consider possible objections to the argument and include them near the end of the essay:

> The idea that the universe exhibits an orderly design and that this design is proof of a purposeful intelligence in the universe is exemplified by the psalmist who sang, "The heavens declare the glory of God, and the firmament showeth his handywork." Yet modern man, in an atmosphere of technical accomplishments and what might be called the new hedonism, often has doubts about the existence of God. In view of modern people's skepticism, is there any evidence that God exists? To many thinkers, proofs of God's existence have always been available, and many of these proofs are just as relevant today as they were in years gone by. One of the most popular of these proofs is the argument from design, which states that *the world must be the work of an intelligent being in the universe because it displays design, order, and harmony.*
>
> Everywhere, *the world displays signs of design, order, and harmony.* The planets revolve around the sun in the same plane. The simplest molecules contain several thousand atoms, all intricately organized. The universe is an intricate and orderly balance of rhythms, forces, and processes. Numbers, scales, times, crystal forms, groups, symbolic forms, sentences, and languages of all kinds reveal order and complexity. Order is a necessary condition for anything in the universe to function: the human body, plants, machines, athletic teams. There are recurrent features in the world which repeat themselves over and over again: the patterns of leaves, the colors in sunsets, the symmetry of plants and flowers, the shapes of birds, the odor of roses, the rhythm of waves.
>
> But some skeptics have serious objections about the argument from design. If the universe exhibits order and harmony, they say, it also exhibits an absence of order and harmony. Does not evil exist in the world? Are there not natural disasters and calamities such as floods, storms, tornadoes, cyclones, and earthquakes? The answer to these questions is that for order and harmony to exist in the universe, it is not necessary for it to be detectable in all parts of the universe. Besides, in order for us to experience disorder, we must first have had to experience some kind of order. If you were to go into a dormitory in which there were a hundred beds and see one unmade bed, would you necessarily conclude that the one unmade bed proves

that disorder is characteristic of that dormitory? What is disorder, anyway? According to some scientists, disorder is the clash of uncoordinated orders, not the absence of order.

When things in the universe, then, show signs of orderly progression, design, and harmony, they cannot be said to do so of their own nature. It follows, therefore, that this order is a matter either of chance or of design, or the product of a designer who had a particular purpose in mind. But as we have seen from numerous examples and analogies, and as you know from personal experience, whatever comes about in this world is not the result of accident. *Therefore, God must be the designer of the universe.*

Exercises

1. Discuss the essay on fraternities. From your experience, give supporting evidence for the thesis "fraternities should be abolished." Then take the opposite point of view, that fraternities should *not* be abolished, and give supporting evidence for your opinion.

2. Bring to class magazine ads that use deductive arguments to sell goods and services. Then discuss the arguments, including the thesis and support.

3. Bring to class a letter to the editor that uses deductive reasoning.

4. Complete the following theses by adding at least three reasons in the form of *because* clauses. Then, for class discussion, choose one or two and consider the evidence you might use to support each reason:

   a. Cheating is wrong.
   b. All wars are immoral.
   c. English is the most valuable subject in the curriculum.
   d. Personality is more important to success than brains.
   e. Gambling should (should not) be legalized.
   f. _____ is a lousy movie.

5. Assume you believe that smokers have a right to smoke in public places:

    a. Write a dialogue that might take place as you try to convince a non-smoking friend of your position.

    b. Write an ad a cigarette manufacturer might use to convince the general public that smoking should be allowed in restaurants.

    c. Write a letter to your parents (who won't let you smoke in their house) which persuades them to let you smoke when you go out with them in public.

6. Write an essay on one of the following. (These topics can also be used for class discussion.) In your essay, add to the thesis at least three reasons in the form of *because* clauses, or include one main reason and several subordinate reasons:

    a. There should (should not) be complete and open honesty between prospective marriage partners before marriage. (In other words, you must tell your fiancé all that you did before marriage.)

    b. Final examinations should (should not) be abolished.

    c. Killing animals for sport should (should not) be prohibited by law.

    d. Shows that depict violence should be banned from television.

    e. Smoking in public places should be prohibited.

    f. Minorities should be given job preferences.

    g. Price controls should (should not) be lifted on gasoline.

    h. Nuclear power plants should be banned.

    i. Peaceful demonstrations should be allowed on college campuses.

    j. The pass-fail system should be allowed for all undergraduate courses.

    k. Lobbying should be prohibited.

l. Congress should pass an emergency gasoline rationing plan.

m. The selling of handguns should be prohibited.

n. A college education should be free.

o. Capital punishment should be abolished (restored).

p. The jury system should be abolished.

q. The president of the United States should be elected by direct popular vote.

r. Women should serve in the armed forces.

s. Universities should provide day-care centers for the children of married students.

t. Colleges should teach only salable skills.

7. To write an argument based on either a hypothetical syllogism or a disjunctive syllogism, you substitute a hypothetical proposition or a disjunctive proposition for a categorical proposition. The following propositions or syllogisms can be used for discussion or for a writing assignment:

a. If a law lacks support, it can't be enforced. The 55 mph speed limit lacks public support. Therefore, it can't be enforced.

b. Nuclear power is either a good way of solving our energy problems or a lousy way.

c. Either price controls will be imposed or there will be a recession.

d. If human beings were basically good, then laws would not be necessary.

e. If telling a certain kind of lie is not always wrong, then telling a lie can sometimes be ethically better than telling the truth.

Errors in Reasoning

A **fallacy** is *an idea or opinion based on faulty logic.* It is an error in reasoning that may be deliberate or due to ignorance. The following fallacies are intended as a checklist to make you alert to possible errors in reasoning in your own arguments and in those of others. Ironically, as strategies of persuasion, they can be very effective. But as logical arguments, they are fallacious.

Begging the Question

This is a fallacy in which you assume the truth of the premise that you are supposed to prove in your argument. If you state, for example, "Everybody knows that minorities commit most of the crimes in large cities," and then argue from that premise, you would be guilty of **begging the question.** Another form that begging the question takes is **arguing in a circle,** that is, assuming the truth of a premise, drawing a conclusion from this premise, and then using the conclusion to prove your initial premise. For example, if a salesperson says to you, "You should buy the new Chevrolet Impala because it's the best car on the market," and you ask why, and he or she answers, "Because it's made by Chevrolet," that's arguing in a circle. Still another form that begging the question takes is the use of prejudicial words in the proposition—for example, "Who wouldn't oppose this *idiotic* piece of legislation?"

Argumentum Ad Hominem

If in an argument you attack or insult the person you are arguing against rather than deal with the issues, then you are guilty of **argumentum ad hominem** (arguing against the person). Opponents of John F. Kennedy, for example, argued that he was unfit for the presidency because he was a Catholic who would owe allegiance to the Pope. Opponents of Nelson Rockefeller criticized him because he had been divorced—as if his being divorced had anything to do with his qualifications for office. Other politicians have been accused of being socialistic or ultraconservative or too radical, the intent being to discredit the person rather than to address the argument.

Name-Calling

This fallacy is similar in some respects to that of the argumentum ad hominem. In arguing, you give bad names to a person, an issue, or an event, rather than examine the issues. Down through the years, people have been called heretics, fascists, communists, demagogues, and troublemakers by adversaries who appeal to hate and fear rather than to logical reasoning. Thus, if someone doesn't agree with an action taken by some group, they can avoid dealing with the action by calling it "communist-inspired," "radical," "left-wing," or "right-wing."

Argumentum Ad Populum

Like the previous two fallacies, this is an emotional appeal in which you turn away from the real argument and appeal to the irrational fears and prejudices of your audience. You can do this by praising your audience extravagantly, praising the American way of life, resorting to appeals of God, country, home, and motherhood. In other words, you associate something good or bad with your argument. Writers who habitually include in their arguments stock appeals for or against "our free enterprise system," "bureaucracy and red tape," "government interference," and "big business" are guilty of appealing to the crowd.

Shifting Ground

This fallacy consists of ignoring the question by shifting from one question or proposition to another when you are cornered. This fallacy is also called **confusing the issue** and the **Red Herring.** You argue beside the point you are trying to prove. In other words, if you can't answer a question or meet your opponent's arguments straight on, you simply ignore the question and raise another one. Pat Brown, the former governor of California, was once asked, "Governor, what's your opinion of the rising crime rate in California?" He answered: "Rising crime is not the decisive factor. It is the increasing efficiency of crime reporting with the more accurate use of computer technology." Here is how his son, Jerry Brown, answered the same question: "Why don't you ask an intelligent question? You sound like you're giving me the Rorschach test, asking me what I think of the crime rate."

The Bandwagon

This is a technique used to get people to follow the crowd. Any time you call for an action or an opinion because it is popular, because "everybody's doing it," you are using the **bandwagon technique** of arguing. Because people are imitative, they like to do what everybody else does and to believe what other people believe. So this appeal has human-interest value. Advertisers use this appeal when they make claims about the popularity of an advertised product, based on the large number of people who buy the product or who remain faithful to a name brand: "Everybody loves delicious Wrigley's Spearmint Gum"; "Today, more people ask for Coke than for any other soft drink."

Slanting

This is a technique in which you phrase a statement in such a way that you encourage your reader to take a favorable or unfavorable view of a subject. You can do this by selecting certain facts and details of your subject that are favorable and omitting others that are unfavorable. Or you can distort the facts in such a way as to suggest things that are not completely true. **Slanting** can be achieved by using words connotatively, by ordering words in a certain way, by italicizing or underlining words you want to emphasize, by punctuating, and by using emotional or charged language. A humorous example of slanting is this conjugation of an irregular verb, attributed to Bertrand Russell: "I am firm; you are obstinate; he is pig-headed."

Either-Or Fallacy

This is a logical fallacy in which you oversimplify an issue by narrowing your reader's options to just two alternatives. The linguistic form of the **either-or** statement forces your reader to think in terms of black or white. If the options are genuine, there is no problem. But sometimes there may be an unnoticed third possibility hidden by the false dilemma. Thus, if someone argues that lifting price controls on gasoline will produce either more oil at cheaper prices or less oil at higher prices, what may go unnoticed is the possibility of producing the same amount of oil at higher or lower prices. The reader can escape the "horns of a dilemma" by going between them—that is, by not being caught by the one or the other, but considering all of the alternatives.

The Complex Question

This is an error in reasoning in which you ask a question in such a way that it assumes an answer to another question, which has not even been asked. The fallacy is committed when a single answer is demanded of the question. "Why" or "how" questions are frequently of this type. Thus, the question "How long are we going to tolerate interference with our national interests by these large international corporations?" assumes that there has been such interference. The question "Why is it that girls are less interested in science than are boys?" contains the answer to the hidden question "Is it a fact that girls are less interested in science than boys?"

Hypothesis Contrary to Fact

If you begin an argument with a hypothesis that is not true or that is speculative and then draw conclusions from it, this is an error in reasoning called **hypothesis contrary to fact.** It takes the form: "What would the consequences have been *if* such and such had been true?" For example: "If the Shah of Iran were still ruler of that country, gasoline prices would be much lower in this country." There is, of course, evidence to show that the Shah encouraged higher prices when he was the ruler of that country. Another example that keeps making the rounds is the statement "If Columbus hadn't discovered America, we wouldn't be living here today."

Argument From Ignorance

This fallacy is committed if you argue that a statement must be true because it has not been proven false, or that it must be false because it has not been proven true. In other words, if you try to justify a belief when there is no evidence for it, you are guilty of **arguing from ignorance.** For example: "There must be life on other planets, because no one can prove that there isn't." Or, "Psychic phenomena must exist, because eyewitnesses have given us reports of them for years, and nobody has ever disproved these reports."

Exercises

1. Identify the errors in reasoning in the following:

   a. Ever since we put men on the moon, we've been having unusual weather.

b. When I get married, either I will run the house or my husband will.

c. I cooked it. That's why it's good.

d. I'd never vote for Carter. I don't like his Southern accent.

e. The ranting of *Time* and the pseudo-Americans over the CIA disclosures would be comical were it not so childish and tragic. What the United States needs is a stronger CIA, and let the chips fall where they may.

f. You accuse me of going over the 55 mph speed limit, but everybody speeds on the highway.

g. Everyone has a new car but me. Why can't I get a new car? After all, I'll be going to college next year.

h. The West would have been won ten years sooner if the pioneers didn't have to stop and ride back forty times a day to pick up their hats.

i. My teacher is a hard grader. Three of my friends got "F's" on the midterm exam.

j. You are either a Republican or a Democrat.

k. The energy crisis could ultimately destroy our economy and bring down the world economy along with it. Such a collapse would precipitate world conflict and probably atomic war. We cannot escape the danger of the atom. But I would rather risk a mishap from a nuclear power plant once every twenty or thirty years than face one nuclear holocaust.

l. Everybody watches the NBC evening news. You ought to watch it, too.

m. The first chapter was so boring I concluded that it must be a lousy book.

2. Bring to class magazine ads that commit the fallacies cited in this and the previous chapter.

3. Bring to class for discussion examples of fallacies taken from letters to the editor in magazines such as *Time* or *Newsweek,* in your local newspaper, or in the campus newspaper.

4. Discuss the arguments and the errors in reasoning in the following letter to the editor:

Dear Editor:

The letter of Mrs. _____ is outstanding in that she links evolution with the proposed sex education in schools supported by tax money.

We are in this fight against great odds and powers, "against spiritual wickedness in high places" (Ephesians, chapter 6, especially verse 12).

With this thought in mind, we should make every effort to withdraw our children from such influence and place them in a Christian school where only dedicated teachers are employed.

If we do not believe the account of Creation and the Flood, then we call God a liar. If we make God a liar, then we cannot believe any part of His word. This is the position of the supporters of evolution.

God, the essense of life, is life itself, the source of life, plant and animal. This the evolutionist denies, and yet he goes to the swamp and steals from God's creation the smallest form of life, a microorganism, the physicochemical basis of living matter that forms the essential part of plant and animal life.

The microscopic bit of life the evolutionist stole from God and placed into a never-never time resembling eternity, namely, billions upon billions of never-never years before time or matter were created. The amoeba is that bit of protoplasm that the evolutionist has made to be his god, his idol, for he has claimed for it the power to evolve itself in billions of never-never years into great animals such as lived before the Deluge.

There is no halfway point between evolution and the Creation, as some would have us believe. As Mrs. _____ says, "It is either evolution or God." The promoters of evolution despise and violate the moral law which contains the law of chastity. This law forbids the practice of the marriage act outside of marriage.

Adultery, fornication, rape, and what have you already have such a hold on our moral life, as a nation, that we do not need sex instruction by licentious teachers to foster a further drop in morality. Go-go girls, miniskirts, Bikini suits: what next?

Remember, Rome and other great nations of the past have gone into oblivion by a similar route.

Paragraphs and Paragraphing

Chapter 10

Paragraphs and Paragraphing

The Paragraph as Part of A Longer Unit

There are several ways of looking at paragraphs. One way is to see the paragraph as a division of a longer piece of writing. Another is to think of the paragraph as a group of logically related sentences, composed of unified parts, based on a single idea. A third way is to view the paragraph as a kind of extended sentence.

Writers paragraph for a variety of reasons—for instance, to change tone, to shift rhythm, or to emphasize a point. One of the most important reasons for paragraphing, however, is for logical considerations. Understanding the logical basis of paragraphing is of primary importance in developing in the writer a sense of form consciousness.

Some writers claim that they are always conscious of paragraphing and of the logical basis of their paragraphing *when they write*. Others assert that they often go back *after they have completed their writing* and then make their paragraph indentations. These are not opposing points of view, in my opinion, but complementary ones. Writers who claim that they go back and paragraph after they have completed their writing usually end up paragraphing similarly to the way in which writers who use the opposite method do. Both kinds of writers know in general the end they want to achieve. Both have an intuitive grasp of the overall structure of their essays. But some writers are more self-conscious about the logical basis of their paragraphing *as they are writing*. Others are less so. Nevertheless, the latter necessarily have to group their ideas into thought units as they are writing, *whether they paragraph them as such or not*. I am not saying that writers cannot go back and paragraph their essays for reasons that have little to do with the logical progression of ideas.

What I am saying is that the logical basis for dividing essays into paragraphs is there, if writers want to avail themselves of it. It is there because composition is an organic development that begins with an intuitive grasp of the whole. The writer knows in general the end he or she wants to achieve. **Paragraphing** is *the process of differentiating the parts within the whole to achieve the writer's purpose.*

The truth of this idea is easy to illustrate. Give an experienced writer a completed piece of writing, one that has been written without traditional paragraph divisions, and he or she can invariably divide that piece of writing into thought units that make sense. Although some writers may disagree slightly as to where some of the paragraph divisions should be, the extent to which they will agree is amazing.

To illustrate this point, let's look at two kinds of writing: the kind of writing that is **overdifferentiated,** in which there seem to be too many paragraph divisions and in which the basis of the paragraph divisions seems to be almost arbitrary, or at least nonlogical; and the kind of writing that is **underdifferentiated,** in which there are few or no paragraph divisions.

Overdifferentiated writing occurs in magazine ads and in newspaper writing, where considerations such as the educational level of the mass audience, the neat, orderly appearance that shorter paragraphs present, the readability of such paragraphs, and the balance achieved by making the paragraphs the same average length are of paramount importance. Underdifferentiated writing occurs in encyclopedia articles, to give just one obvious example.

Overdifferentiated Paragraphing

Let us look at a few examples of overdifferentiated writing, the first an ad for Kitchen Aid disposers:

OTHER DISPOSERS CAN'T COMPARE
TO KITCHEN AID.

Kitchen Aid disposers have a cast
iron drain chamber to fight corrosion.
Other disposers don't.

Kitchen Aid has a push-button Wham
Jam Breaker to break up stubborn jams.
Other disposers don't.
Kitchen Aid has a powerful motor.
Stronger start-up power than any other,
to handle tough stuff like steak bones
and corn husks.
Which some disposers can't.
In fact, when you make a point-by-
point comparison, it turns out there
really isn't much comparison.
And, perhaps, that's why so many
people choose a new Kitchen Aid
stainless steel disposer when it comes
time to replace their worn-out disposers.

This ad appeared in the October 1978 issue of *Better Homes and Gardens.* The paragraphs are written in typical advertising-copy fashion. The copy is broken up into eight short paragraphs. Each contains a single sentence or a fragment punctuated as a sentence, with the exception of paragraph 5, which contains both a sentence and a fragment. Paragraph 1 has eleven words; paragraph 2, three words; paragraph 3, thirteen words; paragraph 4, three words; paragraph 5, twenty-two words; paragraph 6, four words; paragraph 7, eighteen words; paragraph 8, twenty-four words. The average paragraph length is twelve words.

The typical short paragraph in advertising copy is composed of three or four sentences. The paragraphing in this ad is even more extreme. If breaking up a block of printed matter into smaller units makes it easier to read and more inviting to the eye, then it follows that the more you break up the copy, the better it will be.

In the typical short paragraph in an ad, there is little opportunity for extensive internal development. Yet most advertising copy has a logical progression of ideas, found in the various sections of the text. The section in advertising copy is often the equivalent of the paragraph in a longer essay. Naturally, the arrangement of logical units into paragraphs and sections will differ from advertisement to advertisement.

Are advertisers being perverse in writing such short paragraphs? Indeed not. They know a great deal about the psychology of their audiences. Ads with long paragraphs (as in some stereo ads) look like *hard reading* before readers even know what's in them. Short paragraphs look like *easy reading*. They are easy on the eyes. They are simple to follow. They aid emphasis. They get attention and hold it. This is especially important in magazines, where the ad has to compete with stories, feature articles, editorials, and reviews to make its selling point.

Yet despite the copywriter's grouping of the sentences into eight paragraphs, the logical basis for grouping these sentences into new paragraph units is there. A reorganization of the sentences based on logical considerations gives us four paragraphs that look like this:

OTHER DISPOSERS CAN'T COMPARE TO KITCHEN AID

Kitchen Aid disposers have a cast iron drain chamber to fight corrosion. Other disposers don't.

Kitchen Aid has a push-button Wham Jam Breaker to break up stubborn jams. Other disposers don't.

Kitchen Aid has a powerful motor, stronger start-up power than any other, to handle tough stuff like steak bones and corn husks, which some disposers can't.

In fact, when you make a point-by-point comparison, it turns out there really isn't much comparison. And perhaps that's why so many people choose a new Kitchen Aid stainless steel disposer when it comes time to replace their worn out disposers.

This rewritten version uses a point-by-point comparison paradigm. In the first two paragraphs, the first sentence in each lists a feature of Kitchen Aid disposers. The second sentence negates these features in the competitor's product. In the third paragraph, consisting of a single sentence, the first part of the sentence comments on Kitchen Aid's powerful motor and on what it is capable of doing.

The second part denies this capability in the competitor's product. The last paragraph makes the point that there really isn't much of a comparison between Kitchen Aid and other products and concludes with an implicit appeal to the reader to buy Kitchen Aid disposers.

Here is a second example of overdifferentiated paragraphing, this time a slightly more elaborated piece of writing, from a newspaper article:

7,000 Stolen Books Found in NY (Associated Press)

NEW YORK—A middle-aged man with eclectic reading taste and sticky fingers brought public library officials to their knees Monday as they sorted through 7,000 volumes valued at $100,000 that were stashed in his apartment.

Inspectors from the New York and Queens public libraries picked their way delicately through wall-to-wall books stacked in the back bedroom of the Queens apartment abandoned three months ago by Caio A. D'Aurelio.

"It looks like they've all been stolen," said Cecil Greenidge, a Queens library inspector. Some of the books were stamped with library logos as distant as Florida State University in Tallahassee, but most were from libraries here.

"Now we can't be sure this guy stole these books. But somebody sure did," Greenidge said. Authorities at first thought the books had been checked out and never returned.

D'Aurelio rented the apartment for 10 years, said Armando Arias, the building superintendent. He stopped living in the apartment about two years ago, and he stopped paying his monthly $200 rent three months ago. No one has seen him since.

Arias and city marshals entered the apartment a week ago and found a riot of books—on the bed, the floor, even packed into the kitchen cabinets. They included books on Cicero, architecture and design, chemistry and archeology, flowers, Greek and Russian, and a guide to the rhythm method of birth control.

Some were dated as having been taken as long ago as 1952.

D'Aurelio was described by neighbors as an average-looking man in his 50's, with receding red hair and quiet demeanor. Arias said he once worked for the city as an architect, and apparently kept the Queens apartment as a place to work and study.

The street-level, one-bedroom apartment also had a litter of papers and magazines. Arias, once a military librarian in Ft. Polk, La., said he spent four days stacking most of the volumes in the bedroom because it would be easier for library officials to remove them through windows.

Arias said he used a shovel to plow through the strewn books and knee-high yellowed newspapers and magazines—some 11 years old—but it was two days before he could see the apartment's parquet floor.

At 10 cents a day, D'Aurelio's overdue charge in New York City for all 7,000 volumes would amount to $700 daily. Any book overdue since 1952 would have an accumulated fine of about $912. If all had been due back then, the bill would total more than $6.3 million.

Like the paragraph structure of the Kitchen Aid ad, the paragraph structure of this news story is not completely logical. This does not mean that it is less effective, however. As I have previously pointed out, there are many reasons a writer would want to vary his or her paragraph structure: ease of reading, balance, emphasis, and the psychology of the audience being just a few. Like the paragraphs of the Kitchen Aid ad, the paragraphs in this news story contain few sentences. There is a total of eleven paragraphs in this article, ranging in length from one to three sentences.

Although the paragraph structuring is not strictly logical, the overall plan is logical. In typical journalistic fashion, the opening paragraph answers the questions who (public library officials), what (found 7,000 stolen or borrowed books), when (Monday), where (in the apartment of a middle-aged man with eclectic reading taste).

If you regroup the sentences from the original paragraphs and place them together in new paragraphs based on similar ideas, you get the following logical divisions:

7,000 Stolen Books Found in NY (Associated Press)

1

NEW YORK—A middle-aged man with eclectic reading taste and sticky fingers brought public library officials to their knees Monday as they sorted through 7,000 volumes valued at $100,000 that were stashed in his apartment.

2

Inspectors from the New York and Queens public libraries picked their way delicately through wall-to-wall books stacked in the back bedroom of the Queens apartment abandoned three months ago by Caio A. D'Aurelio. "It looks like they've all been stolen," said Cecil Greenidge, a Queens library inspector. Some of the books were stamped with library logos as distant as Florida State University in Tallahassee, but most were from libraries here. "Now we can't be sure this guy stole these books. But somebody sure did," Greenidge said. Authorities at first thought the books had been checked out and never returned.

3

D'Aurelio rented the apartment for 10 years, said Armando Arias, the building superintendent. He stopped living in the apartment about two years ago, and he stopped paying his monthly $200 rent three months ago. No one has seen him since.

4

Arias and city marshals entered the apartment a week ago and found a riot of books—on the bed, the floor, even packed into the kitchen cabinets. They included books on Cicero, architecture and design, chemistry and archeology, flowers, Greek and Russian, and a guide to the rhythm method of birth control. Some were dated as having been taken as long ago as 1952.

5

D'Aurelio was described by neighbors as an average-looking man in his 50's, with receding red hair and quiet demeanor. Arias said he once worked for the city as an architect, and apparently kept the Queens apartment as a place to work and study.

6

The street-level, one-bedroom apartment also had a litter of papers and magazines. Arias, once a military librarian in Ft. Polk, La., said he spent four days stacking most of the volumes in the bedroom because it would be easier for library officials to remove them through windows. Arias said he used a shovel to plow through the strewn books and knee-high yellowed newspapers and magazines—some 11 years old—but it was two days before he could see the apartment's parquet floor.

7

At 10 cents a day, D'Aurelio's overdue charge in New York City for all 7,000 volumes would amount to $700 daily. Any book overdue since 1952 would have an accumulated fine of about $912. If all had been due back then, the bill would total more than $6.3 million.

Paragraph 2 depicts inspectors from the New York and Queens public libraries picking their way through wall-to-wall books in D'Aurelio's bedroom in Queens and records their comments. Paragraph 3 discusses the length of time D'Aurelio stayed in the apartment and when he left. Paragraph 4 gives a catalog of D'Aurelio's eclectic reading tastes. Paragraph 5 describes D'Aurelio. Paragraph 6 emphasizes the litter of books, papers, and magazines. Paragraph 7 gives an account of the overdue charges.

Underdifferentiated Paragraphing

If overdifferentiated writing can be described as the kind of writing in which the writer, for whatever reasons, makes a large number of paragraph divisions, then underdifferentiated writing is the type in which the writer makes few, if any, paragraph divisions. Nevertheless, there are units of thought within this kind of writing that can be separated into paragraphs.

A typical example of this kind of writing is the following article, taken from *The Columbia Encyclopedia:*

Lingua Franca

[A lingua franca is] an auxiliary language, generally of a hybrid and partially developed nature, that is employed over an extensive area by people speaking different and mutually unintelligible tongues in order to communicate with one another. Such a language frequently is used primarily for commercial purposes. Examples are the several varieties of the hybrid pidgin English; Swahili, a native language of East Africa; Chinook jargon, a lingua franca formerly used in the American Northwest that was a mixture of Chinook, other American Indian languages, English, and French; and a variety of Malay (called *bazaar Malay*), which served as a compromise language in the area of British Malaya, the Dutch East Indies, and neighboring regions. The original lingua franca was a tongue actually called Lingua Franca (or sabir) that was employed for commerce in the Mediterranean area during the Middle Ages. Now extinct, it had Italian as its base with an admixture of words from Spanish, French, Greek, and Arabic. The designation "Lingua Franca" [Language of the Franks] came about because the Arabs in the medieval period used to refer to Western Europeans in general as "Franks." Occasionally the term *lingua franca* is applied to a fully established formal language; thus formerly it was said that French was the lingua franca of diplomacy.

The structure of this article is very much like that of many encyclopedia articles. The entire article consists of a single unit the size of a long paragraph. The opening statement is not a complete sentence, but it could be made into a complete sentence by the addition of a main verb. Despite the lack of paragraph divisions, however, this article has a logical progression of ideas that could be paragraphed like this:

Lingua Franca

1

[A *lingua franca* is] an auxiliary language, generally of a hybrid and partially developed nature, that is employed over an extensive area by people speaking different and mutually unintelligible tongues in order to communicate with one another. Such a language frequently is used primarily for commercial purposes.

2

Examples are the several varieties of the hybrid pidgin English; Swahili, a native language of East Africa; Chinook jargon, a lingua franca formerly used in the American Northwest that was a mixture of Chinook, other American Indian languages, English, and French;

and a variety of Malay (called *bazaar Malay*), which served as a compromise language in the area of British Malaya, the Dutch East Indies, and neighboring regions.

3

The original lingua franca was a tongue actually called Lingua Franca (or sabir) that was employed for commerce in the Mediterranean area during the Middle Ages. Now extinct, it had Italian as its base with an admixture of words from Spanish, French, Greek, and Arabic. The designation "Lingua Franca" [Language of the Franks] came about because the Arabs in the medieval period used to refer to Western Europeans in general as "Franks."

4

Occasionally the term *lingua franca* is applied to a fully established formal language; thus formerly it was said that French was the lingua franca of diplomacy.

The logical basis for grouping these sentences into paragraphs is as follows. Paragraph 1 defines a *lingua franca*. Paragraph 2 gives examples of an auxiliary language. Paragraph 3 gives the origin of the word and traces the original language that was used as a *lingua franca*. Finally, paragraph 4 discusses another application of the term.

What, then, can you conclude about paragraphing from the study of overdifferentiated writing and underdifferentiated writing? That the structure of sentences, paragraphs, and sections of the whole essay interact. That paragraphing is the process of differentiating the parts within the whole, whether that differentiation comes as you are writing or after you have completed your first draft. And that paragraphing can be based on a number of considerations, depending on the writer's intention, although the logical basis of paragraphing may be the most important one.

Exercises

1. Rewrite the following news story, regrouping the sentences into new thought divisions:

Chair Commands High Spot in Human History

Michael Kernan
Washington Post

Is civilization possible without the chair?

Think about it. Plenty of animals make their own beds, but did you ever see even the sharpest rat sit in a chair?

The chair is no mere piece of furniture; it's a concept. It says something about human power. Long before the kings of Scotland were crowned on the Stone of Scone, the idea of a throne must have existed.

After all, if you could afford to sit down in the presence of strangers, that is, enemies, and not stand ready for combat, it must mean you didn't fear them very much. Where do you think the word chairman came from?

In our homes, this curiously ambiguous emblem of authority and relaxation is almost a member of the family.

My grandfather, an old soldier from the Gold Rush days, took up wood-carving in his last years and made a marvelous mahogany armchair with claws and scrolls.

It was always my father's chair in the dining room, and mine in my turn. My father also had his special armchair, by the fire in the library, deep, profoundly comfortable, with a high back and generous arms: it was a chair to take a nap in. Sometimes I would sit in this chair to read his paper, but never when he was around.

Something made me get up and offer it to him when he came in the room. Not that he was in the least threatening, or that I was in the least polite. It was something about the chair.

We still have that chair, all but reupholstered to death, and are about to retire it, but people still shy away from sitting in it unless I insist.

Even today, in an executive office, the chair has mojo. Try asking the boss for a raise when you're sitting in a chair lower than the one across the desk.

My mother also had her special chair: elegant, dowell-backed and efficient. It was the chair she sat in to write checks. If she wanted to relax, she would lie on the sofa.

Another one, a fine old wing chair, used to be stationed by a window in the living room overlooking the lawn and the valley beyond. It was in a nook, so you could sit perfectly still in it and someone looking for you to do a chore would walk right past.

I decided to make it my official reading chair. But it was too formal, too sternly straight-backed, so I never warmed to it. We still have that one too, in the attic, too valuable to throw away, not valuable enough to sell. It's as unaccommodating as ever.

Another disaster is the loveseat, which is good for nothing except arm wrestling.

You can tell a lot about a family by its chairs: whether it's socially ambitious, puritanical, lazy or whatever. Some living rooms contain all those springy-bottomed, stiff-backed antique chairs. You can't feel really welcome in such a place, and you wonder if even the people who live there do.

Doubtless those chairs were Louis XVI, Chippendale or some such. Which brings up the question: Why didn't the master chaircrafters make comfortable chairs? Was there some social prestige attached to sitting up straight? Is this the origin of "Don't slouch"?

The more you think about chairs, the stranger they get. The electric chair: Why? Wouldn't it be much more practical to put the poor soul on a stretcher? Even in the gas chamber, the executee sits on a chair. Maybe it is a vestige of the homage paid to the sacrificial victim from times primeval.

2. Rewrite the following encyclopedia article, dividing it into paragraphs that "make sense":

[A *pidgin* is] a LINGUA FRANCA that is not the mother tongue of anyone using it and that has a simplified grammar and a restricted, often polyglot vocabulary. Pidgins that have developed from English and other tongues have been employed in different regions since the 17th century. An example is the variety of pidgin English that resulted from contacts between English traders and the Chinese in Chinese ports. In fact, the word *pidgin* supposedly is a Chinese (Cantonese) corruption of the English word *business*. Another well-known form of pidgin English is the Beach-la-Mar (or *Beche-de-Mer*) of the South Seas. The different kinds of pidgin English have preserved the basic grammatical features of English, at the same time incorporating a number of non-English syntactical characteristics. The great majority of words in pidgin English are of English origin, but there are also Malay, Chinese, and Portuguese elements. As a result of bringing to the Caribbean area large numbers of Negro slaves from West Africa who spoke different languages, other pidgins evolved in that region that were based on English, Portuguese, French, and Spanish.

The Paragraph as a Group of Logically Related Sentences

The paragraph as a group of logically related sentences represents, for the most part, the traditional approach to composition. In this view, the paragraph is a collection of sentences on a single subject. It expresses a single thought, and it contains no idea that does not advance the main topic. The thought of such a paragraph can usually be expressed in a single, concise statement called the **topic sentence,** which is ordinarily stated at the beginning of the paragraph. The **topic sentence** is *the sentence that expresses the main idea of the paragraph.* In this position, all the subsequent ideas in the paragraph are developed from it:

> 1. Apart from teaching him Latin, *Stratford Grammar School* taught *Shakespeare* nothing at all.
> 2. *It* did not teach *him* mathematics or any of the natural sciences.
> 2. *It* did not teach *him* history, unless a few pieces of information about ancient events strayed in through Latin quotations.
> 2. *It* did not teach *him* geography, for the first (and most inadequate) textbook on geography did not appear until the end of the century, and maps and atlases were rare even in university circles.
> 2. *It* did not teach *him* modern languages, for when a second language was taught at grammar school it was invariably Greek.
> —Marchette Chute, *Shakespeare of London.*

In this paragraph, the first sentence is the topic sentence and each of the next four sentences adds a supporting detail. The paragraph is unified because it deals with a single topic, the things that Stratford Grammar School did not teach Shakespeare.

In the traditional view of the paragraph, the relationship of every sentence to every other sentence and to the main idea is made clear and orderly through logical development and proper transitions:

> 1. Applied to language, the adjective *good* can have *two meanings:* (1) "effective, adequate for the purpose to which it is put" and (2) "acceptable, conforming to approved usage."

2. The *first* of *these* is truly a value judgment of the language itself.
    3. In this *sense* the language of Shakespeare, for example, is "good English" because it serves as a highly effective vehicle for his material.
    3. On the other hand, the language of a poorer writer, which does not meet adequately the demands put upon it, might be called "bad English."
2. The *second meaning* of *good* is not really a judgment of the language itself but a social appraisal of the persons who use it.
    3. An expression like *I ain't got no time for youse* may be most effective in the situation in which it is used, and hence "good English" in the first *sense*.
    4. But most people, including those who naturally speak this way, will call it "bad English" because grammatical features like *ain't, youse,* and the double negative construction belong to a variety of English commonly used by people with little education and low social and economic status.

—W. N. Francis, *The English Language*

This paragraph has the form of an extended definition. The opening sentence is the topic sentence. It introduces the term to be defined, *good language.* It also indicates the plan of development. The adjective *good,* the writer states, can have two meanings when it is applied to language: "effective" and "adequate for the purpose," or "acceptable" and "conforming to approved usage." Then he goes on to comment on the two meanings. He does this by dividing the remaining sentences into two groups. Sentence two and the two subordinate sentences related to it extend one part of the meaning of the term (the first meaning of *good,* followed by two examples). The language of Shakespeare is *good* because Shakespeare uses it effectively. The language of a poorer writer is bad, not because it is intrinsically bad, but because the poor writer does not use it effectively. Sentence five and its qualifying sentences take up the second meaning of the term, "a social appraisal of the persons who use it." Most people will label an expression *bad,* regardless of its effectiveness, if it has grammatical features that people of little education and low economic status use, the writer contends in the last two sentences.

In addition to the logical order of ideas, this paragraph uses a number of other methods to achieve unity and coherence:

Parallelism
the first of these is
the second meaning . . . is
in this sense
on the other hand
the language of Shakespeare
the language of a poorer writer

Repetition

the adjective *good*	highly effective
good English	most effective
the second meaning of *good*	language
bad English	the language of Shakespeare
good English in the first sense	the language of a poorer writer
bad English	the language itself
effective	

Synonyms
meanings
these
sense
meaning
sense

Transitional Expressions
in this sense
on the other hand
and hence
but

Exercises

1. Compose five topic sentences to be used in developing paragraphs.

2. Develop a paragraph from one of the following topic sentences:

   a. Education reduces prejudice.
   b. All people are motivated by self-interest.
   c. People should always be honest with each other.
   d. I was startled by what I saw when I entered the room.
   e. There are at least two good arguments to be made against pornography.
   f. Aside from its interest, _____is an informative book (or television show, movie, and so forth).

Modes of Developing Paragraphs

Because writing is a unified process, the same principles which apply at the essay level also apply at the paragraph level. You have learned in earlier chapters that a **mode** is *a way or manner of developing ideas.* At times, I have used the term to refer both to the process of invention and to that of arrangement. But a mode is also a way of developing paragraphs.

Categories such as analysis, classification, comparison and contrast, and cause and effect, besides referring to mental processes and processes of invention and arrangement, also represent methods of developing paragraphs. They appear in paragraphs because our minds think along those lines.

Although it is true that in much writing the modes are mixed, it is useful in the beginning stages of learning to write for you to see them as simple. Just as in invention, the modes rarely appear in pure form (for instance, when you classify, you must also compare), in paragraphs, the modes are often mixed.

The following are typical examples of the modes as they appear in paragraphs. (You might want to go back and review the discussion of modes in the first chapter and in the chapters titled "Arrangement" and "Patterns of Thought.")

Analysis

Organize *analysis paragraphs* by dividing a complex subject into its component parts. In the following paragraph by Bertrand Russell, the topic sentence introduces the term *patriotism* (in the first sentence), and the following sentences break this term into its elements:

> Patriotism is a very complex feeling, built up out of primitive instincts and highly intellectual convictions. There is love of home and family and friends, making us peculiarly anxious to preserve our own country from invasion. There is the mild instinctive liking for compatriots as against foreigners. There is pride, which is bound up with the success of the community to which we feel that we belong. There is a belief, suggested by pride but reinforced by history, that one's own nation represents a great tradition and stands for ideals that are important to the human race. But besides all these, there is another element, at once nobler and more open to attack, an element of worship, of willing sacrifice, of joyful merging of the individual life in the life of the nation. This religious element in patriotism is essential to the strength of the State, since it enlists the best that is in most men on the side of national sacrifice.
>
> —Bertrand Russell, *Why Men Fight*

Description

Descriptive paragraphs consist basically of sentences representing objects arranged in space. In its simplest form, the principle of organization is based on the way you perceive objects in space—left to right, right to left, bottom to top, top to bottom, and so forth. In writing descriptive paragraphs, you can make the scene easier to follow if you use a particular principle of spatial arrangement:

> As you enter the forest, your eyes used to the glare of the sun, it seems dark and shadowy, and as cool as a butter dish. The light is filtered through a million leaves, and so has a curious green aquarium-like quality which makes everything seem unreal. The centuries of dead leaves that have fluttered to the ground have provided a rich layer of mold, soft as any carpet, and giving off a pleasant earthy smell. On every side are the huge trees with their

great curling buttress roots, their thick smooth trunks towering hundreds of feet above, their head foliage and branches merging indistinguishably into the endless green roof of the forest. Between these the floor of the forest is covered with the young trees, thin tender growths just shaken free of the cradle of leaf mold, long thin stalks with a handful of pale green leaves on top. They stand in the everlasting shade of their parents, ready for the great effort of shooting up to the life-giving sun. In between their thin trunks, rambling across the floor of the forest, one can see faint paths twisting and turning. These are the roads of the bush and are followed by all its inhabitants.

—Gerald Durrell, *The Overloaded Ark*

Classification

Classification deals with systems of classes. Begin classification paragraphs with a general statement and support this statement by an enumeration and explanation of the types or subtypes:

> Meteorites are of three general classes: irons—composed 98 percent or more of nickel-iron; stony irons—composed roughly half and half of nickel-iron and of a kind of rock known as olivine; and, finally, stones. The stones are further subdivided, depending on whether they contain tiny bodies (or chondrules) of the minerals olivine and pyroxene. The stones that possess them—more than 90 percent of all known meteoritic stones—are called chondrites. The few stones that lack these minerals are known as achondrites. All these categories offer useful clues to those who try to reconstruct the history of the earth, for not only are meteorites fellow members of the solar system, but radioactive dating indicates that they are as old as the earth itself.

—Time-Life Books, *The Earth*

Exemplification

Exemplification paragraphs use supporting examples to illustrate a generalization. Begin exemplification paragraphs with a general statement and then support this statement by specific examples:

Almost no feature of the interior design of our current cars provides safeguards against injury in the event of collision. Doors that fly open on impact, inadequately secured seats, the sharp-edged rearview mirror, pointed knobs on instrument panels and doors, flying glass, the overhead structure—all illustrate the lethal potential of poor design. A sudden deceleration turns a collapsed steering wheel or a sharp-edged dashboard into a bone-and-chest-crushing agent. Penetration of the shatterproof windshield can chisel one's head into fractions. A flying seat cushion can cause a fatal injury. The apparently harmless glove-compartment door has been known to unlatch under impact and guillotine a child. Roof-supporting structure has deteriorated to a point where it provides scarcely more protection to the occupants, in common roll-over accidents, than an open convertible.

—Ralph Nader,
"The Safe Car You Can't Buy,"
The Nation (April 11, 1957).

Definition

Definition paragraphs tell what a thing is. They also explain what words or phrases mean. One way of developing paragraphs of definition is to lead off with a general statement or with a logical definition. Then expand the general statement by other methods of defining:

"Desert" is an unfortunate word all around and most of its usual associations are inaccurate as well as unfavorable. In the first place the word doesn't even mean "dry," but simply uninhabited or deserted—like Robinson Crusoe's island. In that sense, the expanse about me is far from being a desert, for it is teeming with live things very glad indeed to be right there. Even in its secondary meaning, "desert" suggests to most people the rolling sand dunes of the Sahara. Something like that one may find in Death Valley; perhaps in parts of the Mojave; and especially, with an added weirdness, in the hundreds of square miles of New Mexico's White Sands, where the great dunes of glistening gypsum drift like the snowbanks one can hardly believe they are not. Most of my Lower Sonoran Desert, however, is not at all like that. The sandy soil is firm and hard-packed; it supports life, less crowded than in wetter regions but pleasantly flourishing. Nature does not frown here. She smiles invitingly.

                                                    —Joseph Wood Krutch, *The Desert Year*

Comparison and Contrast

Comparison and contrast paragraphs deal with similarities and differences. One way of organizing such paragraphs is as follows. In the first half of the paragraph, deal with one subject or aspect of a subject, and in the second half, take up the second subject or aspect of the subject to be compared:

> The way of the desert and the way of the jungle represent the two opposite methods of reaching stability at two extremes of density. In the jungle there is plenty of everything life needs except more space, and it is not for the want of anything else that individuals die or that races have any limit set to their proliferation. Everything is on top of everything else; there is no cranny which is not both occupied and disputed. At every moment, war to the death rages fiercely. The place left vacant by any creature that dies is seized almost instantly by another, and life seems to suffer from nothing except too favorable an environment. In the desert, on the other hand, it is the environment itself which serves as the limiting factor. To some extent the struggle of creature against creature is mitigated, though it is of course not abolished even in the vegetable kingdom. For the plant which in the one place would be strangled to death by its neighbor dies a thirsty seedling in the desert because that same neighbor has drawn the scant moisture from the spot of earth out of which it was attempting to spring.
>
>   —Joseph Wood Krutch, *The Desert Year*

Narration

In *narrative paragraphs,* the emphasis is usually on the action, on the connected series of events that take place in chronological order. Of course, description is often included in narrative paragraphs in order to present the action in the most vivid terms. Organize narrative paragraphs chronologically. Since narrative paragraphs seldom use topic sentences, begin with a sentence that gets the action started. Then add sentences to advance the action:

> Slowly the minutes ticked away toward the zero hour. Officers, their watches synchronized, waited with guns in the air, ready to fire the shots that signaled the opening. At last the revolvers barked, and along the line pandemonium broke loose. Men whipped up their horses, wagons careened wildly forward, horses freed from overturned vehicles galloped madly about—all was hurrah and excitement. The Santa Fe trains, streaming slowly forward at a regulated pace which would not give their passengers an undue advantage, disgorged riders along the route as men leaped from roofs or platforms and rushed about in search of a claim. Noise and confusion reigned as the shouts of successful "Boomers," the crash of hammers on stakes, the clatter of wagons, the crash of overturned vehicles, and the curses of disappointed homeseekers mingled to create a bedlam unique in the annals of the nation.
>
> —Ray Allen Billington, *Westward Expansion*

Process

Organize *process paragraphs* chronologically, as you would narrative paragraphs. Place the emphasis, however, on *the steps* involved in the process:

> The process of précis writing is fivefold: (1) The student reads slowly the entire selection he intends to summarize, concentrating his attention on getting at the author's central idea. (2) He then rereads the selection, picking out the essential points or subdivisions; and, if the selection is long, jotting down the points made in successive paragraphs. (3) Either with or without reference to these notes, he next constructs sentences expressing the different points concisely but accurately, and groups these sentences into paragraphs representing sections or larger divisions of the whole. (4) He reads the selection a third time, comparing it with the summary he has prepared, and making sure that nothing important has been omitted,

nothing unimportant included, and nothing at all unclearly expressed. (5) He finally revises and recopies or rewrites his summary. The précis which results from this process will generally be from one-quarter to one-third the length of the original.

—Harry Robbins and Roscoe Parker, *Advanced Exposition*

Cause and Effect

Compose *cause and effect paragraphs* by moving from cause to effect or from effect to cause. The assumption is that an event takes place in time *because* an initial event caused it to occur or because it is part of a causal chain:

> The intellectual life of the nineteenth century was more complex than that of any previous age. This was due to several causes. First: The area concerned was larger than ever before; America and Russia made important contributions, and Europe became more aware than formerly of Indian philosophies, both ancient and modern. Second: Science, which had been a chief source of novelty since the seventeenth century, made new conquests, especially in geology, biology, and organic chemistry. Third: Machine production profoundly altered the social structure, and gave men a new conception of their powers in relation to the physical environment. Fourth: A profound revolt, both philosophical and political, against traditional systems in thought, in politics, and in economics, gave rise to attacks upon many beliefs and institutions that had hitherto been regarded as unassailable. This revolt had two very different forms, one romantic, the other rationalistic. (I am using these words in a liberal sense.) The romantic revolt passes from Byron, Schopenhauer, and Nietzsche to Mussolini and Hitler; the rationalistic revolt begins with the French philosophers of the Revolution, passes on, somewhat softened, to the philosophical radicals in England, then acquires a deeper form in Marx and issues in Soviet Russia.
>
> —Bertrand Russell, *A History of Western Philosophy*

Exercises

1. Analyze the foregoing paragraphs. Usually the topic sentence is the first sentence of the paragraph. Is this true in these paragraphs? What are the specific sentences in each paragraph that relate to the respective modes of development?

2. Write an analysis paragraph, listing the characteristics, features, aspects, or parts revealed by your analysis, based on one of the following topics:

   a. a song lyric
   b. the human body
   c. a day in your life
   d. a landscape
   e. an album cover
   f. a part of your room
   g. some object or possession
   h. a poster
   i. a picture or painting
   j. a magazine ad

3. In a single paragraph, describe a person, an object, or a scene.

4. Write a classification paragraph based on one of the topics listed below:

   a. popular songs
   b. clothing styles
   c. graffiti
   d. people
   e. blind dates

5. Write a paragraph giving examples of:

   a. things that disturb you
   b. prejudiced people
   c. current fads
   d. doublespeak in language
   e. ads that use subliminal appeals

6. In a single paragraph, write an extended definition of one of the following terms: *trashing, grodie, hippie, groupie, myth, romance, love, beauty, truth, success, pacification.*

   Coin a word and then write a paragraph defining it.

7. In a well-written paragraph, compare or contrast:

   a. two songs (rock lyrics)
   b. two people
   c. two dances
   d. two ads
   e. two of anything

8. Write a one paragraph narrative on one of the following subjects: an embarrassing moment, a frightening experience, a college experience.

9. In a single paragraph, describe a process:

   a. how to cook something
   b. how to play a certain game
   c. how to eat a certain dish
   d. how to produce (sell, prepare, build, plan, solve, and so forth)

10. Write a cause and effect paragraph based on one of the following topics:

   a. the effect of inflation on my life
   b. the effects of taking some drug (or of drinking a certain liquor)
   c. the cause of an accident in which you or a friend was involved
   d. the effects of a love affair
   e. the cause of some natural occurrence

The Paragraph as an Extended Sentence

Another way of looking at paragraph structure is to think of a paragraph as an extended sentence. This approach to paragraph construction is based on the work of Francis Christensen, who sees a close relationship between a particular type of sentence that he calls the **cumulative sentence** and the paragraph. According to Christensen, the cumulative sentence begins with a sentence base. This base contains the main subject, the main verb, and any bound or restrictive modifiers:

   1. The boys ate warily,

To the base is added an accumulation (hence the designation *cumulative*) of details, in the form of free or sentence modifiers:

   1. The boys ate warily.
     2. trying not to be seen or heard,
       3. the cornbread sticking,
       3. the buttermilk gurgling,
         4. as it went down their gullets.

—Katherine Anne Porter

The base clause is often stated in general terms. The modifiers add specific details to the base so that there is a deductive movement from the general (level 1) to the particular (levels 2, 3, and 4). The sentence levels are numbered and indented to show the grammatical and logical progression of ideas.

If sentences tend to have a base, to which details in the form of modifiers are added, then paragraphs, according to Christensen, have a similar movement. The paragraph, in this view, is a kind of extended sentence. The top sentence of the paragraph is similar to the base clause of the cumulative sentence. The supporting sentences in the paragraph are similar to the sentence modifiers. The successive sentences in the paragraph are related to each other by coordination and subordination.

If it is possible to consider the paragraph as having the same kind of structure as the cumulative sentence, then clearly some sentences can be rewritten as paragraphs. Below is a rewritten version of the Katherine Anne Porter sentence (cited above) as a paragraph:

1. The boys ate warily.
    2. They were trying not to be seen or heard.
        3. The cornbread was sticking.
        3. The buttermilk was gurgling.
            4. It went down their gullets.

Implicit in Christensen's approach to paragraph construction is the idea than an inductive study of the paragraph can be useful in learning to write paragraphs, that analyzing paragraphs will enable the writer to see what goes with what. Since all writers must necessarily use the same basic compositional principles, one can learn a great deal about these principles by studying the writing of others.

Analyzing Paragraphs

For the purpose of analyzing paragraphs, therefore, Christensen has suggested a sequence of steps that may be described as follows. First, assume that the first sentence of the paragraph is the top or topic sentence of the sequence, not the traditional topic sentence, but the sentence that gets the paragraph going. Give it the number 1. Then examine the subsequent sentences carefully, searching for similarities and differences. If the second sentence in the paragraph is like the first (is parallel in structure or ideas), set it down as coordinate and assign it the same number. If the second sentence differs from the first (gives evidence of subordination of structure or ideas), indent it as subordinate and give it the number 2. Do the same with the remaining sentences.

The following paragraph has been analyzed using the method indicated above. (Key transitional words and phrases are italicized to supplement the indentation and numbering of sentence levels):

1. The intellectual life of the nineteenth century was more complex than that of any previous age.
   2. *This* was due to several *causes.*
      3. *First:* The area concerned was larger than ever before; America and Russia made important contributions, and Europe became more aware than formerly of Indian philosophies, both ancient and modern.
      3. *Second:* Science, which had been a chief source of novelty since the seventeenth century, made new conquests, especially in geology, biology, and organic chemistry.
      3. *Third:* Machine production profoundly altered the social structure, and gave men a new conception of their powers in relation to the physical environment.
      3. *Fourth:* A profound *revolt,* both philosophical and political, against traditional systems in thought, in many beliefs and institutions that had hitherto been regarded as unassailable.
         4. This *revolt* had two very different forms, one *romantic,* the other *rationalistic.*
            5. (I am using these *words* in a liberal sense.)
            5. The *romantic revolt* passes from Byron, Schopenhauer, and Nietzsche to Mussolini and Hitler; the *rationalistic revolt* begins with the French philosophers of the Revolution, passes on, somewhat softened, to the philosophical radicals in England, then acquires a deeper form in Marx and issues in Soviet Russia.
            —Bertrand Russell, *A History of Western Philosophy*

This paragraph has a structure similar to that of the cumulative sentence. The first sentence is the top sentence or base. It also happens to be the topic sentence, the sentence that contains the main idea of the paragraph (the idea that "the intellectual life of the nineteenth century was more complex than that of any other age"). I have given it the number 1. The second sentence (level 2) is subordinate to the first, the word *this* referring to the idea of the complexity of intellectual life. Further, this sentence acts as the organizing sentence for the ideas in the subsequent sentence. (The word *causes* in the sentence "this was due to several causes" leads us to expect an enumeration of causes.) The next four sentences, labeled 3, enumerate specific causes of the complexity of intellectual life. The repetition of the cardinal numbers ("First," "Second," "Third," "Fourth") makes the logical progression of ideas and the tie-in with the word *causes* explicit. The next sentence (level 4) expands the idea in the previous sentence about the philosophical and political revolt, and the next two sentences (level 5) comment on the two forms of this revolt.

Let us look at another paragraph, this time doing a more extensive analysis:

1. It is impossible for Mexicans to produce the humblest thing without *form and design.*
    2. A donkey wears a load of palm leaves *arranged* on either flank in great *green* sunbursts
    2. Merchants hang candles by their wicks to make *patterns* in both *line* and *colour.*
    2. Market coconuts show *white* new *moon strips* above the dark, fibrous *mass.*
    2. Serapes are thrown with just the right *line* over the shoulders of ragged peons, muffling them to the eyes.
    2. Merchants in the market will *compose* their tomatoes, oranges, red seeds and even peanuts into *little geometric piles.*
    2. *Bundles* of husks will be *tied in a manner suitable for suspension in an artist's studio.*
        3. To the traveler from the north, used to the treatment of the cold, dead produce as cold, dead produce, this is a matter of perpetual wonder and delight.

—Stuart Chase, *Mexico*

This paragraph follows a rigid, logical order. The first sentence is the topic sentence. Sentences two, three, four, five, and six are coordinate to each other but subordinate to sentence one. Each gives a specific example of the general idea contained in the topic sentence. Sentence seven is immediately subordinate to sentence six, but the word *this* in sentence seven could also refer to all the previous coordinate sentences.

The logical movement of this paragraph is from the general to the particular. The rhetorical pattern is exemplification. The first sentence states the main idea, the inductive generalization, that Mexicans produce even the humblest things with form and design. The next six sentences give specific examples of humble things with form and design. The load of palm leaves on a donkey are arranged in the shape of great green sunbursts. Candles are hung by their wicks in symmetrical patterns. Market coconuts are cut to show white moon strips. Ragged peons throw serapes over their shoulders with just the right lines. Merchants arrange their produce in geometrical piles. And husks are tied in bundles in such a way that an artist could have arranged them. The last sentence ties all these ideas together and concludes that this attention to form and design in the simplest, everyday objects is a matter of wonder and delight to the traveler from the north.

The logical structure is also developed by the use of synonyms and related ideas that tie together the ideas of form, design, and color. The key lexical patterns can be schematized as follows:

Form and Design
palm leaves . . . *arranged* . . . . in great green *sunbursts*
candles [hung] . . . to make *patterns* in both *line* and *colour*
coconuts [with] . . . white new *moon strips*
serapes . . . thrown with just the right *line*
merchants . . . *compose* their tomatoes, oranges, red seeds and
    even peanuts into little *geometric piles*
bundles of husks . . . *tied in a manner suitable for suspension*
    in an artist's studio

Color
palm leaves . . . in great *green* sunbursts
coconuts show *white* new moon strips
dark, fibrous mass
tomatoes, *oranges, red* seeds

The value of this kind of analysis is that it not only graphically depicts the sentences in a paragraph in relation to each other, but it also enables you to understand the meaning relationships that obtain in paragraphs. You can subsequently use this kind of analysis to check your own paragraph structure, or you could go on to write your own paragraphs, using the same basic principles.

Composing Paragraphs

For the purposes of writing your own paragraphs, you could follow a sequence of steps very much like those listed below:

> *Begin with a base sentence.*
> *Add a supporting sentence.*
> *Add a second supporting sentence.*
> *Add a third supporting sentence.*
> *Conclude with a final supporting sentence.*

Or you could use some variation on the basic pattern:

> *Write a base sentence.*
> *Qualify that base.*
> *Add a specific detail.*
> *Add another detail.*
> *Qualify that detail.*

Visually, the two basic movements of thought in such paragraphs can be depicted as follows:

The Two-Level Paragraph

1. _____
   2. _____
   2. _____
   2. _____
   2. _____

The Multi-Level Paragraph

1. _____
  2. _____
    3. _____
    3. _____
      4. _____

In the two-level paragraph, all the sentences in the paragraph follow from and "depend" upon the base sentence. In a multi-level paragraph, the sentences follow from and "depend" upon each other.

Exercises

1. Some sentences have a structure remarkably like the structure of paragraphs. Transform the sentences below into paragraphs, as in the following example:

Sentence
1. A host of laughing children bestrode the animals,
  2. bending forward like charging cavalrymen, and
  2. shaking reins and whooping in glee.
          —Stephen Crane

Sentence into Paragraph
1. A host of laughing children bestrode the animals.
  2. They bent forward like charging cavalrymen.
  2. They shook the reins and whooped in glee.

1. It was really a lovely day,
  2. the first dandelions making suns,
  2. the first daisies so white.
          —D. H. Lawrence

1. The boys ate warily,
  2. trying not to be seen or heard,

    3. the cornbread sticking,

    3. the buttermilk gurgling,

        4. as it went down their gullets.

                                  —Katherine Anne Porter

1. The dentist began his work,

    2. probing into sensitive cavities,

    2. swabbing the tender area with a dulling liquid,

    2. his fingers pressing the gumline,

        3. searching for the exact spot to insert his needle,

            4. still hidden from the patient's cringing eyes.

    2. As the snow melted on the roof,

1. streams of clear, cold water rippled over the slanted, brown-glazed shingles and slid off the edge,

    2. forming a waterfall which splashed on the grey cement walk below.

1. The old woman prayed alone in the huge cathedral,

    2. her head covered by a dark shawl,

        3. making her round face wide and Slavic,

    2. her elbows leaning heavily on the pew in front of her,

    2. her thick hands cradling her chin and mouth,

        3. the fingers clasped about a wooden rosary,

        3. the large roughened knuckles bent away from the center,

            4. forming a basket with which to collect prayers before releasing them to heaven.

2. Using the kind of analyses illustrated in this section, analyze a few of the example paragraphs, numbering and indenting the levels. Be prepared to discuss the structure, ideas, and language of these paragraphs.

3. Select one or two paragraphs from your own reading and analyze them in the same manner, or bring them to class, put them on the board, and analyze and discuss them.

4. Write a few paragraphs of your own, beginning with narrative and descriptive paragraphs, and then move on to expository paragraphs. Try writing two-level as well as multi-level paragraphs.

Throughout this chapter, my assumption has been that one good way to learn to write effective paragraphs is to look carefully at the principles that other writers use to achieve their purposes and then to use these principles in your own writing. When you write, you are carried along by the movement of the prose, by the flow of ideas, by the logical, spatial, or temporal progression. Often you may have an intuitive sense of paragraph structure, but this is not enough. Good writers usually have a developed sense of form consciousness, and often they can be self-conscious about their writing when there is a need to be. Good writing is planned in such a way as to exploit all the resources of language—the sentence structure, the word choice, and the paragraph structure. Learning to write is in part learning to recognize and to use the best available resources of the language.

Achieving Coherence

The best way of achieving coherence in your writing is to develop your powers of consecutive thinking so that your paragraphs unfold in a logical, step-by-step manner. Sometimes, however, it may be helpful to your reader if you use **transitional devices** to make the relationship among the parts of your essay clear. You can achieve coherence by breaking your writing into logical units, but sometimes you need *connecting words and phrases to make the flow of your thoughts smooth and effortless.*

Careful writers use transitional words and phrases to show connections in thought. These coherence devices link words within a sentence, sentences within a paragraph, and sentences between paragraphs. The following are some typical examples:

Addition

Use connectives to suggest simple addition to the thought in the preceding sentence: *and, too, also, again, and then, moreover, further, indeed, in addition to, plus, likewise, besides, together, jointly.*

This is a wine to enjoy with your dinner. You will *also* enjoy its delicious flavor with fruit, cheese, and dessert after dinner is over.

Ask to visit several classrooms. *Also* make the most of parent–teacher conferences.

Series

Use transitional devices to link items in a series: *first, second, third; next, again, last; primarily, secondarily; in the first place, in the second place; finally, additionally, first and foremost, the former, the latter.*

At first, it may be Grand Prix's beautiful styling that captivates you the most. *The next time*, it may be Grand Prix's luxurious interior that charms you.

First we let blueberry pie dry on a dessert dish overnight. *Then* we washed it with Electrasol.

Pronoun Reference

Use a pronoun to refer to a noun, another person, or a clause in the preceding sentence: *this, that, these, those, he, she, it, you, they, we, such, some, many, none.*

Welcome to *Hawaii. It* is a place as unique and varied as *its* flowers.

Some *people* dream of relaxing on a secluded island. *Others* dream of more lavish surroundings.

Repeated Word

Repeat a key word, or a word derived from the same root: *told/tell, arrived/arrival, rare/rarity, moisture/moistness/moisten/moist, depth/deep, mix/mixture/admixture/mixed.*

There are crippled *children* who want to walk so badly it hurts. *There are children* for whom even the simple act of moving a pencil becomes an agonizing test of determination. *There are children* whose courage in therapy would astonish you.

He *arrived* early. His *arrival* filled us with dread.

Synonyms

If the repetition of key words gets tiresome or if variety is needed, use a different word or phrase to refer to an element in the preceding sentence: *car/automobile,   spectator/onlooker/observer/viewer, purchase/buy, join/unite/connect, exterior/outside, mere words/ nonsense.*

One of the hottest topics in public education today is *"back to the basics."* PTA meetings resound with debates on the *subject.*

It was a rare *caper,* planned to the second and full of acrobatic derring-do: thieves dropped in through the roof at San Francisco's De Young Memorial Museum and made off with several Dutch paintings, including Rembrandt's "The Rabbi," worth about a million dollars. Such elaborate *heists* are becoming increasingly common nowadays.

Whole-Part

Use a word or a phrase that names a whole in one sentence, and then use another word or a phrase that names a part of the whole: *television/picture tube, stereo/tuner, water/wave, flower/petal, book/chapter/section/paragraph, landscape/meadow.*

The roof on this house is made of a new kind of *nonwood shingle.* The *edges* are thick and irregular.

The creosote *bush* is a wispy shrub. It has scraggly *branches* two to five feet high.

Class-Members

Name a general class in one sentence and a member of that class in another: *vehicle/car, sound/noise, fluid/water, fuel/coal/gas, fragrance/perfume, span of time/decade, place of worship/cathedral.*

> Supersoil is a superbly balanced *nutrient potting mix.* It contains rich *sphagnum peat, redwood, fir bark,* and *granite-based river sand.*

> In speed, power, and appetite, the *shark* is a formidable ocean predator. The little we know of this dangerous, unpredictable *fish* has been learned at a high cost in human life.

Emphasis

Use connectives to reinforce the thought in a previous clause or to give emphasis to that thought: *obviously, certainly, perhaps, surely, naturally, really, to be sure, in truth, very likely, undoubtedly, assuredly, without fail.*

> Add fresh taste and variety to your salad with country-fresh mushrooms. They're full of flavor and *surprisingly* low in calories.

> *Naturally,* a teething baby or even a small child cannot be expected to brush its own teeth. But you can—and must.

Comparison

Use connectives that reveal to the reader significant likenesses in thought: *equally important, similarly, in the same way, also, comparably, corresponding, equally, like.*

> Animal life on the desert is *like* life anywhere else. It is completely dependent upon plant life for sustenance.

The killer whale is one of the most dangerous marine animals. *Equally* dangerous is the moray eel.

Contrast

Connect sentences with linking devices that show contrast and that reveal to the reader significant differences in thought: *but, yet, however, still, nevertheless, on the contrary, on the other hand, in spite of, conversely, although, unlike, be that as it may.*

Until now, all bran cereals were made from wheat. *But* many people think corn tastes better.

Taking care of wood is a constant job. *Unlike* wood, vinyl siding takes care of itself.

Result

Use transitional devices when you want to show result: *consequently, therefore, thus, as a result, for this reason, on this account, it follows that, accordingly, hence, so, necessarily.*

The color of the roof is soft and muted. *So* it blends in naturally with the architecture and the surroundings.

No matter how many trash cans you buy, it always seems that there isn't enough room for the trash. *That's why* a Kitchen Aid trash compactor is so worth having.

Example

Use transitional words and phrases to introduce illustrations or examples: *for instance, for example, namely, that is, thus.*

The new cars are quieter than last year's models. You will be surprised, *for example,* by the almost complete absence of road noise and body vibrations.

Nouns which consist of two or more root words are called compound nouns. Often they are written as one word, but they can be written as two words. "Ice cream," *for instance*, is just as much of a compound as is "blueberry."

Parallel Structure

Repeat in the second clause a grammatical structure similar to that in a previous clause: *in the morning/in the evening, some things will never change/some things will always be the same.*

Have you ever seen a killer whale or a live shark up close? Have your children ever touched a real dolphin?

Come and watch Kabuki, a Japanese drama. Visit gilded palaces in Bangkok. Admire ancient temples in Malaysia.

Place

Use linking devices that indicate place or change of place: *here, there, above, under, near by, beyond, on the other side, opposite, adjacent to, in.*

Spend your vacation in *British Columbia.* Your American dollar's worth much more *there.*

Odors used to be an everyday problem *in my house* until I started using Lysol Disinfectant Spray every day. *In the bathroom*, Lysol doesn't just cover up odors, it eliminates them fast.

Time

Use connectives that indicate time or a change of time: *not long after, then, soon, now, after a short while, meanwhile, immediately.*

During the day, you can swim, sun, relax, and play. *At night*, you can watch a floor show.

When your cab pulls up in front of the London Hilton, you can expect a most gracious welcome from our doormen. *When* they open your cab door, they'll tip their hats and usher you in with a friendly smile.

Exercises

1. Analyze the following paragraphs. What methods are used to achieve coherence? Mark each paragraph in detail to illustrate the use of transitional devices (for example, put one line under pronouns and their antecedents, two lines under connectives, circle appropriate words and phrases, draw arrows, use squiggly lines, etc.). Then be prepared to discuss these paragraphs in class.

   a. Italians are convinced that it is good to be alive, and they spend considerable time and energy proving themselves right. With gusto, they sail on warm seas and chill lakes, bowl in the nearest back yard, race about sun-baked soccer fields or argue among themselves at a sidewalk café. But nothing reflects their enjoyment more than their cookery, which is as diverse as the nation's regions, as imaginative as the Italian character. Whether the cook presides in a swank hotel or an ancient farmhouse, the meal is likely to be superb. For, to an Italian, to eat is to live.
   —*Italy*, Life World Library

   b. For no other art do the Italians have more natural talent than they have for dramatic vocal music. The most extroverted and demonstrative people of the Mediterranean, they have since Dante and Petrarch spoken a language that is the most melodious in the world. Furthermore, the Italians seem peculiarly blessed with throats which naturally emit sweet, free-flowing sounds. Perhaps this is because they have been essentially a pastoral people free from many of the tensions of urban life—even when living in cities.
   —*Italy*, Life World Library

   c. Another farsighted practice of the English was to bring along their women. This made for a more homogeneous society than that of the French and Spanish colonies, in which men took native wives. And it also meant the family unit was to provide a solid core for a racially well-knit people, who early indicated that they had come to stay. For the next 300 years, as the descendants of these early settlers pushed westward across the continent, building the nation, it was the presence of the women and of the unit that provided stability and permanence to the new communities. It was they who demanded schools, religion, and order. It was their presence that encouraged a cultural uplift and broke down some of the rough-house tendencies of the masculine frontier. While the Spanish and French ranged over vast stretches of land, unhampered by any family ties, except momentary domesticity with occasional native women, the English stayed close to home. The result was a family type of frontier, characterized by small farms, that remained much more compact, more easily defended, and permanent in nature.

—*The New World*, American Heritage

2. Select an article from your reader or from a magazine. Identify the words and phrases that are used as explicit transitions *from paragraph to paragraph*.

Introductory Paragraphs

Have formal introductions gone out of style? According to some writers, they have. Because of television and the mass media, readers are impatient with long and formal introductions. They want you to get right to the point.

But even if you decide to keep your beginning paragraphs brief and informal, you must not forget that in your opening paragraphs, you make a commitment to your readers that you are expected to fulfull.

What should you do in your opening paragraph or paragraphs? At the very least, give your readers some idea of what you are going to write about, state your purpose, and indicate your plan of development. If your subject is a difficult one, you might also want to include a preliminary explanation.

Introductory paragraphs, then, should lead into the subject. But they should do more. They should also arouse the curiosity and interest of your readers and create the proper tone.

In considering strategies for your opening paragraphs, it might be helpful to ask yourself the following questions:

1. *Who are my readers?*
2. *Do they have any knowledge of my subject?*
3. *Do they have any interest in my subject?*
4. *How can I best gain their attention?*
5. *Is my purpose to present my readers with new ideas or information, to persuade them to take a certain course of action, or to entertain them?*
6. *How can I best convey to my readers my own interest in and attitude toward my subject?*

Experienced writers use a number of strategies in their opening paragraphs. Here are a few you may want to try.

Begin With Descriptive Details

Staring from the poster, they looked like a nightmare of what might be, that terrifying day when the street gangs take over the city, any city. Some of them wore leather vests over bare chests. Others had on Arab headdresses. A few, their faces painted harlequin colors, wore baseball uniforms and carried bats. Massed as far as the eye could see, all looked menacing, and the threat was underscored by the text above the picture: "These are the Armies of the Night. They are 100,000 strong. They outnumber the cops five to one. They could run New York City. Tonight they're all out to get the Warriors."

That Paramount ad was chillingly effective, bringing into 670 theaters around the country thousands of youths keen to see *The Warriors*—and eager for trouble. Since the film opened on Feb. 9, three young men have been killed by *Warrior*-inspired fights, and other brawls have broken out at moviehouses in several cities. More than a half a dozen theaters have dropped the film entirely; others are hiring some muscle of their own, which Paramount will pay for. In Washington, D.C., two full-time guards were on duty last week at the Town Downtown and will stay there until *The Warriors* finishes its run. Not since Stanley Kubrick's *A Clockwork Orange* opened in 1971 has a movie generated such anxiety about the seeming power of a film to engender gang violence in those who see it.

—"The Flick of Violence," *Time*

Begin With An Anecdote

Nearly five years ago I sat in the courtyard of a household in the village I call Tudu, Niger, haranguing the head of the household in an attempt to determine the year his first son was born. His replies were desultory as I sought to find out whether the son was older or younger than other men whose ages I knew fairly well. In the middle of this important but tedious part of demographic data collection, the man's daughter-in-law came out of her hut with an infant in her arms. She hurried over to me, and with tears running down her cheeks, her body shaking with sobs, she placed the baby in my lap and pleaded, "Ladi just stopped breathing in her sleep. Can you do anything?" Ladi—her stomach distended, the bones of her arms and legs like fragile spindles—was dead, and Ladi's mother, in spite of her question, knew that there was nothing I could do. At that moment my inability to help in a tangible way, as well as the needlessness of Ladi's death, ignited my anger and frustration at the effects of the Sahelian drought.

The drought in West Africa south of the Sahara was due to four straight years of poor rainfall—from 1970 to 1973—each year worse than the one before. The drought was reported to the United States and Europe in terms of thousands of deaths, hundreds of thousands made homeless, the encroaching Sahara, and somber declarations of international relief aid for the region.

—Ralph H. Faulkingham,
"Where the Lifeboat Ethic Breaks Down," *Human Nature*

Begin With a Quotation

"We cannot tolerate the Cubans to go swashbuckling unchecked in Africa, the Middle East and other areas, nor can we tolerate the Cubans of the Orient to go swashbuckling in Laos, Kampuchea or even in the Chinese border areas. Now some people in the world are afraid of offending them, even if they do something terrible. These people wouldn't dare take action against them."

So said China's Vice Premier Teng Hsiao-p'ing last week, puffing on a Panda cigarette as he aimed an unmistakable rebuke at what Peking considers the jelly-bellied Western response to adventurism by the Soviets and their clients. Teng also gave the fullest explanation yet of the motives behind China's two-week-old "punitive" invasion of its southern neighbor, Viet Nam. In an effort to placate international alarm, he repeated assurances that the operation "will be limited in degree and will not last a long time," perhaps no longer than China's four-week invasion of India in 1962. There were reports at week's end, in fact, that the Chinese were considering a cease-fire and might begin pulling back this week.

—"Suck Them In and Out—Flank Them," *Time*

Begin With the Thesis Statement

A revolution was spinning out of control. With nonviolent protests and uncommon discipline, the people of Iran had ended the tyranny of the Shah. Their rewards was not freedom but chaos, as the forces united around Ayatullah Ruhollah Khomeini last week showed the first dread signs of schism. Suddenly, guns were everywhere, in every hand, as self-styled "freedom fighters" liberated weapons from police stations and army barracks. In Tehran, Tabriz and other cities, sporadic fighting raised the death toll for the week to an estimated 1,500. A bewildering motley of forces was involved: troops loyal to the Shah, ethnic separatists, *mojahedeen* (literally, crusaders) who backed the new government of Prime Minister Mehdi Bazargan, and, ominously, Marxist *fedayeen* (sacrificers) who felt that the revolution had not moved far enough to the left.

—"Guns, Death, and Chaos," *Time*

Begin With a Question

Is it possible that a cigar-shaped spaceship descended over the tiny town of Aurora, Texas (pop. 237), and crashed into Judge J. S. Proctor's windmill? And that a tiny spaceman was buried in the Aurora cemetery?

That was the tale sent to newspapers in nearby Dallas and Fort Worth one April day in 1897 by a local correspondent named S. E. Hayden. It was generally ridiculed at the time, and most citizens of Aurora still scoff. "Hayden wrote it as a joke and to bring interest to Aurora," says Etta Pegues, 86. "The railroad bypassed us, and the town was dying."

—"Close Encounters of a Kind," *Time*

Begin with a Figure of Speech

Like fast-approaching storm clouds, the consequences of the political turmoil that shut down Iran's oil fields became clearer last week, presaging a period of trouble and uncertainty for Western nations. Higher fuel prices and some scarcities are inevitable in the U.S. President Carter warned that though the situation created by the Iranian cutoff is "not critical" yet, it "certainly could get worse." He said that the difficulties might be manageable if Americans "honor the 55-mph speed limit, set thermostats no higher than 65° and limit discretionary driving." Otherwise, the President added, "more strenuous action" would be needed to curb fuel use.

—"The Price of Stormy Petrol," *Time*

Begin with a Cryptic Statement

Winnipeg is jumping. Airline reservations to the frostbitten Canadian city (pop. 560,000) have been booked for months. Hotels are full up too. The cause of this midwinter madness: the last solar eclipse over the continental U.S. until 2017. On Monday, Feb. 26, the moon will slip between the earth and sun, and progressively blot out the solar disc along a so-called path of totality that begins in the Pacific Ocean west of Washington State, cuts northeast over Canada, then darts off and away toward Greenland.

—"A Matter of Night and Day," *Time*

Begin with an Analogy

From Florida to Maine there is a war. Between man and man, fish and bird, wave and sand. The battle rages and storms over the coast. Yet the battlefield is strangely quiet. Grasses bend softly in the wind. Herons stalk silently through shallow waters. This war is being fought in the narrow green-and-tawny band of salt marsh that stretches along our eastern shore.

For millenniums there could be no final victory or defeat. Nature's contending forces stayed in balance. The rising sea stole from the marshland, and the marshland rebuilt its defenses. The marsh grass died and, decaying, nourished the animal life of the estuaries. Fish warred on fish and the birds on them, but all at last fell in the battle, and, in dissolution, fed the grass roots. The circle closed, and the battle was joined again.

Now, however, we humans can impose a final decision in this immemorial war of the wetlands along all our coasts. We even have it in our power to obliterate the battlefield. And if we do, will that be victory or defeat? Are we about to conquer nature, or about to conquer ourselves?

The salt marshes are disappearing before the onslaught of factories, dump and fill, homes with a seaward view. As chemicals and sewage pollute the wetlands, the encroachment of industrialists and developers is also the route of oyster dredgers, clammers, crabbers, sportsmen, and lovers of nature.

—Stephen W. Hitchcock,
"Can We Save Our Salt Marshes?"
National Geographic

Concluding Paragraphs

The concluding paragraph should conclude. Nothing could be so obvious or so simple. Yet inexperienced writers often have a difficult time concluding their essays. When they run out of something to say, they just stop.

If your writing is to have any effect on your readers, it ought to have an appropriate ending. If your essay is relatively short, you might end it with the most important point. If your essay is relatively long, you might repeat the main points you made in the body of your paper. If your ideas are difficult, you might want to summarize in your concluding paragraph what you have said in the body of your paper. In brief, you want to leave your readers with the feeling that your essay is complete.

Here are some suggestions for concluding your essays:

1. *End with the most important point of your essay.*
2. *Repeat the main points of your essay.*
3. *Present your reader with a summary of your main ideas.*
4. *Conclude with a call for action.*
5. *End with a question.*

6. *Conclude with a prediction or forecast.*
7. *Give your reader an opinion, based on your previous discussion.*
8. *Discuss the broader implications of your subject.*
9. *End with an anecdote.*
10. *Conclude with a striking example.*

The following are a few examples of concluding paragraphs.

End with a Restatement of Your Main Points

The rules that govern the act of kissing, in short, are complex and varied. The human kiss has evolved a long way from its probable origins in the sniff of animal recognition and the warmth of human bonding. It can be a reflexive gesture of greeting or deference, or a carefully planned sign of personal feeling. The first deep kiss, a passionate kiss from one's beloved, the last kiss exchanged between close friends or relatives, the happy kisses for a newborn baby—all evoke powerful emotions that are remembered for life. The simple kiss carries complex meaning, which poets will continue to praise, scientists will continue to explain, and all of us will continue to practice.

—Leonore Teifer, "The Kiss," *Human Nature*

End with a Generalization

Nothing in the universe has more grandeur than the infinity of the human mind. Even pea-sized computers capable of forecasting the movement of the galaxies are not more wondrous than the mysterious human creature that produced them. The ultimate frontier is not geographical or spatial but intellectual.

—Norman Cousins, "The Conquest of Pain," *Saturday Review*

End with a Quotation

Sir Richard Livingstone, late vice-chancellor of Oxford, once wrote that "true education is the habitual vision of greatness"—the study of great individuals, great events, and great art and literature. Teachers of English should demand greatness in what their students read and aim for greatness in what their students write. To do less is to condemn the next generation to mumbling mediocrity.

        Edward T. Hall, "Why Americans Can't Write," *Human Nature*

Exercises

1. Discuss the following introductory paragraphs in class. What method is used to begin each paragraph or set of paragraphs? Do they arouse your interest? Why or why not? How do they lead into the body of the paper?

    a. The China-Viet Nam War wilted like a frostbitten blossom last week. China's 100,000 or so infantry and armored troops arrested their languid advance 15 to 20 miles inside the Viet Nam border, wheeled, and began a gradual, piecemeal withdrawal. Vietnamese artillery and front-line units of the 70,000-man-strong border defense force put on a show of hot pursuit but coolly refrained from any real, obstructive attack. Judging from the ferocity of each side's victory claims, it seemed safe to conclude that neither side had won—or lost.

        "Windup of a No-Win War," *Time*

    b. "Maps speak, and through the language of a map speaks the mind of a society," wrote Barbara Aziz (August 1978). Aziz skewered any lingering beliefs a citizen might have that maps are somehow independent of the people who create them. A 20th-century sophisticate, after all, is likely to regard a Rand-McNally atlas or an *Encyclopedia Britannica* geographical sketch as revealed truth.

        But, as Aziz has demonstrated, geographic reality is culturally determined: "Maps, like language, select certain features and ignore others, and like language, maps are cultural expressions of elements significant to a society."

        "Maps and the Mind," *Human Nature*

    c. Seething gases and liquids mask its rocky core. Its frigid atmosphere consists mostly of hydrogen and helium. Great cyclones and hurricanes swirl in its turbulent sky, with brilliant red and orange clouds constantly merging and breaking apart in ever changing patterns. Often the turbulence creates trails of sinuous white vapors thousands of miles long. The awesome, forbiddingly beautiful world is that of Jupiter, a planet so large it could swallow more than 1,300 earths.

"Intimate Glimpses of a Giant," *Time*

d. Skimming down a steep, snow-covered road at Camp David in Maryland's lovely Catoctin Mountains, Jimmy Carter was enjoying the brisk air of an afternoon in the woods when the tip of one of his thin skis caught beneath a crust of rough ice. The President of the United States went down hard. The consequences of this tumble were clearly visible when he returned to snow-paralyzed Washington the next day: an ugly purple bruise the size of a silver dollar over his right eye, several bright red scratches on his cheek, a puffy lip and a slight limp. It took the deftest ministrations of his makeup woman to hide the wounds before public appearances.

> The bruising of the President did not stop all week. Despite Carter's efforts to appear decisive and determined in his handling of the nation's affairs, he kept encountering hidden obstacles. And as his standing in U.S. public opinion polls once again sank, world events seemed conspiring to prove his frequently repeated assertion that "the United States cannot control events within other nations."

"Carter: Black and Blue," *Time*

e. What if it were possible to cut heating costs to a fraction of the current rate? Wouldn't this be worthwhile—particularly if it could be done without spending billions for solar retrofits and insulation, and if the final result would be a healthier, more satisfying heat like that provided by a fireplace or an old-fashioned potbellied stove? I believe we could do it if we would remember that regardless of the problem that faces us, it makes no sense to ignore human nature. In this case, the problem under discussion is the transaction between human beings and a variety of heat sources.

> There is an abundance of data on the thermal requirements of heating buildings and none on heating people. We heat buildings in order to heat people (and even that job is often done rather badly). We behave like the mythical primitive who burned down his house in order to cook his pig.

Edward T. Hall, "Let's Heat People Instead of Houses," *Human Nature*

f. In ten summers of rewarding work at Aphrodisias, a great ruined city of the Greco-Roman age in Turkey's Anatolian uplands, I have learned that past and present often merge. For example, as we excavated the city's agora, or marketplace, we came upon some 300 fragments of inscribed stone panels. Fitted together like a giant jigsaw puzzle, they proved to be exactly what Americans find posted in neighborhood supermarkets today—a table of fixed prices.

In A.D. 301, runaway inflation had threatened to destroy the economy of the Roman Empire. To deal with this situation so closely paralleling that of our own era, the Emperor Diocletian froze all prices. It was his edict, and the prices he established, that we discovered in the agora of Aphrodisias. The roster of items is exhaustive, including commodities as varied as melons and marble, kerchiefs and cattle. Violations of the edict drew severe penalties, even death.

> Kenan T. Erim, "Aphrodisias: Awakened City
> of Ancient Art," *National Geographic*

g. A man in bright orange trousers asked me to close my eyes and hold his hand. I did as he said. In my other hand he put one end of a forked plastic rod. He held the other side. Then he told me to breathe deeply, clear my mind, and think only of water. The rod pointed into the sky, but as we walked slowly across the grass it was pulled down as if by a magnet. I opened my eyes and saw the rod pointing directly to the ground in front of the fire hydrant on the green in Danville, Vermont.

Dowsing, also called divining, witching, wishing, or striking, is the process of discovering hidden objects by means of a divining rod. Many dowsers claim that the practice goes back to Biblical times, citing the story in Numbers of Moses striking a rock with his rod and water spurting forth. Some say that the Chinese relied on it for the placement of their houses. The image of a man pacing the earth with a divining rod in hand is certainly part of American folklore, but it is an imported rather than native-born practice. The first clear-cut account of dowsing is a report on German mining by Georgius Agricola in *De Re Metallica*, published in 1556. From Germany it spread to the rest of Europe and finally to the United States.

> Nancy Hechinger, "Discovering Human Nature,"
> *Human Nature*

2. Bring to class at least three closing paragraphs from current magazine articles. Be prepared to discuss the techniques used for concluding the respective articles.

3. Write three introductory paragraphs, using one of the methods previously discussed.

4. Write three different types of concluding paragraphs, making sure to leave your reader with a sense of completeness.

Revising Paragraphs in Relation to Purpose and Audience

In strict logical terms, your paragraphing ought to contribute to the unity of the whole composition. Each paragraph ought to have a unity of its own. But it is quite possible that because of considerations of purpose or audience or kind of writing (for example, if you are writing an ad or a news story), you will want to go back after you have finished your writing and change the length of your paragraphs or change your overall organizational pattern. I am not suggesting that you write one- or two-sentence paragraphs, although at times a one-sentence paragraph might be very effective. I am suggesting, however, that you might learn something from advertisers about paragraphing, about the psychology of audiences, and about readability.

Short paragraphs can help you achieve emphasis in your writing. They are easy to read and to follow. However, in essay writing, an excess of short paragraphs might become tiresome. Sometimes long paragraphs are necessary to make a long, involved point. They can also give your reader the effect of reason and deliberation.

To illustrate these ideas more concretely, I'd like to take you through the stages of rewriting and reparagraphing a magazine ad to show you how copywriters skillfully adapt their copy to their purposes and audiences and to suggest paragraphing strategies that can be adapted for different purposes and audiences.

The ad I have chosen is a Suntory Royal Whiskey ad that appeared in the November 14, 1977, issue of *Time* magazine. The general audience is that of *Time* magazine, and the specific audience is Scotch drinkers. The purpose of the ad is to persuade Scotch drinkers to buy Suntory Royal Whiskey rather than Scotch. The dominant mode is process analysis. The copy reads as follows:

SUNTORY ROYAL.
SLIGHTLY EAST OF SCOTCH.

1

For over 50 years, we've been making our Suntory Whiskies just the way the very best Scotches are made.

2

To create Suntory Royal
we begin with fine barley malt
and clear mountain water.
Patiently we smoke the grain
over rich Scottish peat.

3

The mash is then distilled
in real copper pot stills. With
tedious, painstaking control.

4

To let it age and mellow,
we store the distillate in
genuine white oak barrels,
delicately steeped in sherry.

5

After ageing, the mature
whiskies are drawn from the
barrels and carefully married
according to time-honored
tradition.

6

We then store the blend
again, allowing the subtle
richness of the flavors to become one magnificent taste.

7

No, our Suntory Royal is
not Scotch.

8

And although it is made
the very same way, from the

very same ingredients, it still
retains a unique character
all its own. Smoother, lighter
and more distinctive.

9

Suntory Royal may be
close to Scotch, but it's still
about 10,000 miles apart.

This ad consists of nine paragraphs, each ranging in length from one to two sentences. Paragraph 1 contains one sentence. Paragraph 2 contains two sentences. Paragraph 3 contains a sentence and a prepositional phrase punctuated as a sentence. Paragraphs 4, 5, 6, 7, and 9 contain single sentences. Paragraph 8 consists of a complete sentence and a series of adjectival modifiers punctuated as if it were a complete sentence.

Paragraph length is interesting. Paragraph 1 consists of nineteen words; paragraph 2 has twenty-three words; paragraph 3, thirteen; paragraph 4, nineteen; paragraph 5, seventeen; paragraph 6, eighteen; paragraph 7, seven; paragraph 8, twenty-eight; paragraph 9, fourteen. Paragraphs 7 and 8 provide just enough variety in sentence length to keep the copy from getting monotonous. The other paragraphs are approximately the same length. If you look at the shape of the paragraphs in the overall plan, you will see that they are balanced and pleasing to the eye.

The mode of development is process analysis. But if you look closely at the way the stages of the process are organized into paragraphs, you wonder if the copywriter knows what he or she is doing. The ingredients of the product are listed in the second paragraph. But rather than separating the stages of making this whiskey into separate paragraphs or perhaps grouping all of the stages into a single paragraph, the writer puts the first stage of the operation in the second paragraph. Also, curiously, the writer switches person, from *we've* and *we* to *the mash,* to *we,* to *the mature whiskies,* to *we.* Doesn't this advertiser know how to write process copy? If you were to switch from the first person to the third or from the second to the third in writing a process essay, your instructor would probably mark you down for changing the point of view. However, this is not the description of a scientific process, but the use of process analysis *in the service of persuasion.* So the writer is deliberately breaking the conventions of process writing for a particular purpose.

If you were to follow the conventions of process analysis in rewriting this ad, you might use the first person almost exclusively. *The effect would be to put the emphasis on the maker of the product,* as in the following rewritten version:

> For over 50 years, *we*'ve
> been making our Suntory
> Whiskies just the way the
> very best Scotches are made.

> To create Suntory Royal
> *we* begin with fine barley malt
> and clear mountain water.
> Patiently *we* smoke the grain
> over rich Scottish peat.

> *We* then distill the mash
> in real copper pot stills. With
> tedious, painstaking control.

> To let it age and mellow,
> *we* store the distillate in
> genuine white oak barrels,
> delicately steeped in sherry.

> After ageing the whiskies,
> *we* draw the mature whiskies
> from the barrels and carefully
> marry them according to time-
> honored tradition.

> *We* then store the blend
> again, allowing the subtle
> richness of the flavors to be-
> come one magnificent taste.

> No, our Suntory Royal is
> not Scotch.

> And although it is made
> the very same way, from the
> very same ingredients, it still
> retains a unique character
> all its own. Smoother, lighter
> and more distinctive.
>
> Suntory Royal may be
> close to Scotch, but it's still
> about 10,000 miles apart.

You could also write the ad in the third person. *The effect would then be to put the emphasis on the product,* as in the rewritten version below:

> For over 50 years, *Suntory
> Whiskies* have been made just
> the way the very best Scotches
> are made.
>
> Fine barley *malt* and clear
> mountain *water* are used to create
> Suntory Royal. The *grain* is
> smoked over rich Scottish peat.
>
> The *mash* is then patiently
> distilled in real copper pot
> stills. With tedious, pains-
> taking control.
>
> So that it can age and mellow,
> the *distillate* is stored in genuine
> white oak barrels, delicately
> steeped in sherry.
>
> After ageing, the mature
> *whiskies* are drawn from the
> barrels and carefully married
> according to time-honored
> tradition.

The *blend* is then stored again,
allowing the subtle richness of
the flavors to become one magnificent taste.

No, Suntory Royal is not Scotch.

And although it is made
the very same way, from the
very same ingredients, it still
retains a unique character
all its own. Smoother, lighter
and more distinctive.

Suntory Royal may be
close to Scotch, but it's still
about 10,000 miles apart.

But the copywriter decided to switch back and forth between
the first person and the third, to emphasize both the maker of the
product and the product itself. Think for a moment about the strategies involved. Suntory Royal is made in Japan, not Scotland. It is
not Scotch whiskey, but according to the advertiser it's better than
Scotch. How can you convey this idea to the reader? *By stressing
both the process and the character of the makers of Suntory Royal.*
In other words, the advertiser is combining an ethical appeal with a
logical appeal. If Scotch drinkers trust the manufacturer, they will
buy the product. If they understand how well the product is made,
they will buy the product. So the shift from the pronoun *we,* which
stresses the manufacturer, to the nouns *(mash, whiskey)* that stress
the process is calculated.

The language of the ad reinforces the organizational strategies.
Adjectives such as *fine, rich, best, genuine, magnificent, unique,*
and *distinctive* emphasize the quality of the product. Adverbs such
as *patiently* and *delicately* and adjectives such as *tedious* and
painstaking stress the care that the manufacturer takes in making
the product. The line "patiently we smoke the grain over rich Scottish
peat" thus directs the reader to the patience of the manufacturer
in smoking the grain and to the process of smoking the grain.

If the advertiser had decided to follow the conventions of writing a scientific process, with logical paragraphing and a logical development of the ideas, the result would be something like the following:

> For over 50 years, Suntory
> Whiskies have been made just
> the way the very best Scotches
> are made, with barley malt
> and clear mountain water.
>
> To begin with, the grain
> is smoked over Scottish peat.
> Then the mash is distilled
> in copper pot stills. So that
> it can age and mellow, the dis-
> tillate is stored in white
> oak barrels steeped in sherry.
> After ageing, the mature whisk-
> ies are drawn from the barrels
> and blended. The blend is then
> stored again, allowing the fla-
> vors to become one.
>
> No, Suntory Royal is not
> Scotch. And although it is made
> the very same way, from the
> very same ingredients, it still
> retains a character all its own.
>
> Suntory Royal may be made
> like Scotch, but it's actually
> better.

Notice the difference in tone and in purpose in this version of the ad. Instead of nine paragraphs, there are four. The first paragraph consists of a single, long sentence of twenty-five words, which combines the first two sentences of the original. This paragraph lists the ingredients used in making the product. Paragraph 2 contains five sentences, for a total of sixty-one words. Each sentence in this paragraph enumerates a stage in the process. Paragraph 3 contains twenty-eight words. It stresses the quality of the process. Paragraph 4 contains eleven words. It makes the comparison with Scotch explicit.

You will notice that this version combines all of the sentence fragments into grammatically correct sentences, sticks to the third person, and neutralizes the language by taking out most of the emotion-laden and impressionistic diction. The result is a more scientific tone in which the emphasis is more on the process than on the character of the manufacturer.

I hope that this analysis reveals the importance of a self-conscious awareness of paragraphing and of organizational patterns. The extent to which many writers neglect organizational strategies is surprising. Unlike advertisers, many writers prefer to stress the uniqueness of a piece of writing rather than its conventionality. But advertisers have discovered that certain organizational conventions work better than others, that paradigms are important because they have a psychological reality, and that structure, rather than being constricting, can bring the writer freedom. The more structures you have available, the freer you are. Freedom depends on choices.

Exercises

1. Bring to class some very short magazine ads. Be prepared to discuss the mode of development and the paragraphing in relation to the writers' purposes.

2. Rewrite a short magazine ad, using different methods of paragraphing for each rewritten version.

3. Rewrite a news story, regrouping the paragraphs into new thought divisions.

4. Bring to class other examples of writing in which the writer paragraphs for other than logical reasons.

5. Bring to class an essay that uses paradigmatic structure (for example, comparison, classification, exemplification, process, cause and effect, and so forth).

Style:
The
Sentence

Chapter 11

Style: The Sentence

It is almost impossible to separate the rhetoric of a sentence from its grammatical form. Grammatical constructions have rhetorical consequences, and good writers usually have a firm grasp of grammatical principles, even though they cannot always bring this knowledge to conscious awareness. For this reason, I would like to put our discussion of the sentence on a firm grammatical basis.

Almost all writers know that sentences tend to fall into patterns that can be called "basic sentence patterns." These sentence patterns are *minimal grammatical structures* consisting of a few words and cast in an active, declarative form. Some linguists call these sentences "kernel sentences." The term is certainly interesting, suggesting the core or the essential part of something. It is a good term to describe the basic sentence types. Simply by examining the sentences you read in books and in magazines, you will notice that certain patterns recur with some frequency. Despite your increasing linguistic sophistication, you will find that it is still useful to work with these patterns.

Basic Sentence Types

The following sentences may be considered basic sentence types:

> *Subject-Verb*
> The slaves revolted.
> Tension mounted.
> Tastes differ.
> Prices rose.
> TV can talk.

Subject-Verb-Object
Death can unite a family.
Dracula wears dentures.
Education makes a difference.
Cars clogged the streets.
Some plants will eat insects.

Subject-Verb-Indirect Object-Object
We'll give the devil his due.
He offered her fame.
Joan gives her family trouble.
Children ask everyone questions.
Money can't buy you love.

Subject-Verb-Object-Objective Complement
He named his daughter Sandy.
Joan considered Jan neurotic.
His friend elected him secretary.
Van Gogh painted the sky orange.

Subject-Linking Verb-Noun
Loyalty is a virtue.
Posters were a weapon.
Their fears were legitimate.
Tokyo is many things.

Subject-Linking Verb-Adjective
The landscape is flat.
The weather was cold.
IBM is punchy.
The cup is empty.
Order seemed assured.

You are probably already familiar with most of these patterns, and you can write them quite easily. More interesting, perhaps, is their rhetorical effect. The sentence base, in its most concise form, is stark and striking. Because it is so striking, it can be used to empha-size:

Progress was slow.

Because it is so concise, it can present ideas clearly and directly:

Practice makes perfect.

Standing alone, it takes on an aphoristic quality:

Boys will be boys.

Exercises

1. Using the basic sentence types as models, compose five sentences for each of these pattern types:

    a. subject-verb
    b. subject-verb-object
    c. subject-verb-indirect object-object
    d. subject-verb-object-objective complement
    e. subject-linking verb-noun
    f. subject-linking verb-adjective

2. Discuss the basic sentence types in the following sentences:

    a. Factories proliferated.
    b. Sleeping Beauty takes Nytol.
    c. Skylab is falling.
    d. Planes crossed the alps.
    e. Reaction was strong.
    f. Audiences grew restless.
    g. Everyone imitated the Americans.
    h. Sonic booms are unsound.
    i. Not all whales are large.
    j. Marie Curie discovered radium.

Expansion by Modification

It should be obvious that these basic sentence types can be made more complex by making a few transformations. In English, these transformations constitute stylistic choices. These stylistic changes are many and varied, but most involve some sort of syntactic change. There is no need to go into complicated rules of grammar to learn how to make these changes. You already know intuitively how to make many of them. But you can exert a more conscious control over these processes with just a little effort.

One important means of transforming basic sentences into more complex sentences is by modification. **Modification** is *the process of supplying additional information about a word or word group to which the modifier is attached.* A modifier usually comments on, qualifies, or limits the word that it modifies. A modifier may be a word, a phrase, or a complete clause.

One way of expanding the basic sentence types is by adding **adjective modifiers** to a noun in the base sentence:

Adjective Modifiers
The *black* smoke poured out the chimney.
A *velvety* mold covers the walls.
The farmer picked the *golden, ripe* fruit.
The *decrepit old* house was abandoned.

Another way you can expand the basic sentence types is by adding **participial modifiers:**

Participial Modifiers
Chanting rhythmically, they file through the streets.
Picasso has a *fragmented* iris.
Broken hearts will mend.
The child, *kicking* and *screaming*, irritated the visitors.
Bruised and *battered*, he awaited the enemy.

A third way you can expand basic sentence patterns is to add **relative clauses** as modifiers of the noun:

Relative Clause Modifiers
All that *glitters* is not gold.
I like people *who are thoughtful*.
We admired the car *which he recently bought*.
Everything *that I am* I owe my parents.

A fourth way you can expand the sentence base is to add to the noun **prepositional phrase modifiers:**

Prepositional Phrase Modifiers
Paris is the central jewel *of the French crown*.
A sense *of humor* is important.
The explanation *in this book* is confusing.
The car *by the side of the road* has been abandoned.

Just as you can expand basic sentence types by adding modifiers to the noun, you can also expand them by *adding modifiers to the verb*.

For example, you can add a single **adverb** to the base:

Adverb Modifier
Golden ages *never* last long.
Summer is *here*.
Lately I can't sleep.
He *usually* eats breakfast.
The cost is *surprisingly* low.

You can add a **prepositional phrase:**

Prepositional Phrase Modifier
Immigrants poured *into America*.
Balloons bob *in the wind*.
He drove the car *into the ditch*.
In the morning, he watches television.
At first, I was afraid.

Or you can include a **subordinate clause:**

Subordinate Clause Modifier
Whales do not breathe *while they are under water*.

Take things *as you find them.*
If it is grape season, the gutters will be purple with leavings.
The alarm sounded *while she was sleeping.*

Expansion by Substitution

Another way of expanding the basic sentence types is by *substituting* words, phrases, or clauses for nouns in noun positions.

You can substitute a **gerund** for a noun:

Gerund Substitute
Facing a shark always takes courage.
Jan's *singing* drove me crazy.
Destroying the rain forest could upset the climate all over the world.
Shoveling snow is difficult.

You can put an **infinitive** or **infinitive phrase** in place of a noun.

Infinitive Substitute
We can't afford *to run* out of ideas.
Bullfrogs like *to croak.*
To act that way is unforgiveable.
He would have liked *to have believed* her.

Or you can substitute a **complete clause** for a noun:

Clause Substitute
Nostalgia isn't *what it used to be.*
What he did surprised me greatly.
You can believe *whatever she tells you.*
It depends upon *how they react.*

The rhetorical effect of expanded sentence types is not too much different from that of the minimal sentence types. Like minimal sentence types, expanded sentence types can be clear, concise, striking, forceful, direct, and aphoristic.

Exercises

1. Compose ten expanded sentences, using a different kind of modifier in each base.

2. Combine the following bases, changing one sentence in each set into a modifier (adjective, relative clause, participial phrase, prepositional phrase) in the other sentence. For example:

> Cinderella has a foot.
> The foot is dirty.
> Cinderella has a *dirty* foot.

   a. The widow kneels silently.
   The widow is wearing her grief like a cloak.

   b. The French people sometimes refer to their country as a hexagon.
   The French people greatly admire mathematical elegance.

   c. Her eyelashes waved at the world every time she blinked.
   Her eyelashes were heavy.
   Her eyelashes were false.

   d. The puppy had a long, skinny tail.
   The tail was in the shape of a parenthesis.

   e. The brook gurgled by.
   It was splashing and splattering.

   f. The moon peered down on the black world below.
   It was like the eye of a cyclops.

   g. *Sumō* calls itself the national sport.
   Sumō is the oldest form of Japanese wrestling.

   h. The raindrops fell against the window.
   They were tapping rhythmically against the glass.

   i. His hair formed waves.
   The waves were down the back of his head.

j. Her hands sat quietly in her lap.
They were thin and transparent.

3. Combine the following sentences so that the second sentence in each
set becomes a gerund, an infinitive, or a subordinate clause when embedded in the first. For example:

> Insomnia cures something.
> Someone is snoring.
> Insomnia cures *snoring.*

a. He asked me something.
I should leave at once.

b. Something is forbidden.
Someone carries firearms.

c. I hate something.
I get up early.

d. Something is no easy task.
Someone is a doctor.

e. We just got a report.
The president was assassinated.

f. It is understandable.
You are irritated about the economy.

g. Something can change the ecology of a whole region.
Someone is damming a river.

h. The evidence convicted him.
The jury considered the evidence.

i. I have read something.
Hank Aaron broke Babe Ruth's home-run record.

j. Something is an active process.
Someone is reading photographs.

4. Make one sentence into an adverbial modifier (adverb, prepositional phrase, subordinate clause). For example:

>   It is summer.
>   The heat is unbearable.
>   The heat is unbearable *in the summer.*
>   *or*
>   *When it is summer,* the heat is unbearable.

   a. It is autumn.
     The leaves begin to fall.

   b. You smoke too much.
     You will get cancer.

   c. We will meet.
     The bridge crosses the river.

   d. She spoke the words.
     Then there was a dead silence.

   e. He promised not to do it.
     He did it.

Expansion by Coordination

A third way of expanding the basic sentence types is by *coordination.* Because you employ coordination so often in everyday speech, it seems rather foolish to suggest that this is another sophisticated way that good writers have of manipulating sentences. Yet coordination is in fact an important way of transforming basic sentence patterns. It is important to learn something of grammatical coordination because it is basic to understanding the rhetorical concepts of parallelism and antithesis.

The Parallel Sentence

Parallelism is a special kind of coordination. It is *the process of linking two or more grammatical units using similar grammatical forms.* You can join *two* words in parallel structure:

You cannot serve God and
                    Mammon.
Climate and landscape play an important role in the formation of
every civilization.

You can join a *series* of words or phrases in parallel order:

Apples,
peaches,
pears,
plums—he arranged them all in pleasing piles.

Suddenly he stopped,
            jumped straight up, and
            arched the ball toward the basket.

Or you can join *complete sentences* in parallel structure:

Insects cannot close their eyes; they sleep with them open.

The mountains are behind, and the thirsty plains lie ahead.

An apple a day keeps the doctor away. . . .
An onion a day keeps everybody away.

If you link two or more words, phrases, or clauses together without a conjunction, this has the effect of speeding up the line, affording
economy of expression, and achieving emphasis and climax:

I came, I saw, I flunked.
Whole armies, whole fleets vanished.

If, however, you join words, phrases, and clauses with many
connectives, this has the effect of slowing up the line:

The muddy groundswell lifts and breaks and falls and slides away.
                    —John Gould Fletcher, *The Groundswell*

The raisins and almonds and figs and apples and oranges and
chocolates and sweets were now passed about the table and Aunt
Julia invited all the guests to have either port or sherry.
                    —James Joyce, ''The Dead''

Linking grammatical constructions with many conjunctions can be a means of emphasis because each word or phrase is presented to the mind in such a way that each word stands out. In addition, it can be a source of prose rhythm.

If you set forth words, phrases, or clauses in such a way that the final item in the series gains in force and intensity, the result is a parallel series ending in a climax:

> He who loses money loses much;
> he who loses a friend loses more;
> he who loses his nerve loses all.

> Because of a nail a horse was lost,
> because of a horse a battle was lost,
> because of a battle a war was lost, and
>   all for the want of a horseshoe nail.

The principle of expressing parallel ideas in parallel structures can be applied to grammatical constructions of all kinds:

> Sharks will swallow anything: sea turtles,
>   birds,
>   fish,
>   lobsters,
>   horseshoe crabs,
>   garbage,
>   coal,
>   people.

> But if thought corrupts language;
> language can also corrupt thought.
>   —George Orwell, *Politics of the English Language*
> Rainbows,
> halos,
> coronas—these are born of the action of atmospheric components
>   on light.

Parallel structure has a variety of uses in writing. It can be used to organize parallel ideas. It can be used to catalog a sequence of ideas in serial order. It can be employed to develop a climactic order of ideas. It can be used to secure balance and harmony. And it can be a source of prose rhythm.

Exercises

1. Write five sentences using words or phrases in a series.

2. Write five sentences using subordinate clauses in a series.

3. Compose five parallel sentences using independent clauses in a series.

4. Discuss the effect of the parallel structure in the following sentences and phrases:

    a. The Roman empire had many virtues and many vices.

    b. The river deepens and slows and loses its clarity.

    c. There were paintings everywhere—on store fronts, inside factories, and in private houses, where they sometimes decorated the rooms from floor to ceiling.

    d. Without the atmosphere no animal or plant, bird or fish, tree or blade of grass could exist.

    e. The world is coming to an end—repent and return those library books.

    f. In the trunks of trees, in dead limbs, in weathered fence posts, and in the wooden structures that man builds, myriad insects dig, bore, and tunnel, carving out nests and nurseries for their young.

    g. Whether they're Contemporary or Moroccan, Rya or Oriental, hand-made or machine-made, the great classic rugs are wool.

The Antithetical Sentence

The **antithetical sentence** is *a special type of parallel sentence in which contrasting ideas are juxtaposed in balanced or parallel structures*. Antithesis, like parallelism, is a form of coordination, and the rules of coordination also apply to antithesis.

In contructing antithetical sentences, you can juxtapose *words* and *phrases:*

> *War:* 2,485,321; *Peace:* 0.
> Use *soft* words and *hard* arguments.
> Easy *come,* easy *go.*

Or you can link complete *clauses* or *sentences:*

> As there are valleys on land,
> so there are valleys under the sea.
>
> If a free society cannot help the many who are poor,
> it cannot save the few who are rich.
> > —John F. Kennedy

In joining two or more clauses or sentences, you can use conjuctions or conjunctive adverbs:

> The spirit is willing, *but*
> the flesh is weak.
>
> Hope for the best *and* prepare for the worst.
>
> Jesus was a fisher of men, *not* a keeper of the aquarium.

Or you can simply juxtapose two or more sentences by means of punctuation:

> Moths spin cocoons;
> butterflies do not.
>
> What time you go to sleep is your business.
> What time you wake up is ours.

> Order is comic;
> chaos is tragic.
> —John Updike

Antithesis is based upon the principle of contrast. By using antithesis, a writer can convey his or her ideas more clearly because of the emphasis afforded by the contrast. Thus, good can be contrasted with evil, love with hate, virtue with vice, peace with war, cowardice with bravery, and so forth. For example, in the graffiti

> Make love, not war.

> Plant flowers, not bombs.

the effect of the antithesis is to emphasize the idea that people should do something constructive, not destructive, in the modern world. Thus, life (love, procreation, conservation) is contrasted to death (hate, destruction, war).

Antithesis, like parallelism, is invaluable in achieving an effective prose style. It can be used to emphasize, to clarify, to sharpen an effect, to express a contradiction, to intensify ideas, or to discriminate between opposing ideas. Because antithesis is founded upon such a deep principle of human nature, you will find it in proverbs, maxims, wise sayings, dialogues, and formal debates.

Exercises

1. Pick out the word or words that form the basis of the antitheses in the following sentences. What effect do the antitheses have in relation to the meaning?

   a. The atmosphere is clearly not a calm ocean of air, but a tossing, unquiet sea.

   b. Do as I say; not as I do.

   c. There are no separate oceans; there is only the sea, single and all-encompassing.

d. For every mountain that is obliterated from the earth, a new one comes into being.

e. You can't control the purity of your tap water, but you can control the purity of your drinking water.

f. He that cannot obey, cannot command.

g. Every leaf, every flower, every garland is carved by hand.

h. Man proposes; God disposes.

i. Neither a borrower nor a lender be.

—Shakespeare

j. One man sows, and another reaps.

2. Compose five antithetical sentences.

The Cumulative Sentence

Thus far we have seen that the basic sentence types are the foundation of an effective style. But to achieve a mature style, you need to draw upon other stylistic principles, such as modification, substitution, and coordination, to expand your stylistic resources.

In addition to these stylistic types, another important sentence type is the cumulative sentence. The *cumulative sentence* is a particular sentence type first described and discussed by Francis Christensen. According to Christensen, the **cumulative sentence** is *one that begins with a sentence base.* The base contains the main subject and the main verb together with any *bound modifiers* (modifiers such as articles, adjectives, participles, and prepositional phrases that cannot be freely moved about in the sentence). Then to that base are added *free* or *sentence modifiers* in the form of phrases and clauses. These phrases and clauses are usually set off by commas, and they can be freely moved to other positions in the sentence without distorting the essential meaning of the sentence. For example:

Slowly and laboriously, the car climbed up the hill.

The car, slowly and laboriously, climbed up the hill.

The car climbed up the hill, slowly and laboriously.

In the cumulative sentence, the main idea is stated in the sentence base, and the subordinate or qualifying ideas are stated in the free modifiers.

The following student sentence is a good example of the cumulative sentence.

1 Her hands sat quietly in her lap,
   2 thin and nearly transparent with age, (A + A)
   2 the blue veins forming ridges from the wrists to the knuckles, (Abs)
      3 jutting from the wasted flesh, (VP)
   2 the crooked, skinny fingers bent around each other in her clasp, (Abs)
      3 like the claws of a bird clutching a tree limb. (PP)

This sentence begins with a base clause ("Her hands sat quietly in her lap"). This base clause is followed by a sequence of free modifiers (numbered and indented for visual effect) that add concrete details to the base. The modifiers labeled 2 are parallel to each other, but subordinate to the base clause (level 1). They add descriptive details to the base. The modifiers labeled 3 are subordinate to the level 2 modifiers immediately above them. Sentence elements are coordinate when they show similarity of structure of parallel ideas. Sentence elements are subordinate if they give evidence of subordination of ideas. There is a deductive movement in the sentence from the more general statement of the base to the less general and more specific descriptive details in the modifiers. The symbols in parentheses are shorthand terms to describe the grammatical nature of the modifiers (A + A, adjectives in a series; AC, adjective cluster; Abs, absolute construction; VP, verbal phrase; PP, prepositional phrase; RC, relative clause; SC, subordinate clause).

The cumulative sentence often begins with the sentence base, but there are variations on the basic pattern, as the following student sentences illustrate.

It may begin with free modifiers, followed by the sentence base, to which are added other modifiers:

> 2 As the snow melted on the roof, (SC)
> 1 streams of clear, cold water rippled over the slanted, brown-glazed shingles and slid off the edge,
> > 2 forming a waterfall which splashed on the grey cement wall below. (VP)

> 2 Stone naked, (AC)
> > 3 except for our skimpy underwear, (PP)
> 1 we stood like stalagmites,
> > 2 our feet anchored to the floor of the cavernous room, (Abs)
> > 2 our bodies shooting upwards. (Abs)

It may begin with a series of free modifiers, with the sentence base suspended until the very end:

> 2 Making a low, thunderlike rumble that progresses to a shriek as it barely clears the barn, (VP)
> 2 rattling every window in the house, (VP) and
> 2 terrifying the cattle, (VP)
> 1 the huge jet roars over the house.

> 2 Into the darkened room, (PP)
> 2 like a silver arrow, (PP)
> 1 the light filtered.

The cumulative sentence seems to be more fluid, more natural than some of the other sentence types. In the cumulative sentence, the ideas seem to run along easily, almost as if one were thinking aloud or engaging in a free-flowing conversation. In fact, the style of the cumulative sentence is very much like the style of spoken prose, in which the speaker makes a point, amplifies it, and then expands, limits, or illustrates it by successive phrases and clauses.

Although the cumulative sentence is perhaps more common in narrative and descriptive prose, it can be used very effectively in expository prose as the following example illustrates:

1 The cumulative sentence in unskillful hands is unsteady,
  2 allowing a writer to ramble on, (VP)
    3 adding modifier after modifier, (VP)
      4 until the reader is almost overwhelmed, (SC)
        5 because the writer's central idea is lost. (SC)

The above sentence, like the narrative sentence examples, begins with a sentence base ("The cumulative sentence in unskillful hands is unsteady"). Added to the base are four free modifiers (levels 2, 3, 4, 5), each one subordinate to the modifier above it, each one expanding the main idea in the sentence base.

It is relatively easy to write a cumulative sentence. Begin with a base:

1 Dark specks moved on the horizon,

Add a modifier:
  2 gliding across the ocean like white seagulls across the sky,

Add another modifier:
  2 their features slowly coming into view—

Add several more modifiers, making them subordinate to the previous modifier or modifiers:

    3 white sails,
    3 inverted v-shaped hulls,
    3 tall masts.

—Student sentence

The cumulative sentence is an especially good sentence to use in narratives because it enables the writer to enrich a sentence with concrete, specific detail. But it has other rhetorical uses also. It can be used in expository prose to define a topic, to limit it, to expand it by means of examples, or to qualify it in some way. It can also be an excellent source of prose rhythm.

Exercises

1. Compose ten cumulative sentences using the following base clauses:

    a. The fire raged.
    b. April had come again.
    c. The door began to open slowly.
    d. The music began.
    e. The sky outside was changing.
    f. The dentist began his work.
    g. The speaker approached the podium.
    h. The aroma was tantalizing.
    i. He released the ball.
    j. The clouds floated by.

2. Compose five original cumulative sentences. In at least one or two sentences, add as many free modifiers as possible to the base.

3. Bring to class five cumulative sentences and analyze their structure and their effectiveness.

4. Bring to class a paragraph composed almost exclusively of cumulative sentences. Then analyze the sentences and discuss their purpose and effectiveness.

I think it should be clear by now from our discussion of the grammar of the sentence that almost every sentence in English presents the writer with innumerable choices. Many beginning writers, however, are almost completely unaware that they have syntactic stylistic options and that these options have rhetorical consequences. Too often, writers concentrate more on word choice, assuming that the sentence structure will somehow take care of itself. Careful writers are able at times to choose deliberately, weighing their alternatives. At the very least, they can go back and revise their sentences after they have written them. Sentence style consists of using minimal grammatical patterns and of transforming these basic patterns into more complex patterns.

Summary Exercises

1. Write an essay in which you analyze the style of graffiti. Be sure that in your analysis, you show how the sentence structure is used to make a point.

2. Write an essay in which you do a stylistic analysis of proverbs.

3. Write an essay in which you do a stylistic analysis of advertising slogans and headlines.

4. Identify the sentence types in the following passages and discuss their use:

a.   Soon afterwards they retired, Mama in her big oak bed on one side of the room, Emilio and Rosy in their boxes full of straw and sheepskins on the other side of the room.
     The moon went over the sky and the surf roared on the rocks. The roosters crowed the first call. The surf subsided to a whispering surge against the reef. The moon dropped toward the sea. The roosters crowed again.
     The moon was near down to the water when Pepe rode on a winged horse to his home flat. His dog bounced out and circled the horse yelping with pleasure. Pepe slid off the saddle to the ground. The weathered little shack was silver in the moonlight and the square shadow of it was black to the north and east. Against the east the piling mountains were misty with light; their tops melted into the sky.
                  —John Steinbeck, "Flight"

b.   It came on great oiled, resilient, striding legs. It towered thirty feet above half of the trees, a great evil god, folding its delicate watchmaker's claws close to its oily reptilian chest. Each lower leg was a piston, a thousand pounds of white bone, sunk in thick ropes of muscle, sheathed over in a gleam of pebbled skin like the mail of a terrible warrior. Each thigh was a ton of meat, ivory, and steel mesh. And from the great breathing cage of the upper body those two delicate arms dangled out front, arms with hands which might pick up and examine men like toys, while the snake neck coiled. And the head itself, a ton of sculptured stone, lifted easily upon the sky. Its mouth gaped, exposing a fence of teeth like daggers. Its eyes rolled, ostrich eggs, empty of all expression save hunger. It closed its mouth in a death grin. It ran, its pelvic bones crushing aside trees and bushes, its taloned feet clawing damp earth, leaving prints six inches deep wherever it settled its weight. It ran with a gliding ballet step, far too poised and balanced for its ten tons. It moved into a sunlit area warily, its beautifully reptile hands feeling the air.

—Ray Bradbury, "A Sound of Thunder"

c.   None of them knew the color of the sky. Their eyes glanced level, and were fastened upon the waves that swept toward them. These waves were of the hue of slate, save for the tops, which were of foaming white, and all of the men knew the colors of the sea. The horizon narrowed and widened, and dipped and rose, and at all times its edge was jagged with waves that seemed to thrust up in points like rocks. Many a man ought to have a bathtub larger than the boat which here rode upon the sea. These waves were most wrongfully and barbarously abrupt and tall, and each froth-top was a problem in small-boat navigation.

—Stephen Crane, "The Open Boat"

d.   We observe today not a victory of party but a celebration of freedom—symbolizing an end as well as a beginning—signifying renewal as well as change. For I have sworn before you and Almighty God the same solemn oath our forebears prescribed nearly a century and three-quarters ago.

The world is very different now. For man holds in his mortal hands the power to abolish all forms of human poverty and all forms of human life. And yet the same revolutionary beliefs for which our forebears fought are still at issue around the globe—the belief that the rights of man come not from the generosity of the state but from the hand of God.

We dare not forget today that we are the heirs of that first revolution. Let the word go forth from this time and place, to friend and foe alike, that the torch has been passed to a new generation of Americans—born in this century, tempered by war, disciplined by a hard and bitter peace, proud of our ancient heritage, and unwilling to witness or permit the slow undoing of those human rights to which this nation has always been committed, and to which we are committed today at home and around the world.

Let every nation know, whether it wishes us well or ill, that we shall pay any price, bear any burden, meet any hardship, support any friend, oppose any foe to assure the survival and the success of liberty.

—John F. Kennedy, inaugural address, 1961

e. To everything there is a season, and a time to every purpose under heaven:
   2. A time to be born, and a time to die; a time to plant, and a time to pluck up that which is planted;
   3. A time to kill, and a time to heal; a time to break down, and a time to build up;
   4. A time to weep, and a time to laugh; a time to mourn, and a time to dance;
   5. A time to cast away stones, and a time to gather stones together; a time to embrace, and a time to refrain from embracing;
   6. A time to get, and a time to lose; a time to keep, and a time to cast away;
   7. A time to rend, and a time to sew; a time to keep silence, and a time to speak;
   8. A time to love, and a time to hate; a time of war, a time of peace.

—Ecclesiastes, chapter 3, King James Version of the Bible.

The Devil (mortified): Senor Don Juan: you are uncivil to my friends.

Don Juan: Pooh! Why should I be civil to them or to you? In this palace of lies a truth or two will not hurt you. Your friends are the dullest dogs I know. They are not beautiful: they are only decorated. They are not clean: they are only shaved and starched. They are not dignified: they are only fashionably dressed. They are not educated: they are only college passmen. They are not religious: they are only pew-renters. They are not moral: they are only conventional. They are not virtuous: they are only cowardly. They are not artistic: they are only lascivious. They are not prosperous; they are only rich. They are not loyal, they are only servile; not dutiful, only sheepish; not public-spirited, only patriotic; not courageous, only quarrelsome; not determined, only obstinate; not masterful, only domineering; not self-controlled, only obtuse; not self-respecting, only vain; not kind, only sentimental; not social, only gregarious; not considerate, only polite; not intelligent, only opinionated; not progressive, only factious; not imaginative, only superstitious; not just, only vindictive; not generous, only propitiatory; not disciplined, only cowed; and not truthful at all—liars every one of them, to the very backbone of their souls.

—George Bernard Shaw, *Man and Superman*

Style:
Word
Choice

Chapter 12

Style: Word Choice

Whether or not you write extensively, you are still faced constantly with the problem of choosing between two or more words. Quite often, you make your choices unconsciously, but the choice still has to be made. Many students have an intuitive feeling for language, but the problem is using words effectively in writing. Communication of some kind can be carried on with a small or imprecise vocabulary, and such communication can at times be moderately effective. But to have a small number of words at your disposal is to limit your resources, and intelligent choices among words cannot be made unless you have a store of words from which to choose.

"But I don't know much about words," one student protested, and then proceeded to write an imaginative and original paper about diction.

No Experience

While I'm thinking to myself, "What dialect? I haven't had any experience with dialect!" a sudden but not uncommon wail is heard through the hall. "Ay-un, kin I borrrr-oww you-ur pi-unk le-o-tards?" (TRANSL: Ann, can I borrow your pink leotards?) "Whaaaaa?" is the extremely nasal and immediate reply. "Pi-unk le-o-tards, do ye-u hay-ave iny I kin way-er?" Ignoring another "Whaaaaa?" the Voice goes on to implore, "Tha-ey hay-ave te-u be pi-unk, I cay-n't way-er bu-lack ones. I'ull wash they-um ou-oot ay-und ever-y-th-yang. Pu-lease?" The resultant reply from down the hall is very long and very unintelligible, but it doesn't daunt the seeker-of-leotards. "Way-ell, tha-ey cay-un be ao-paque whe-ite wuns. Way-ell?" Then, just as suddenly as it began, it is over. How can I concentrate on dialects with such interruptions?

Dialect, dialect, it's driving me bananas! A friend wanders in, momentarily halting my leap from the window.

"Hi. Yeah, well . . . watcha doin'?"

"Uh. Nothin' . . . Inglish . . ."

"Uh . . ."

"Well, I can't write anything, ya know?"

"Um . . . yeah . . . I know . . ."

"Um . . ."

"Ya know what I mean?"

"Um . . ."

After another half-hour or so of mutual commiseration, the friend wanders out and once again I am left without an idea in my head.

Before I can really get into some deep thinking on the subject, my mother calls. And while "discussing" money matters with her I hear another conversation in the background. "Oh, you sweet wittle baby-kins," my sister croons to the dog. "You is such a good wittle doggie-poo. Yes, um is de sweetest . . ." etc., etc. After hanging up, still nothing—except homesickness for my doggie-poo. I try thinking of something other than dialect, such as jargon, slang, idioms. Nothing!

Turning on the TV with the desperate hope of finding inspiration, I hear some impeccably dressed newscaster intone the words, "And this, just in. A usually reliable Pentagon source, who declined to be identified, has vigorously denied suggesting that published speculation, admittedly based on fragmentary and unconfirmed reports not available to the press, regarding allied troop movements in or near unspecified areas of Indochina and purportedly involving undisclosed numbers of South Vietnamese, Cambodian, Laotian, and perhaps American armed personnel is false, although he cautioned that such published speculation could be dangerously misleading and potentially divisive." The mind is boggled! And the sad truth being that a boggled mind with no experience with the subject might as well abandon all hope of an English paper.

If you are like this student, you have had considerable experience with diction, but you cannot always bring this knowledge to conscious awareness. Therefore, perhaps you need more formal approaches to word choice and vocabulary study.

Much of the traditional advice offered for enlarging your vocabulary is sound:

1. Buy a good dictionary and use it frequently.
2. Obtain a good thesaurus.
3. Try to bring new words into your writing and conversation.
4. Read widely in literature of all kinds.
5. Read aloud passages of unusual force and beauty.

Exercises

1. Write an essay, similar to the student essay on dialects, in which you transcribe as accurately as you can the speech of friends, relatives, acquaintances, radio or television newscasters, and the like, and place these transcriptions into a coherent narrative.

2. Bring to class five new words in the context of a short passage from a magazine ad, a newspaper, or a book, and discuss their meanings, their effectiveness in context, and their possible origins.

In addition to these more traditional ways of developing your vocabulary, another way of enlarging your vocabulary and increasing your sensitivity to language is by formal study, and it is with the formal study of words that we will be primarily concerned in this chapter.

Denotation and Connotation

Choose words for their literal as well as for their suggested meanings. The **denotation** of a word is *its literal or dictionary meaning.* The **connotation** of a word is *the sum total of its suggested or associative meanings.* Denotations are emotionally or morally neutral, while connotations convey an attitude toward their referents. Words have meanings beyond those in the dictionary. For example, if you look up the word *house* in the dictionary, you will find that the word refers to "a building or shelter that serves as living quarters for people." Then if you look up the related word *home*, you will notice that one of its primary meanings is "a family's place of residence." The **dictionary meaning** of these words is called their *denotative* meaning. In addition to their literal meanings, these words also evoke feelings and emotions and various associations. The word *house* seems to be the more neutral of the two words. You seldom hear or read about someone defending a house, but books and movies are filled with stories about people defending their homes. The movie *Straw Dogs* is one example. So the word *home* seems to carry with it stronger connotations than the word *house*. In fact, each of the following synonyms for the words *house* and *home* has slightly different meanings and different connotations from the others:

habitation	residence	retreat
abode	homestead	haunt
dwelling	hearth	nest
lodging	fatherland	quarters
domicile	country	hiding place

The first step in using a word in your writing, then, is to be sure that you understand its basic meaning, its referential meaning. If you do not, look it up in the dictionary. The second step is to consider its context, since the context of a word is also an important determinant of its meaning. Notice, for example, the difference in meaning in the words *house* and *home* in the following contexts:

People make houses.
People construct houses.
People make homes.
People construct homes.
People build houses, families make homes.

A third step is to consider the associated meanings of the word you are using. Would a reader be offended by the word, indifferent to it, aroused by it, or persuaded by it? Consider, for example, the differences in connotation of the following sentences, achieved by the substitution of a single word:

It's not much, but it's my *home*.
It's not much, but it's my *habitation*.
It's not much, but it's my *dwelling*.
It's not much, but it's my *residence*.
It's not much, but it's my *domicile*.
It's not much, but it's my *lodging*.
It's not much, but it's my *quarters*.
It's not much, but it's my *hiding place*.

Many connotations are individual and personal and depend on the writer's past experiences with the word and with the idea or thing to which the word refers. For example, for some people the word *snake* has unpleasant associations. For others, the words *country, patriotism, communism, fascism, totalitarianism, socialism, left wing, right wing, radical, liberal, conservative, Republican,* and *Democrat* have emotional overtones. In addition to any personal meanings and associations that words might have for us, there are some meanings and associations that are shared with people as a group. If you were brought up in a certain country and lived in a particular state, or city, or neighborhood, you would hold in common with the people there certain attitudes, beliefs, and feelings about words and about the things to which they refer. But more often than not, the connotation of a word is less fixed than its denotation.

Exercises

1. Explain the differences in denotation and connotation of the following sets of words:

   a. exist, be, subsist, live, vegetate, prevail, pass the time
   b. confusion, disarray, jumble, mess, turmoil, ferment, disturbance, uproar, rumpus, fracas, disorder
   c. crowd, gathering, throng, multitude, rabble, mob, horde

    d. child, brat, kid, urchin, youngster, tot, youth
    e. spit, sputter, splutter, drool, drivel, slaver, slabber, slobber
    f. meal, repast, spread, banquet, feast, feed
    g. hard, rigid, stubborn, stiff, firm, starchy, unbending, unyielding, inflexible
    h. sea, ocean, main, briny deep, waters, deep, high seas
    i. woman, skirt, lady, broad, female, the fair sex, chick, dame
    j. fat, corpulent, plump, stout, portly, burly, well-fed, fleshy, pudgy, paunchy, chubby

2. Make up sentences illustrating as accurately as possible one of the following sets of words. Use your dictionary if necessary.

    a. rash, incautious, imprudent, heedless, careless, reckless, wild, foolhardy

    b. loathe, dislike, resent, detest, hate, abhor, disgust, scorn

    c. vain, conceited, self-assured, self-satisfied, pretentious

    d. friend, acquaintance, intimate, associate, buddy, bosom pal, comrade, chum, sidekick

    e. fondness, love, affection, tenderness, attachment, passion, rapture, adoration, enchantment

3. Discuss the differences in connotation of the following proper names:

    a. Lulu, Lucile, Matilda, Agatha, Maggie, Percy, Elmer, Hugh, Jud, Edgar, Francis, Henry

    b. Gloria, Ruby, Christy, Stella, Laura, Sylvia, Robin, Scarlet

    c. Josephine/Josie, Marian/Mary, Robert/Bob, William/Will, Susan/Sue, Stephen/Steve, Katherine/Cathy, Thomas/Tom

    d. Jennifer, Elizabeth, Roberta, Florence, Alicia, Madeline, Melanie, Emily

    e. Achilles, Atlas, Hercules, Alfred, Atilla, Merlin, Casanova, Richard, Leonardo, Hero, Aristotle

4. Write an essay in which you discuss the denotative and connotative meanings of words in a letter to the editor or in a magazine advertisement.

5. Discuss the differences in connotation of the following brand names:

   a. Tide, Duz, Lux, All, Rinso, Cheer, Oxydol, Cold Power

   b. Winston, Camels, Lucky Strike, True, Kent, Salem, Viceroy, L&M, Virginia Slims, Marlboro

   c. Duster, Dart, Cheyenne, Pinto, Mustang, Charger, Continental, Imperial, Monarch, Jaguar, Rabbit, Bug

   d. Colgate, Aim, Pepsodent, Crest, Close-up, Pearl Drops, McCleans, Strike, Gleem

   e. Ivory, Palmolive, Dove, Joy, Downy, Borax, Clorox, Purex

6. Write five sentences in which you use the same word in each sentence, each time changing the connotation slightly.

Some categories of words seem to have the power to produce an immediate reaction in people. One category is words pertaining to everyday living such as *mother, father, home, marriage, bride, groom, divorce, widow,* and *God.* Another category is abstract words, such as *honor, virtue, pride, patriotism, truth, love, justice, valor, respect, duty, piety, freedom,* and *liberty.* A third category consists of proper names, especially the names of people who are in the public eye and who stir up emotional reactions: for example, Andrew Young, Ayatollah Khomeini, Castro, and Arafat. A final category is taboo words. Taboo words, especially profane and obscene words, shock and offend many people. They may be used to create attention, to discredit someone, to provoke confrontations, and to provide a kind of catharsis for the user.

Exercises

1. Give ten examples of emotion-laden words with which you are familiar and discuss their effects on you and the reasons for their effects.

2. What obscene words do you find offensive? Why do you find them offensive?

3. What makes a word obscene or taboo? Are people's attitudes toward taboo words changing? Is there a context in which obscenity might be justified?

4. Discuss the use of euphemisms that people employ to avoid mentioning the blunter taboo words.

Concrete and Abstract Words

Use concrete words to present a vivid picture to the reader's mind. **Concrete words** refer to *actual, specific things in experience.* More than any other words, concrete words bring us closest to immediate sensation. They appeal to the reader's sense of touch, taste, smell, sight, or hearing. They can be especially effective in narrative and descriptive writing, as the following student sentences illustrate:

> The teakettle sat on the stove boiling, the water rumbling against the metal sides, the steam rising in puffs through the top, disappearing into the air only moments after its escape, blowing a shrill whistle as I ran to lift it from the fire.

> About noon, Mom sliced up thick, uneven chunks of homemade bread, covering them with slabs of pink ham and wedges of creamy cheese; then she set out tumblers of foamy milk and clinking glasses of cola.

Not all writing can be concrete, nor does it necessarily have to be. But even in expository writing, you can be very concrete in your choice of supporting details, in your examples, and in your illustrations.

Abstract words *are words that refer to qualities (hot, cold, good, bad), relationships (existence, quantity, order, number), and ideas (curiosity, inquiry, judgments, brief, credulity).* They tend to be Latinate words and are usually, but not necessarily, longer and more complex than Anglo-Saxon words.

Abstract words are frequently used to express complex ideas. They can give fine distinctions to thought, and they are often used to convey technical or specialized ideas. They are often learned words, words found more in written than in spoken English. If you are going to engage in any serious discussion of ideas from law, science, medicine, psychology, philosophy, or politics, you will make some use of abstract words. You must be careful, however, in using abstract words. If you do not use them carefully, your writing can become vague, obscure, and inaccurate, as in the following passage taken from a student theme:

> Loneliness is an appalling ordeal, encasing its victim in a desolate world. If he is to survive, the individual must learn to cope with his dilemma. To dispossess this perplexity requires the careful observance of the sufferer's habitat, recreation, and thoughts.
>
> The victim of loneliness must use the eyes of Argus when choosing his environmental habitat. He should try to find a location in the midst of a mass of extroverts. Their gregarious characteristics might draw the victim into their circle, curing him of his problem. If this desired location cannot be found, his abode should be in the approximate area of a center of communal entertainment. This will, in all likelihood, give him a temporary reprieve from the torment of his plight. Under no circumstances should the individual choose a secluded dwelling. Seclusion only adds to the pain, driving him deeper into the depths of his despair.

Phrases such as "appalling ordeal," "dispossess this perplexity," "the sufferer's habitat," "environmental habitat," and the like obscure rather than advance this writer's thought. Not only does the misuse of the abstract words obscure the writer's full meaning, but these words also make the writing seem stuffy and affected. Do not, then, indulge in a fondness for abstract words for their own sake. When you do use them, try to use them with some clarity and precision. Your main task as a writer is actually to combine the abstract with the concrete. If you have been operating at a very high level of abstraction in your writing, you will want to narrow down occasionally and give some concrete illustrations.

General and Specific Words

Choose general words to express general ideas. Use specific words to supply exact details.

A **general word** is *one that applies to many things, to a collectivity, to the whole.* Any word that takes in a group of particulars, in which these particulars are thought of as parts of a whole, is a general word. If, however, a word refers to only a few of these particulars, to the parts, the word is specific. A **specific word** is *one that applies to particular, unique, and distinctive things.* A specific word calls forth a distinct mental image. Thus, the word *clothing* is general, but the term *yellow striped pants* evokes a specific image.

General and specific words should not be confused with abstract and concrete words. A general word is not necessarily an abstract word, nor is a concrete word necessarily specific. For example, the word *dog* is a general word because it can refer to many animals, but it is obviously not abstract. On the other hand, neither is it very specific, although it is concrete. To make the idea to which the word *dog* refers specific, you would want to make the word more particular. For instance, the words *cur, mutt,* and *hound* call forth much more distinct mental images than does the word *dog.* Usually, when your instructors ask you to make your writing more concrete, they want you to be both concrete and specific.

It is often pointed out that the terms *general* and *specific* are relative. A word may be specific in relation to one word, yet general in relation to another. Words specify in varying degrees. In writing, the context often indicates whether a word is being used in a general sense or in a particular sense. *Athlete* is more general than *fighter,* but *fighter* is more general than *Muhammad Ali. Fragrance* is more definite than *odor. Bird* is more general than *thrush; thrush* is more general than *robin.* In your writing, you want to be sure that you are aware of the difference. At times you will want to use general terms, but other times you may want to choose a more vivid and precise word to present the mind of your readers with a more definite picture.

Exercises

1. What is the purpose of the abstract words in the following sentences? What happens to the meaning if concrete words are substituted for the abstract words? Why do the writers of these sentences use abstract words instead of concrete words?

   a. Today's L&M is rich, mellow, distinctively smooth.

   b. Volvo gives you luxury, quality, and a sense of elegance that other so-called luxury cars can't match.

   c. Winston gives me real taste and real pleasure; in my book, that's the only reason to smoke.

   d. Armstrong carpets give you the easy elegance and warmth of rich autumn hues.

   e. Through the years, V.O. has stood apart as a whiskey uncompromising in quality, with a tradition of craftsmanship that has made it The First Canadian in smoothness.

2. Discuss in class your attitudes toward abstract words such as *truth, honor, courage, patriotism, virtue, love,* and *loyalty.* Cite specific experiences in the use of these words, avoidance of them, attempts to articulate them, and so forth.

3. Rewrite the following sentences. Substitute specific concrete details for the more abstract and general words (for example: general—*It was a cold morning;* concrete—*It was twenty degrees below zero*).

   a. We went shopping to get some food.
   b. He walked down the street in an unsteady manner.
   c. They tried to get money from him by dishonest means.
   d. The dishes fell to the floor with a loud noise.

e. The dog gave a high, excited bark.
f. He looked at her in an angry way.
g. She had a funny expression on her face as she talked.
h. Slowly he departed from the room.

4. Describe a scene, an event, or an experience using abstract words. Then describe the same scene using concrete words.

5. Paraphrase the following proverbs, eliminating the concrete and specific diction, including the figures of speech:

a. A stitch in time saves nine.
b. A rolling stone gathers no moss.
c. A new broom sweeps clean.
d. When the cat's away, the mice will play.
e. Every cloud has a silver lining.
f. A bird in the hand is worth two in the bush.
g. You can't teach an old dog new tricks.
h. Birds of a feather flock together.
i. Barking dogs never bite.
j. Still water runs deep.

Figurative Language

Use figures of speech to increase concreteness and to secure vividness in your writing. One student began a paper about an experience she had while working in the library with this vivid figure of speech:

> Maybe I shouldn't write on this particular topic, but at the moment it is the only thing on my mind. The experience is too fresh and disturbing. It lingers like a grease burn from a popcorn popper, stinging and irritating my thoughts.
>
> —Patti

Not only did the grease-burn comparison effectively convey her feelings about her experience in a way that few abstractions could, but also it was interesting. It captured my attention. It made me want to read on.

The **figurative meaning** of a word is *based on a comparison of unlike things*. To illustrate this, let us look at a couple of examples:

The leopard cannot change his spots.
When the wolf comes in the door, love creeps out the window.

In the first sentence, the leopard is obviously not a leopard but a metaphor for man. The spots of the leopard symbolize the ways of men, so the figurative meaning of the statement is that men cannot change their ways. In the second statement, the wolf is a metaphor for poverty, and the meaning of the proverb is that if young people marry before they have enough money to support themselves, their love will not last very long.

The **literal meaning** of a word is *its dictionary meaning*, its usual and customary meaning, as opposed to its figurative meaning. The literal meaning of the word *dog* is "a domesticated carnivorous mammal, having four legs." But you can call an unattractive person "a dog," as in the sentence "I went out last night with a real dog," and it is obvious that the statement is not literally true. Or you can use the word *dog* or the related word *cur* to refer to a miserable, contemptible person, as in the expression "You cur," and it is apparent that you are not speaking literally. When you transfer the reference of a word so that it covers other meanings and includes new associations, you are writing figuratively.

Three common figures of speech used by prose writers are the *simile*, the *metaphor*, and *personification*.

A **simile** is *a direct comparison in which two things, essentially unlike, are likened to one another*. The comparison is made explicit by the use of *like* or *as*. Similes can be used to express feelings as well as ideas, as the introductory paragraph from this student theme on the generation gap indicates:

> I have a problem which is eating away on my insides *like acid on a car battery*. Putting it down on paper won't solve anything, but it will make me calm down.
>
> —Christine

The figurative comparison of the student's problem with acid that eats away on a car battery captures the turbulence of the student's feelings in a way that literal language cannot.

Here is another example from a student theme of an effective use of similes to describe a wheat harvest:

> This weekend we took a short trip to the country and the countryside was beautiful. To begin with, the day was a beautiful day, such a blue sky, blue *like a lake on a clear day.* The grass was a kelly green which seemed to boast of a freshness that belongs only to the country.
>
> The wheat, *like golden waves,* shimmering in the sun, promised a bountiful harvest for the farmers. Seeing the wheat waving in the wind brought back old memories of the farm and of the yearly wheat harvest. Dad used to let me ride in the wheat bin of the combine, and I can still (very plainly) see the grasshoppers hopping and jumping to keep on top of the rising mound of golden grain that was pouring into the bin from an overhead spout, *resembling water being forced from an old-fashioned pump.*
>
> You know, I think wheat is the most beautiful crop that is grown on a Nebraskan farm. It always seems to be promising so much, *like a treasure chest full of golden coins.*
>
> —Shirley

The simile is such a natural form of expression that it is common in folk speech, where it draws its comparisons from everyday objects, animals, and events:

as fit as a fiddle	as blind as a bat
as steady as a rock	as strong as a horse
as clean as a whistle	as alike as two peas in a pod
as stiff as a board	like water off a duck's back
as stiff as a poker	like a bolt from the blue

A **metaphor** is *an implicit comparison in which two unlike things are likened to each other without the uses of* like *or* as. A metaphor can make abstract ideas concrete. It can describe, clarify, delineate, and point out logical relationships between things. It can also reveal attitudes and feelings and make judgments about the subject of the metaphor.

In the following passage from a student paper, the student uses a series of metaphors, combined with the vulture simile, to give her impressions of the gluttonous behavior of her friends one evening when they were dining out. The figurative language seems to capture the experience much better than an objective description of the scene might.

> Dinner tonight was a festival for gluttons. The people at the table where I was sitting were *ravenously* hungry, and we attacked our food *like vultures gleefully chomping on freshly killed meat.* We were gluttonous, sucking up our food, and when that was gone, scrounging for food at other tables. We were *snow cleaners*, inhaling a constant stream of victuals and seemingly exhaling it somewhere else so we could inhale more. We were *guerrilla fighters*, sneaking our *spoils of war* slyly (usually from the *jungle* of a neighboring table) so that we wouldn't have to share them with our *fellow fighters*. We were *Roman banqueters*, rolling in an *orgy* of good food, boisterous conduct, and riotous table manners. Even after exhausting the supply of food from every source possible, we clamored for more. We were insatiable and uncouth, and Emily Post would have been mortified!
>
> —Lynn

Like the simile, the metaphor is also a natural form of expression in everyday speech:

the apple of my eye	bury the hatchet
know the ropes	at the crossroads
in a nutshell	dark horse
sit on the fence	bone of contention
pull up stakes	nothing to sneeze at

Personification is *attributing to inanimate objects and abstractions, human qualities.* It is closely related to metaphor. In fact, personification is sometimes called personal metaphor. The tendency to ascribe life to inanimate objects seems to be universal.

> Truth has a good *face*, but bad *clothes*.
> Walls have *ears*.
> Love is *blind*.

Exercises

1. Write five sentences in which you use original figures of speech.

2. Discuss the use of figurative language in the following passages:

   a. Wit is a lean creature with a sharp inquiring nose, whereas humor has a kindly eye and comfortable girth. Wit, if it be necessary, uses malice to score a point—like a cat it is quick to jump—but humor keeps the peace in an easy chair. Wit is a better voice in a solo, but humor comes into the chorus best. Wit is as sharp as a stroke of lightning, whereas humor is diffuse like sunlight. Wit keeps the season's fashions and is precise in the phrases and judgments of the day, but humor is concerned with homely eternal things. Wit wears silk, but humor in homespun endures the wind.
   —Charles Brooks, "On the Difference Between
   Wit and Humor"

   b. The high gray-flannel fog of winter closed off the Salinas Valley from the sky and from all the rest of the world. On every side it sat like a lid on the mountains and made of the great valley a closed pot. On the broad, level land floor the gang plows bit deep and left the black earth shining like metal where the shares had cut. On the foothill ranches across the Salinas River, the yellow stubble fields seemed to be bathed in pale cold sunshine, but there was no sunshine in the valley now in December.
   —John Steinbeck, "The Chrysanthemums"

3. Pick out the figures of speech in the following sentences. What is being compared? Are the figures of speech effective?

   a. Ring and your room steward appears like a genie.

   b. The Mitsubishi Clean Air Engine is a pure engineering jewel.

   c. The Sheraton-Waikiki, like a gigantic ship of sail, stands poised on the crest of Waikiki Beach.

   d. Your air-conditioned room is a sunburst of Polynesian color.

e. The whirling, clattering helicopters, with the flexibility of humming birds, carry their passengers across green canyons and over the clawing fingertips of mountains from desert to rain forest.

f. Roads became black bands snaking their way through the fields.

g. The walrus is a relative of the seal with the wrinkled skin of an old oak.

h. These islands look like a strand of jade green beads splashed down in the middle of a cobalt blue sea.

i. Hawaii has magnificent beaches, blue-mirrored lagoons, high, wind-whipped cliffs that tumble majestically into the sea.

j. The starfish has a spokelike design.

4. Rewrite the passage from Steinbeck using literal language.

5. Select a brief prose passage almost completely lacking in figurative language. Then rewrite the passage using figurative language.

Doublespeak

Doublespeak is *the use of language to obscure the truth.* Increasingly, critics of contemporary culture are pointing out that when politicians, corporate executives, or advertisers deliberately distort language for their own gain, they are also distorting values. Consequently, the general public ought to be aware of the verbal techniques used to "overload our verbal circuits." These techniques include the use of jargon, meaningless abstractions, euphemisms, slogans, clichés, and so forth.

For example, advertisers attach adjectives such as *amazing, sensational, revolutionary, bold,* and *proud* to products as though these words had concrete referents. But what do these words really mean? Can the latest look in clothing, for example, really be called revolutionary?

More alarming, perhaps, than the use of meaningless abstractions is the use of euphemisms to hide the truth. A **euphemism** is *the substitution of a softened or less explicit expression for a more offensive one.* For example, during the Vietnam War, some government officials used euphemisms to hide from the American public the extent of the United States involvement in Vietnam. In the early stages of the war, despite the presence of United States troops in Vietnam, the word *troops* was never used. Instead, the United States was supposedly employing "advisers," and our role there was "indirect" and "political" rather than military. To soften public reaction to the waging of the war, apologists for the war used such words and expressions as "antipersonnel device" for gun, "routine improvement of visibility" for defoliation and crop destruction, "technical errors" for bombing errors in which civilians were killed, and "harassment and interdiction" for artillery fire. Slogans such as "waging the peace," "peace with honor," and "conducting a peace-keeping action" were also used to present the war in Vietnam in a more favorable light.

Both government deception (from the secrecy involving the U-2 affair in 1960 to the Watergate conspiracy) and corporate deception (lying in advertising; doubletalk used by corporate executives who give bribes and kickbacks to foreign officials) have occasioned a great deal of public distrust and have diminished confidence in the government and in the business community. The best way to react to doublespeak is to avoid it in your own language by using words, insofar as you are able, with truth, candor, and precision, and to insist upon a similar use of language on the part of government officials, public figures, and advertisers.

Exercises

1. Bring to class examples of gobbledygook from your textbooks or some other source. Discuss the stylistic features that make the writing gobbledygook and then try to rewrite the passage in clearer language.

2. Bring to class some recent advertisements that use jargon, slogans, clichés, or meaningless abstractions to make a point.

3. Examine the language of advertisements and discuss those which actually tell something about the product and those which merely influence us to buy.

4. Some critics argue that sometimes euphemisms are necessary to make events (jobs, death, and so forth) more bearable. Discuss.

Dialects

In its broadest sense, the word **dialects** refers to *varieties of language based on geographical, educational, or social differences, and writing conventions.* Dialects based on geographical differences are called *regional dialects.* Those based on educational or social differences are called *social dialects.* And those based on writing conventions are called *functional dialects.*

All students have a right to whatever language skills and conventions are necessary to enable them to carry on the tasks of the everyday world and to ensure them a moderate degree of success and happiness. But there is disagreement among scholars and speakers of nonstandard dialects about the best possible means to these goals. Must everyone learn to write in the standard dialect?

Whatever may be true of spoken dialects, there is no doubt that written conventions are very rigid and codified. The student who insists upon using the less formal conventions of spoken English in writing will find himself under a great handicap if he wishes to get a job that demands formal writing skills. Most employers would find the following student sentences unacceptable:

> It take a femail to have children.
> Then there were some black who escape the cruelty of the white man.
> Whites says that blacks are not human beings.
> The police claimed to have heard they reply, "Shoot it out."
> That was all that happen no conversation no nothing.
> So, White Americans, watch out of what you say or do concerning the Black Race.
> He was young and dress in today fashion.

To me seems like the Mexican-American find themselves in an alien environment.

He taken it.

Very slowly the man what up and pickup the red rose as she had just dropped on a mudded of water.

The dialect features in these sentences are characteristic of those found in many nonstandard social dialects: omission of the plural marker on nouns, omission of the possessive marker, omission of tense markers, a different use or the omission of the auxiliary, spelling errors, and so forth. Whereas in certain kinds of writing dialect features would be perfectly acceptable, in more formal writing, such as professional writing or business writing, dialect features could interfere with clarity and effectiveness of expression.

To use dialect features to report spoken conversation or to use them in writing that is personal or expressive (as in diaries, journals, or autobiographies) is perfectly acceptable, and perhaps even desirable, as the following student paper illustrates:

Mama

Well she was born in a log cabin, in the back woods, black woods of Mississippi. She drank moonshine and chewed tobacco. Raised thirteen children all by herself. Never looked much like a lady. You see, she was too busy providing and raising her babies. Spent her evening sitting in her rocking chair. Never had much of nothing, but was always willing to share.

I'm talking about Mama, my mama.

Education she didn't have none. Never had a sick day in her life. She was as good and strong as any man who ever lived. You better believe she was. Now look here. When papa died, she swore on the good book up and down on it that she would not love nobody else. Made sure we were in church every Sunday. Papa would of wanted it that way, that was what she would always say.

Yes, I'am talking about Mama, yea!! I am talking about the lady who raised me.

Every once and a while when Mama would get depressed, she would go to the closet and get Pa's guitar. She would sit herself down in her rocking chair, start humming and strumming. This was

Ma's way of letting off steam. In plain old english we could see, that Ma was doing her thing.

Ma is a very emotional woman. She gets very mad if someone ever tries to do us harm in any way. For example: A school teacher gave my little brother a hard time in his school and in a flash she was on the scene to straighten things out.

She always told us to stick together no matter what instances occurred. Because we would need each other one day as we grew older.

We always appreciated the things she done for us. We never gave her a hard time as we were going through our life cycles.

Till this day, Ma is the same as she was before taking care of her children as she has always have done. And I love her deeply because, without her I wouldn't of been here now. Mom thanks!!!!

—Larry

The repetitions, the fragments, the use of punctuation, and other features are characteristic more of the spoken than the written dialect in this student paper. You can almost "hear" the writer intoning the phrases:

I'm talking about Mama, my mama.
Never looked much like a lady.
Raised thirteen children all by herself.
Yes, I'am talking about Mama, yea!!!

To criticize such a highly personal paper as this would be to criticize the writer's self-image. Nor is there a need to, since the language is perfectly suited to the subject and the mode of discourse. But to use these same conventions in more formal writing would be inappropriate. All students, then, should be encouraged to do some kinds of writing in their own dialects, but they should also be given an opportunity to master the conventions of the standard dialect.

Exercises

1. Point out the dialect features in the following student sentences. Do they interfere with communication? Are they expressive? Appropriate? Inappropriate?

   a. The one room school house is no longer use because the childrens are now bused to a town twenty miles away.
   b. My grandfather used to set on his front porch and tell us of the old times.
   c. He stopped and look at the young girl whom dress in all red.
   d. With this kind of things happening, almost every city is a danger spot.
   e. Today only one city has a majority of black.
   f. Many solution are so simple that they are overlook.
   g. The music at this point liven up.
   h. His only recognition come through sports.
   i. Since you are not knowing much about the campus, I will give you a first hand ride through.
   j. When I first saw he, I could hardly believe it.

2. Write a personal narrative using your own regional or social dialect features.

3. Write a narrative in which you try to capture the language use and dialects of someone you know.

Summary Exercises

1. Discuss the word choice in the following ads. What effect is achieved by the word choice? Consider the denotation and connotation of words, abstractions, concreteness, specificity or lack of specificity, jargon, clichés, figurative language, dialect features, and so forth.

   a. Arandas captures a True Sunrise for those who are into the real McCoy, the legit, the right on, coming clean, on the level, straight goods, Simon Pure in the Grove, and all kinds of sweet vibrations.

Taste the Sun! Pour 1½ ounces Arandas Tequila (White or new Oro) and 4 oz. orange juice into a tall ice-filled glass. Stir. Add ¾ oz. grenadine (more or less) and a squeeze of fresh lime; then drop the lime wedge right in. Now you have a True Sunrise . . . and nothing can outshine it.

b. *Cobra bites man.* Both live. And once bitten, there is no known cure except a long, quick drive down a snakelike road where Cobra II can show off its rack-and-pinion steering. Not to mention the slithering four-speed stick shift, and 2.3 litre engine. And with front/rear spoilers, black louvered back lite and quarter windows, hood scoop, sporty tires, wheels (car shown with optional aluminum wheels), and stripes, this is one snake that doesn't have to shed its skin. So if you're looking for some snake-bite remedy, see your local Ford Dealer.

c. You have to go beyond moisturizing to deter premature aging.
You must have noticed a woman's skin can often look older than it should.
For this kind of needless aging, new Ultra Vera can be a real deterrent.
First, it has an abundance of moisture elements to shelter your skin from the dryness that may cause little lines.
But Ultra Vera goes beyond that.
You see, contrary to what many women believe, just moisturizing isn't enough to keep your skin youthful-looking.
That's why Ultra Vera Facial Lotion is formulated with aloe vera and UV screen.
Consider the legendary aloe vera gel. It's not by chance aloe has been regarded throughout history as nature's gift to skin beauty. Cleopatra herself is said to have relied on it.
As for our UV screen, a PABA derivative, many dermatologists recommend it to help block out ultra-violet rays. Make no mistake, continual exposure to these rays even in ordinary daylight can wither your skin and add years to the way it looks. Ultra Vera lets you guard against that.
So why limit yourself to just moisturizing? Use Ultra Vera every day, alone or under makeup. It's a big step toward attaining that priceless asset. Ageless-looking skin.

d. *This Smuggler Coat Does Everything But Stop Bullets.* Like it stops chicks, for instance, dead in their tracks. Only who's got time for chicks when you got a little business to attend to.

Like lining your pockets with maybe 12 boxes of Cuban cigars, 6 gross Swiss watches, one case good Scotch, 2 snow leopard skins, one German P-38 and 2 solid gold bricks.

Which with a little imagination you can do easy with this coat.

Or take that big collar.

Most guys see it as maybe a pain in the neck, what with keeping it down so it don't mess up your hair.

But any guy sees past his nose sees himself in an open boat in a sudden twister up the Florida Keys, with collar up high to protect the back of his head from taking an awful dousing.

Same goes for the icy blast of a Labrador northeaster down from Fundy.

Or the cold hard stare of a U.S. agent at customs.

There's just about nothing this coat won't do for you when the going gets rough.

Find yourself caught in a tight squeeze on the back of a truck in between a shipment of Picassos and a bunch of Greek vases and you can sleep through the whole night's events and shake off the wrinkles in the AM because the coat's 100% texturized Dacron polyester.

e. *Kama baba, kama mwana.* Through his father, a son's eyes are opened to the world. He learns about pride at his father's side. The pride of being black, of being a man.

He learns, too, about pride in his culture and that this beautiful natural is the outward expression of that pride.

And nothing grooms and conditions a proud natural better than Afro Sheen. Afro Sheen makes the difference you can see in your hair. Your natural takes on new body, lustrous and alive. Afro Sheen, the complete product for father . . . for son . . . and for you . . . naturally.

Imitation
and
Style

Chapter 13

Imitation and Style

A number of important artists and writers down through the years have attested to the value of imitation as *one* way of achieving an original style. "The imitation of other artists," contends Lewis Mumford, "is one of the means by which a person enriches and finally establishes his own individuality, and on the whole such imitation is more promising than an icing of originality that hardens too quickly." "The originals are not original," wrote Ralph Waldo Emerson. "There is imitation, model and suggestion to the very archangels, if we knew their history." Vincent Van Gogh, the painter, complained that "we painters are always asked to compose of ourselves. . . . Heaps of people do not copy; heaps of others do—I started it by chance and I find that it teaches me things."

Some writers are very specific as to the manner in which they began to use imitation. "I began to compose by imitating other authors I admired," stated William Dean Howells, "and I worked hard to get a smooth, a rich, classic style." Robert Louis Stevenson confessed that "whenever I read a book or passage that particularly pleased me . . . in which there was either some conspicuous force or some happy distinction in the style, I must set myself to ape that quality. . . . That, like it or not, is the way to learn to write." Somerset Maugham is very explicit about his methodology, in his autobiography, *The Summing Up:*

> I studied Jeremy Taylor's *Holy Dying*. In order to assimilate his style, I copied out passages and then tried to write them down from memory.
>
> Later the prose of Swift enchanted me. I made up my mind that this was the perfect way to write and I started to work on him in the same way as I had done with Jeremy Taylor. . . . As I had done before, I copied passages and then tried to write them out from

memory. I tried altering words or the order in which they were set. . . .

    The work I did was certainly very good for me. I began to write better.

The improvement of style can be achieved by creative imitation. This approach to style assumes that in assimilating the best features of a writer's style, you will produce writing that in time will come to rival the model itself. You can best do this by following a sequence of steps that may be described as follows:

1. *Select a short passage from a writer's work that seems to have excellencies of style and that seems to be relatively complete in itself.*

2. *Read the model carefully, preferably aloud at first to get the full impact, in order to get an overview of the dominant impression.*

3. *Analyze the model carefully, noting the sentence length, the sentence types, and the word choice.*

4. *Then do either a close or loose imitation of the model by selecting a subject that differs from the model's but is suitable for treatment in the model's style.*

Ideally, you will follow these steps exactly as outlined. In practice, however, there may be considerable overlapping.

Model Analysis 1

In order to exemplify one method of using models for imitation, I would like to analyze a few short selections so as to present at least one workable approach to improving style.

    The model I have chosen for analysis is the introductory paragraph of the short story "The Eighty Yard Run," by Irwin Shaw. The passage describes an eighty yard run made in a scrimmage by Darling, the main character in the story. Ironically, this run is the climax in Darling's football career as well as in his life. The rest of the story follows his declining fortunes as his wife gradually takes over the dominant position in the marriage. Because the story is told by means of a flashback, which begins with the second paragraph, the opening paragraph is relatively complete in itself, and thus it makes a suitable model for imitation.

The pass was high and wide and he jumped for it, feeling it slap flatly against his hands, as he shook his hips to throw off the halfback who was diving at him. The center floated by, his hands desperately brushing Darling's knee as Darling picked his feet up high and delicately ran over a blocker and an opposing linesman in a jumble on the ground near the scrimmage line. He had ten yards in the clear and picked up speed, breathing easily, feeling his thigh pads rising and falling against his legs, listening to the sound of cleats behind him, pulling away from them, watching the other backs heading him off toward the sidelines, the whole picture, the men closing in on him, the blockers fighting for position, the ground he had to cross, all suddenly clear in his head, for the first time in his life not a meaningless confusion of men, sounds, speed. He smiled a little to himself as he ran, holding the ball lightly in front of him with his two hands, his knees pumping high, his hips twisting in the almost girlish run of a back in a broken field. The first halfback came at him and he fed him his leg, then swung at the last moment, took the shock of the man's shoulder without breaking stride, ran right through him, his cleats biting securely into the turf. There was only the safety man now, coming warily at him, his arms crooked, hands spread. Darling tucked the ball in, spurted at him, driving hard, hurling himself along, his legs pounding, knees high, all two hundred pounds bunched into controlled attack. He was sure he was going to get past the safety man. Without thought, his arms and legs working beaufitully together, he headed right for the safety man, stiff-armed him, feeling blood spurt instantaneously from the man's nose onto his hand, seeing his face go awry, head turned, mouth pulled to one side. He pivoted away, keeping the arm locked, dropping the safety man as he ran easily toward the goal line, with the drumming of cleats diminishing behind him.

The passage describes the climactic momemt in a scrimmage, just as the halfback is breaking away for a long, broken-field run.

As you read, you are caught up in the intense excitement of the action. The narrative movement is vivid, conveying a sense of rapid motion and dynamic action. The descriptive details are sharp and intense.

The paragraph consists of ten sentences. Sentence 1 contains thirty-three words; sentence 2 has thirty-seven words; sentence 3, eighty-six words; 4, forty words; 5, thirty-nine words; 6, sixteen words; 7, twenty-six words; 8, twelve words; 9, forty-one words; 10, twenty-seven words. The shortest sentence is 8, with twelve words; the longest sentence is 3, with eighty-six words. The total number of words in the paragraph is 357. The average number of words per sentence is 35.7. Most of the sentences are relatively long. Sentence length seems to contribute to the overall effectiveness of the passage in two ways: first, it gives variety to the sentences, and second, it lends rhythmic movement to the prose. Notice the difference in effect that is achieved by breaking up sentence number 3, the longest sentence in the paragraph, into shorter sentences:

> He had ten yards in the clear. He picked up speed. He breathed easily. He felt his thigh pads rising and falling against his legs. He listened to the sound of cleats behind him. He pulled away from them. He watched the other backs heading him off toward the sidelines. The whole picture was suddenly clear in his head. It was not a meaningless confusion of men, sounds, speed. The men were closing in on him. The blockers were fighting for position. He had to cross the ground.

Not only is the sense of vivid and intense action lost in this version, but this rendering also completely distorts the writer's purpose, which is to show that all these activities are taking place simultaneously. The rewritten version destroys the simultaneity and gives the impression of a sequence of separate actions.

In a preliminary reading of the selection, you seem to perceive the dynamic action and the descriptive details as being sharp and intense. To support this intuition, you naturally tend to look closely at what the verbs and verbals are doing. Yet when you make a word count, you find that of the twenty-six main verbs in the passage, only eleven are concrete and specific (*jumped, smiled, shook, headed, diving, tucked, stiff-armed, floated, swung, spurted, pivoted*). And of the twenty-eight present participles, approximately half are concrete and particular (*brushing, twisting, hurling, breathing, rising, pounding, biting, pumping,* and so forth). On the basis of the evidence, you are forced to conclude either that earlier intuitions were inaccurate or that Shaw is using other strategies to achieve his purpose. To offset the less specific verbs and verbals, Shaw uses a large number of manner adverbs to depict action and to add concreteness to the description:

> *Adverbs*
> feeling it slap *flatly* against his hands
> his hands *desperately* brushing Darling's knee
> picked his feet up *high*
> *delicately* ran over a blocker and an opposing lineman
> breathing *easily*
> all *suddenly* clear in his head
> his knees pumping *high*
> holding the ball *lightly* in front of him
> his cleats biting *securely* into the turf
> coming *warily* at him
> his arms and legs working *beautifully* together
> feeling blood spurt *instantaneously* from the man's nose
> seeing his face go *awry*
> ran *easily* toward the goal line

In addition, although many of the participles are somewhat general, because they are present participles, they increase the sense of rapid motion felt by the reader. The *-ing* ending helps to create this vivid sense of movement. And finally, the movement of the verbs is strengthened by the fact that there are few auxiliaries to slow the action. The burden of the action is carried directly by the main verbs: *stiff-armed, floated, spurted, pivoted,* and so forth.

With the exception of sentence 8, the predominant sentence type is the *cumulative sentence:*

1

1 The pass was high and wide and
1 he jumped for it,
   2 feeling it slap flatly against his hands, (VP)

   3 as he shook his hips to throw off the halfback who was diving
at him. (SC)

2

1 The center floated by,
   2 his hands desperately brushing Darling's knee as Darling picked
his feet up high and delicately ran over a blocker and an opposing
lineman in a jumble on the ground near the scrimmage line.
(Abs)

3

1 He had ten yards in the clear and picked up speed,
   2 breathing easily, (VP)
   2 feeling his thigh pads rising and falling against his legs, (VP)
   2 listening to the sound of cleats behind him, (VP)
   2 pulling away from them, (VP)
   2 watching the other backs heading him off toward the sidelines,
(VP)
      3 the whole picture, / , all suddenly clear in his head, for the
first time in his life not a meaningless confusion of men,
sounds, speed. (Abs)
         4 the men closing in on him, (Abs)
         4 the blockers fighting for position, (Abs)
         4 the ground he had to cross. (Abs)

4

1 He smiled a little to himself as he ran,
   2 holding the ball lightly in front of him with his two hands,
(VP)
   2 his knees pumping high, (Abs)
   2 his hips twisting in the almost girlish run of a back in a broken
field. (Abs)

5

1 The first halfback came at him and
1 he fed him his leg, then swung at the last moment, took the shock
of the man's shoulder without breaking stride, ran right through
him,
   2 his cleats biting securely into the turf. (Abs)

6

1 There was only the safety man now,
  2 coming warily at him, (VP)
    3 his arms crooked, (Abs)
    3 hands spread. (Abs)

7

1 Darling tucked the ball in, spurted at him,
  2 driving hard, (VP)
  2 hurling himself along, (VP)
    3 his legs pounding, (Abs)
    3 knees high, (Abs)
      4 all two hundred pounds bunched into controlled attack. (Abs)

8

1 He was sure he was going to get past the safety man.

9

  2 Without thought, (PP)
  2 his arms and legs working beautifully together, (Abs)
1 he headed right for the safety man, stiff-armed him,
  2 feeling blood spurt instantaneously from the man's nose onto his hand, (VP)
  2 seeing his face go awry, (VP)
    3 head turned, (Abs)
    3 mouth pulled to one side. (Abs)

10

1 He pivoted away,
  2 keeping the arm locked, (VP)
  2 dropping the safety man as he ran easily toward the goal line, (VP)
    3 with the drumming of cleats diminishing behind him. (Abs)

The cumulative sentences lend a sense of rapid motion to the prose and advance the action.

    Another interesting stylistic feature that Shaw employs to convey rapid movement is the deliberate omission of conjunctions between the main verbs. This is one technique that may be used to speed up the action in a narrative.

> The first halfback *came* at him and he *fed* him his leg, then *swung* at the last moment, *took* the shock of the man's shoulder without breaking stride, *ran* right through him, his cleats biting securely into the turf.
> Darling *tucked* the ball in, *spurted* at him, driving hard, hurling himself along. . . .
> . . . he *headed* straight for the safety man, *stiff-armed* him, feeling blood spurt instantaneously from the man's nose. . . .

Imitation Exercises

Once you go through this kind of analysis, you can then do imitation exercises based on the principles discovered in the models chosen for study. One kind of exercise would consist of writing sentences of varying levels, beginning naturally enough with two-level narrative or descriptive sentences and then adding more complex levels. Within each sentence, the use of participial phrases and absolute constructions would be stressed. So also would the use of active verbs, manner adverbs (those that relate how an action is completed), and present participles. The omission of conjunctions between verbs might be emphasized in a few sentences, as would variety in the length of sentences. Finally, the choice of vivid and precise words appealing to the senses would also be suitable for imitation.

More important, however, the sentences chosen for imitation should be part of a larger unit so that you might see the effect that a stylistic technique has in a particular context. The most useful approach is to begin with a close imitation of the model, putting your own ideas and experiences into the structure of the whole. Then, at the same time that you are attending to the stylistic principles within the individual sentences as well as within the paragraph, you are also attending to the manner in which content interacts with form to produce a mature style.

The following student paper is a good example of a close imitation based on the Shaw model.

Close Imitation

(Situation: A grease monkey has only four cars left to lube before he can leave the gas station. He hopes to finish before the other shop workers.)

The Cadillac was long and wide and he jumped for its underside, feeling the suspension with his hands, as he shook his feet to throw off the piece of bubble gum sticking to him. The manager floated by, his finger desperately shaking at Ernie's face as Ernie picked his feet up high and delicately ran over a hydraulic lift and a spare tire in a jumble on the floor near the storage rack. He had three cars in the clear and picked up speed, sighing despondently, feeling his greasy overalls rising and falling against his legs, listening to the sound of tune-ups behind him, pulling away from them, watching the alignment boys heading him off toward closing time, the whole picture, the men trying to finish before him, the other lube specialists fighting for the grease gun, the cars he had to finish, all suddenly clear in his head, for the first time in his job not a meaningless confusion of grease monkeys, machines, speed. He smirked a little to himself as he worked, holding the grease gun tightly in front of him with his two grubby paws, his legs stretching high, his hips twisting in the almost clumsy style of a bull in a china shop. The first car came to him and he filled it with grease, then swung at the last moment, took the shock of several more drops of grease on his face without breaking stride, walked right over some more, his tennis shoes slipping wildly on the slick concrete floor. There was only the Volkswagen left now. Ernie approached it warily, his arms crooked, legs spread. Ernie shoved the grease gun out, spurted at the "bug," driving hard, hurling himself along, his heart pounding, arms high, all one hundred twenty pounds stretched into an awkward attack. He was sure he was going to finish before the tune-up man. Without thought, his arms and legs working somewhat together, he headed right for the oil pan, knocked the plug off, feeling hot oil spurt instantaneously from the spout onto his head, seeing the manager's face go awry, head turned, mouth pulled to one side in an obscenity. Ernie pivoted away, keeping the arms forward, dropping the grease gun as he ran for his own car, with the thunder of boots diminishing behind him.

—Bruce

Contrary to what you might think, this kind of imitation is not mere copying, nor is it merely slavish imitation. This kind of assignment demands a high degree of skill. It demands a sensitivity to style and structure, a feeling for the nuances of language, and a knowledge of what type of content goes best with what type of structure.

Here is another student imitation that uses the same style but a different subject matter.

Close Imitation

The toy was pink and cuddly and he clutched it, feeling it squash within his chubby hands, as he wobbled to free himself from his mother's confining grasp. His brother scurried by, his arm jarringly knocking Jamie's shoulder as Jamie swerved to his left and desperately avoided a hard plastic horse and an imposing red wagon in a heap on the living room floor. He had five feet in the clear and became a bit steadier, gurgling loudly, feeling his terry-cloth pajamas stretch around his fat tummy, listening to the encouraging cheers behind him, venturing away from them, unconscious of the restraining relatives heading him into the center of the room, the entire picture, the thrust of the starting push, the relatives reaching with unneeded hands, the soft carpet he had to cross, all new and amazing in his mind, for the first time in his life not a distorted view of people and things from a crawling position. He grinned a little as he stepped, clinging to the toy frantically with his fat little palms, his head wobbling up and down, his pink bottom wiggling in the humorous fashion of a bouncing baby. The first aunt came at him and he shoved her with his bent elbow, then stumbled at the last moment, crashed to the floor, struggled to regain his footing by raising his bottom first, his determination exhibited in his serious little face. There was only an uncle now, squatting in the center of the floor, his arms cocked, his eyes busily watching. Jamie still clung to the toy, toddled toward his uncle, giggling repeatedly, hurling himself along, his legs pumping, free arm flopping for balance, all 19 pounds wobbling forward across the living room. Without thought, his arms and legs working awkwardly, he headed straight toward his uncle, arm flying, knocking his uncle off balance with the slightest brush, his uncle's startled eyes gawking at the tiny child. He waddled past, arm still swinging, then reaching for a huge hand, the safety of his daddy, with excited cheers from the gallery behind him.

—Jeanne

A second kind of useful exercise is based on a looser imitation of the model. In this type of exercise, you are asked to model your sentences on those of the original, but in any order and in varying lengths. The following is an example of a student imitation which uses a looser form of imitation.

Loose Imitation

The lively notes of the piano began and so did her action, as the three criticizing judges watched, their pencils poised, ready to deduct points. She executed a step-kick-lunge with great ease, her hands and arms reaching upward in perfect time to the smooth music filling the room. Now halfway through the first run of the pattern, she felt her black leotard stretch over her arched body, listening for the cue to continue with a quick front roll, breaking into a high leap, cartwheel, and back roll. She landed lightly on her knees and pointed toes, thinking of what was to come next. The second run, her easiest, was performed with grace and speed. She smiled as she rose to her toes, ran three short steps, did a high hitch kick, toes pointed, a cat leap, then going right into a step-hop, right toe pointed straight back. Next came four leaping steps and a pose, her right hand ending its movement high above her head, her eyes following its path. Abruptly she raised both hands, held a handstand and somersaulted into a flat position on the mat, her arms above her head, then quickly rolled a complete turn and sat up, her back arched, her knees bent. Straightening her right knee, then her left, she stood and turned. Without thought, her arms and legs keeping perfect time to the music, she executed her final run, sliding her right leg to her left, hopping left, sliding her left leg to right, then pivoting abruptly, her hands at the small of her back. Three swift turning steps followed, then two perfect cartwheels, her knees straight, her legs directly over her head, her exhibition ending exactly with the music in a lunge, her back arched, her head proudly held high, her heart pounding with success.

—Linda

Exercises

1. Using the Irwin Shaw model, do either a loose or a close imitation in which you depict a subject in motion (for example, a skier, a swimmer, a basketball player, a skater, an animal, a robot). Use cumulative sentences, with an extensive number of free modifiers. Use active participles, manner adverbs, and active verbs. Choose words that appeal to the senses.

1. The *periodic sentence* is the inverse of the cumulative sentence. The following passage uses both kinds of sentences. Do an imitation of this selection, but first analyze and discuss in class the sentence structure, the use of repetition and restatement, the images, the sound devices, and the rhythm of the prose.

Some Things Will Never Change

"Some things will never change. Some things will always be the same. Lean down your ear upon the earth, and listen.

"The voice of forest water in the night, a woman's laughter in the dark, the clean, hard rattle of raked gravel, the cricketing stitch of midday in hot meadows, the delicate web of children's voices in bright air—these things will never change.

"The glitter of sunlight on roughened water, the glory of the stars, the innocence of morning, the smell of the sea in harbors, the feathery blur and smoky buddings of young boughs, and something there that comes and goes and never can be captured, the thorn of spring, the sharp and tongueless cry—these things will always be the same.

"All things belonging to the earth will never change—the leaf, the blade, the flower, the wind that cries and sleeps and wakes again, the trees whose stiff arms clash and tremble in the dark, and the dust of lovers long since buried in the earth—all things proceeding from the earth to seasons, all things that lapse and change and come again upon the earth—these things will always be the same, for they come up from the earth that never changes, they go back into the earth that lasts forever. Only the earth endures, but it endures forever.

"The tarantula, the adder, and the asp will also never change. Pain and death will always be the same. But under the pavement trembling like a pulse, under the buildings trembling like a cry, under the waste of time, under the hoof of the beast above the broken bones of cities, there will

be something growing like a flower, something bursting from the earth again, forever deathless, faithful, coming into life again like April."
—Thomas Wolfe, *You Can't Go Home Again*

Model Analysis 2

The second model chosen for analysis is taken from a novel by Virginia Woolf entitled *To the Lighthouse*. Like the Irwin Shaw passage, it is relatively complete in itself, and it also is an interesting model for imitation. Its style and structure contrast nicely with that of the Irwin Shaw passage.

The house was left; the house was deserted. It was left like a shell on a sandhill to fill with dry salt grains now that life had left it. The long night seemed to have set in; the trifling airs, nibbling, the clammy breaths, fumbling, seemed to have triumphed. The saucepan had rusted and the mat decayed. Toads had nosed their way in. Idly, aimlessly, the swaying shawl swung to and fro. A thistle thrust itself between the tiles in the larder. The swallows nested in the drawing room; the floor was strewn with straw; the plaster fell in shovelfuls; rafters were laid bare; rats carried off this and that to gnaw behind the wainscots. Tortoise-shell butterflies burst from the chrysalis and patterned their life out on the windowpane. Poppies sowed themselves among the dahlias; the lawn waved with long grass; giant artichokes towered among the roses; a fringed carnation flowered among the cabbages; while the gentle tapping of a weed at the window had become, on winter's nights, a drumming from sturdy trees and thorned briars which made the whole room green in summer.

This model describes the desolation of an abandoned house. Unlike the intense excitement conveyed by the movement of the prose in the Shaw passage, however, the prose in this passage seems to be static. The tone is somber.

This paragraph consists of ten sentences. Sentence 1 has eight words; sentence 2 contains twenty-one words; sentence 3, twenty words; 4, eight words; 5, six words; 6, nine words; 7, ten words; 8, thirty-three words; 9, fourteen words; 10, fifty-six words. The shortest sentence is 5, with six words. The longest sentence is 10, with fifty-six words. The total number of words in the paragraph is 185. The average number of words per sentence is 18.5, in marked contrast to the 35.7 words per sentence of the Shaw passage. The sentences, therefore, have good variety in length.

In reading this passage, you seem to perceive the action and the descriptive details as static. To support this intuition, you naturally look at how the verbs are used. A careful analysis reveals that of the twenty-four main verbs in the passage, four are static verbs *(was, was, seemed, seemed);* three are in the passive voice *(was deserted, was strewn, were laid bare);* five are in the past perfect tense *(had left, had rusted, had decayed, had nosed, had become);* and twelve are in the past tense, active voice *(swung, thrust, nested, fell, carried, burst, patterned, sowed, saved, towered, flowered, made).*

The static nature of the description can be accounted for in part by the static verbs, but the verbs in the passive voice and the verbs in the past perfect tense work more or less in the same fashion as the static verbs. The static verbs (the verb *to be* and the verbs of appearance) are followed by predicate adjectives or some kind of complement that moves back toward the subject and comments on it. The past participal forms of the verb following the auxiliary *was (were)* work in the same manner, as kinds of adjectivals moving back toward the subject. Similarly, the main verbs after the auxiliary *had* (in the past perfect tense verbs) act like adjective complements and refer to the subject. The result is that the forward motion of the prose is impeded, and the effect is static. The following scheme illus-trates this point:

Static Verbs

the *house* was *left*

it was *left* like a shell on a sandhill

the long *night* seemed *to have set in*

the trifling *airs* seemed *to have triumphed*

Passive Voice Verbs

the *house* was *deserted*

the *floor* was *strewn* with straw

rafters were *laid bare*

Past Perfect Tense Verbs

life had *left* it

the *saucepan* had *rusted*

the *mat* [had] *decayed*

toads had *nosed* their way in

the gentle *tapping* of a weed . . . had become . . . a *drumming*

In addition, there is a large number of verbs, adjectives, and adverbials, which through their meaning give the sense of desolation and aimlessness:

Verbs
the swallows *nested* in the drawing room
the plaster *fell* in shovelfuls
tortoise-shell butterflies . . . *patterned* their life out on the windowpane

Adjectives
the *long* night
the *trifling* airs
the *clammy* breaths

Adverbials
idly
aimlessly
to and fro

Besides these words, the use of reflexive pronouns referring back to the subject adds to the static nature of the description:

Reflexives

a *thistle* thrust *itself*

poppies sowed *themselves* among the dahlias

There is some movement carried by the active verbs (*swung, thrust, nested, carried, burst, patterned,* among others), but these stand in stark contrast to the static verbs and reinforce the somber tone. The word choice in general conveys this sense of desolation and futility. The plants and flowers, which at first seem to impart life to their surroundings and add color, are growing wild. Everything is overgrown, random, and the plants are prickly or thistly:

long grass
poppies . . . among the dahlias
a fringed carnation among the cabbages
giant artichokes among the roses

In sharp contrast to the cumulative sentences that convey action in the Shaw passage, most of the sentences in this model are balanced sentences, or sentences that give the sense of being balanced:

1

1 The house was left;
1 the house was deserted.

2

1 It was left like a shell on a sandhill to fill with dry salt grains now that life had left it.

3

1 The long night seemed to have set in;
1 the trifling airs,
   2 nibbling, (VP)
1 the clammy breaths,
   2 fumbling, (VP)
      3 seemed to have triumphed.

4

1 The saucepan had rusted and
1 the mat [had] decayed.

5

1 Toads had nosed their way in.

6

  2 Idly, (Adv)
  2 aimlessly, (Adv)
1 the swaying shawl swung to and fro.

7

1 A thistle thrust itself between the tiles in the larder.

8

1 The swallows nested in the drawing room;
1 the floor was strewn with straw;
1 the plaster fell in shovelfuls;
1 rafters were laid bare;
1 rats carried off this and that to gnaw behind the wainscots.

9

1 Tortoise-shell butterflies burst from the chrysalis and patterned
 their life out on the windowpane.

10

1 Poppies sowed themselves among the dahlias,
1 the lawn waved with long grass;
1 giant artichokes towered among the roses;
1 a fringed carnation flowered among the cabbages;
  2 while the gentle tapping of a weed at the window had become,
  / , a drumming from sturdy trees and thorned briars which made
  the whole room green in summer.(SC)
  3 on winter's nights, (PP)

The coordinate and balanced structures combine with the static verb
structures to convey a desolate picture of the abandoned house. The
cumulative sentences in the Shaw passage move the action forward.
The balanced sentences in this passage impede the action and force
the movement backwards, as base clause piles up upon base clause,
giving no sense that the prose is going anywhere.

 One final stylistic feature in the Virginia Woolf passage is the use of sound devices to give a sense of parallelism and balance. Its effect is similar to that of the syntactic parallelism:

Sound Parallelism
the *s*waying *s*hawl *s*wung to and fro
a *th*istle *th*rust i*t*self be*t*ween the *t*iles in the larder
the floor was *str*ewn with *str*aw
the *l*awn waves with *l*ong grass
a *f*ringed carnation *f*lowered among the cabbages

The net result of all these stylistic devices is to convey a strong sense of desolation and futility. The somber tone is felt strongly as a single impression.

Imitation Exercises

As with the analysis of the Shaw model, once you go through this analysis you can do an imitation using balanced sentences, static verbs, verbs in the passive voice, and words that convey a desolate tone.

The following student imitation, based on the Virginia Woolf passage, is a good illustration of how one student handled the assignment.

Close Imitation

The ship was abandoned; the ship was forsaken. She was left like a wreck in a junkyard now that her usefulness had ended. The long day seemed to have its effect on her; the hot sun, burning, the humid air, corroding, seeming to have conquered. Her hull had rotted and her bow caved in. Fish had ambled their way in. Idly, purposelessly, the tattered flag flapped to and fro. Seaweed made its way between the boards in the hull. Some doves made nests in the ballroom; the floor was covered with debris; part of the ceiling had fallen in; the rafters were now exposed; rats had long ago deserted the corroding shell. Gray-colored seagulls tiptoed noiselessly among musty life jackets and then flapped aimlessly about the upper deck. Coral had attached itself to her bottom; crustaceans implanted themselves among the coral; a gray shape glided past in silence; while the gentle movement of a wave at the hull had become, on a still summer's day, a pounding which echoed from the bow to the stern.

—Jackie

The student imitation reprinted below follows the model in some detail, but in a looser fashion.

The church was empty; the church was abandoned. It resembled an old deserted ship, alone and forsaken. The pages of the hymn books in the pews had corroded and their covers rotted. Mice transported bits and pieces of the pages to nibble between the walls. Dark brown moths implanted themselves in the tattered cloth chairs near the altar, never to escape. Doves nested in the corners of the church, piling dried sagebrush together for a haven. The gloomy fall day appeared to be a sign of winter approaching, the damp brisk air rattling, the gray sky emerging through the broken stained-glass windows. The organ was enveloped in a network of mildew and moss, collecting slowly, spreading like a cancer over the keyboard. Cacti were springing up here and there on the earth visible through cracks in the floorboards. An ocotillo growing near the doorway fastened itself to a piece of dead wood; while the soft thumping of a bottlebrush tree, dwarfed against the giant church door, carried, on these fall afternoons, a pleasing scent to counteract the foul air inside the church. Loudly, continuously, a large, rusty bell above the doorway of the church repeated its mournful sound.

—Scott

Exercises

1. Write an imitation of the Virginia Woolf passage in which you describe a deserted mine, a ghost town, a cemetery at night, an antique shop, a junk shop, an abandoned house, or some other, similar subject. Try to achieve a dominant impression of desolation. Do either a loose or a close imitation. Use balanced sentences, with a sequence of coordinate clauses. Intersperse these with short sentences of single clauses that when combined with the coordinate sequences give the impression of being coordinate with them. Use static verbs, verbs in the passive voice, or verbs that give the sense of being static. Choose words whose meaning conveys desolation, futility, or the tone you want to achieve. If you like, use

sound devices such as alliteration that will give a sense of parallelism and balance.

2. At the end of the chapter on the sentence, there are three excellent selections that use balance and parallelism effectively: Kennedy's inaugural address, the selection from Ecclesiastes, and the passage from *Man and Superman*. Choose one of these passages, analyze it in class, and then do an imitation, using the style of the original.

3. Choose a short passage using parallel structure, by a writer you admire. Then do an imitation of that passage.

Model Analysis 3

The final model chosen for analysis is taken from Mark Twain's *Autobiography*.

The Farm

As I have said, I spent some part of every year at the farm until I was twelve or thirteen years old. The life which I led there with my cousins was full of charm and so is the memory of it yet. I can call back the solemn twilight and mystery of the deep woods, the earthy smells, the faint odors of the wild flowers, the sheen of rainwashed foliage, the rattling clatter of drops when the wind shook the trees, the far-off hammering of woodpeckers and the muffled drumming of wood-pheasants in the remoteness of the forest, the glimpses of disturbed wild creatures scurrying through the grass—I can call it all back and make it as real as it ever was, and as blessed. I can call back the prairie, and its loneliness and peace, and a vast hawk hanging motionless in the sky with his wings spread wide and the blue of the vault showing through the fringe of their end-feathers. I can see the woods in their autumn dress, the oaks purple, the hickories washed with gold, the maples and the sumachs luminous with crimson fires, and I can hear the rustle made by the fallen leaves as we plowed through them. I can see the blue clusters of wild grapes hanging amongst the foliage of the saplings, and I remember the taste of them and the smell. I know how the wild blackberries looked and how they tasted; and the same with the pawpaws, the hazelnuts, and the persimmons; and I can feel the thumping rain upon my head of hickory-nuts and walnuts when we were out in the frosty dawn to scramble for them with the pigs, and the gusts of wind loosed them and sent them down. I know the stain of blackberries and how pretty it is, and I know the stain of walnut hulls and how little it minds soap and water, also what grudged experience it had of either of them. I know the taste of maple sap and when to gather it, and how to arrange the troughs and the delivery tubes, and how to boil down the juice, and how to hook the sugar after it is made; also how much better hooked sugar tastes than any that is honestly come by, let bigots say what they will.

This passage is written in the form of a reminiscence. Twain uses the order of memory to organize the descriptive details. The first two sentences announce the subject, the memories of a man who lived on a Missouri farm when he was twelve or thirteen years old:

> As I have said, I spent some part of every year at the farm until I was twelve or thirteen years old. The life which I led there with my cousins was full of charm and so is the memory of it yet.

The subsequent sentences add concrete and sensory images, detailing the memories of the farm.

The predominant sentence type is the *parallel series*. The structure of the sentences is relatively simple, each one beginning with a similar kind of base ("I can call back," "I can see." "I can hear," "I can feel"). Then to the base is added a *catalog* of sights, sounds, smells, and tastes of things found on a Missouri farm. The following are examples of the sentence structure, presented in graphic form.

    1 I can call back
        2 the solemn twilight and mystery of the deep woods,
        2 the earthy smells,
        2 the faint odors of the wild flowers,
        2 the sheen of rainwashed foliage,
        2 the rattling clatter of drops when the wind shook the trees, the far-off hammering of woodpeckers and the muffled drumming of wood-pheasants in the remoteness of the forest,

    2 the snapshot glimpses of disturbed wild creatures scurrying
      through the grass—
1 I can call it all back and make it as real as it ever was, and as
  blessed.

1 I can call back
    2 the prairie, and
        3 its loneliness and peace, and
    2 a vast hawk hanging motionless in the sky with his wings spread
      and
        3 the blue of the vault showing through the fringe of their end-
          feathers.

1 I can see
    2 the woods in their autumn dress,
        3 the oaks purple,
        3 the hickories washed with gold,
        3 the maples and the sumachs luminous with crimson fires, and
1 I can hear
    2 the rustle made by the fallen leaves as we plowed through them.

1 I can see
    2 the blue clusters of wild grapes hanging amongst the foliage of
      the saplings, and
1 I remember
    2 the taste of them and the smell.

1 I know
    2 how the wild blackberries looked and
    2 how they tasted; and
    2 the same with
        3 the pawpaws,
        3 the hazelnuts, and
        3 the persimmons; and
1 I can feel
    2 the thumping rain upon my head of
        3 hickory-nuts and
        3 walnuts
           4 when we were out in the frosty dawn to scramble for them
             with the pigs, and

        4 [when] the gusts of wind
            5 loosed them and
            5 sent them down

    1 I know
        2 the stain of blackberries and
        2 how pretty it is, and
    1 I know
        2 the stain of walnut hulls and
        2 how little it minds soap and water,
        2 also what grudged experience it had of either of them.

    1 I know
        2 the taste of maple sap and
        2 when to gather it, and
        2 how to arrange
            3 the troughs and
            3 the delivery tubes, and
        2 how to boil down the juice, and
        2 how to hook the sugar after it is made;
        2 also how much better hooked sugar tastes than any that is
          honestly come by, let bigots say what they will.

In a passage that uses a cataloging technique to convey a sequence of sensory experiences, you would expect the sentences to be fairly long, and your expectations are fulfilled. The shortest sentence contains twenty-one words. The longest sentence is eighty-five words. The average sentence length is 43.5 words. So the *sentence length* is effective in achieving Twain's purpose. The following scheme illustrates the variety in sentence length:

Sentence 1	22 words
Sentence 2	21 words
Sentence 3	85 words
Sentence 4	38 words
Sentence 5	42 words
Sentence 6	26 words
Sentence 7	62 words
Sentence 8	37 words
Sentence 9	59 words

The word choice is predominantly concrete and specific, with some use of imagery and figurative language. The vocabulary is too extensive to permit an exhaustive sampling, but the following examples are representative:

Images of Sight
the snapshot glimpses of disturbed *wild creatures scurrying* through the *grass*

a vast *hawk hanging motionless* in the *sky* with his *wings spread wide*

the *blue* of the *vault* showing through the *fringe* of their *end-feathers*

the *oaks purple*
the *hickories* washed with *gold*
the *maples* and the *sumachs luminous* with *crimson fires*
the *blue clusters* of wild *grapes* hanging amongst the *foliage* of the *saplings*

Images of Sound
the *rattling clatter* of drops when the wind shook the trees
the *far-off hammering* of woodpeckers
the *muffled drumming* of wood-pheasants in the remoteness of the forest

the *rustle* made by the fallen leaves as we plowed through them

Images of Smell
the *earthy smells*
the *faint odors* of the *wild flowers*
the *smell* . . . of *wild grapes*

Images of Taste
the *taste* of *maple sap*
[taste] of hooked *sugar*
[taste] of *wild blackberries*

Tactile Images of Touch
the *thumping rain* upon my head of *hickory nuts* and *walnuts*
the *frosty dawn*
the *gusts* of *wind*

Figures of Speech
the far-off *hammering* of woodpeckers
the muffled *drumming* of wood-pheasants
the *snapshot* glimpses of disturbed wild creatures
the blue of the *vault*
the woods in their autumn *dress*
the hickories *washed* with gold
the maples and the sumachs *luminous* with *crimson fires*
the thumping *rain* upon my head of hickory-nuts and walnuts

The effect of the concrete and specific images and the figures of speech is to allow the reader to share the sensations and vivid experiences of a Missouri farm experienced by the writer.

Imitation Exercises

The Mark Twain passage lends itself well to the imitative method. Following this model, you would want to write a short reminiscence of your own, using parallel sentences with series of words and phrases in balanced constructions. The word choice should be concrete and specific, using images that appeal to the senses and figures of speech that present a vivid picture to the reader's mind.

The following student imitation follows fairly closely Mark Twain's model.

The Farm

Until I was thirteen or fourteen, I spent at least a week or more on the farm each year. The life there with my cousins was delightful and I still have memories of it yet. I can call back the brilliant sunlight and the expanse of the open farmland, the earthy smells, the pleasant aroma of cut alfalfa, the glistening of dew-drenched foliage, the crinkle and flap of corn leaves in the wind, the far-off roar of a tractor in the field and the sound of a single truck raking and grinding the gravel as it passed, and the split-second glimpses of prairie dogs scurrying across the pasture into their underground shelters—I can call it all back and see it as real as the day I was there. I can call back the farmland, and its apparent loneliness and peace, and a hen pheasant safely leading her brood of chicks through the tall brush in search of food. I can see the farmland in its summer dress, the corn green, the pastures brown from the scorching heat, the wheat golden ripe and ready for harvest, and I can hear the rustle of the tall grass and weeds as we plowed through them. I can see the pink clusters of wild plums hanging amongst the foliage of the brush down in the bottoms, and I can remember the sweet taste of the jelly we made from them. I know how the wild mulberries looked and how they tasted; and the same with the strawberries, the raspberries, and the cherries; and I can feel the thud of over-ripe peaches hitting my shoulder as we passed under the trees, as the wind loosened them and caused them to fall. I know the stains of raspberries and strawberries and how red they are, and I know only too well how they resist soap and water. I know how to irrigate, and when this job should be done, and how to arrange the plastic dams and siphon tubes, and when enough water has been applied, and how long it will be before water is to be added again; also how much better it is to irrigate than to farm dry land, let bigots say what they will.

—Jim

Here is another student paper that uses the same model, with an unusual choice of subject matter:

The Morgue

I seldom mention it, but while I was in the Army I spent two years in Japan working in a mortuary. The life in death which I led with my sergeants, the embalmers, Japanese morgue attendants, and physical anthropologists was full of charm and so is the memory of it yet. I can call back the ominous midnights and the mystery of the deep dark preparation room, the smell of embalming fluid, mingling with the faint odor of perking coffee from the front office, the rattling clatter of the doors and windows when the wind shook them, the faroff sound of a refrigerator motor starting up, the sound of a plane flying over which sounded exactly like the back door sliding open, the snapshot glimpses of disturbing shadows I swore were scurrying across the floor as I looked up. I can call it all back and make it as real as it ever was, and as frightfully blessed. I can call back the identification room with its tables of bones and their loneliness and peace, and a vast skeleton hanging motionless in a cabinet with its arms dangling and the green of the cabinet showing through its yellowish white ribs. I can see the Japanese morgue attendants in their work uniforms, white jackets with white trousers stiff with starch, their hands in red plastic gloves, their heads in white dome caps, making them look incongruously like Santa's elves working around a gigantic doll, and I can still hear their laughter as they scrubbed, stuffed, and stitched. I can see the sponge with different sized needles hanging on the wall, and I remember the purpose of each needle and its feel. I know how the viewing chapel looked and how it smelled, and the same with the casket room, the carpenter shop, and the embalming room, and I can feel the dull slap on my buttocks caused by the motion of the corpse's hand as I worked nervously trying to lift the legs in order to take the body off the draining braces at two in the morning, and I can feel the gust of wind I made as I ran like hell down the long dark hall. I know the stain of blood and how undistinguished it looks, and I know the stain of embalming fluid and how little it minds soap and water, also how hard it is to scrub to get rid of either of them. I know the look of a dead body and how to embalm it, and how to arrange the hoses and tubes, and how to start the fluid, and how to stop the flow when it is complete, also how much better cremated remains are than those that aren't, let the Pope say what he will.

—Dale

In writing an imitation, you need not use the same subject as in the original model. In fact, part of the challenge is to put your own ideas into different kinds of styles and structures, as both the previous student papers and this one illustrate.

The Dorm

As many others can say, I spent nine months one year in a dorm when I was 17 or 18 years old. The existence which I led there with the other dormies was fascinating and so are the memories of

it yet. I can call back the noisy nights and the scariness of the dark
halls, the perfume smells, the faint odors of popcorn, the piles of
freshly washed clothes in the laundry room, the scrambling clatter
of feet when the alarm clocks pierced the air, the nearby hammering
on doors and the muffled roar of stereos in the adjoining rooms,
the snapshots of funny friends clowning in the halls—I can call it
all back and make it as real as it ever was, and as pleasing. I can
call back the lounge, and its furniture and terrible acoustics, and a
small TV hanging immobile on the wall with its antennas spread
wide and the orange of the wall showing through the maze of its
wires and cords. I can see the coeds in their fall wardrobes, the coats
bright, the brunettes striking in golds, the blondes and the redheads
glowing in greens, and I can hear the whistles from the freshman
guys as we walked past them. I can see the long lines of hungry
students waiting on the stairs of the cafeteria, and I remember the
taste of the food and the smell. I know how the desserts looked
and how they tasted; and the same with the salads, the meats, and
the vegetables; and I can feel the clunking upon my tray of knives
and forks when we went over in the early morning to grab for them
among the early risers, and the press of classes rushed us and sent
us on. I know the drape of fishnet and how pretty it is, and I know
the problems of thumbtack holes and how hard they are to cover,
also what frustrating experiences I had with them. I know the taste
of rum in coke and when it is safe to drink it, and how to conceal
it and get it to the room, and how to hide the bottles, and how to
keep it a secret after it is hidden; also how much better drinks in
your room taste than in any legal place, let the regents say what
they will.

—Christy

Exercises

1. From your own experience, write a reminiscence similar to Twain's, using
the rhetoric of the series. Use concrete imagery, sensory details, and figures
of speech.

2. The use of light is interesting in the following description by James Baldwin. Pick out the images, such as "pale end-of-winter sunlight," and discuss them. What other images does Baldwin use to create a certain impression of the kitchen? Discuss Baldwin's use of word repetition, parallelism, and the series to reinforce the description. What effect does the grammatical structure have? Then write a description of a room using the Baldwin passage as a model. Focus on one or two details; the smell (floral, musty, damp), the colors, the clutter or order of the objects in the room, and so forth.

The Kitchen

Their mother, her head tied up in an old rag, sipped black coffee and watched Roy. The pale end-of-winter sunlight filled the room and yellowed all their faces; and John, drugged and morbid and wondering how it was that he had slept again and had been allowed to sleep so long, saw them for a moment like figures on a screen, an effect that the yellow light intensified. The room was narrow and dirty; nothing could alter its dimensions, no labor could ever make it clean. Dirt was in the walls and the floorboards, and triumphed beneath the sink where roaches spawned; was in the fine ridges of the pots and pans, scoured daily, burnt black on the bottom, hanging above the stove; was in the wall against which they hung, and revealed itself where the paint had cracked and leaned outward in stiff squares and fragments, the paper-thin underside webbed with black. Dirt was in every corner, angle, crevice of the monstrous stove, and lived behind it in delirious communion with the corrupted wall. Dirt was in the baseboard that John scrubbed every Saturday, and roughened the cupboard shelves that held the cracked and gleaming dishes. Under this dark weight the walls leaned, under it the ceiling, with a great crack like lightning in its center, sagged. The windows gleamed like beaten gold or silver, but now John saw, in the yellow light, how fine dust veiled their doubtful glory. Dirt crawled in the gray mop hung out of the windows to dry.

—James Baldwin, *Go Tell It on the Mountain*

The kind of imitation I am advocating is not "mere copying" or slavish imitation, but *imitation based on a thorough understanding and assimilation of the principles* of a writer's style. There are formal principles in all writing that recur from one writer to another, and it is valuable to learn something about these principles. Imitation may not make you a James Joyce, a Mark Twain, or a Virginia Woolf. Only natural ability will. But it can help you to achieve an effective and pleasing style.

Summary Exercises

1. Analyze in class the following selection from *The Yearling*, by Marjorie Kinnan Rawlings. Discuss the sentence structure, word choice, imagery, and figures of speech. Then, for a subsequent assignment, do an imitation in which you depict some subject in motion.

Two Bears

Two male bears were moving slowly ahead down the road, a hundred yards distant. They were on their hind legs, walking like men, shoulder to shoulder. Their walk seemed almost a dance, as when couples in the square dance move side by side to do a figure. Suddenly they jostled each other, like wrestlers, and lifted their forepaws, and turned, snarling, each trying for the other's throat. One raked his claws across the other's head and the snarls grew to a roar. The fighting was violent for a few moments, then the pair walked on, boxing, jostling, harrying. The wind was in Jody's favor. They could never smell him. He crept down the road after them, keeping his distance. He could not bear to lose sight of them. He hoped they would fight to a finish, yet he should be terrorized if one should end the fight and turn his way. He decided that they had been fighting for a long time and were exhausted. There was blood in the sand. Each attack seemed less violent than the others. Each shoulder-to-shoulder walking was slower paced. As he stared, a female walked out of the bushes ahead with three males following her. They turned silently into the road and walked on in single file. The fighting pair swung their heads a moment, then fell in behind. Jody stood until the procession passed from sight, solemn and ludicrous and exciting.

2. The following selection from "The Lagoon" by Joseph Conrad has some interesting characteristics of style: the tone (somber, brooding, heavy, still), the position of the conjoined adjectives after the noun, the use of alliteration and other sound devices, and the use of negatives. After reading and analyzing this passage, do the following exercises:

   a. Do a statistical count in which you give the total number of words in the passage, the number of words in each sentence, and the average sentence length.

   b. Isolate those sentences with sound devices and underline the sounds that are repeated.

   c. Discuss the use of the conjoined adjectives in this passage. What is the effect of their position after the noun?

   d. Discuss those characteristics of style that support the tone in this passage.

   e. Make a list of all the adjectives in the passage. Do they fall into certain semantic clusters? Discuss their use in the passage. Make similar lists for the adverbs, verbs, and nouns. What characteristics do these words have?

   f. Discuss the use of imagery and figures of speech in this passage.

   g. Do an imitation of this model, choosing a subject that lends itself to a somber tone.

The Lagoon

The Malay only grunted, and went on looking fixedly at the river. The white man rested his chin on his crossed arms and gazed at the wake of the boat. At the end of the straight avenue of forests cut by the intense glitter of the river, the sun appeared unclouded and dazzling, poised low over the water that shone smoothly like a band of metal. The forests, sombre and dull, stood motionless and silent on each side of the broad stream. At the foot of big, towering trees, trunkless nipa palms rose from the mud of the bank, in bunches of leaves enormous and heavy, that hung unstirring over the brown swirl of eddies. In the stillness of the air every tree, every leaf, every bough, every tendril of creeper and every petal of minute blossoms seemed to have been bewitched into an immobility perfect and final. Nothing moved on the river but the eight paddles that rose flashing regularly, dipped

together with a single splash; while the steersman swept right and left with
a periodic and sudden flourish of his blade describing a glinting semicircle
above his head. The churned-up water frothed alongside with a confused
murmur. And the white man's canoe, advancing upstream in the short-lived
disturbances of its own making seemed to enter the portals of a land from
which the very memory of motion had forever departed.

3. Analyze the following passage by James Joyce. Then do a free association
   or a surrealistic imitation, playing around with words, experimenting with
   language.

> In long lassoes from the Cock lake the water flowed full, covering
> green-goldenly lagoons of sand, rising, flowing. My ashplant will float away.
> I shall wait. No, they will pass on, passing chafing against the low rocks,
> swirling, passing. Better get this job over quick. Listen: a four-worded
> wavespeech: seesoo, hrss, rsseeiss ooos. Vehement breath of water amid
> seasnakes, rearing horses, rocks. In cups of rocks it slops: flop, slop, slap:
> bounded in barrels. And, spent, its speech ceases. It flows purling widely
> flowing, floating foampool, flower unfurling.
>
> Under the upswelling tide he saw the writhing weeds lift languidly
> and sway reluctant arms, hising up their petticoats, in whispering water
> swaying and upturning coy silver fronts. Day by day: night by night: lifted,
> flooded and let fall. Lord, they are weary: and, whispered to, they sigh.
> Saint Ambrose heard it, sigh of leaves and waves, waiting, awaiting the
> fullness of their times, *diebus ac noctibus iniurias patiens ingemiscit.* To
> no end gathered: vainly then released, forth flowing, wending back: loom
> of the moon. Weary too in sight of lovers, lascivious men, a naked woman
> shining in her courts, she draws a toil of waters.
>
> Five fathoms out there. Full fathom five thy father lies. At once he
> said. Found drowned. High water at Dublin bar. Driving before it a loose
> drift of rubble, fanshoals of fishes, silly shells. A corpse rising salt-white
> from the undertow, bobbing landward, a pace a pace a porpoise. There he
> is. Hook it quick. Sunk though he be beneath the watery floor. We have
> him. Easy now.
>
> —James Joyce, *Ulysses*

Revising and Editing

Chapter 14

Revising and Editing

You have probably read enough about making movies to realize that although film directors may follow a script closely, much of their important work is done after the shooting, in the editing of the film. At this time, they must arrange the individual shots or scenes in a desired order. The result is a version of the film called a **rough cut.** In making a rough cut, film directors or editors may reject certain shots or rearrange them. While doing this, they may focus on organization and transitions, but they will also consider other aspects of the composing process. Then they must prepare a final version of the film called the **fine cut,** in which the film is virtually ready for approval. So important is the process of editing (or revision) in making films that the Russian film director V. I. Pudovkin has flatly asserted that "the foundation of film art is editing."

Writers generally agree with Pudovkin about the importance of editing or revision in the art of composition. Thomas Huxley maintained that he wrote essays a half-dozen times before he could "get them into proper shape." Robert Louis Stevenson vehemently declared: "When I say writing, O, believe me, it is rewriting that I have chiefly in mind." Yet many student writers believe that the main task of writing is complete once they have put the last word down on paper.

Despite time-honored advice given by professional writers and artists about the importance of revision, however, very few students revise their work. Perhaps they make a few mechanical corrections after they have finished the first draft, but **revision** is more than correcting mechanical errors. At its best, it is *making improvements in the original paper by rearranging and reorganizing ideas* (and, if need be, entire paragraphs), *rephrasing sentences, deleting extraneous material, and adding completely new material.* It often requires *a total reconception of the subject and of the writer's approach to the subject.* Some writers make a distinction between revision and editing or proofreading. **Revision,** in this sense, refers to *reconstructing a theme, improving weak passages, adding new material,* whereas **editing** or **proofreading** refers to *correcting grammatical errors, rewriting misspelled words, and changing punctuation.* Both revising and editing are necessary for a finished piece of work.

In the beginning stages of learning to write, it may be difficult for you to cultivate the habit of self-criticism. Yet this is exactly what you must do if you want to be a good writer. Until you learn how to check your own work for proper organization and development of ideas, as well as for mechanical correctness, no matter how diligent you may be in writing your paper, the final result may be a paper that is incoherent, digressive, and a waste of your valuable time and that of the instructor. Never mind that in the process of composition you seemed suitably inspired, filled with the satisfaction that often results when the words come easily, almost unbidden from your mind. *Good writing often demands rewriting.*

After you have finished your first draft, therefore, *get to work immediately and read your paper.* Some writers recommend that you wait at least several days to let your work cool, and this is good advice. But be realistic. If you are taking several classes, or if your schedule prevents your being able to put your work aside for awhile, or if you are the kind of person who procrastinates, who puts off even the first draft until the very last minute, you should read your work immediately. Reading your work after several days have gone by, however, does have this advantage—it allows you to become somewhat detached and dispassionate in your appraisal of it, so that in rereading it, it is almost as if you were reading someone else's work. Then you can bring to your criticism a kind of objectivity that you seldom get in the actual process of composing.

If it is at all possible, after you have handwritten your first draft, *type your paper.* You will find it amazing the degree to which problems in organization and in mechanics stand out after you have typed your paper. In a handwritten paper, your sentences and paragraphs are spread over several pages, so that it is difficult sometimes to take them in as a unit. In a typewritten paper, however, your sentences and paragraphs can usually be taken in at a glance.

Whether you decide to type your paper or to write it out in

longhand, after you have finished the first draft, *read your paper aloud*. This is fairly traditional advice, but it does work. Quite often, in reading your paper aloud, your ear will detect some problem that your eye may overlook. By reading your paper aloud, you can test, first of all, the logical flow of ideas. You can determine if the ideas connect with each other, if the pieces fit together, if the thrust of the essay is what you really want. You can literally *hear* the effect of the writing as it impinges on your consciousness. You can detect obscure passages, badly punctuated sentences, repetitive phrases, and monotonous expressions. You can also detect wordiness, the lack of grammatical correctness, and awkward combinations of words.

Revision Checklist

As you read, ask yourself certain pertinent questions, beginning first of all with *questions pertaining to the paper as a whole:*

1. Do I have a suitable introduction? Is it interesting and appropriate? Will it make my readers want to read on?

2. Do I have a clearly defined thesis sentence, or is my main idea at least implicit in my introduction?

3. Does my introduction clearly indicate my plan of development?

4. Is the body of my paper arranged according to some convenient plan? Are the successive steps easy to follow? Are there transitions from one part to another?

5. Have I used supporting details in such a way that they strengthen the general ideas in the body of the paper?

6. Is my evidence appropriate, and is my reasoning sound? Have I considered possible objections?

7. Does my conclusion follow logically from all that has gone before? Is it free from new or irrelevant material?

8. Is my conclusion effective? Does it leave my readers satisfied?

9. Is my paper as a whole clear? Have I included as many details as are necessary? Have I remembered that my audience may know little or nothing about my subject and that it is my responsibility to fill in the gaps?

10. Have I maintained a consistent point of view, or have I shifted unaccountably from one person to another, from one viewpoint to another?

11. Do I have an appropriate title? Does it reveal a close relationship to my central idea?

12. Finally, have I kept the commitment I implicitly made to my reader in my opening sentences?

After you have examined your paper as a whole, *consider the individual paragraphs:*

1. Is each paragraph logically developed?
2. Does it function well in the plan of the paper as a whole; for example, as a support for a general idea or as a means of going from one part of the essay to another?
3. Does it observe the rules of unity and coherence?
4. Is it punctuated properly?
5. Does it have good (that is, grammatical and effective) sentences?

Consider next the individual sentences, both isolated from the context and in the context of the sentences nearest to them:

1. Are my sentences varied in form?
2. Are my sentences varied in length?
3. Is each sentence clear and complete in itself?
4. Are the modifiers close to the words they modify?
5. Is there agreement between the subjects and the verbs?
6. Are subordinate ideas grammatically subordinated?
7. Are coordinate ideas properly coordinated?

8. Is each sentence properly punctuated?
9. Can some of the sentences be written more concisely?
10. Does each sentence relate logically and stylistically to the sentences around it?

Then, within the context of each sentence, *consider the word choice*, and ask yourself:

1. Is my wording clear and accurate?
2. Is it appropriate in context?
3. Is it free from jargon and trite or stale expressions?
4. Does it generally follow the conventions of language? That is, is it formal when it should be formal, idiomatic when it should be idiomatic, conversational when it is appropriate that it be so?
5. Is it free from vagueness or from unwarranted generalities?
6. Can I find a better word or phrase than the one I am currently using?

Finally, go through the entire essay and check for *mechanical correctness*, asking the following questions:

1. Have I checked all doubtful spellings? Words I habitually misspell? Hyphens? Capitals? Apostrophes?

2. Is my puncutation both correct and appropriate? Commas? Dashes? Semicolons? Colons? Periods?

3. Are quotations properly credited and enclosed in quotation marks? Are ellipses and interpolations properly marked?

4. Is my manuscript neat and clean? Few or no blotted or crossed-out lines?

5. Does this paper honestly represent my best effort?

A revision checklist can be very helpful in assisting you to read and revise your own work. But in addition to keeping a revision checklist, you may want to keep a record of your chronic faults.

You will discover that many of the weaknesses in your writing are caused by the same recurring types of faults. The following are suggestions for correcting some of the kinds of errors that recur in student writing.

Wordiness

Improve sentences and paragraphs that are needlessly wordy. Notice that this kind of advice is not necessarily the same as that which encourages you to write simply and directly. There are times when complex ideas should be expressed in complex grammatical structures. Nor is the injunction to avoid wordiness merely a matter of asking you to cut down on the length of a statement or a passage.

One type of wordiness you will want to avoid in your writing is **tautology,** *the needless repetition of the same meaning in different words.* For example, in the following student sentence, the words *carelessly discarded* are not necessary to make out the sense of the sentence:

> Among the increasing tons of *carelessly discarded* litter befouling the country's beautiful scenery are hundreds of thousands of beer cans.

Since the word *litter* means "trash that has been carelessly discarded," the phrase *carelessly discarded* is a tautology that should be eliminated.

Similarly, in the following student sentence, there is no need to use the word *necessary* before the word *prerequisites.* The word *prerequisites* contains the meaning of "necessary."

> I don't think I have the *necessary* prerequisites for graduation.

Another type of wordiness you will want to avoid is **redundancy,** that is, *using more words than are absolutely necessary.* Quite often, redundancy is the result of padding or of an inability to see how words work. In the revision process, therefore, you will want to cut out the padding.

For example, in the following student sentence, the word *today* can be substituted for the phrase "in this day and age" since both mean the same thing. The substitution immeasurably improves the sentence.

> *In this day and age*, a bachelor's degree is becoming commonplace.
> *Today*, a bachelor's degree is becoming commonplace.

Some kinds of wordiness are so obvious that they should be relatively easy for you to spot:

> Dates with persons of the opposite sex, *be they male or female,* can be classified in many ways.

You can improve this sentence merely by deleting the phrase "be they male or female," since this information is already contained in the words *persons of the opposite sex.*

Other kinds of wordiness may not be as obvious, but with a little practice you will be able to spot these as well. The following student sentence is grammatically correct, but the revised version, which is less wordy, is much more effective:

> As long as *there are pressures from parents to force students to try and obtain* a college degree, *there will be the problem of the overcrowding of disinterested students* in the universities.
> As long as parents pressure students to get a college degree, uninterested students will crowd the universities.

In revising your paper to eliminate wordiness, sometimes you may want to combine several sentences within a paragraph, as in the following student example:

> Have you ever had the misfortune to own a misconceived piece of junk better known as a late-model car? Well, if you have or do own one of these lifelong lemons and want to sell or unload it, please listen close. If you follow the following steps, you can be successful.

The rewritten version is not only more concise, but it is also more effective:

> If you own a late-model car which is a lemon and if you want to unload it, follow these simple steps and you will be successful.

Jargon

Improve sentences that contain jargon. Jargon is characterized by the following:

1. *Using several words when one word will do:*

exhibits a tendency	tends
in an efficient manner	efficiently
make inquiry regarding	inquire
a not inconsiderable number	many
resembling in nature	like
reach a decision	decide
render operative	fix
causative factor	cause

2. *A preference for abstract nouns ending in* -tion, -ity, -ment, -ness, -ance, -ative, -ate, -ous, -cy, -ist, *and the like:*

utilization	dentition
nullity	pertinacity
apportionment	exigency
credulousness	diplomatist
discountenance	parsimonious

3. *Excessive use of words with Latin or Greek prefixes:*

abnegation	debriefing
circumspect	upgrade
contravene	antitechnology
nonpreferential	bioelemetric
intrazonal	dishabituate

4. *The use of stock phrases:*

   in the final analysis
   other things being equal
   from the point of view of
   within the framework of
   in the event that

5. *The substitution of euphemisms for less explicit or offensive terms:*

terminal living	dying
mortician	undertaker
defensive maneuver	retreat
mild irregularity	constipation
bathroom tissue	toilet paper
loan expert	pawnbroker
senior citizens	old people
underprivileged	delinquent
criminally assaulted	raped
liquidation	assassination

6. *The overabundant use of clichés:*

lock, stock, and barrel	one and all
as thick as thieves	a grievous error
all to the good	null and void
blank amazement	safe and sound
pick and choose	fair and square

7. *The extensive use of the passive voice rather than the use of the more direct active voice:*

   Job opportunities may be increased by higher education.
   Higher education may increase job opportunities.

   Competitive activities should be avoided.
   Avoid competitive activities.

   The report has been solicited by the committee.
   The committee has solicited the report.

Almost all of these characteristics of jargon, of course, need qualifying. Occasionally, a long phrase such as *along the lines of* might be more appropriate for your purpose than *like.* You can't always avoid abstract nouns, especially if you need to refer to the special vocabulary of a particular discipline or profession. Latin and Greek prefixes often add flexibility to the language. Stock phrases such as ''with reference to'' sometimes enable your thoughts to flow more smoothly than do single words, and aid the rhythm of your sentence. It might be necessary occasionally to use euphemisms to avoid offending your audience, especially if you are dealing with death or bodily functions. Sometimes clichés add intensity to the language. Finally, there are times when you can't avoid the passive voice, especially when you don't know the agent of the action in your sentences.

Here are some guidelines that you may want to keep in mind in revising your sentences to avoid jargon.

> *Substitute short words for long words.*
> *Avoid an excessive use of abstractions.*
> *Substitute Anglo-Saxon words wherever possible for those of Latin or Greek origin.*
> *Eliminate clichés and stock phrases.*
> *Take out the euphemisms.*
> *Change the passive voice to the active voice, unless you have a particular reason for using the passive voice.*

Clearly, all of these guidelines must be modified in relation to your purpose, your audience, and the occasion. But much of the writing that you do will be of the kind that emphasizes economy of language for a general audience.

Shift in Point of View

Improve passages in your writing that contain unnecessary or illogical shifts in point of view. Illogical shifts in point of view may be the result of moving from one person or number to another, from one subject to another, or from one voice or tense to another.

Avoid illogical shifts in person and number. Notice how, in the following student theme, the writer shifts confusingly from *pilot* to *he* to *you* to *one.* I have included the pronoun *you* in places where it is understood.

A Preflight Inspection of Aircraft

A preflight inspection of an aircraft is a must before every flight. If the *pilot* does not make a preflight inspection, *he* will not know if the aircraft is fit for flight. *He* will be endangering the passengers' lives as well as his own. There are several checkpoints *one* must inspect in making a preflight check.

The first checkpoint is the cockpit. In the cockpit, *you* should first turn the main switch on and check the fuel gauges and the generator light, then turn the main switch off. Also, *you* should make sure the ignition switch is off and the fuel valve is on.

The second checkpoint is the rudder. *One* should check the rudder for proper movement and do the same for the elevator. Then *you* should disconnect the tail tie-down.

At checkpoint three, [*you* should] look for lumps or cracks in the wing. Also, [*you* should] check the flaps and ailerons for proper movement.

Checkpoint four is in the front of the wings. There *you* should check the main wheels for proper inflation. *One* should also make sure that the airspeed static source is not clogged.

Checkpoint five is the cowling. At this checkpoint, *you* should check the oil level and fill if necessary. Next [*you* should] make sure the propellor is free of nicks and cracks and that it is attached securely. Then [*you* should] check the carburetor for cleanliness and the fuel supply for quantity and contamination. In addition, [*you* should] make certain the tire is properly inflated.

Checkpoint six is at the end of the left wing. At this checkpoint, *one* should remove the pilot tube covering and check the pilot tube for stoppage. [*You* should] check also the stall warning vent for interference.

A *pilot* should make this preflight inspection before every flight so it becomes a habit. If *he* does not, *he* may get off the ground, but *he* might never come down.

You can improve this paper by rewriting it, keeping consistently to the same person and number, as in the following revision:

A preflight inspection of an aircraft is a must before every flight. If you do not make a preflight inspection, you will not know if the aircraft is fit for flight. You will be endangering the passengers' lives as well as your own. There are several checkpoints you must inspect in making a preflight check.

The first checkpoint is the cockpit. In the cockpit, you should first turn the main switch on and check the fuel gauges and the generator light, then turn the main switch off. Also, you should make sure the ignition is off and the fuel valve is on.

The second checkpoint is the rudder. You should check the rudder for proper movement and you should do the same for the elevator. Then you should disconnect the tail tie-down.

At checkpoint three, you should look for lumps or cracks in the wing. Also, you should check the flaps and ailerons for proper movement.

Checkpoint four is in the front of the wings. There you should check the main wheels for proper inflation. You should also make sure that the airspeed static source is not clogged.

Checkpoint five is the cowling. At this checkpoint, you should check the oil level and fill if necessary. Next you should make sure that the propellor is free of nicks and cracks and that it is attached securely. Then you should check the carburetor for cleanliness and the fuel supply for quantity and contamination. In addition, you should make certain the tire is properly inflated.

Checkpoint six is at the end of the left wing. At this checkpoint, you should remove the pilot tube covering and check the pilot tube for stoppage. You should check also the stall warning vent for interference.

You should make this preflight inspection before every flight so it becomes a habit. If you do not, you may get off the ground, but you might never come down.

There are other problems in this student paper, of course, but keeping consistently to the same person and number improves the paper considerably.

Avoid illogical or confusing shifts in subject, as in the following example:

The new cars are not very comfortable, but you can drive in relative safety.

In this sentence, there is a shift from talking about the comfort of new cars to talking about *your* driving them in relative safety. You can correct this by keeping to the same point of view:

> The new cars are not very comfortable, but they are relatively safe.

Avoid also confusing shifts in voice (from active to passive or from passive to active). The following student paragraph shifts awkwardly from the active to the passive voice:

> Still another ad shows an endless amount of sand, sunlight, and heat. Then the camera is zoomed in and is focused on a can of underarm deodorant. The announcer's voice then explains that X deodorant will keep you dry.

You can rewrite this paragraph and make it more effective by changing the passive-voice verbs to the active voice:

> Still another ad shows an endless amount of sand, sunlight, and heat. Then the camera zooms in and focuses on a can of underarm deodorant. The announcer's voice then explains that X deodorant will keep you dry.

Avoid, finally, awkward shifts in tense where such shifts are not clearly warranted, as in these student sentences:

> The pitcher *came* up quickly and *tries* to strike out the batter.
> Laura *asks* the doctor about her brother's condition but *received* an evasive answer.
> She *goes* her way silently and no one *took* notice of her.
> By getting back to town late, they *missed* the sale and thus *lose* the opportunity to buy the TV.

You can make these sentences clearer and more effective by sticking to one particular tense:

> The pitcher *came* (comes) up quickly and *tried* (tries) to strike out the batter.

Laura *asked* (asks) the doctor about her brother's condition but *received* (receives) an evasive answer.

She *went* (goes) her way silently and no one *took* (takes) notice of her.

By getting back to town late, they *missed* (miss) the sale and thus *lost* (lose) the opportunity to buy the TV.

Revising the Whole Theme

In addition to revising your paper along the lines suggested thus far, you may need to make more extensive changes in your paper, in keeping with your original intention, your organizational plan, and your audience. Some of the questions in the revision checklist that pertain to the paper as a whole would be appropriate here. Remember that to revise is not merely to make superficial changes in your paper or simply to recopy it. It is rather to see your work again with a new vision, to improve it over your first effort.

The following student paper is a good example of a revision that goes beyond making a few mechanical changes. The paper is an analysis of an ad for Lindsay olives that appeared in *Sunset* magazine. The picture depicts a young boy dressed in the manner of a character from a Charles Dickens novel. He gazes longingly at a huge sandwich which is in the foreground of the picture. The sandwich has layers of ham, salami, and cheese, with olives generously sprinkled about. The text reads as follows:

The Oliver Twist
from Lindsay!

(It beats the Dickens out of ordinary sandwiches.)

Great Expectations! Feed a family of four with fun and frivolity. It's easy! Just slice, hollow and butter a loaf of round bread. Then pile on slices of ham, salami, cheese and anything else your family loves in a sandwich. Add pimiento pieces, lettuce and fresh onion rings. Now sprinkle a generous handful of Lindsay Ripe Pitted Black Olives between the layers. They add a special nutlike mellow flavor—plus added color and excitement. That's the Oliver.

Now the Twist: Press your sandwich to blend the ingredients together. Slice, serve and enjoy! That's the Oliver Twist from Lindsay—a Dickens of a great sandwich!

An olive is just an olive . . . unless it's a Lindsay.

Now here is the student paper, which was written in response to an assignment to analyze an ad and evaluate its effectiveness in relation to its intended audience.

With Oliver Twist (or possibly his literary first cousin, David Copperfield) gazing longingly in the background at a huge sandwich called "The Oliver Twist," Lindsay foods presents a clever ad in the December 1978 edition of *Sunset* magazine. By using heavy literary allusions, a little alliteration, and sophisticated manipulation of puns, the ad is successful in presenting and marketing Lindsay olives.

The ad is rich in literary allusions, both visually and textually. The sanwich itself, made of round bread suggests a by-gone era to the world of 24 slice one pound loaves, as well as forming the triangle base that eventually leads the eye to the waif in the background, heavily reminiscent of Oliver Twist asking for "some more."

The literary allusions are continued in the text. The headline mentions Oliver Twist, the secondary headline recalls the author, Dickens, and *Great Expectations* (another Dickens work) leads off the body copy. These references appeal to the more learned audience as they would be unintelligible to anyone not familiar with Dickens, they also form the base for the sophisticated use of puns.

By far the most successful stylistic device is the use of puns. The primary headline develops the frame of mind needed for the two major plays on words. The Oliver Twist, we are told, "beats the Dickens out of ordinary sandwiches." The use of literary allusions, but especially the puns, causes the audience to keep reading. *Great Expectations* is another play on words as it parallels the reader's anticipation as well as continues the literary theme. After detailing the process of making the sandwich (appropriately called the Oliver), the audience is told there's a "Twist"—completing the second major point. The pun cycle is completed with Dickens again being used in a different wordplay.

The simple expository sentences, heavy in parallelism, are

momentarily suspended with a strong alliterative "f" causing a sense of frivolity. This sense of frivolity causes the reader to continue.

By appealing to a literary audience, developing a general sense of frivolity, and by using sophisticated puns, the Lindsay ad causes the reader to finish the ad and envision himself using the product. These are features of a successful ad.

This paper is good in parts, but it certainly needs more than the correction of mechanical and grammatical errors. These consist primarily of a lapse in spelling or editing *(sanwich),* a run-on sentence ("These references appeal to the more learned audience as they would be unintelligible to anyone not familiar with Dickens, they also form the base for the sophisticated use of puns"), and a dangling modifier ("After detailing the process of making the sandwich, appropriately called the Oliver, the audience is told there's a "Twist"—completing the second major point").

What this student has failed to do is to develop and explain his ideas fully, especially in the fourth and fifth paragraphs. He needs to give more examples, explain them, and quote from the text. Finally, he needs to rewrite some sentences that are awkward or in which the meaning is not too clear.

The following is a revised version of this paper.

With Oliver Twist (or probably his literary first cousin, David Copperfield) gazing longingly in the background at a huge sandwich called "The Oliver Twist," Lindsay foods presents a clever ad in the December 1978 edition of *Sunset* magazine, the magazine of western living. The ad uses literary allusions, puns, alliteration, and parallel structure to sell Lindsay olives.

The ad is rich in literary allusions. The waif in the background of the illustration is heavily reminiscent of Oliver Twist, a character in the Dickens novel of the same name. The sandwich itself is made of a round bread that could have been made in the nineteenth century. The sandwich is cut into two pieces and arranged in the shape of a triangular wedge that leads the reader's eye to the young boy who is looking hungrily at the sandwich.

The literary allusions are continued in the text. The headline, which reads "The Oliver Twist from Lindsay," is a reference not only to the sandwich, but also to the character Oliver Twist, in the Dickens novel. The next line ("It beats the Dickens out of ordinary sandwiches") is a play on the word *dickens* and an allusion to Charles Dickens. The opening line of the copy ("Great Expectations!") refers literally to what the reader could expect from a can of Lindsay olives and is an allusion to the title of another of Dickens's novels. The ad concludes with two more allusions: to Oliver Twist ("That's the Oliver Twist from Lindsay") and to Charles Dickens ("a Dickens of a great sandwich!").

By far the most successful stylistic device is the use of puns. "The Oliver Twist," we are told, "beats the Dickens out of ordinary sandwiches." The puns on the words *Oliver Twist* and *Dickens* can be understood in at least two senses. Oliver Twist is the name of the sandwich and the name of the young boy in the Dickens novel. The word *dickens* refers to Charles Dickens, and it is also a mild oath. Other puns similar to these can be found in the lines "That's the Oliver," "Now the Twist," "That's the Oliver Twist," and "a Dickens of a great sandwich."

Alliteration is used effectively in the line "Feed a family of four with fun and frivolity." The alliteration (the "f" sounds) seems to reinforce the playful tone of the ad.

Finally, the parallel structure combines with the word choice to convey a concrete, descriptive picture of the "makings" that go into the sandwich: "Just slice, hollow, and butter a loaf of round bread"; "Then pile on slices of ham, salami, cheese and anything else your family loves in a sandwich"; "Add pimiento pieces, lettuce, and fresh onion rings."

The reader of *Sunset* magazine is probably a person who has some education and money for leisure living, since the contents of the magazine have to do with food, outdoor living, and travel. Such a reader would be delighted by the allusions to Charles Dickens, by the playful language, and by the alliteration and parallelism. These stylistic devices, combined with the illustration, make for a very effective selling appeal.

Exercises

1. Before turning in your next composition, bring it to class. Then read your paper aloud to the class. The other members of the class should criticize it, using the revision checklist and offering constructive suggestions for revision.

2. As an in-class project, exchange papers with one of your classmates and make suggestions on the paper for revision.

3. Ask your instructor to put one of your themes on an overhead projector or an opaque projector and then have the class analyze it and offer constructive criticism.

4. Discuss in class the problems in the following student essays, and suggest ways of improving these essays.

Doodles

People who doodle during passive periods often reveal more about themselves than they do about their artistic ability. Although doodling is merely a means of relieving nervous tensions, it often times is a graphic manifestation of an individual's unconscious mind. Therefore, doodles in fact, can be insights to an individual's personality, thoughts, and even sexual attitudes.

Generally speaking, a person's personality is determined by the way in which the individual acts and reacts. People who do not outwardly express themselves through actions and verbal communication may do so through doodling. People with different personalities will doodle in a different manner. For example, a person who is meek and timid might doodle with thin lines and unattached figures. The thin line indicates that the person is very frail and afraid to bear down when faced with perplexing problems. Also, meekness can be equated with an inferior feeling about themselves. Thus, an inability to assert a solid position in a particular situation or circumstance. The unconnected configuration is also a sign of meekness. This type of figure illustrated an inability to cope with any task which is too hard to complete. Rather than attack the problem at its base the timid person would rather let it drop with the excuse of being too difficult. Other doodles that might indicate meek personalities are: unshaded squares and geometric figures; indicating emptiness and loneliness, and circles; which relates to a continuous fear of inferiority.

On the other hand, in a strong, dominating personality the doodles change radically in the opposite direction. A person with this type of personality is most often very sure of intended actions and will usually see a problem through to the very end. Their doodles are usually bold, precise, and definite in shape and size. Such doodles are objects, and depending upon artistic ability, closely resemble the object as it appears in real life. The objects might include human caricatures; indicating a positive relationship with others, animals, and a three-dimensional-objects; indicating solidity of thought and firmness of mind.

A person's thoughts can also be interpreted by analyzing their casual scribblings. By looking at their doodles it is possible to determine what mood or state of mind the person was in at that particular time. For example, if the doodles are made up of cross-hatched lines or a series of broken-line designs this could show an existant state of confusion in the mind of the individual. Moods of happiness, sadness, and loneliness can also be seen in the doodles of the individual. Doodles which might indicate happiness are quick, curly, and generally take the form of flower-like sketches. A person might unknowingly draw this type of doodle while speaking to someone whom they haven't seen in a long period of time. Sadness can also be a factor in determining the type of doodle which is produced at that particular instant. For example, a mood of sadness can be linked with small circular-like objects; denoting emptiness and a sense small and unimportant. Other doodles which also seem to indicate sadness are first names of an actual person. Such a case might involve the departure or break-up of friends or lovers. The sad individual might write the other person's name over and over, thus showing an actual mood of sadness because the other person has left. In most cases, loneliness is a factor of sadness and, therefore, the doodles are similar to those of sadness.

In most cases, doodles can reveal the sexual attitude or tendency of an individual. A person who is pre-occupied with the thought of sex will doodle in a very distinct manner. All the doodles will indicate sexual body parts and sexual ideas. Those doodles which might be equated with sexual thoughts are short straight lines, rounded objects, circular objects with depth, and the intersection of circles and lines. Logically, the circular and rounded objects indicate the female body, and the straight-line objects represent the male body. All of these types of doodles might indicate the desire to take part in sexual relationships. Although this is not a positive means of determining sexual attitudes it does, in fact, give a good indication of it.

In conclusion, by analyzing the doodles of an individual it is possible to determine certain aspects of that individual's character at a particular time. Doodles often leave a picture of the mood a person was in while drawing them. Doodles can determine a person's personality, thoughts, and sexual attitudes.

How To Survive Loneliness

Loneliness is an appalling ordeal, encasing its victim in a desolate world. If he is to survive, the individual must learn to cope with his dilemma. To dispossess this perplexity requires the careful observance of the sufferers habitat, recreation, and thoughts.

The victim of loneliness must use the eyes of Argus when choosing his environmental habitat. He should try to find a location in midst a mass of extroverts. Their gregarious characteristics might draw the victim into their circle, curing him of his problem. If this desired location can not be found, his abode should be in the approximate area of a center of communal entertainment. This will, in all likelihood, give him a temporary reprieve from the torment of his plight. Under no circumstances should the individual choose a secluded dwelling. Seclusion only adds to the pain, driving him deeper into the depths of his despair.

When the pangs of loneliness strike, the victim must find some way to salve his feelings. People are the only balm which can truly help this attack. If no people can be reached, a movie or play could prove helpful. He should show discretion in picking his subject, making sure not to choose one that would bring an old memory to surface. This memory would only be likely to increase his pain. To become a Bacchanalian is another route. It is not as desirous as the others because of an unwanted self-reproach which accompanies such indulgences. This self-reproach can cause a more serious problem than the symptom it was to have cured. It occurs the individual should abandon this means immediately.

The person afflicted with loneliness will find, in the long run, only he can find his own cure. No lasting results can be achieved unless the individual convinces himself that loneliness is just a state of mind. He should start by telling himself that he is equal to the next man. This has a tendency to lower the barriers separating him from others. It is only when those barriers of the difference are lowered can loneliness be uprooted and expelled. The suffering individual should not, at any time, feel sorry for himself. If he should start feeling this way, it will increase his feeling of isolation, causing him to slide further into desolation.

If an individual is to defeat his loneliness, he must meet it head on. There are an infinite number of ways a person may vie with this feeling. I have shown you the three that have helped me the greatest in my struggle with this adversary. It is through these eternal battles that I found that a careful regulation of habitat, recreation, and thoughts prove effective as a nemesis of loneliness.

Don't Be Fooled by Advertisements

Don't be fooled into thinking advertisements are innocent. They will stoop to any means to manipulate your mind. The diabolical weapons of the advertiser include slanted language, inferences, sly use of connotation, generalization with no supporting fact and claims that certain things will happen after buying their product. Our best defense against these diabolical weapons is objective analysis.

"It could well be the world's most wanted car," is the opening statement of an advertisement for 1972 Cadillac. Look at how extremely general and shallow the statement is. General, in the sense that it could be applied to any car. Shallow, in the sense that it doesn't say anything specific. A classic example of generalization without factual foundation. Working upon the assumption that the reader has accepted this primary statement we proceed. "Some want it for the way it looks . . . its beauty of line and form." Line and form are used for their connotative meanings. These words are used in description of art like great paintings and sculpture. An example of the sly use of connotation is seen here. It is ridiculous to equate a mass produced car with a sculpture of Michelangelo. A parallel statement appears later in the advertisement. "The finest of the automaker's art." The word "art" is used to deceive reader into thinking each car is tediously worked upon like a sculpture of Michelangelo. The word "achievement" is important to look at as well. It has a connotation of something that has been accomplished successfully, especially by means of exertion, skill, practice or perseverance. It reinforces the art connotation very well. "Some for what it says about them to others." This phrase exhibits a terrible lack of specifics. What does it say to others? Instead of answering the question in words, the advertiser cleverly uses a picture. Above the picture of the car, appears a group of affluent people at an expensive restaurant. A faint image of a flower appears over the scene. The importance of the restaurant scene is it shows what image you will, supposedly, produce if you own a Cadillac. The importance of the flower is it has a connotation of beauty and elegance. Owning a Cadillac is no indication of how elegant and affluent you are. If a person has 8,000 dollars he or she can own a Cadillac. This is regardless of how beautiful or affluent they may be. An illustration of how things will happen if you buy our product is seen here. "Some for its resale value, traditionally highest of any car in the land." Strange, recently, on television, I heard Skylark had the highest resale value. Factual information seems to be lacking in this claim. "Some for what it represents in driving peace of mind." Peace of mind has the connotation of inner contentment, calm and serenity. Driving a Cadillac doesn't remove the fears and dangers of driving. These factors exist no matter what type of car you're driving. Peace of mind is a phrase people love to hear because of what it implies. Mrs. Merritt, a well-known figure, once said, "If you put things into nice language, you can make anything sound nice." Cadillacs don't produce peace of mind in driving but by using the nice phrase "peace of mind" they are tricked into accepting it. "It could well be everything you've ever wanted in an automobile." Does the form look familiar? It should, they are using the same ambiguity they used to begin the advertisement to end it. The statement infers Cadillac is everything you've ever wanted in a car. However, by using the word "could" the company has completely detached itself from all liability. Meaning, that if their car isn't what you wanted you can't hold it against them because they said "it could be everything you've ever wanted," not it *is* everything you've ever wanted. Appearing at the bottom of the page is an article about how GM is progressively reducing exhaust emissions was because of government action. Don't believe they care more about the consumer than their profits. If they did care they would have taken more action earlier and on a much larger scale.

Now for an overall look at the advertisement. The language is sophisticated to express the prestige of the car and appeal to the class of people who buy it. The word "some" is used over and over again. There are two reasons behind it. The first reason is because it has a connotation of individualism. Knowing the society stresses rugged individualism, the advertiser wants to make you feel like one. This advertisement used language usage integrated with visual suggestion fantastically. Advertisements are extremely subversive. I urge the reader to really consider the points I have made. The next time you see an advertisement don't automatically swallow it hook, line and sinker, use objective analyzation!!!!

The Research Paper

Chapter 15

The Research Paper

The research paper should be a logical outgrowth of the kinds of papers you have been doing all semester. For example, if for a particular classroom assignment you are asked to go to your book of essays and read two articles about the same subject and to discuss the point of view taken by each writer about his or her subject, as soon as you begin to analyze and evaluate the ideas in each article, synthesize them, and come to some kind of conclusion about what you have read, you are in effect laying the foundation for a research paper. For a typical 500-word theme, you might be asked to write a comparison and contrast paper about what you have read. If in your paper you support your ideas by including a few footnotes based on the two articles you were required to read, you are in effect writing a miniature research paper.

But the word *research* suggests not a 500-word theme, but an "extended" investigation or inquiry into some particular subject. So if you add to the two articles a few books and several more articles and you read, analyze, evaluate, and synthesize the ideas from these sources into a coherent discourse, then you will have written a research paper about the different points of view concerning your subject.

In most of the papers you do in a composition course, you do not have time to do more than scratch the surface of a topic. But the research paper encourages you to think long and deeply about some subject.

The process of writing a research paper breaks up into steps something like the following: (1) choosing a general subject, (2) limiting the subject and formulating a thesis, (3) finding material and making a tentative bibliography, (4) evaluating your material and taking notes, (5) making a rough outline, (6) writing the paper, (7) documenting it, and (8) making the bibliography. Needless to say, there may be considerable overlapping in these steps.

Choosing a General Subject

In chapter 1, we discussed places where you can go to get general subjects to write about: the table of contents of magazines such as *Time* or *Newsweek*, the dictionary, the alphabetically arranged subject index or table of contents of a textbook or an essay anthology, the subject heading of the card catalog in the library, periodical indexes such as the *Reader's Guide to Periodical Literature*, and a good encyclopedia. Obviously, you should first select a subject you would enjoy reading about and writing about. But a second consideration is choosing a subject about which there is sufficient information.

The following topics were compiled by the library staff of Arizona State University. Each topic was researched by a member of the staff to be certain that there were sufficient library resources (books, periodicals, newspapers, government documents, and so forth) to enable students to complete their research. It may be, of course, that you will not find many of these subjects interesting, but at least you have a starting place.

Advertising	Migrant laborers
Astrology	Minorities
Camping	Nutrition
Censorship	Organic gardening
Conservation	Overpopulation
Consumer protection	Pollution
Demonology	Propaganda
Divorce	Riots in the United States
Drug abuse	Transplantation of organs
Earthquakes	War crimes
Gambling	Wildlife conservation
Ghettos	Women's liberation

Limiting the Subject and Formulating a Thesis

As you consider the subjects listed above, you will soon realize that each is too broad for a relatively short research paper (between ten and fifteen typed pages, double-spaced). Therefore, you need to limit your subject, to make clearer your approach to the subject, to tell the reader more precisely what you intend to cover. You can begin by dividing the subject into its parts. For example, you can divide the subject of censorship as follows:

censorship
  books
  films
  newspapers

Or better yet, you can formulate a thesis sentence that will express clearly and precisely your central idea. Your thesis sentence will provide a frame of reference so that when you begin to do your research, you can frequently return to it to get your bearings. Your thesis sentence will be the working idea of your paper.

The following thesis sentence was formulated by a student after she had become interested in the general subject of demonology:

My thesis is that devil worship does exist in the modern world, that it has become quite widespread in the '60s and '70s, and that there are a number of reasons for this new interest in devil worship and in the occult.

It is possible, of course, that after you have formulated your thesis you will want to change your mind about it and qualify it or discard it completely after you begin your research. But the formulation of a thesis sentence will give your research a particular direction, it will enable you to limit your subject, and it may even suggest to you an organizational plan when you finally begin to write your paper.

Finding Your Material and Making a Tentative Bibliography

Assuming now that you have chosen a general subject that interests you and you have formulated a thesis statement, your next step is to go to the library and find your material. Go first to an encyclopedia article and read it. You will find the encyclopedias in the reference room of the library. By reading the article, you will be able to get an overview of your subject. The article will also contain key ideas and some terms you can use later on in your searching. In addition, it may contain a brief bibliography at the end of the article, which you can copy down and use to begin your research.

Your next step is to go to the card catalog in your library. The card catalog will usually have three cards for each book: one under the *author's last name,* one under the *title,* and a third under the *subject.* In addition to information about the author, the title, and the subject, each card will have a *call number* in the upper left corner, which tells you where the book is located.

From the card catalog, begin to compile your bibliography. Jot down on 3×5 cards the bibliographical material you will need to conduct your reading. Put the information on your card in the same form that you will use in your bibliography. For example, the author's last name comes first, then his first name, followed by a period. Next comes the title of the book, underlined, followed by a period. The place of publication, followed by a colon, comes afterward; then the name of the publisher, followed by a comma; and finally the date, followed by a period.

The following are examples of an author card, a title card, and a subject card for one book.

Author Card

```
                Rudhyar, Dane, 1895--
BF                  The lunation cycle. A key to the under-
1701            standing of personality.
R778            Wassenaar, Netherlands, Servire;
                distributed by Llewellyn Publications,
                St. Paul: Minn. [1967]

                    Bibliography of the author's work:
                    p. 157-158.

                1. Astrology    I. Title

BF 1701.R778            133.5               68-117119
```

Title Card

```
              The lunation cycle

         Rudhyar, Dane, 1895--
BF             The lunation cycle. A key to the under-
1701     standing of personality.
R778     Wassenaar, Netherlands, Servire;
         distributed by Llewellyn Publications,
         St. Paul: Minn. [1967]

             Bibliography of the author's work:
             p. 157-158.

         1. Astrology    I. Title

BF 1701.R778              133.5              68-117119
```

Subject Card

```
                    ASTROLOGY

         Rudhyar, Dane, 1895--
BF             The lunation cycle. A key to the under-
1701     standing of personality.
R778     Wassenaar, Netherlands, Servire;
         distributed by Llewellyn Publications,
         St. Paul: Minn. [1967]

             Bibliography of the author's work:
             p. 157-158

         1. Astrology    I. Title

BF 1701.R778              133.5              68-117119
```

A typical entry on your card will look like this:

Lindsey, Hal. *Satan Is Alive and Well on Planet Earth.* Grand Rapids, Mich.: Zondervan Publishing House, 1972.

The bibliographical form for books usually follows this format:

One Author
Hopkins, Jerry. *Elvis: A Biography.* New York: Warner Paperback
    Library, 1972.

Two Authors
Shulman, Arthur, and Roger Youman. *The Television Years.*
    New York: Popular Library, 1973.

Three or More Authors
Burns, Robert E., et al. *Episodes in American History.* Lexington,
    Mass.: Ginn and Co., 1973.

An Edited Book
Wise, Herbert H., ed. *Professional Rock and Roll.* New York:
    Collier Books, 1967.

A Book in Several Volumes
Gosse, Edmund. *English Literature an Illustrated Record.* 4 vols.
    New York: Grosset and Dunlap, 1908.

After you have put the bibliographical material about books that you need on separate 3×5 cards, do the same with articles. Go first to the *Reader's Guide to Periodical Literature*, which indexes hundreds of periodicals containing articles of general interest. This guide lists the author's name, the title of the article, the source, and the number of pages. For any particular piece of information, you can look under the subject, the author, or the title.

Then put the appropriate bibliographical information for magazine articles on your 3×5 cards, just as you did for books. The author's last name comes first, then his first name, followed by a period. Next comes the title of the article in quotation marks, followed by a period. The name of the magazine, underlined (or italicized) comes next, followed by a comma, the volume number, then the month and the year in parentheses, followed by a comma, and finally the page numbers, followed by a period.

Typical entries on your 3×5 bibliography cards will look like this:

Signed Article
Lardner, John. "Devitalizing Elvis," *Newsweek* (16 July 1956),
    59.

Anonymous Article
"All About That Soviet Wheat Deal," *U.S. News & World Report* (9 October 1972), 28–30.

In addition to the *Reader's Guide to Periodical Literature*, you may need to consult other indexes, such as the *Book Review Digest*, the *Biography Index*, the *Education Index*, and the *Social Sciences and Humanities Index*, for information pertaining to your paper. Almost every major discipline has its own indexes that you might want to consult. You can find these reference sources in the card catalog under such specialized subject names as anthropology, linguistics, literature, philosophy, political science, psychology, and so forth. The librarian will be happy to show you where these reference books may be found.

Other important reference sources you will want to consult are dictionaries and encyclopedias such as the *Oxford Classical Diction-*

ary, the *Oxford English Dictionary*, the *Congressional Record*, the *Encyclopedia of Educational Research*, the *Encyclopedia Britannica*, and *Bartlett's Familiar Quotations*.

Finally, at times, you will undoubtedly want to use *The New York Times Index* as well as indexes from newspapers from all parts of the country. Many of these, however, may be on microfilm. A typical bibliographical entry from a newspaper will look like this on your card:

Signed Article
May, George O. "An Analysis of the Problem of Taxation." *The New York Times*, 9 May 1937, Sec. 4, p. 8.

Unsigned Article
"Presley Termed a Passing Fancy." *The New York Times*, 17 December 1956, Sec. 5, p. 28.

Evaluating Your Material and Taking Notes

Now that you have built up a fairly good bibliography, look up a few of the most interesting references. You might start with the magazine articles, then the newspaper articles, and then books. Read the articles and/or books carefully. As you read, take notes on 5×8 note-cards. Notice conflicting points of view, clashes of authority, knowledge of the field, unsupported or sweeping generalizations, facts, and the use of supporting details. Notice contradictory statements, disagreements, and lines of reasoning. Remember that the notes you take will become the rough material of your paper.

At the top of each notecard, put a brief description of the contents of the card, for example, "Devil Worshippers Turn to Christianity." Then, when you are finished your note-taking, you can sort the cards by categories. The result will be a kind of rough organization of your material. At the bottom of the last notecard dealing with a particular reference source, put the name of the author, the title, the volume number, the page, and so forth in footnote form.

On the card itself, put specific facts and quotable words or passages. At times, jot down these facts in outline form. At times, when the author's exact words are not required, paraphrase them. Quote the exact words of the writer if she or he has said something extremely well, or concisely, or if she or he is a particularly important authority on the subject. Be sure to enclose exact words in quotation marks. Other times, summarize the author's ideas, and from time to time record your own comments about what you are reading. As you jot down specific ideas about what you have read, be sure to put the page numbers from the original articles or books in the appropriate places on the notecards.

The following are typical examples of a notecard that uses the paraphrasing method and one that quotes the author's exact words.

The Paraphrase

Murder linked to devil worshippers

In Switzerland, an ex-priest, who had become a member of a religious cult, and his mistress were charged with the murder of a young girl. The reason for the murder, the killers later stated, was that the young girl had been physically and sexually possessed by the devil. p. 146

Henry Ansgar Kelly, "Death of the Devil?" *Commonweal*, 6 Nov. 1970, p. 146.

The Direct Quote

> Reasons for the renewed interest in Satan
>
> "The Satanic Age started in 1966. That's when God was proclaimed dead, the Sexual Freedom League came into prominence, and the hippies developed as a free sex culture." p. 29
>
> Hal Lindsey, *Satan Is Alive and Well on Planet Earth* (Grand Rapids, Mich.: Zondervan Publishing House, 1972), p. 29.

In the process of taking notes, you may discover references to other books and articles about your subject. If you think them important, add these to your list and read them.

Making a Rough Outline

After you have finished your reading and your note-taking, organize your cards so that you can make an outline from them. Many teachers and students feel that an outline is an artificiality that simply does not take into account the way people actually compose. But a rough outline need not be complex or detailed. If you have been careful in formulating your thesis, it can provide you with a guide for making the simplest kind of tentative outline. At the very least, such an outline will suggest the main divisions of your paper.

For example, the student who did her research paper on devil worship and the occult worked up this simple outline:

Devil Worship in Modern Times

I. Introduction

Devil worship does exist in the modern world, it has become widespread in the '60s and '70s, and there are reasons for this new interest in devil worship and the occult.

II. Body

A. Devil worship does exist in the modern world.

B. It has become widespread in the '60s and '70s.

C. There are reasons for this new interest in devil worship and the occult.

III. Conclusion

A. Some speculate that a Second Coming is at hand.

B. Others see the birth of a new consciousness.

The form that your outline will take will in some measure be determined by the nature of your material, but in general the organizational plan of a research paper will not differ markedly from that of a shorter theme. The pattern may be logical or chronological, a division into parts or classes, comparison or contrast, or a pattern that deals with origins or causes. Each subject will suggest its own organizational plan.

Writing the Paper

Your reading has been done; your notes have been taken; your outline is finished. You are ready to begin writing. In your introduction, state your thesis, your purpose, and the scope of your paper. After you have done this, proceed with the body of the paper. You can use your outline as a guide, but do not hesitate to depart from the outline if new ideas or a slightly different organizational plan occurs to you as you are writing. Keep your notecards nearby and refer to them as the need arises. Everything you have learned previously about the writing of themes should be brought to bear on the writing of this paper: the use of a suitable introduction; the arrangement of the body of your paper according to some plan; the use of supporting details to strengthen the general ideas in the paper; the maintenance of a consistent point of view; an effective conclusion; and finally (as it relates to the paper as a whole), a check to see that you have kept the commitment you made to your reader in the opening sentences.

As you write, you may have to reword your notes so that the ideas fit smoothly into the body of your paper. At times, of course, your original paraphrase or a quotation can be copied exactly as is. As you go along, keep your thesis clearly in mind, checking back from time to time to be sure that your paper is progressing in a logical manner.

When you use a direct quotation, try to incorporate it gracefully into your text. Remember to put direct quotations in quotation marks. When your paper warrants a footnote, put it in the appropriate place in your text, numbering the footnotes consecutively throughout the paper. Finally, after you have finished the body of the paper, try to make your conclusion as natural as possible. Do not just stop. You may want to summarize or to comment on the significance of the ideas, but at this point you do not want to include any new ideas not warranted by what has gone before.

Documenting the Paper

Since the purpose of the research paper is to present the results of an investigation into some subject of importance or personal interest, you should give proper credit for your sources. You need not give credit, of course, to ideas that are common property, but any information that you get from an author should be footnoted if the ideas are original with him or her.

This, of course, brings up the idea of originality. In learning to write a research paper, you will be primarily concerned with learning a method. The success of your paper, therefore, will be determined by the extent to which you are able to integrate the ideas derived from your reading into a reasonable and coherent whole. As for originality, your paper will be original to the degree that you can arrange the material from your reading into a clearly focused, well-thought-out paper that moves toward a particular goal.

I have said that in documenting your paper, you should insert a number in your text just after the part you wish to footnote. Raise the number a little above the line (like this: ¹). This number will refer the reader to a similar number, followed by the appropriate footnote information, either at the bottom of the page (properly called "footnotes") or at the end of the paper (properly called "notes").

If you use footnotes, draw a line from margin to margin under the last line of your text. Then, under this line, type the footnotes, single-spaced, in the same order as they appear on that particular page.

The footnote information for books is usually arranged as follows:

1. Put the first name of the author first, then the last name, followed by a comma.

2. After this, place the title of the work, and underline (or italicize) it.

3. Then enclose the place and date of publication in parentheses, followed by a comma.

4. Finally, include the page number, followed by a period.

Representative examples of footnotes, including some variations, will look like this:

One Author
   [1] Ulric Neisser, *Cognitive Psychology* (New York: Appleton, 1967), pp. 232–233.

Two Authors
   [2] R. E. L. Masters and Jean Houston, *The Varieties of Psychedelic Experience* (New York: Holt, Rinehart and Winston, 1969), p. 61.

More Than Two Authors
   [3] Richard Young, et al., *Rhetoric: Discovery and Change* (New York: Harcourt Brace Jovanovich, 1970), p. 72.

A Book of Several Editions
    [4] Kenneth Burke, *Counter-Statement*, 2nd ed. (Los Altos, Calif.: Hermes Publications, 1953), pp. 141–142.

An Edited Book
    [5] Gyorgy Kepes, ed., *Structure in Art and Science* (New York: George Braziller, 1965), p. 7.

A Translation
    [6] Karl R. Popper, *The Logic of Scientific Discovery*, trans. Julius and Lan V. Fried (London: Hutchinson and Co., 1959), p. 31.

A Work in Several Volumes
    [7] William R. Parker, *Milton*, II (Oxford: Clarendon Press, 1968), p. 640.

The footnote information for articles may be arranged as follows:

1. Put the first name of the author first, then the last name, followed by a comma.

2. After this, place the name of the article, followed by a comma, in quotation marks.

3. Then write the name of the journal or magazine, underlined (or italicized), followed by a comma.

4. Next put the volume number, the month and year enclosed in parentheses, followed by a comma.

5. Finally, put the inclusive page numbers, followed by a period.

The following are a few examples of footnotes for articles, including variations.

Article from a Professional Journal
    [8] Robert M. Gorrell, "Structure in Thought," *College English*, XXIV (May 1963), 592–594.

Article from a Weekly Magazine
[9] Hennig Cohen, "Why Isn't Melville for the Masses?" *Saturday Review* (16 Aug. 1969), 19–20.

Article from a Monthly Magazine
[10] Irving Howe, "James Baldwin: At Ease in Apocalypse," *Harper's* (Sept. 1968), 93–97.

Newspaper Article
[11] David Hapgood, "The Diploma: A Meaningless, If Powerful, Piece of Paper," *Los Angeles Times*, 3 Aug. 1969, Sec. F, p. 1.

Signed Encyclopedia Article
[12] Arthur Knight, "Motion Pictures," *The World Book Encyclopedia*, 13 (1970), 716.

Unsigned Encyclopedia Article
[13] "Bilingualism," *Encyclopedia Britannica*, Micropaedia 2 (1974), 17.

Book or Film Review
[14] Linda Wolfe, "Free and Nervous," rev. of *The New Chastity and Other Arguments Against Women's Liberation*, by Midge Decter, *Saturday Review* (21 Oct. 1972), 72–74.

Editorial
[15] "Survival of a Free Society," Editorial, *The New York Times*, 7 June 1970, Sec. 4, p. 16, cols. 1–2.

Interview
[16] Joyce Roberts, personal interview with Charles Manson, Phoenix, Arizona, 10 July 1971.

Essay in a Collection
[17] Lancelot L. Whyte, "Atomism, Structure, and Form," in *Structure in Art and Science*, ed. Gyorgy Kepes (New York: George Braziller, 1965), p. 20.

In documenting your paper, you will undoubtedly cite your authorities more than once. Rather than citing such references fully each time, you will want to use certain abbreviations.

To cite the same author and title used immediately before, use the last name of the author and the page number. You may also use "ibid." (Latin for "in the same place"), followed by the page number, when only one reference is cited in the previous note; but current practice is to avoid cumbersome Latin words or phrases that irritate some readers.

Whyte, p. 19.
Ibid., p. 19.

To cite the same author and title used on a different page, use the last name of the author and the page number:

Kepes, p. 7.

To cite the same author for whom you may have used two or more books or articles, cite the title of the book or article:

Structure in Art and Science, p. 20.
"Structures in Thought," p. 492.

Making the Bibliography

After you have documented your paper, if during your research you have made a separate bibliographical entry for each of your sources (see beginning of this chapter), you need only to arrange your cards in alphabetical order and copy their contents. Below is a typical example of a completed bibliography:

Bibliography

"All About That Soviet Wheat Deal." *U.S. News & World Report* (9 Oct. 1972), 28–30.
"Bilingualism." *Encyclopedia Britannica,* Micropaedia 2 (1974), 17.

Burns, Robert E., et al. *Episodes in American History.* Lexington, Mass.: Ginn and Co., 1973.

Gorrell, Robert M. "Structure in Thought." *College English*, XXIV (May 1965), 592–594.

Gosse, Edmund. *English Literature an Illustrated Record.* 4 vols. New York: Grosset and Dunlap, 1908.

Hopkins, Jerry. *Elvis: A Biography.* New York: Warner Paperback Library, 1972.

Knight, Arthur. "Motion Pictures." *The World Book Encyclopedia,* 13 (1970), 716.

Lardner, John. "Devitalizing Elvis." *Newsweek* (16 July 1956), 59.

May, George O. "An Analysis of the Problem of Taxation." *The New York Times,* 9 May 1937, Sec. 4, p. 8.

"Survival of a Free Society." Editorial, *The New York Times,* 7 June 1970, Sec. 4, p. 16.

Whyte, Lancelot L. "Atomism, Structure, and Form," *Structure in Art and Science.* Edited by Gyrogy Kepes. New York: George Braziller, 1965.

Wise, Herbert H., ed. *Professional Rock and Roll.* New York: Collier Books, 1967.

Wolfe, Linda. "Free and Nervous." Review of *The New Chastity and Other Arguments Against Women's Liberation,* by Midge Decter. *Saturday Review* (21 Oct. 1972), 72–74.

At this point, you have finished the rough draft of your research paper. All that remains to be done is to read your paper carefully and to revise it, if revision is necessary. In the revision process, you may feel that you have to expand portions of your paper or cut out some material, as well as revise for grammatical correctness. (See the chapter on revision.) But primarily, you will be concerned with making sure that your paper has a good introduction, a clear statement of your thesis, sufficient and appropriate supporting details, proper organization and unfolding of the ideas, and a suitable conclusion.

The Final Form

Your finished paper will have four or five parts: the title page, a table of contents, the paper itself, the notes (if you do not use footnotes), and the bibliography. The title page will contain the title on one or two lines, your name on a separate line, preceded by the word *by*, the title of the course, the name of the school, and the date, each on a separate line. The table of contents should be carefully numbered, lettered, and indented. The paper should be typed neatly, double-spaced throughout, with the pages numbered at the top, in the middle or in the right-hand corner. The bibliography should be arranged alphabetically by author, or by title if the author is unknown.

When you hand in your paper, it may look something like the following student paper.

Devil Worship in Modern Times

That devil worship existed in the past there is no doubt. Volumes have been written about devil worship in the Middle Ages alone. But does devil worship still exist in what many of us presume to be an enlightened, scientifically sophisticated age? My thesis is that devil worship does exist in the modern world, that it has become quite widespread in the '60s and '70s, and that there are a number of reasons for this new interest in devil worship and in the occult.

That devil worship (and interest in the occult) does exist in the modern world and that it has become quite widespread in the '60s and '70s can be substantiated quite easily. For example, Marcello Truzzi, in the *Sociological Quarterly*, recounts the claim of a New York bookstore that its occult sales have zoomed 100 percent in the past three years (1969–1971). Truzzi also reports that after forty years of poor sales, over two million Ouiji boards were sold in 1961, outdistancing the sale of Monopoly. Both *Time* magazine and *The Wall Street Journal* relate that a mystical renaissance is everywhere, according to Truzzi. But the most startling figures of all are that the Church of Satan in San Francisco claims 7,000 contributing members. This figure does not include people who occasionally come to a service.[1]

I could continue to quote from general sources and give statistical figures about this new interest in devil worship and related activities, but instead I will give some specific examples that perhaps will illustrate my thesis more dramatically.

In Switzerland, an ex-priest, who had become a member of a religious cult, and his mistress were charged with the murder of a young girl. The reason for the murder, the killers later stated, was that the young girl had been physically and sexually possessed by the devil.² In Kanab, Utah, a twenty-eight-year-old man was arrested for the murder of a young couple, whom he later buried in a shallow grave. A witness stated that he claimed the devil made him commit this act.³ More recently, an article in *Newsweek* related that citizens around Strunk Lake, Nebraska, believed that several gruesome killings in the area had been committed by members of a local Satanic cult. These citizens further believed that a house in nearby McCook, Nebraska, served as the scene of many ritualistic Satanic ceremonies. Their evidence included the ritualistic, mutilated remains of animals and the body of a dead baby found in a pit nearby.⁴

Television entertainer Flip Wilson may grin and jokingly say, "The devil made me do it." But Mike Warnke and Johnnie Todd, former devil worshippers who have turned to Christianity, believe that joking about the devil is serious business. They led lives, they claimed, that were almost ruined by the devil. Warnke and Todd revealed that their involvement in Satanism included "mocking the Christian faith during rituals," indulging in sex orgies, and "controlling drug traffic in their areas."⁵

Warnke, who was once the high priest in the Church of Satan of Southern California, is now the president of an antioccult ministry called the Alpha Omega Outreach. He has turned his life over to Jesus Christ, he says, and he is out to win the 1,000 souls for Christ that he formerly had converted for Satan. The one thing lacking that is necessary to hold these Satanic followers together in a meaningful relationship, he proclaims, is forgiveness. The absence of forgiveness has made itself evident in the appalling number of suicides among witches and Satanists and their commitment to mental institutions and violent wards of hospitals.⁶

Johnny Todd, like Warnke, searched for something more fulfilling than Satanism. Yet Satanism was a natural thing for Todd to turn to before he embraced Christianity because Todd's whole family "did nothing but practice witchcraft." But Todd got to the point where he "couldn't even look himself in the face, because his eyes were so full of hate."⁷ That is when he found Christ and forgiveness, said Todd.

Allegiance to Satan also has its commercial overtones, but underneath it all is a deadly seriousness. In Hollywood, a dancer who is known as Princess Leda Amun Ra, every evening in a nightclub called the Climax, dances a salute to Satan. The Princess covers her chalk-white skin with black feathers. Her stark black hair and mad eyes, ringed with black smudges, call attention to her face. Gold fishnet loosely hangs over her bare breasts. Her dance is a tribute to Satan and to lust. The Climax is a haven for members who come not only to see the Princess dance, but also to view old vampire films and to make convulsive movements before a twenty-foot Satan's head. The Princess herself, it is reported by residents who live in her Hollywood Hills neighborhood, is as bizarre as the members of the Climax club. One story has it that she lies out by her pond with a fullgrown black swan, screaming, "I will conceive by this swan."[8]

If these antics by followers of Satan seem bizarre, the actual ceremonies and ritualistic services held to worship the devil are even more so. The services vary from sect to sect, but most contain sexual activities and aberrations, drug trips, and sometimes human sacrifice. About the use of human scarifices in devil worship, Hal Lindsey, in his book, *Satan Is Alive and Well on Planet Earth*, states categorically that

> There has never been a society or culture that got into occult practice that didn't break out into sacrifices (whether animal or human). I have known of little children who have been offered. There was a nine month old baby boy sacrificed in the Church of Satan in Berkeley.[9]

As if "mere killing" is not enough, some of the cults engage in cruel and unusual treatment. Commander Bob Vernon of the Los Angeles Police Force encountered one case in which a part of the ceremony required the skinning of a dog without killing it. Vernon related that it was a very careful job and one of the most pitiful sights he'd ever seen.

One of the most complete accounts of a service devoted to the worship of the devil is that of a ritual held in El Sereno, California. According to the news reporter who attended the service, the ceremonies began as a naked girl (supposedly a virgin) draped herself over a black cloth on a table. Participants then dimmed the lights and lit black candles. Everyone present then took off their clothes and sprinkled ashes on the floor. Then someone covered a Raggedy Ann doll with wine, cursed it, and stabbed it in the heart. Afterwards, the participants placed walnuts on the virgin's chest, along with bunches of purple grapes. Then someone set yellow marigolds in her hair and painted a blood red cross on her body. After this was done, the leader read a Catholic mass backwards, while the others chanted hymns, begging Satan for a gift of money. When the chanting was over, the members fell to the floor in various sexual couplings. Their backs soon bore a host of red scratches. During this time, a wooden cross was burned to ashes, before which the individuals later bowed. Strange movements, which passed for dancing, became visible, and as it grew lighter, the Satanists got dressed and left. Only the naked girl on the altar remained . . . apparently sleeping.[10]

These examples illustrate better than any statistics might that devil worship and interest in the occult are increasing today. But why in this "Age of Reason" is Satanism gaining so many advocates? In a book called *The Flight from Reason,* James Webb suggests that in the past many people embraced Satanism in times of rapid change and social revolution. During such times, people are faced with the destruction of values and relationships which lie deep in the psyche. As a consequence, they become filled with fears and anxieties and turn to a world beyond, as represented by the occult.[11] Some critics feel that Webb's argument is just as relevant to our time as to past ages.

A complementary reason that people are turning to Satan and to the occult, according to Gorony Rees, is that the turn of the twentieth century has witnessed the death of God and the triumph of science. These two things gave birth to an astonishing variety of sects and movements dedicated to the idea that the only real world is the world beyond. So the widespread interest in Satanism is a response to one of the most powerful of human needs, the need for contact with and control over a world beyond the world of the senses.[12]

Commander Vernon, of the Los Angeles Police Force, comments:

I know there is a spiritual hunger among people today. Many of them have gone to a church and haven't found the answer to that hunger. Someone comes along and offers them a feeling of belonging, a sense of being loved by a group, and they fall for it. There are other reasons, of course, but the longing for acceptance and a place in the world is what I see as being a very important part of the insane direction many are taking into the supernatural.[13]

Anton LaVey, the high priest of the First Church of Satan in San Francisco, offers this explanation for the renewed interest in Satan:

The Satanic Age started in 1966. That's when God was proclaimed dead, the Sexual Freedom League came into prominence, and the hippies developed as a free sex culture.[14]

Henry A. Kelly, in his article the "Death of the Devil?" offers probably the shortest and most commonsensical reason for the renewed interest in Satanism: "diabolical possession is caused by a belief in diabolical possession."[15] T. K. Oesterreich supplements Kelly's explanation with one of his own:

In all periods of transition when a people's highest faith weakens and is threatened with destruction, and before the somewhat higher, new forms have as yet definitely developed, the more primitive, old beliefs emerge from the lower depths of the popular mind.[16]

What does all of this renewed interest in Satan and the occult portend? To the religious, perhaps that the second Coming is at hand. But to the nonreligious, that we seem to have entered a new stage in the evolutionary process, the beginning perhaps of a new consciousness.

Notes

[1] Marcello Truzzi, "The Occult Revival as Popular Culture: Some Random Observations on the Old and the Nouveau Witch," *Sociological Quarterly*, 13 (Winter, 1972), 16–36.

[2] Henry Ansgar Kelly, "Death of the Devil?" *Commonweal* (6 Nov. 1970), 146.

[3] "Murder Suspect Blamed Devil, Witness Testifies," *The Arizona Republic*, 11 Nov. 1973, p. A-15, cols. 7–8.

[4] "Nebraska Gothic," *Newsweek* (26 Nov. 1973), 37.

[5] Gene Luptak, "Devil Worshippers Turn to Christianity," *The Arizona Republic*, 18 Nov. 1973, p. B-1, cols. 6–8.

[6] Luptak, p. B-1, cols. 1–3.

[7] Luptak, p. B-1, cols. 1–2.

[8] Tom Burke, "Princess Leda's Castle in the Air," *Esquire*, 73 (March 1970), 104–111.

[9] Hal Lindsey, *Satan Is Alive and Well on Planet Earth* (Grand Rapids, Mich.: Zondervan Publishing House, 1972), p. 18.

[10] Trudy Taylor, "Witchcraft Is Everywhere," *Los Angeles Free Press*, 28 Sept. 1973, p. 5.

[11] Quoted in Gorony Rees, "Making Friends with Darkness," *Encounter*, 39 (Aug. 1972), 58.

[12] Rees, p. 56.

[13] Lindsey, p. 26.

[14] Lindsey, p. 29.

[15] Kelly, p. 148.

[16] Traugott Konstantin Oesterreich, *Possession Demonaical and Other Among Primitive Races, in Antiquity, the Middle Ages and Modern Times*, trans. D. Ibberson (New York: University Books, 1966), p. 170.

Bibliography

Bell, L. Nelson. "Recognize Your Enemy." *Christianity Today* (19 July 1968), 21–22.

Burke, Tom. "Princess Leda's Castle in the Air." *Esquire*, 73 (March 1970), 104–111.

Kelly, Henry Ansgar. "Death of the Devil?" *Commonweal* (6 Nov. 1970), 146–149.

Lindsey, Hal. *Satan Is Alive and Well on Planet Earth*. Grand Rapids, Mich.: Zondervan Publishing House, 1972.

Luptak, Gene. "Devil Worshippers Turn to Christianity." *The Arizona Republic*, 18 Nov. 1973, pp. B-1 – B-2, cols. 1–5.

Marty, Martin E. "Satan: Alive and Relevant?" *Christian Century* (10 Jan. 1973), 55–56.

McCasland, S. Vernon. *By the Finger of God*. New York: The Macmillan Co., 1951.

"Murder Suspect Blamed Devil, Witness Testifies." *The Arizona Republic*, 11 Nov. 1973, p. A-15, cols. 7–8.

"Nebraska Gothic." *Newsweek* (26 Nov. 1973), 37.

Oesterreich, Traugott Konstantin. *Possession Demonaical and Other Among Primitive Races, in Antiquity, the Middle Ages and Modern Times.* Translated by D. Ibberson. New York: University Books, 1966.

Rees, Gorony. "Making Friends with Darkness." *Encounter,* 39 (Aug. 1972), 56–58.

Roscoe, Judith. "Church of Satan." *McCalls* 97 (March 1970), 74–75, 133–36.

"Speak of the Devil," *Newsweek* (1 Jan. 1973), 39.

Taylor, Trudy. "Witchcraft is Everywhere." *Los Angeles Free Press,* 28 Sept. 1973, p. 5.

Truzzi, Marcello. "The Occult Revival as Popular Culture: Some Random Observations on the Old and the Nouveau Witch." *Sociological Quarterly,* 13 (Winter 1972), 16–36.

—Toni Konopisos

This paper has a very simple organization. In the opening paragraph, the student introduces her subject (devil worship and the occult) and states her thesis ("My thesis is that devil worship does exist in the modern world, that it has become quite widespread in the '60s and '70s, and that there are a number of reasons for this new interest in devil worship and in the occult.") Then, in successive paragraphs she takes up each point in turn, beginning first with a few quotations and statistics supporting the idea that devil worship is not just a thing of the past, but that it exists in the modern world and is increasing in popularity. After this, to dramatize her point, she narrows down and gives specific instances of people and events related to devil worship. In the last section of her paper, she cites reasons for the renewed interest in devil worship and in the occult, and she concludes by speculating upon the meaning of it all.

Since she began with a clearly defined thesis, in the writing of the paper all she had to do was to follow her notecards dealing with specific incidents of devil worship and work them into a logical progression and then do the same with the material dealing with the reasons for the devil worship. Since her cards were grouped together according to a central idea, it was relatively easy for her to sort them out and leaf through them, incorporating the specific examples into a progressive pattern. As she did this, she sometimes copied her paraphrases verbatim, putting in the notes as she went along, or she reworded the material from her cards to make it fit the context of her paper, or she quoted directly from a particular author.

This kind of paper is not too different, then, from the traditional theme. One obvious difference, of course, is that the process of invention comes about through research and from external sources. But the selection of a topic, the limitation of that topic, the formulation of the thesis, and the arrangement of ideas are the same steps you would use in writing a 500-word theme.

The Inductive Research Paper

An alternative to the deductive approach to writing the research paper is the inductive approach. The inductive research paper is the kind of paper in which you will be asked to consider some idea, event, personality, or topic about which differing opinions, attitudes, or perspectives may be found, to gather source materials relating to these ideas, events, or personalities, to classify them, and to come to some sort of conclusion about them. Your conclusion will be the thesis of your paper. The process is essentially inductive, but you may want to present your conclusions deductively, in the form of a thesis statement and supporting details in the actual writing of your paper.

For example, one student got interested in the critical furor that accompanied the CBS television special "The Guns of Autumn," a program that dealt with hunting and gun control in the United States. She wanted to trace the varying critical responses to that program. What were the different points of view toward hunting and gun control, she asked herself, and more specifically, what were the critical reactions to the CBS program? Were certain critics receptive or hostile to the CBS program? Why? What was the point of view of the program? Was it biased? Or was there an attempt to be as objective as possible? What was the basis of the acceptance or rejection of the point of view taken in the CBS special? How would you classify the positions taken for or against the program?

At this time she had a focal point, but no real thesis. So she went to sources such as the *Reader's Guide to Periodical Literature*, which indexes hundreds of periodicals, got some information there about the program, and then began to read in newspapers and magazines what different critics had to say about the program. Her task essentially was to gather the individual accounts, look for signs of differences of opinion among them, classify them, treat each classification as objectively as possible, and then come to some sort of conclusion about them, a conclusion that was not emphasized in the descriptions of each.

Then she made a rough outline, formulated an introductory statement, and wrote her paper. The result was the following paper.

The Guns of Autumn

I. Introduction
   A. The CBS program, "The Guns of Autumn," attracted strong and varied responses.
   B. The major emphasis in this paper is on a survey of these critical responses.
II. The pro-hunting reaction was predictably strong.
   A. Pro-hunting factions defended hunting as big business.
   B. Some pro-hunting groups gave game management as a justification for hunting.
   C. Pro-hunting supporters blocked much of the commercial advertising for the program.
III. The anti-hunting reaction was also predictably strong.
   A. Anti-hunting factions countered the game management arguments.
   B. Many critics likened hunting to warfare.
IV. The non-partisan reaction to the program varied.
   A. The United Fund was an innocent victim because of a public-service announcement.
   B. The general public reacted predictably both for and against the program.
V. Conclusion
   A. CBS tried to present the opposing viewpoints as fairly as possible.

B. Nevertheless, CBS did effectively present a controversial issue
    for public discussion and debate.

The Guns of Autumn

Early this fall, CBS televised a controversial documentary entitled
"The Guns of Autumn." Irv Drasnin wrote, produced, and directed
this ninety-minute video essay about hunting and the need for some
form of gun control in the United States. CBS newsman Dan Rather
narrated the program. The program attracted strong and varied
responses because some critics were questioning the legitimacy of
hunting as a sport, and others the need for gun control legislation.
Even before its nationwide airing on September 5, 1975, reactions
to the forthcoming program had already reached sizable proportions.
So vigorous were the reactions of special interest groups prior to air
time that a second documentary, to be called "Echoes of the Guns
of Autumn," was planned.

My major purpose in this paper will be to survey the varying
critical responses to the program and to try to determine just who
had the strongest feelings about this program and why. The critical
responses can be broken down into three categories: the pro-hunting
reaction, the anti-hunting reaction, and (for lack of a better term)
the non-partisan reaction.

My sources are primarily newspapers and magazines because they
provided immediate reactions to the program and because they seem
to represent the reaction of a greater part of the population. Other
sources include books and, of course, the television program itself.

The pro-hunting reaction to the program was predictably strong.
Many pro-hunting factions defended hunting as a sport and a big
business. Those who have financial interests in guns and hunting
equipment naturally were not eager to have hunting presented in
what they considered to be a detrimental light. Irv Drasnin, the
producer of the show, in an interview which appeared in the *Christian
Science Monitor*, remarked that a representative of the National
Shooting Sports Foundation told him that even if the show was
objective, he would consider it anti-hunting.[1] After all, hunting is a
two billion dollar a year industry in the United States. A half billion
alone goes for guns and ammunition.[2] Information I was able to obtain
from television about "Echoes of the Guns of Autumn" indicated

that private game preserves received seventeen and a half million dollars last year in hunting fees and licenses.[3] In numerical terms, hunters represent a considerable portion of the population. Hunters are estimated to number twenty million in the United States or approximately ten percent of the entire population.[4]

Some pro-hunting groups gave game management as a justification for hunting. They argued that hunting is beneficial to game management. For example, "the Wildlife Society recognizes 'sport hunting as one legitimate and desirable use of wildlife resources.' The Izaak Walton League says, 'hunting should be a valuable management tool.' The American Forestry Association believes in hunting as a 'tool of management by owners of large forest and rangeholdings.' Such documentaries [as "The Guns of Autumn"] can only swell the 'killing animals is wrong' psychology that has grown so rapidly in the United States of late, and this societal attitude may be reaching a point of ecological counter-productivity."[5]

Critics who supported the game management theory as a justification for hunting reached strongly to "The Guns of Autumn." Robert Thomas, in an article in *The Arizona Republic*, protested that "shooting preserves got a black eye in a recent CBS film, 'Guns of Autumn,' but preserves, when properly managed, can be a needed addition to hunting recreation."[6] John Russo, the chief of game management for the Arizona Game and Fish Department, agreed. "Hunting is the game manager's most important tool for complete and controlled management," he declared.[7]

So strong were the feelings of the hunting advocates against CBS airing "The Guns of Autumn" that pro-hunting supporters blocked much of the commercial advertising for the program. Lost advertising revenues due to the success of the campaign against CBS were estimated to be $100,000.[8] Before the program was even aired, the National Rifle Association obtained the names of the advertisers for "The Guns of Autumn." By broadcast time, all of the scheduled companies except the Block Drug Company had withdrawn their commercials.[9] This incident showed how effectively organizations such as the National Rifle Association could organize its members and supporters for a protest.[10]

The anti-hunting reaction was also predictably strong. Anti-hunting factions countered game management arguments by contending that nature follows the law of the survival of the fittest in weeding out the sick and the aged animals, but that man aims for the biggest and strongest.[11] There is no doubt that a tremendous number of strong and healthy animals are killed annually—2 million deer, 100,000 elk, 17,000 bear, 11 million ducks, and 1½ million geese.[12] And as CBS graphically demonstrated the once solitary contest between the hunter and these animals has come more to resemble modern warfare, complete with walkie-talkie, than a sport.

This comparison of hunting with modern warfare is not accidental. Many critics have likened hunting to warfare. For example, the anthropologist Lionel Tiger, in a fairly recent book entitled *The Imperial Animal*, has argued that *"organizing predatory violence* has always been a male monopoly, whether practiced against game animals or those enemy humans defined as 'not men' (and hence also a kind of prey animal). This is the important step in the move toward human warfare."[14]

Closely allied to the idea of hunting as modern warfare is the connection of hunting with assassination. Although the connection between these two ideas is slight, the relationship of all of these ideas to gun control legislation is important. For example, the two recent attempts (September 5 and September 22, 1975) on President Gerald Ford's life has increased public reactions against hunting and for gun control legislation. And, of course, the CBS program "The Guns of Autumn" itself brought angry reactions against hunting and for some form of gun control legislation. As *Time* magazine reported: "CBS and the Block Drug Company combined to make the unlikeliest gunfighters since Batman and Robin. Together they stood off the one-million strong National Rifle Association and its allies, the firearms manufacturers and game-preserve associations. That is more than Congress has been able to accomplish."[15]

Non-partisan reactions to the program varied. The United Fund was an innocent victim because of a public service announcement. Because CBS had lost a number of advertisers for "The Guns of Autumn," regular commercial time was filled with public service announcements. One announcement was a plea to aid the United Fund. Because some viewers thought that the United Fund was one of the sponsors of the program, they reacted strongly. According to one newspaper account, "angry television viewers in at least twelve cities, including Phoenix and Tucson, have told the United Fund they won't contribute this year because they thought the charity sponsored a controversial CBS hunting documentary. . . ."[16] Complicating the gun control issue for the United Fund was the fact that the Young Women's Christian Association and the Urban League, both local United Fund agencies, sanctioned gun control.[17] "If you're angry at CBS News," said Charles Collingwood, the narrator of the follow-up program, "Echoes of the Guns of Autumn," "that's one thing, but don't blame the United Fund."[18]

The general public reacted predictably both for and against the program. Many offered a variation on the theme, "We may hate people like Cleveland Amory [the president of the Fund for Animals], but some of what they are saying is true. Some forms of hunting are more cruel and the endangered species list continues to grow which means . . . don't put a bad name on hunting but look for better management."[19] Other opinions concerned individual hunters. "To picture us all [hunters] as cruel and ruthless is unfair. . . . It is not the "Guns of Autumn" that gives us the bad image, but the type of jerk we all know from time to time. There [are] people who indeed have some kind of cruel streak in them and unfortunately they sometimes fancy themselves hunters."[20] Finally, Henry Mitchell, of the *Washington Post*, felt compelled to comment, "The show is neither anti-hunting nor pro-hunting. . . ."[21] Supposedly, CBS was trying to be as objective as possible.

Both "The Guns of Autumn" then, as well as the companion program "Echoes of the Guns of Autumn" elicited reactions not only from formal organizations, clubs, and journalists, but also from the general public as well. Richard Salant, the CBS News president, observed that "never in all my years of broadcasting have I seen such an outpouring of reaction preceding an airing."[22]

The evidence seems to suggest that CBS did try to present the opposing viewpoints about hunting and gun control as fairly as possible. On the one hand, hunters viewed the pursuit of game as a natural part of their heritage. They saw nothing cruel or inhumane about something which seemed a part of nature. On the other hand, conservationists objected to the slaughtering of game for the sake of personal gratification. Whatever may have been true of hunting in the past, they declared, today because some forms of hunting are unnecessarily cruel and because hunting threatens to make some species of animals extinct, hunting should be severely limited. The CBS program effectively presented controversial issues for public discussion and debate. Both environmental and gun control issues were effectively brought before the public as well as the morality of killing animals, along with the deeper implications of killing, assassination, and warfare. Whether the program will continue to spur discussion and debate remains to be seen, but for a time "The Guns of Autumn" will press on the consciences of many.

Notes

[1] Arthur Unger, "CBS Won't Alter Friday's Controversial Look at Hunting," *Christian Science Monitor*, 4 Sept. 1975, p. 26, cols 1–4.

[2] John J. O'Connor, "The Guns of Autumn Hunted and Hunters," *The New York Times*, 14 Sept. 1975, Sec. 2, p. 25, cols. 1 and 2.

[3] Judith Betz, personal notes on "Echoes of the Guns of Autumn," 28 Sept. 1975.

[4] Robert N. Butler and Myrna I. Lewis, *Aging and Mental Health* (Saint Louis: The C. V. Mosby Company, 1973), p. 5.

[5] Kevin Phillips, " 'Guns of Autumn' Misses Bull's Eye But Still Scores," *TV Guide* (27 Sept. 1975), A-3 and A-4.

[6] Robert Thomas, "Bird Shooting Vitalizing," *The Arizona Republic*, 21 Sept. 1975, p. D-12, col. 1.

[7] "Role of Hunter Aids Game Growth," *The Arizona Republic*, p. D-12, col. 2.

[8] "Intimidated Advertisers," *Des Moines Register*, 10 Sept. 1975, p. 6-A, cols. 1 and 2.

[9] "Gunfight," *Time* (22 Sept. 1975), 73.

[10] "Intimidated Advertisers," p. 6-A, cols. 1 and 2.

[11] Judith Betz, personal notes on "Guns of Autumn," 5 Sept. 1975

[12] Gregg Kilday, "Hunting, Less Sport Than Harvest," *Los Angeles Times*, 5 Sept. 1975, part IV, p. 22, cols. 1 and 2.

[13] Kilday, part IV, p. 22, cols. 1 and 2.

[14] Lionel Tiger and Robin Fox, *The Imperial Animal* (New York: Holt, Rinehart, and Winston, 1971), p. 213.

[15] "Gunfight," p. 73.

[16] "United Fund Blamed for Hunting Show," *The Arizona Republic,* 29 Sept. 1975, p. A-5, cols. 3–6.

[17] "United Way Official Discounts Impact of Show on Gun Control," *The Arizona Republic,* 8 Oct. 1975, p. C-5, cols. 1 and 2.

[18] "United Fund Blamed for Hunting Show," p. A-5, cols. 3–6.

[19] J. Leo King, Editorial Commentary, "Some Are Jerks!" *The Arizona Republic,* 28 Sept. 1975, p. A-7, col. 1.

[20] J. Leo King, p. A-7, col. 1.

[21] Henry Mitchell, "Ready, Aim, Misfire," *Washington Post,* 5 Sept. 1975, p. B-1, col. 1 and B-11, cols. 1–5.

[22] Phillips, pp. A-3 and A-4.

Bibliography

Butler, Robert N., and Myrna I. Lewis, *Aging and Mental Health.* Saint Louis: The C. B. Mosby Company, 1973.

"Guns Issue Hurts Drive for United Way." *The Arizona Republic,* 7 Oct. 1975, p. B-1, cols. 1–3.

"The Gun Thugs." *The New York Times,* 7 Sept. 1975, Sec. 4, p. 16, col. 2.

"Gun-buff Judge Tough on Robbers." *The Arizona Republic,* 28 Sept. 1975, p. A-9, cols. 5–8.

"Gunfight." *Time* (22 Sept. 1975), 73.

"Intimidated Advertisers." *Des Moines Register,* 10 Sept. 1975, p. 6-A, cols. 1 and 2.

Kilday, Gregg. "Hunting, Less Sport Than Harvest." *Los Angeles Times,* 5 Sept. 1975, part IV, p. 22, cols. 1 and 2.

King, J. Leo. Editorial Commentary. "Some Are Jerks!" *The Arizona Republic,* 28 Sept. 1975, p. A-7, col. 1.

Lamson, Edward W. Editorial Commentary. "Weed Out Slob Hunters." *The Arizona Republic,* 3 Oct. 1975, p. A-7, cols. 1 and 2.

Mann, E. B. "Our Endangered Tradition: 'By Their Words Ye Shall Know Them.'" *Field and Stream* (Aug. 1975), 30 and 32.

———— "Our Endangered Tradition: Do Gun Laws Work?" *Field and Stream* (June 1975), 107–108.

Mitchell, Henry et al. Editorial Commentary. " 'Guns of Autumn' in Hot Crossfire." *The Arizona Republic,* 11 Sept. 1975, p. D-6, cols. 3–6.

———— "Ready, Aim, Misfire." *Washington Post,* 5 Sept. 1975, p. B-1, col. 1 and p. B-11, cols. 1–5.

O'Connor, John J. "The Guns of Autumn Hunted and Hunters." *The New York Times,* 14 Sept. 1975, Sec. 2, p. 25, cols. 1 and 2.

Phillips, Kevin. " 'Guns of Autumn' Misses Bull's Eye But Still Scores." *TV Guide* (27 Sept. 1975), A-c and A-4.

"Role of Hunter Aids Game Growth." *The Arizona Republic,* p. D-12, col. 2.

Samson, Jack. Editorial Commentary. *Field and Stream* (July 1975), 4.

Tiger, Lionel, and Fox, Robin. *The Imperial Animal.* New York: Holt, Rinehart, and Winston, 1971, p. 213.

Thomas, Robert. "Bird Shooting Vitalizing." *The Arizona Republic,* 21 Sept. 1975, p. D-12, col. 1.

———— " 'Guns' Stirs Furor." *The Arizona Republic,* 7 Sept. 1975, p. D-10, cols. 2 and 3.

Unger, Arthur. "CBS Won't Alter Friday's Controversial Look at Hunting." *Christian Science Monitor,* 4 Sept. 1975, p. 26, cols. 1–4.

"United Fund Blamed for Hunting Show." *The Arizona Republic,* 29 Sept. 1975, p. A-5, cols. 3–6.

"United Way Official Discounts Impact of Show on Gun Control." *The Arizona Republic,* 8 Oct. 1975, p. C-5, cols. 1 and 2.

Wheeler, Norma. Editorial Commentary. "Was Squeaky's Action Really an Anti-gun Ploy?" *The Arizona Republic,* 20 Sept. 1975, p. A-7, col. 6.

—Judith Betz

Notice how this approach to the research paper differs in some respects from that of the other research paper:

1. It begins with a *focal point,* not with a subject or thesis per se. The **focal point** is *an idea, event, personality, or any-*

thing about which differing opinions, attitudes, or perspectives may be found.

2. The actual **subject** of the paper is *the variety of opinions, attitudes, perspectives, or interpretations surrounding the focal point.*

3. In most cases, the **thesis** will be *a specific formulation of the idea that a better or more complete understanding of _____ can be obtained by observing certain opinions, attitudes, or perspectives about some focal point.*

4. The **source materials** will necessarily be limited, in terms of *media, availability of material, and subject, and the limitations of the sources must be strictly indicated to enable the reader to judge the validity of the conclusions.*

5. The approach is essentially inductive, analytical, and classificatory.

Your choice of a focal point and a subject will determine in large part a good deal of the success of your paper. In choosing a focal point, you should consider, among other things, your *interest* in the material and the *amount of material* available to you about the subject. In addition, you would want to choose a subject about which there are varying opinions or perspectives. The following focal points will give you some idea of how you might go about getting a topic of your own:

1. Reactions to some kind of controversial issue or subject such as those presented on CBS's *Guns of Autumn* or *Helter Skelter.*

2. Critical reactions to any segment of a television program such as CBS's *60 Minutes, The Dick Cavett Show,* or *The David Susskind Show.*

3. Differing critical opinions about some aspect of a major novel, story, poem, or play.

4. Reviews and critical reactions to best sellers and movies such as *Helter Skelter* and *Coming Home*.

5. A survey of opinions about the conclusion of *Huckleberry Finn* in critical books and essays.

6. A survey of critical comments about movies such as *The Deer Hunter, Apocalypse Now, The Warriors*.

7. Attitudes about disco music, jazz, rock, or some other kind of music.

8. Magazine views of Jackie Kennedy as First Lady, grieving widow of President Kennedy, newly married to Onassis, widow of Onassis, and so forth.

9. Attitudes toward controversial or interesting public figures as depicted in newspapers, magazines, and books.

10. Critical reactions to public events such as the capture and trial of Patty Hearst, the murder of Sharon Tate, The Three Mile Island, and so forth.

11. Differing points of view given in books, newspaper articles, or magazine articles for supporting or opposing behavioral modification, abortion, nuclear energy, and so forth.

12. A review of the attitudes of participants or nonparticipants in some particular war in American history (for example, the Civil War, the war in Vietnam).

In the event you decide to write about one of these topics, your focal point will be some topic such as The Three Mile Island, Jackie Kennedy, or *The Warrior* but your subject will be the varying opinions, attitudes, and perspectives about these movies, books, events, people, ideas, or things.

Once you have chosen your focal point and your subject, you go through the usual steps of locating your material, making a tentative bibliography, evaluating your material and taking notes, writing the paper, documenting it, and so forth.

Index